LAWS AND CUSTOMS OF ISRAEL.

COMPILED FROM THE CODES

CHAYYE ADAM ("Life of Man")

KIZZUR SHULCHAN ARUCH ("Condensed Code of Laws")

IN FOUR PARTS.

דת ודין

ע"פ חיי אדם וקצור שלחן ערוך.

TRANSLATED FROM THE HEBREW BY

GERALD FRIEDLANDER

PREACHER, WESTERN SYNAGOGUE, LONDON.

British Library Cataloguing-in-Publication Data
A catalogue record for this book is available from
the British Library

PREFACE.

THE present work is an endeavour to provide for the home a condensed résumé of the Laws and Customs of Israel, and also a text book for Jewish schools in the upper standards. The title דת ודין[1] "Law and Custom" explains the nature of its contents. The "Laws and Customs" of Israel are set forth in the great code of Maimonides, *Yad Hachazakah* (יד החזקה), in the *Tur* (טור) of R. Asher ben Jechiel, and in R. Joseph Karo's *Shulchan Arukh* (שלחן ערוך). These monumental writings and many more have been summarised in R. Abraham Danziger's *Chayyé Adam* (חיי אדם) and *Chokhmath Adam* (חכמת אדם) as well as in R. Solomon Ganzfried's *Kizzur Shulchan 'Arukh* (קצור שלחן ערוך). The labours of these learned Rabbis have been epitomized in R. Bernard Abramowitz's "Law of Israel." These books have been laid under contribution in the preparation of the present work.

The present book contains much material that is suitable for use in Hebrew classes. It is believed that the intelligent study of this work will lay the foundation of a thorough knowledge of Hebrew and Jewish Law and will enable the reader and student to gain an insight into the great codes on which they are founded. With this aim in view the translation is as literal as possible. The entire work consists of 4 volumes. For the greater convenience of students the translation appears opposite each page of the original. This edition comprises 3 volumes in English only. A glossary and a complete index appears in the fourth volume.

GERALD FRIEDLANDER.

Feb. 12, 1915-5675.

[1] See Esther i. 13.

TO THE MEMORY

OF

DR. HERMAN ADLER, C.V.O. (ל״צז)

CHIEF RABBI.

CONTENTS OF VOL. I.

CONTENTS OF VOL. II.

Contents of vol. ii. (continued) :—

CONTENTS OF VOL. III.

CONTENTS CONTINUED.

THE
LAWS & CUSTOMS
OF ISRAEL.

1. "I have set the Lord always before me" (Ps. xvi. 8). This text helps one to fear God and to dread sin. If a man will realize that God, who fills the universe with His glory, is ever with him watching his actions, as it is said: "Can any hide himself in secret places that I shall not see him ? saith the Lord. Do not I fill heaven and earth ?" (Jer. xxiii. 24), he will assuredly keep far away from sin and indecency.

2. The first daily thought of man should be concerning the God of his salvation and His many lovingkindnesses, because He has restored to him his soul and health, making him like a new creature. Let him thank God for this with all his heart, and whilst on his bed let him say: "I thank Thee, O eternal King, because Thou hast graciously restored my soul to me, great is Thy faithfulness." This prayer may be said, although he has not yet washed his hands, because the name of God is not mentioned therein. Let him strengthen his will to rise quickly and zealously; if he accustom himself to do this four or five times, he will find no difficulty thereafter.

3. When he arises he must not walk four cubits unless he has washed his hands, except in cases of emergency. Prior to his ablution he must not touch his mouth, nostrils, eyes or ears, nor may he touch any food. Water must be poured three times on each hand alternately as far as the wrist or at least to the joints of the fingers, then the face and mouth must be washed and whilst drying his hands he says the benediction על נטילת ידים. The water with which he washed must not be used for any other purpose.

1

4. The hands must be washed every morning in a basin with water which one applies by his or her personal effort on each occasion of ablution, just as we must do when washing before meals. But in cases of emergency, when all that is requisite is not available, and one wishes to pray, it is permissible to wash in any utensil and with any kind of water without any personal effort (involved by pouring the water over the hands) and the benediction על נמילת ידים can be said. If there be at hand a river or even snow he can dip his hands therein three times, and if neither be available he can wipe his hands thoroughly with any material and say the benediction על נקית ידים. Afterwards when he finds water he can wash his hands without any further benediction.

5. On the following occasions the hands must be washed : on awakening from sleep in the morning, on coming from the lavatory or bath, after cutting the nails or hair, after taking off one's boots, after attending a funeral or going into the house where the corpse lies, or after touching anything unclean or any part of the body usually covered.

RULES AS TO DRESS.

1. Purity is a very important principle which every one must seek and observe even when alone in one's secret chamber. Habit is second nature, therefore when dressing one must avoid as much as possible having the body uncovered, whether by night or by day.

2. One's garments must not be torn or soiled, for even though a person be indifferent to his own sense of shame, the honour due to humanity must be respected.

3. The right hand is more esteemed than the left and generally preference should be shown to the right. In taking off one's boots the left one is removed first. With regard to tying knots, the left hand is more esteemed because the Tephillin are placed on the left arm. Therefore if one ties the bootlaces into a knot, that of the left foot is tied first.

4. The first garment which a male puts on is the "Arba Kanfos," for he must not go four cubits without ציצית, and he should say the benediction על מצות ציצית. If he had not yet washed his hands he should not say the benediction. He should not walk four cubits or utter any holy words (of prayer) with uncovered head.

5. It is written: "Let thy camp be holy, that He see no unclean thing in thee" (Deut. xxiii. 15), hence the sages learn that wheresoever we do any holy service the place must be clean and nothing unclean or impure should be there. If there be any doubt on this matter, no holy service may take place until the place has been examined.

6. As regards the body of a woman, the uncovering thereof of the size of a span of any portion that is usually covered is held to be indecent and her presence in this condition prevents the due performance by a man of any holy observance. This regulation applies to one's own wife as well as to any other woman. If one hear the song of women and it be impossible to stop it, one need not on this account neglect to say the שמע or the שמנה עשרה or to study the Torah, but let him fortify himself to direct his attention to the holy service with which he is occupied and let him pay no heed to the song.

7. As soon as it is dawn, when the time of prayer commences, a man must not begin any work or occupation, or start on a journey before he has prayed, as it is said: "Righteousness shall go before Him; and He shall make its footsteps a way to walk in" (Ps. lxxxv. 13). It is even prohibited to commence to study as soon as dawn has begun, but if one is wont to go to Synagogue and he does not fear that the time of prayer will pass by, he may study. Likewise if one teaches others and if they do not learn then they will lose their study, he may teach them, for the merit of helping the many is a great principle. In this case care must be taken that the time of prayer shall not slip by.

8. Before prayer it is prohibited to eat or drink and to the transgressor the Scripture text applies: "and Me hast thou cast behind thy back" (I Kings xiv. 9). But in the case of an old and weak man, who cannot wait for his food till the congregation come out of Synagogue on Sabbaths and Holydays when the services are prolonged, it is right to permit him to say the morning prayer in his home and then to say the Kiddush and to partake of some food. Thereafter he can go to the Synagogue and attend devoutly to the morning prayers of the congregation and afterwards he must say the Mussaph with them. For reasons of health it is permitted to eat and drink before

3

prayer and likewise if he be unable to pay attention to his prayers unless he has had food, then he may partake thereof before praying.

SOME RULES CONCERNING THE BENEDICTIONS.

1. "Thou shalt not take the name of the Lord thy God in vain" (Ex. xx. 7), therefore before one utters any benediction he must know which one he has to say, so that when he mentions God's name, he knows why he does so. It is prohibited to do anything else when he says a benediction and he should not pray in a hurry, but attend to the meaning of the words and when he prays his mouth must be clean.

2. One must be careful not to mention God's name in vain, but only for praise or blessing or when studying (the Bible). Even then he must attend to what he utters. In ordinary conversation one must not mention God's name either in Hebrew or in any language. This name must not be written out in full lest it be treated with contempt, but he may write a letter such as 'י or 'ה as an abbreviation. When he wishes to mention this name, let him say השם (the Name), but not אדושם as the ignorant people do, for this has no meaning.

3. It is necessary to be careful not to utter a benediction in vain, but if this happened or if one pronounce the Divine Name unnecessarily he should forthwith say: ברוך שם כבוד מלכותו לעולם ועד. If one should say ברוך אתה, or ברוך אתה ה' and then he remembers that there is no need to conclude the benediction, he should add למדני חוקיך (Ps. cxix. 12) so that the benediction be not purposeless.

4. A doubt as to the benediction is not a reason for stringency, e.g., if one be in doubt if he had said a certain benediction or not, he does not say it again except in the case of Grace after Meals and the benedictions over the Law and therefore if the least doubt arise concerning them they must be repeated.

5. Prior to the performance of any precept the benediction is said. No interruption between the benediction and the observance of the precept is allowed, a prolonged silence is not even permitted. If an interruption has taken place the benediction is repeated, but if the interruption took place because of the precept involved, the benediction is not repeated.

LAWS AND CUSTOMS OF ISRAEL

6. One should say at least one hundred benedictions daily, a support for this is given in the Torah : "Now, O Israel, *what* (מה) does the Lord thy God require of thee" (Deut. x. 12). Do not read מה (*what*) but read מאה (*one hundred*). On Sabbaths, Holydays and Fast Days when the number is diminished, compensation is afforded by paying attention to the benedictions recited by the Reader when repeating the Amidah and by the benedictions in connection with the reading of the Law and the Prophets, אמן is to be said after these benedictions. The number may also be completed by the blessings said when enjoying the gifts of God.

7. When one says: ברוך אתה ה' the listener answers ברוך הוא וברוך שמו and when the benediction is concluded אמן is said. אמן means "it is true" and one should believe that the benediction said is true (and he admits :) "I believe this." In benedictions which include prayer, the listener in responding אמן implies that the benediction is true and he prays thereby that the prayer may be answered.

8. If a congregant owing to his prayer be unable to join in the responses, he must not say ברוך הוא וברוך שמו, even in the case when by listening he would fulfil his obligation *e.g.*, the benediction over the Shofar (Ram's Horn) or that over the Scroll of Esther, because the response would be an interruption.

9. It is necessary to say the word אמן properly, neither dropping the first letter nor the last. We must not say אמן before the one saying the benediction has concluded, for this is termed a "snatched" אמן ; one should not delay in responding אמן for this is called an "orphan" אמן ; but immediately after the benediction has been completed, אמן should be said and one should not raise his voice in doing so above that of the person who says the benediction.

10. A person does not respond אמן to his own reading of the benediction, except in the Grace after Meals or similar instances (where אמן is part of the benediction). Should a congregant conclude a benediction with the Reader, he does not respond אמן, but if he happen to say a different benediction to that said by the Reader, and they conclude together, he should say אמן after the benediction of the Reader.

THE LAWS OF THE FRINGES. (ציצית)

1. The precept of the ציצית is great, because Scripture connects therewith all the commandments (of the Law) because it is said : "And

5

ye shall see it (i.e. ציצית) and remember *all* the commandments of the Lord" (Num. xv. 39), therefore every male must wear an "Arba' Kanfos." He should also have a Tallis (Praying Scarf) in which he should enwrap himself at the time of prayer. The benediction over the "Arba' Kanfos" is על מצות ציצית and when he puts on the Tallis he says להתעטף בציצית.

2. The precept of the ציצית applies only by day; women are absolved from this precept; for it is an affirmative one limited to a fixed time. A blind person is bound by this precept although it is said concerning the same : "and ye shall *see* it" (*ibid.*), nevertheless in another text it is said : "Thou shalt make thee fringes upon the four corners of thy vesture, wherewith thou coverest thyself" (Deut. xxii. 12).

3. Since it is written : "upon the fringe of each corner" (Num. xv. 38) we infer that the material of the ציצית should be the same as that of the corner, it is therefore proper to make woollen fringes for a woollen Tallis, or silk fringes for a silk Tallis. The correct method of observing this precept is to have a woollen Tallis with woollen fringes. The threads of the ציצית must be woven and twisted for the special purpose of observing this precept.

4. The following is the method of fixing the ציצית. Make an aperture in each of the four corners not less than a thumb's breadth from the edge and not more than the width of three fingers either in length or in breadth. Take the four threads and put them as far as their half length through the aperture, thereby they will be doubled, i e. eight threads. One of them must be longer than the rest. Then take these four threads on the one side (of the material) and four on the other and tie them with two knots and with the long thread twist round the rest seven times, and again make two knots, then twist eight times with the long thread and tie again two knots, then twist eleven times and tie two knots, and finally twist thirteen times and make two knots.

5. The length of the ציצית is not less than twelve thumb-breadths (measured) from the edge of the corner. If one ציצית be missing, even though the rest be in order, then the Tallis is defective and it is forbidden to put it on. If one thread of the ציצית be broken off, the Tallis is fit for use, for indeed the missing part is only half of a doubled thread. But if two threads be broken off, then, perchance they are both the two halves of the doubled thread, and if so a complete thread is missing and the ציצית is unfit for use.

6. Since it is written : "Thou shalt make thee fringes" (Deut. xxii. 12) we explain "*thou shalt make*" as excluding that which has been made (for other occasions). That is to say, that thou shalt make the fringes for this garment (Tallis or Arba' Kanfos). Therefore if he made the fringes according to regulation and afterwards put them on this (particular) garment, or if he took the ציצית from another garment and put them on this garment accor-

ding to rule, or even if the corner be torn and the ציצית fell off and he replaced it and afterwards mended the rent, in all these cases the ציצית is invalid because the rule is "thou shalt make" and not use that which has already been made. In these instances it is necessary to untie the ציצית entirely and to put it on again according to the rule.

7. Prior to saying the benediction over the ציצית one should daily examine the threads to see whether they are in order since it is natural that they should break off. When the שמע (Deut. vi. 4-9. xi. 13ff. and Num. xv. 37 ff.) is read he should take hold of the ציצית with his left hand opposite his heart, as it is said : "And these words shall be . . . upon *thine heart*" (Deut. vi. 6). It is a custom to kiss the ציצית after its benediction and each time we say the word ציצית. All this is a token of our love for God's precepts.

8. One must not enter a lavatory with a Tallis, but it is permissible to do so with an "Arba' Kanfos." It is prohibited to enter a cemetery or to be within four cubits of a corpse with exposed ציצית of the "Tallis" or "Arba' Kanfos."

9. It is permitted to take the Tallis of anyone who is a casual companion even without his knowledge and to pray therewith and to say its benediction. But it must not be taken out of the house where it happens to be. If it be folded, the user must fold it again. On Sabbath he should not fold it. If one borrow a Tallis from his companion to go to the reading of the Law, the Tallis benediction is not said ; but if he take a Tallis belonging to the congregation, if only for the reading of the Law, it is necessary to say the Tallis benediction. A Tallis belonging to partners requires ציצית.

10. If one take off the Tallis with the intention of putting it on again, even though he go to the lavatory, when he puts it on again he need not repeat the benediction. But if it was not his intention to put it on again and he changed his mind and put it on he must say the benediction. If he took it off without thinking whether he would put it on again, but he wears the Arba' Kanfos, he does not say the blessing (when he puts it on again) ; but if he should not then wear the Arba' Kanfos he must say the benediction (when he puts it on again). If the entire Tallis fall off, but a part is still in his hand it is necessary to say the benediction when replacing it.

THE RULES OF TEPHILLIN.

1. It is an affirmative precept to lay Tephillin on the hand and head, as it is said : "And thou shalt bind them for a sign upon thine hand, and they shall be for frontlets between thine eyes" (*ibid*. 8). This is one of the precepts of especial value enjoined upon Israel for several times the word "sign" is mentioned in connection therewith, that is to say, this precept is a sign that we are sons of our Father in Heaven and that we are members of the community of our

great and holy people. The Tephillin are bound to our bodies, and our sages interpret the text : "All the peoples of the earth shall see that the name of the Lord is called *upon thee*" (*ibid.* xxviii. 10) as referring to the Tephillin. In placing the Tephillin upon the arm opposite the heart and upon the head opposite the brain, the intention is to make not only our senses but also our thoughts and desires sub-servient to our Creator and Ruler, the only Unity, and to give thanks unto Him for His loving kindnesses which He has bestowed upon us from the time when He brought us forth from Egypt and took us to be unto Him a chosen people to observe His commandments and statutes so that we might become a wise and understanding people and a holy nation.

2. Any Jew who does not use Tephillin is reckoned among the class of transgressors in Israel who sin with their body. If one use defective Tephillin, not only does he fail to observe the precept but he utters many benedictions in vain. Therefore one must be careful that the Tephillin should be in good and proper condition, and he must see to it that they are in order and that the capsules and straps are black. If the Tephillin become defective even in a very slight degree or if the sewing become undone or even if the edges of the capsules are not as they should be, they must be speedily repaired by a competent workman.

3. It is a general custom that a lad should not put on Tephillin until he becomes Bar Mitzvah, *i.e.*, until he has completed his thirteenth year, nevertheless he begins to put them on about a month before he is Bar Mitzvah, in order that he may accustom himself to the precept. Women are exempt from this precept.

4. The time for putting on the Tephillin is at the morning service on week-days, they are not used on Sabbath or Festivals because it is written about the Tephillin : "And it shall be for a *sign* unto thee" (Ex. xiii. 9). Sabbath and Festivals are also a sign between God and Israel, as it is said : "It is a *sign* between me and the children of Israel for ever" (*ibid.* xxxi. 17). Owing to the fact that the precept of ציצית is applicable daily whereas the Tephillin are used on week days only, therefore the Tallis is put on before we use the Tephillin, because that which is more frequent in use has the preference over that which is less frequently used. In some places Tephillin are not used on the Intermediate Days of Festivals, but some people put them on without any benediction. Care must be taken that in a Synagogue a uniform procedure should obtain.

5. The Tephillin for the hand and for the head are two separate precepts. and the failure to observe one does not prevent the perform-ance of the other, so that if only one be available or by reason of some compulsion the user can only put on one, he does so ; if it be the hand

LAWS AND CUSTOMS OF ISRAEL

Tephillah, the benediction להניח תפלין only is said, if it be the head
Tephillah the benedictions להניח תפלין and על מצות תפלין are said and
then he says ברוך שם כבוד מלבותו לעולם ועד.

6. In holy things we progress but we do not deteriorate. The
head Tephillah possesses a higher sanctity than the hand Tephillah
and therefore the strap belonging to the former may not be used for
the latter, but the latter may be used for the former.

7. We stand when the Tephillin are put on and speaking is then
prohibited. The Tephillin must be placed next to one's flesh. Care
must be taken that the knot of the hand Tephillah is not shifted
from the capsule even when in the bag. The black side of the strap
should be to the front (i.e. visible).

8. The hand Tephillah is put on the muscle of the left arm with
the rim of the capsule upwards inclining slightly towards the heart.
The capsule of the head Tephillin must be on the forehead, midway
between the eyes with the lower edge placed where the hair begins
to grow; the strap must exactly fit the head measured round the
forehead, the knot being at the base of the skull where the hair begins.

9. A left-handed person puts the Tephillah on his right arm,
whether the habit is natural or acquired. If all work be done with his
right hand except writing or vice-versa, than the writing hand is considered the right and the Tephillah is placed on the other. An ambi-
dextrous man puts the Tephillah on the left arm. A man, although
not born left-handed, who accustoms himself to write with the left
hand but does all his work with the right hand, puts the Tephillah on
the left arm.

10. The Tephillin must be taken out and not shaken out of the
the bag to obviate the slighting of a divine precept. The hand
Tephillah is put on first and before the knot is tightened the benediction להניח תפלין is said. The knot is then tightened and the strap
wound seven times round the arm, then the head Tephillah
immediately placed on the head and the benediction על מצות תפלין is
said, after fixing it properly ברוך שם כבוד מלבותו לעולם ועד is said,
because there is a slight doubt with reference to this benediction and it

9

should therefore be said silently. No interruption is permitted between the placing of the Tephillah on the hand and on the head. If an interruption be made, even to respond יהא ש"ר or קדושה, the benedictions להניח and על מצות are repeated when putting on the head Tephillah. Even on the Intermediate Days of Festivals, or when using the Tephillin of Rabbinu Tam, when no Tephillin benedictions are said, no interruption is allowed between putting on the hand and the head Tephillin, but in these cases it is permitted to respond אמן יהא ש"ר or קדושה. להניח is not repeated if the interruption be in connection with the Tephillin. After the head Tephillah has been adjusted, the strap of the hand Tephillin is wound thrice round the middle finger, once over the middle joint and twice on the bottom joint and the remaining strap is wound round the palm of the hand so that the letter ש is formed on the back of the hand and ד on the palm and י is formed near by the capsule, thus making שדי. Whilst winding the strap round the finger he says: וארשתיך לי וכו' (Hos. ii. 19, 20).

11. One's attention must not be diverted from the Tephillin whilst wearing them. It is customary to touch them when the precept concerning them is said. When he says וקשרתם לאות על ידך he should touch the hand Tephillah and kiss (that with which he has touched it) and when he says והיו לטטפת בין עיניך he should touch the head Tephillah in like manner. If he must remove the Tephillin during prayer, then the benedictions must be repeated when they are replaced.

12. When one has no Tephillin and the congregation is praying, he should wait till the end of the service so as to borrow Tephillin from another, so that he can say the שמע and שמנה עשרה with the Tephillin on, rather than to pray with the congregation without Tephillin.

13. Tephillin should be put on in the morning as soon as it is light enough to recognize one's acquaintance at a distance of four cubits. While wearing the Tephillin a meal is prohibited, but casual refreshment is allowed; sleep is prohibited under any circumstances while wearing Tephillin.

14. If the strap of the hand Tephillah be broken where the knot is tied and one wishes to use a piece of the strap below the knot so that it becomes a part of the section above the knot, this is prohibited. Likewise with the strap of the head Tephillah, it is prohibited to change what was contained within the knot so that it becomes outside the knot.

15. The Tephillin are not taken off until the קדושה in ובא לציון has been said, after the words יהי רצון . . . שנשמור. On the New Moon we take them off before Mussaph. On the Intermediate Days of

10

Tabernacles everyone takes off the Tephillin before Hallel, on the Intermediate Days of Passover the congregation take them off before Hallel, whilst the Reader does so after Hallel.

16. We stand when the Tephillin are removed, first the strap round the finger, then the head Tephillah and finally the hand Tephillah are removed. It is customary to kiss the Tephillin when putting them on and off. They must not be removed in front of a scroll of the Law or before one's teacher, one must in these cases turn aside to remove them.

17. The Tephillin must not be placed in their bag one over the other, but side by side, so that the hand Tephillah can be taken out first. The bag with the Tephillin should be placed in the Tallis bag beneath the Tallis, so that the Tallis is first to hand. They must be handled with reverence, and even when in their bags they must not be allowed to fall on the floor. The Tephillin bag must be made specially for this purpose and it must not be used for anything profane.

18. The capsules of the Tephillin should be examined twice in seven years. If the capsules are broken the parchment must be examined, this also applies if the capsules fall into the water.

RULES CONCERNING THE MEZUZAH.

1. In proximity to the precept concerning Tephillin, the Creator has commanded us: "And thou shalt write them upon the doorposts of thy house, and upon thy gates" (Deut. vi. 9). Just as the Tephillin are a sign of holiness upon our hands and between our eyes, so is the Mezuzah to be a similar sign upon the houses wherein we dwell. It is good to kiss the Mezuzah when coming in and going out, and in the latter case to say : ה' שׁומרי ה' צלי על יד ימיני (cf. Ps. cxxi. 5).

2. It is an affirmative precept to fix the Mezuzah upon every door, also on the gates of courts and yards. Even if one has many apartments and each apartment has many doors for use, but only one is actually in use, they must nevertheless each have a Mezuzah, even if the use of dwelling therein be diminished and he only has need of using one door, still each one requires a Mezuzah. If there be a particular door which was made merely for bringing in goods occasionally, and there be another door for entrance and exit, then the former does not require a Mezuzah.

11

LAWS AND CUSTOMS OF ISRAEL.

3. An unoccupied house needs no Mezuzah. A house which is hired must have a Mezuzah, even if hired from a non-Jew.

4. A Mezuzah must be fixed and a benediction said: (a.) If the house be four cubits square; (b.) If it have two doorposts and a lintel on top of them; (c.) If the house have a roof; (d.) If it have doors; (e.) If the doors be at least 10 cubits high; (f.) If it be built for man to dwell therein (g.) in honour and (h.) as a permanent dwelling.

5. Therefore a Synagogue does not need a Mezuzah as it is not a dwelling house. Since people sit in a Beth Hamidrash all day it is necessary to fix a Mezuzah, but without saying the benediction. A wash-house, a tannery and a ritual bath do not require a Mezuzah; this applies to a סוכה used during the Feast of Tabernacles and also to booths which are erected for fairs and thereafter pulled down again since they are not used as permanent dwellings.

6. A cellar with its doorposts and door underground needs no Mezuzah, for the term "doorposts of thy house" (Deut. vi. 9) is only applicable when the doorposts stand above ground.

7. A house belonging to partners requires a Mezuzah, although it is written "thy house" (ibid.) in the singular, nevertheless since it is written "that your days may be multiplied" (ibid. xi.21) we infer that this precept applies to the many. This only refers to partners who are Israelites (on whom the Law is enjoined). But where the partner is a Gentile or in the case where there is a court where Israelites and Gentiles dwell, even if the former be in the majority, the law of Mezuzah does not apply, lest the Gentiles might take it and it would cease to be used for a holy purpose. This rule applies wherever it is feared that the Mezuzah might be stolen, then it may only be fixed in such wise that it cannot be taken. In cases of emergency it may be fixed inside behind the door, but only on the doorposts and not on the wall. It must not be a cubit away from the doorway, otherwise it is useless.

8. A Mezuzah must not be fixed until the doorposts are erected, for the rule applies: "Thou shalt make it" expressly, and not let it be the result of something done previously (see supra p. 6.). For this reason a Mezuzah is not required if there be no door.

12

9. It is necessary to fix the Mezuzah on the right side of the entrance. There is no difference in this case whether a person be left-handed or not. If the door be between two rooms and doubt arises as to which side he ought to affix the Mezuzah, in this case we notice where the hinge is, and where the door opens and leads to is the chief part of the house, and the Mezuzah is to be affixed on the right side where one enters. This rule applies only when the two rooms are used alike, but if one be used more than the other, then the Mezuzah is fixed on the right side of the entrance to this room which is chiefly used even if the door opened directly into the other room.

10. The position where the Mezuzah is to be fixed is in the first third part of the door (measured downwards), and it should be slanting with its top inclined towards the house ; if it be not affixed but only suspended it is useless. It is therefore necessary to fix it permanently with nails at the top as well as at the bottom.

11. Before affixing it the benediction לקבוע מזוזה must be said. If many Mezuzoth have to be affixed one benediction suffices for all of them. If the Mezuzah fell down and he refixes it, it is necessary to repeat the benediction, but if he removed it in order to examine it, there is some doubt whether he should repeat the benediction.

12. When one is removing from a house and another Israelite is coming to dwell there, then the former must not remove the Mezuzoth, but he must leave them and his successor must recompense him.

13. The Mezuzah of a private person must be examined twice in seven years, but that belonging to a society is examined twice in a jubilee.

PRAYER.

THE RULES OF THE HOUSE OF PRAYER.

1. It is written : "To serve Him with all your heart" (Deut. xi. 13). Our sages of blessed memory ask : Which is the service with the heart ? This is prayer. Prayer is the most suitable means of fortifying our spiritual garrison, to strengthen within us the knowledge that a man lacks power, and that the provision of our needs depends solely upon God. And although we have the right to pray for our needs at all times and in any matter we think proper, nevertheless we

13

should not deviate from the formulæ of the prayers and benedictions instituted by our sages in olden days in the Hebrew language. Just as there are fixed times for prayer, likewise should a man have a fixed place in the congregation for his prayers. For apart from the fact that " the glory of the King is the multitude of the people " (Prov. xiv. 28) the locale itself helps in stirring up holy thoughts, as it is said : " To the House of God let us go *with feeling* " (Ps. lv. 14).

2. If one cannot go to Synagogue or to the House of Study, or even to some regular place where a Minyan (quorum of ten males) is to be found, one should try to arrange for ten men to meet, so that he may pray at home with the status of a congregation. If this be impossible, he should pray under all circumstances simultaneously with the congregation for that is a propitious time. Likewise if one dwell in a place where there is no Minyan, he should pray at such time as the congregation pray ; and he should direct his attention to that prayer which the congregation pray at that time, so that his prayer will not be that of an individual in all respects.

3. The inhabitants of a place compel one another to build a Synagogue or House of Study, to buy books for study and where there is no Minyan they should come continually to form Minyan so that the religious community should not cease. Teachers are forced to come to Minyan even if they be debarred from teaching, for the time of teaching the Torah is distinct from the time of prayer.

4. The sanctity of the Synagogue and of the House of Study is very great, and we are warned concerning them to fear the One who dwells therein, as it is written : " And ye shall reverence My sanctuary " (Lev. xix. 30). This refers not only to the Temple but to every place which has been sanctified. The Synagogue and the House of Study are each called "a little sanctuary," as it is written : "And I will be unto them for a little sanctuary " (Ezek. xi. 16). It is therefore forbidden to gossip or to be frivolous or indecorous therein, and concerning those who act thus it is said : "Who has required this at your hands, to trample My courts " (Is. i. 12). A Synagogue and a House of Study which have been destroyed still retain their sanctity.

5. It is forbidden to eat, drink, sleep or even to doze in a Synagogue. We should not kiss our little sons therein, because it is not meet to distract one's attention from the love of God.

LAWS AND CUSTOMS OF ISRAEL

6. It is permitted to make a House of Study out of a Synagogue, but not vice-versa. It is forbidden to sell a Synagogue unless there is another; if it be the only one, it must not be sold or demolished until they have another one ready, unless it be in danger. If a new one be built, then the old one may be demolished with the consent of the congregation and its leaders, and its sanctity then ceases and is transferred to the new one. The old Synagogue may be transformed in any way desired.

THE RULES AS TO MINYAN.

1. We neither say קדיש, ברכו, and קדושה, nor do we read the Torah (with benedictions) unless there be ten male adults present. An adult is one who has passed his thirteenth year.

2. If one were born in the month of Adar in an ordinary year and when he reaches maturity it is a leap year, he does not become Bar Mitzvah (*i.e.* an adult) until the second Adar, but if he were born in a leap year in the first Adar he becomes Bar Mitzvah in the first Adar also ; but if at his birth it was a leap year and when he becomes Bar Mitzvah it is an ordinary year, whether his birth took place in the first Adar or the second Adar, he becomes Bar Mitzvah on the particular day in Adar of that ordinary year.

3. Some authorities allow, in a case of emergency, such prayers (permitted only when a Minyan is present) to be said when nine adults and a boy more than six years old are present. But the later authorities do not approve this.

4. Care is to be taken not to count the people in a direct manner in order to know if there be Minyan, for it is not permissible to count Israel in a direct manner even for the purpose of fulfilling a precept, as it is written : " And Saul summoned the people, and numbered them *with lambs*" (I Sam. xv. 4). We are accustomed to count the Minyan by saying the verse הושיעה את עמך וגו' (Ps. xxviii. 9) which contains ten words.

5. It is necessary that all the ten should be in one place and the Reader should be with them ; but if some of them be in one room and some in another they are not associated (in the matter of Minyan) although the door is open between the two rooms. Even if a majority of the Minyan be in the synagogue and a minority are in the courtyard in front of the Synagogue, the latter are not counted with the majority to be associated with them, and all this is with reference to

15

completing the Minyan. But if there were ten in one place and they were saying קדיש, ברכו or קדושה, then everybody who hears their voice can join in the response even if many houses intervene. For even a partition of iron cannot separate Israel from their Father in Heaven. We are accustomed to stand for קדיש, ברכו, and קדושה.

6. If there be only a Minyan in the Synagogue every one of them is forbidden to go out, and with reference to such as go out it is said : "And they that forsake the Lord shall be consumed" (Is. i. 28). If one or more depart, that portion of the service which was commenced when the Minyan was present is completed, providing the majority of the Minyan be still present. Thus, if the Reader had commenced to repeat the שמנה עשרה, he completes the שמנה עשרה with קדושה and the priestly benediction, but neither do the priests pronounce the blessing, nor is קדיש said after the שמנה עשרה, for these are separate parts of the Service. If they began to read the Torah with Minyan and a minority has departed, they complete the portion already commenced, but they do not call up any more, neither do they call anybody to read the Haphtora, but the last one called to the Torah reads the Haphtora without benedictions.

RULES FOR THE READER.

1. Only a fit person is appointed as a Reader. A fit person is one who has a good reputation, and is not known as a transgressor, even as a youth. He must be modest and pleasing to the congregation. He must have a pleasant and sweet voice which touches the heart. He must be accustomed to read the Law, the Prophets and the Hagiographa, so that the Scripture texts in the prayers may be fluent in his mouth. If they do not find a person with all these qualifications, they must select from among the candidates the best as regards knowledge and morals.

2. A beardless person may not be appointed permanently, but may be appointed temporarily. Any male who is more than thirteen years old may read the prayers.

3. It is accounted disgraceful for a Reader to prolong the service so that the congregation may hear his voice, it is said of such : "She hath uttered her voice against me ; therefore I have hated her" (Jer. xii. 8). He should pray with decorum and stand in awe and dread. The service must not be unduly prolonged.

4. If one's garments be torn and his elbows be bare he must **not** officiate. A blind man may officiate.

5. A Reader may not be dismissed unless he be guilty of some fault. Even if he take an oath that he will not continue in his **evil** ways, he must not officiate until he has sincerely repented. He must not be dismissed because of gossip; if he be of bad repute the Beth Din must hear all witnesses thereto and, if proved guilty, he must be inhibited. A Reader who is a Shochet must not read Service in soiled garments; if he be unwilling to change he must be discharged (**as** Reader). He must always change his dress after his work (as Shochet), so as to avoid ill-feeling among his fellow-men. A Reader who is prone to speak foul language must be rebuked, and if he pay no heed **he** must be inhibited.

6. A Reader who has a life appointment may in his old **age** appoint his son to assist him occasionally, although the son's voice **may** not be as sweet as his own; if he be his substitute in other **matters** he has the preference before all others, provided his voice be not so untuneful as to be disagreeable to the congregation. The original appointment permitted him to delegate his duties when unable **to** perform them. Therefore his son has the preference. In all cases of appointments the sons have the preference except in the case of **a** teacher or a judge.

7. To obviate individual objections after his appointment, a permanent Reader must be appointed by the majority of the paying members of the congregation. But if engaged for a period, his appointment is not considered binding and a new agreement is necessary when the period of time has expired. This applies also to other appointments. In some places they make the appointment **and** have a witness to confirm the appointment; all such rules **depend** upon the custom of the place.

LAWS REGULATING PRAYER IN GENERAL.

1. He who prays must know that the Shechinah is before **him,** as it is said: "Pour out thine heart like water before the face of the Lord" (Lam. ii. 19) and he must remove all alien thoughts so that his mind and will are devoted entirely to his prayer. For if he **were to** speak before a temporal king, verily would he prepare his words **and** be very much concerned lest he stumble; much more so is **it** necessary to direct his attention before the King of Kings, the Holy One, blessed be He; for before Him the thought of man is **revealed.**

Before prayer he should think about the exalted state of God and the lowliness of man. He should put aside all material enjoyment from his heart.

2. One should fix one's mind on the words of prayer uttered—a little with devotion is better than much without devotion. At times of prayer one should feel humble and direct his heart to his Father who is in Heaven. If alien thoughts come to him whilst praying, let him be silent and wait until they pass away.

3. One's voice should be subdued and never louder than that of the Reader. His eyes should be downcast and his heart heavenward.

4. It is good to pray with a prayer book so that all his thoughts should be concentrated on his prayer. Rabbi Elijah of Wilna found a hint for this in the Book of Esther : " And when she (Esther) came before the King (God) He said *with the book* so that the evil decree should be turned aside" (Est. ix. 25).

5. If one be intoxicated so that he cannot speak before a great and noble man, he is forbidden to pray ; but if he disobey and pray, his prayer is an abomination and he must repeat his prayer when he is sober. If he missed the time of prayer let him compensate with the prayer following, according to the rule of one who errs through ignorance or compulsion.

THE RULES OF THE MORNING PRAYER.

1. The time for morning prayer is at daybreak, as it is said : " They shall fear Thee with the sun " (Ps. lxxii. 5). If he prayed after sunrise he has done his duty and this applies to a third of the day, but it is prohibited to delay overmuch. If one had delayed even intentionally he can still pray until mid-day, although he has not the merit of praying at the right time nevertheless he has some merit (from his prayer). If a person deliberately delay till after mid-day without praying, there is no means of compensation and concerning this it is said : " That which is crooked cannot be made straight." (Eccl. i. 15).

2. The morning prayer is divided into four sections corresponding, according to the Cabbalists, to the four worlds, this world, the world of the spheres, the world of the angels and the heavenly world. (1) The morning blessings are from the benediction על נטילת ידים up to

18

LAWS AND CUSTOMS OF ISRAEL

ברוך שאמר ;(2) the verses of the Psalms from ברוך שאמר up to
ישתבח ;(3) the reading of the שמע and its benedictions up to the שמנה
עשרה ;(4) from the end of שמנה עשרה up to the conclusion of the
service.

3. Up to ברוך שאמר it is permitted to make an interruption
between one benediction and another even for a matter of minor
importance and, of course, for any matter connected with Divine
Worship; but from ברוך שאמר till after תחנון (Supplication) it is prohibited to interrupt for any reason ever so urgent, for this is
a serious transgression.

The Rules Concerning the Morning Service Benedictions.

1. There is a doubt whether one should respond אמן or not after
the benediction לעסוק בדברי תורה. Some hold that the end of the
benediction is not here but that והערב נא is part of it, for it is all one
benediction, therefore one should not respond אמן. Others hold that
the benediction ends here and that והערב נא is another benediction and
we should respond אמן. Therefore one should say this benediction in
silence so that his companion should not hear it and be in doubt
as to whether he should respond or not.

2. The benediction אשר נתן לשכוי בינה should not be said until
daylight.

3. The benediction פוקח עורים may be said by a blind person for
he has the benefit that others point out the way for him.

4. After המעביר שנה מעיני ותנומה מעפעפי we do not say אמן for the
conclusion of the benediction is not here at this passage, since ויהי
רצון belongs also to this benediction and the end thereof is גומל חסדים
טובים לעמו ישראל.

5. If one be awake all night, he says in the morning all the morning benedictions, except על נטילת ידים, אלהי נשמה and המעביר שנה. There
is a doubt whether the benediction over the Law should be said or not,
and therefore it is right to hear others say these benedictions and to
respond אמן.

6. If he had not said all the morning benedictions before he said
the prayers proper, he can say them after the other prayers. The only
exceptions are the benedictions על נטילת ידים and אלהי נשמה.

LAWS AND CUSTOMS OF ISRAEL

The Rules Concerning the Special Verses of the Psalms
(פסוקי דזמרה)

1. ברוך שאמר is praise exceedingly esteemed and it should be said word by word standing. All the special verses of the Psalms should be said quietly and sweetly and not hurridly. One should say (Ps. c.) מזמור לתודה with gladness ; we do not say it on Sabbath or Holydays for the thanksgiving offering (תודה) was not brought thereon, it is omitted also on the Intermediate Days of Passover, the day before Passover and the day before the Day of Atonement.

2. Our sages have instituted the rule to say (Ps. cxlv.) תהלה לדוד thrice daily. This psalm is exceedingly beautiful and should be said with deep devotion.

3. Whilst standing he should say ויברך דוד as far as לשם תפארתך. או ישיר משה should be sung joyfully.

4. After commencing ברוך שאמר until the end of the עשרה שמנה it is forbidden to interrupt with a single word even in Hebrew. Nevertheless with reference to an interruption for the sake of obeying a precept there is a difference, on the one hand, between the special verses of the psalms and the benedictions thereof, and on the other hand, the reading of the שמע and its benedictions. In saying the special verses of the Psalms, between ברוך שאמר and ישתבח if he hear any benediction it is permissible to say אמן, and likewise when the congregation say the שמע he should say the verse שמע ישראל וגו' (Deut. vi. 4) with them. Much more so is it permitted to interrupt the psalms in order to respond קדושה, קדיש, אמן and ברכו. But the response ברוך הוא וברוך שמו and the prayer יתברך וישתבח usually said when the Reader says ברכו do not warrant an interruption even while saying the psalm verses. This rule also applies to the benediction usually said when washing the hands after leaving the lavatory.

5. If one enter the Synagogue and find the congregation praying and whilst he puts on Tallis and Tephillin the congregation say the benediction יוצר, he should begin this benediction with them and join in prayer with them, and after the prayers he should say the פסוקי דזמרה omitting the benedictions ברוך שאמר and ישתבח.

The Rules for קדיש and ברכו.

1. A Minyan is required for the recital of קדיש, ברכו and קדושה. We do not read the Torah (with its benedictions) unless a Minyan be in the place where it is to be read. Only those actually inside the room (place of worship) are reckoned in the Minyan.

20

2. After ישתבח the Reader says Half-Kaddish. But if ten adults were not present when ישתבח was said, but the number was completed thereafter, the Reader must not say Kaddish, for this is not to be said except after that section of the prayers which has been said with the Minyan (ten adults). Therefore they should wait until the Minyan is complete before they say ישתבח. The period of waiting should be within half-an-hour. They should not wait longer than this but they should say ישתבח and then wait, and when the Minyan is there they should say a few verses of Psalms and thereafter the Reader says Half-Kaddish.

3. Even though one did not hear the Reader say ברכו but he hears the congregation responding ברוך, he may join with them in the response. One should try to say the קדושה of the יוצר Prayer with the congregation, and if it be impossible it can be said individually.

RULES FOR THE READING OF THE שמע AND ITS BENEDICTIONS.

1. It is an affirmative precept of the Torah to read the שמע twice daily, morning and evening, as it is written "And thou shalt speak of them *when thou liest down and when thou risest up*" (Deut. vi. 7). The sages have ordained that two benedictions should precede it and one benediction is said after it.

2. The commencement of the time for reading the שמע of the morning service is the same as applies to Tephillin and it extends to a quarter of the day, be it a long or a short day. The day is reckoned from daybreak till the time when the stars begin to shine. The ideal fulfilment of the precept is to read it as the saints did. In any circumstance it is necessary to be very careful not to delay the time after the first quarter of the day. Thus to take a special instance, in the summer days when the day is long in our lands, sometimes it happens that the end of the period (of reading the שמע) is before the seventh hour in the morning. In any case if it had happened that he had passed the time limit, he is permitted to read the שמע with its benedictions up to a third of the day, but thereafter they have

prohibited the recital of the benedictions, but one may read the שמע by itself even all day long.

3. The reading of the שמע with its benedictions is sub-divided into sections, namely, הבוחר בעמו ; אהבה רבה is distinct from יוצר המאורות ; ישראל באהבה is distinct from שמע ישראל ; ובשעריך is distinct from והיה אם ; ויאמר is distinct from על הארץ ; שמע. Between these sections it is permitted to respond אמן after every benediction ; much more so is it permitted to make the responses to קדיש, ברכו and קדושה. He must not say שמע ישראל and ברוך הוא וברוך שמו with the congregation. Whilst in the middle of a section he should not respond אמן except after שומע תפלה and האל הקדוש. In the קדיש he should respond only אמן up to יהא שמה רבא עלמיא, he should also say אמן after דיאמירן בעלמא ואמרו. At the קדושה he should respond only קדיש וכו' and ברוך כבוד. Should he hear ברכו said by the Reader or by one called to the Law, he should respond ברוך וכו' and also אמן after the benediction over the Law. If the congregation respond מודים, he should also bow and say מודים אנחנו לך.

4. Every interruption is prohibited whilst saying the verse שמע ישראל or the phrase ברוך שם כבד וכו' or between אני ה' אלהיכם and אמת ויציב. Even if a king addressed the worshipper, no reply may be given whilst saying these prayers.

5. Before the reading of the שמע, when he says והביאנו וכו' he takes the ציצת in his hand and whilst saying the שמע holds them in his left hand opposite his heart, and when he reads the section ויאמר which contains the portion dealing with the ציצת he also takes hold of them with his right hand. When he says וראיתם אותו he puts them on his eyes and looks at them and kisses them. We are accustomed to kiss them each time we say the word ציצת and we hold them till we say ונחמדים לעד when they are kissed and no longer held.

6. The שמע may be read either sitting or standing, and if one happened to be sitting then it is prohibited to adopt the strict rule of standing. It it not permitted to read it whilst lying down.

7. Before he begins he must direct his attention to fulfil the precept of reading the שמע which God has commanded us. When he says שמע ישראל he must pay heed to its meaning, namely, that the Lord who is our God is the only Lord, one and alone in heaven and on earth.

8. When he says אני ה' אלהיכם he must add forthwith the word אמת, for there must be no pause between them. The Reader, in like manner when reading this portion, says אלהיכם אמת ה'.

22

LAWS AND CUSTOMS OF ISRAEL

Everyone should give heed to hear these words recited by the Reader, for these three words complete the 248 words in the reading of the שמע corresponding to the 248 members in man's body. Thereafter ויציב is said, but אמת must not be said again. If one pray privately, he says אל מלך נאמן before reading the שמע in order thereby to complete the 248 words.

9. If one had read the שמע and then he enters a Synagogue whilst the congregation are reading the שמע, it is necessary to read it with them on every occasion, and it will be accounted as though he had read the Torah.

10. The prayer for Israel's redemption (גאולה) must precede תפלה (Prayer *par excellence*) and it is prohibited to interrupt between them even to respond to קדיש and קדושה. It is proper to conclude גאל ישראל with the Reader, so that there is no need then to respond אמן. The duty of joining גאולה to the תפלה is greater than that connected with the recital of the תפלה in a congregation.

THE RULES OF THE SHEMONEH ESREH.

1. When one is about to say the prayer שמנה עשרה let him arise, put his feet close together and devote his attention to this prayer.

2. He must turn his face towards the land of Israel and the Holy of Holies, as it is said: "And they shall pray unto thee" (1 Kings viii. 48); therefore we, who dwell in the west of the land of Israel, turn towards the east, even if the Ark be placed in another direction. People living in the east turn towards the west, those dwelling in the north turn towards the south, and such who live in the south turn towards the north—with the result that all pray towards one place, namely towards Jerusalem and the Holy of Holies.

3. If one should not know the correct position, let him direct his thought to the Holy of Holies. If he should stand towards the north or the south and then remember his error, it is not permissible to shift his feet towards the east, but let him turn his face eastwards. If this be impossible or if he face the south, let him direct his thoughts towards the Holy of Holies, but he must not move his feet. Likewise if he pray in a place where there are drawings on the eastern wall, he must not pray towards that side but should turn to some other side although it be not the east, and if pictures should be hanging there let him close his eyes. Therefore it is not right to paint pictures in a Synagogue unless they be higher than a man's stature.

23

4. The feet should be placed together and the head slightly bent, the eyes closed or, if using a prayer book, the eyes should not be raised from the book. His heart should be humble and reverent, and he should remember that only by the will of God can his prayers be answered. Let him pray with a perfect heart, and utter every word distinctly and quietly so that one standing by him should not hear his voice, as it is written of Hannah : "only her lips moved but her voice was not heard " (I Sam. i. 13).

5. It is necessary to bend the knees and bow four times whilst saying the שמנה עשרה, at the beginning and end of the first benediction, and at the beginning and end of the benediction מודים. When he says ברוך he bends the knees and when he says אתה he bows so that the joints of the spine protrude and he bends his head, and before he pronounces the divine name he again bends slowly. So at מודים he bends the knees and bows, and before he utters God's name he again, bends. He must not overdo the bowing down for this is the way of pride. An old man and an invalid to whom bending the knees is painful need only incline the head. It is prohibited to increase the occasions for bowing down when saying the other benedictions, either at their beginning or at their end. After the שמנה עשרה he should say יהי רצון. After אלהי נצור and before עשה שלום he should bow and take three steps backward, the steps must not be excessive.

6. The time for saying the morning תפלה (on week days שמנה עשרה) is from sunrise up to a third of the day. In cases of necessity one may pray at daybreak. He may delay till mid-day, but if he intentionally delay till after mid-day no compensation is permissible ; but if he delay through ignorance or compulsion he should effect compensation in the service which follows that which has been missed. And likewise if one made a mistake in his תפלה with reference to a matter which it was necessary to repeat and if he remember this at the next תפלה, or if he thought that he had time to say his תפלה and unknowingly the time passes, or if he be likely to incur a loss and is thus prevented from saying it at the proper time ; in all these cases he can make compensation by saying it after the תפלה of the one omitted. Thus if he had not said the Evening Service, then after the תפלה of the Morning Service he should say תחנון and אשרי and then say the תפלה for compensation. If he had not said the Morning Service he can effect compensation in the Afternoon Service, that is to say, after the תפלה of this Service he should say

התחזון and אשרי and say the תפלה instead of the one omitted. If he did
not say the Afternoon Prayer, then he should pause after the Evening
Service for such time as it takes to go four cubits, and then he should
say the prayer in lieu of the one which he had omitted.

7. If the whole day had passed and he did not say the Mussaph,
there is no means of compensation. The Reader may utilize his
repetition of the תפלה as compensation for an omitted תפלה in the
preceding service.

8. Whilst saying the שמנה עשרה every movement is prohibited. No
interruption is allowed, even to say responses, but he should stop and
silently pay attention to that which the congregation are saying.
He may join in all responses, including אמן after saying יהי רצון which
follows אלהי נצור.

9. It is not permitted to sit within four cubits of one who is
saying שמנה עשרה either in front or behind him or at his side. One
studying Torah may sit behind or at the side of the worshipper. No
objection can be taken if one who is weak desires to sit.

RULES CONCERNING משיב הרוח, ענינו, יעלה ויבא and טל ומטר.

1. If one forgot to say משיב הרוח ומוריד הגשם and he became aware
of the omission before saying the benediction מחיה המתים, he may say
the omitted words where he remembered his error, provided it be not
in the middle of a sentence. Thus if he remembered his error after he
had said ומקים אמונתו he must first add לישני עפר and then say משיב הרוח
וכו׳ and then he continues with מי כמוך וכו׳. But if he does not become
aware of the omission until after he has concluded the benediction
מחיה המתים, it is necessary to recommence the שמנה עשרה. It would not
be sufficient if he began with the words אתה גבור; for the first three
benedictions are here considered as one, so that if he conclude the
benediction improperly he must repeat the entire תפלה.

2. If one forgot to say טל ומטר, but became aware of the omission
before concluding the benediction מברך השנים, he says there ותן טל ומטר
לברכה על פני האדמה ושבעני וכו׳ and he concludes the benediction as is
proper. If he became aware of the omission after he had concluded
the benediction he continues the prayer and when saying the benediction שמע קולנו, after the words ריקם אל תשיבנו let him say ותן טל ומטר.

לברכה כי אתה שומע וכו'. And even if he did not remember his mistake until after he had said ברוך אתה, but if he had not said the Divine Name, he can say ותן טל ומטר לברכה כי אתה שומע וכו'. But if he only remembered the error after he had concluded the benediction שומע תפלה he repeats from ברך עלינו וכו'. If he recalled his mistake after saying יהי רצון וגו' he repeats the שמנה עשרה.

3. If he be in doubt whether he said משיב הרוח or not, then if it be more than 30 days since this formula has been included in the liturgy, so that he had said it 90 times as is proper, the presumption is that he has said it, since he is now accustomed to do so. If this occur during the 30 days, he must repeat the שמנה עשרה. Likewise with טל ומטר if the doubt arise after he had already said it 90 times in the שמנה עשרה as is proper, we rely upon the presumption that now also he has said it; but if less than 90 times the שמנה עשרה must be repeated.

4. If he forgot to say יעלה ויבא on the New Moon in the Morning or Afternoon services, or during the Intermediate Days of Festivals and he remembers his omission before saying יהי רצון he begins again at רצה; if he remember his omission before the benediction המחזיר שבינתו לציון he says יעלה ויבא there and concludes with ותחזינה עינינו וכו'. If he only remember his omission after he has said יהי רצון he must repeat the whole שמנה עשרה. If he forget to say יעלה ויבא on the New Moon in the Evening service, whether there be one or two days New Moon, as soon as he has said ברוך אתה ה' he cannot commence again that benediction, but must conclude with the words המחזיר שבינתו לציון and he must finish the שמנה עשרה. The reason for this procedure is that the New Moon was not sanctified at night.

5. If he forgot to say יעלה ויבא on New Moon or the Intermediate Days of Festivals in the Morning Service and although he only recalls his omission after the Mussaph in which he has made reference to the New Moon or to the Festival; nevertheless he must repeat the morning Amidah and if the time for doing this has passed, he must make compensation at the Afternoon Service.

6. Whenever he has to repeat the שמנה עשרה he must wait so long as it is takes to walk four cubits.

26

7. If the Reader made a mistake whilst saying his תפלה silently, he does not repeat it silently so as not to vex the congregation by the delay, as he has to say it aloud and this suffices.

8. On a fast day, whether it be for the congregation or an individual, in the afternoon עננו, שמנה עשרה is said in the benediction שמע קולנו and when one comes to the words בכל עת צרה וצוקה one concludes with the words כי אתה שומע וכו'. If he forgot to say עננו and does not remember the omission until after he had said the Divine Name in the benediction שומע תפלה, he does not repeat the benediction in order to say עננו, but after אלהי נצור before he moves his feet he says עננו, up to בכל עת צרה וצוקה and concludes with יהי רצון וכו'. If he remember his omission after he has moved his feet he does not say it at all.

[*NOTE.—This rule concludes with the procedure to be observed in case* שמנה עשרה *has been forgotten or omitted. The instructions are the same as for the* תפלה *which has been omitted see pp. 24, 25.*]

THE RULES CONCERNING THE READER'S REPETITION.

1. In the Reader's repetition, *i.e.*, when the Reader reads aloud the שמנה עשרה, everyone present must be careful to be silent and to hearken attentively and with devotion to what is being said, and to respond ברוך הוא וברוך שמו and אמן to each benediction as is proper. It is forbidden to study during the Reader's repetition. It is unnecessary to add that it is essential to avoid conversation. Everyone who is able should stand, just as though he himself said the שמנה עשרה.

2. In the repetition, as the Reader has already prayed silently and only repeats for the sake of the listeners, it is therefore necessary that at least nine people should listen and respond so that the Reader's benedictions be not in vain.

LAWS AND CUSTOMS OF ISRAEL

3. At the קדושה everyone must put his feet together and when they say קדוש and also ברוך and ימלך he should raise his body and it is the custom to look upwards.

4. When the Reader says מודים, all the congregation bow and say מודים דרבנן.

5. On a public fast, if there be in the Synagogue ten persons who fast the whole day, the Reader says עננו between גואל and רפאנו in the morning and afternoon תפלה. If he forgot to say it and remembered his omission before he mentioned the Divine Name of the benediction רופא הולי, he repeats and says עננו and רפאנו. If he remembered his omission after mentioning the Divine Name, he completes the benediction and says עננו in שמע קולנו like the individual. If he forgot even there, he says it after the end of the תפלה without any concluding benediction.

6. If an individual say the שמנה עשרה at the same time as the Reader the rule for קדושה is as follows : if he say the morning שמנה עשרה whilst the Reader recites the Mussaph, or vice-versa, and they both come to the words מחיה המתם then the individual must join the congregation in responding to the קדושה, but if the Congregation say the קדושה of the יוצר prayer or that of ובא לציון, he should not join the Congregation when he reaches מחיה המתים because the importance of the various forms of the קדושה varies.

7. In all such cases where an individual must repeat if he had made a mistake, the Reader also must repeat if he made a mistake in reading aloud the תפלה, except at the Morning Service of the New Moon or of Intermediate Days of Festivals, for if he omitted יעלה ויבא and did not remember his omission until after he had finished the תפלה, he does not repeat it because of the vexation inflicted upon the Congregation (if a repetition took place), we therefore rely upon the reference to the special occasion to be made in the Mussaph. If he remembered the omission before he finished the תפלה he begins again at רצה and this will not vex the Congregation.

The Rules Concerning Supplication.

1. After the שמנה עשרה of the Morning Service תחנון is said and if it be said in a place where there is a Sepher Torah prostration is performed. This is done by bending the head and reclining it on the left arm. At the Morning Service, since the Tephillah is on the left arm, we recline on the right.

28

LAWS AND CUSTOMS OF ISRAEL

2. The rite of prostration is performed sitting, but it may, in cases of emergency, be done standing.

3. On Monday and Thursday the supplications are increased and before תחנון we say the supplication והוא רחום standing and with devotion, slowly as is the custom when saying supplications, but it is not said on such days when we omit תחנון.

4. After תחנון half-Kaddish is said, followed by אשרי and למנצח.

5. On Monday and Thursday after the half-Kaddish following תחנון, we say אל ארך אפים and call up three adults to the Law, reading the first section of the portion of the ensuing Sabbath.

6. תחנון is not said on the following days : Sabbaths, Festivals, New Moon, Chanucah, Purim and Shushan Purim and the two days of Purim Katon (in leap years); the 33rd day of the Omer, the entire month of Nisan, the day after the three great festivals, between the Day of Atonement and Tabernacles, between the New Moon of Sivan and Pentecost, the Fast of Ab, the 15th of Ab and Shebat and the 2nd Passover (14th Iyar). תחנון is omitted at the Afternoon Service preceding all these occasions. At the Afternoon Service immediately preceding the day before New Year and the day before the Day of Atonement תחנון is said as also at the סליחות (Propitiatory Prayers) on the day before the New Year, but after סליחות it is not said that day.

7. We do not say תחנון in a Synagogue where a circumcision takes place or when the father of the child to be circumcised or the godfather or the circumciser pray therein even though the circumcision be elsewhere. If Afternoon Service be read in the house of the circumcision before the repast in honour of the rite takes place or during the repast, תחנון is not said. If Afternoon Service be read after Grace has been said, then תחנון is to be said but it is omitted even then by the father of the child, the godfather, and the circumciser because it is their festival.

8. It is not said in a Synagogue where a bridegroom is present during the seven days of bridal festivity, this applies when neither the bridegroom nor the bride had been married previously. But a widower who marries a widow enjoys this exemption concerning תחנון for three days only. When the Afternoon Service is read just before a wedding תחנון is omitted.

9. On the following week-days אל ארך אפים and למנצח are omitted :
29

New Moon, Chanucah, Purim and Shushan Purim and the two days of Purim Katon, the day before Passover, the day before the Day of Atonement, and the Fast of Ab.

10. In a mourner's house we do not say תחנון or אל ארך אפים or למנצח.

RULES FOR THE READING OF THE LAW.
GENERAL RULES.

1. It is a tradition of our sages that our teacher Moses instituted the custom in Israel of reading the Law in the congregation at fixed times, and that Ezra the scribe extended this custom, which it is necessary to observe very carefully.

2. We do not read in the Scroll of the Law unless it be written according to the proper rules. If three mistakes be found therein it is prohibited to read it until it be corrected, for the presumption holds good that it contains other mistakes. If a parchment sheet be torn or if the majority of the sewing be broken, it is prohibited to read it until repaired.

3. If a Minyan pray in a house and they have no Scroll of the Law, a Scroll must not be brought to them for the purpose of reading the Law, even if they be in prison and it be the New Year or the Day of Atonement. But if they prepare an Ark or a reading desk a day or two previously so that they have a fixed place for a Scroll of the Law, it is permitted to have the Scroll. Some authorities hold that it is not considered a fixed place unless they have read there three times consecutively. For the sake of an invalid who is a worthy man it is permitted to bring a Scroll merely for the purpose of the reading of the Law. Such people who take a Scroll from the Synagogue on the Holydays and Festivals and bring it to a place which has not been destined for the purpose, but they do so merely for the sake of the merit of being called to the Law, their reward is equal to their loss (owing to the infraction of the rule), and it is proper to prevent this custom.

4. In a place where there is no Scroll, someone should read aloud the portion from a printed Pentateuch and the congregation must listen, so that the reading of the Law should not be forgotten.

5. When the Scroll is carried from the Ark to the reading desk, it is to be carried northwards, i.e., to the right of the one who carries it and when it is taken back it is to be carried southwards. It is the

custom that all who are honoured with the privilege of taking out, and putting away the Scroll and also lifting it and rolling it up should follow it. When it is lifted up or when it is being carried all stand, even if some cannot see it.

6. When it is to be read it is the custom for the Warden or his substitute to stand at the side of the Scroll and he is called "Segan."

7. The number called to the Torah is as follows : On Monday and Thursday, public fasts, Sabbath afternoon, Chanucah and Purim three people are called up ; on New Moon and Intermediate Days of Festivals four people ; on the three chief Festivals and the New Year five people and the one to read the Haphtora (מפטיר) ; on the Day of Atonement six people and the Maphtir ; on Sabbath seven people and the Maphtir and the same when a Festival happens on the Sabbath. On the Rejoicing of the Law we increase the number if necessary. In some congregations they increase the number on Sabbath and in a few places also on the Festivals. As soon as the reading has commenced the entire congregation must be perfectly silent even in the interval between the calling up of the people. All must pay attention and it is not permitted to leave the Synagogue then, but if very urgent one may leave in the interval between the calling up of the people.

8. Whilst the people are being called up the Scroll must be covered and if the מי שברך be prolonged it must be covered with its mantle. It is also covered when קדיש it said prior to the Haphtorah. If three Scrolls are required and only two are available, then the first one used (which has already been rolled up and covered with its mantle) should be placed back on the reading desk, and rolled to the place where the third one, if available, would have been used.

WHO ARE TO BE CALLED TO THE LAW.

1. Of the priest it is written : "and thou shalt sanctify him" (Lev. xxi. 8) hence we learn that the priest must be honoured with the first privilege in all matters of holiness, as follows :

2. If a Priest (כהן) be in the Synagogue he must be called first to the Law and it makes no difference even if he be willing to waive his right. After the Priest we call a Levite and if the latter be not there, we call in his stead the Priest who had been called up and we say במקום לוי. If there be no Priest we call in his stead a Levite or an Israelite (ישראל), and we say : אין כאן כהן, לוי במקום כהן

31

or ישראל במקום כהן‎. If an Israelite be called up instead of a Priest, then a Levite must not be called up after him.

3. If the Priest be occupied in saying the שמע‎ or its benedictions or the Amidah, even if no other Priest be present, he is not called up and there is no need to wait for him, for delay is vexatious to the congregation. We call up a Levite or an Israelite and do not say אין‎ כאן כהן‎ but we say לוי אוי ישראל במקום כהן‎. Should the Priest, however, be called up and if he happened to be saying the שמע‎ and its benedictions, he goes to the reading desk and says the benedictions, but he must not read with the Reader but only listen. If he were saying the Amidah or just about to begin the Amidah, even if they called him up he must not go. If he were saying פסוקי דזמרה‎ he must be called up, if there be another Priest present, he should not be called up and this rule applies to a Levite also.

4. If a Priest or a Levite be called up and if neither be present they do not call up another person by name, so that people should not say that the one called up first was unfit to go to the Torah. The son of the absent person may be called up by his name. If a Priest or Levite cannot go up because he was saying the Amidah, another person may be called up by name, for all can see that he does not go to the Torah because he cannot. If they call up an Israelite and he is not present, they can call up another Israelite by name because no question of unworthiness applies in this case. Likewise if they called up a Priest or a Levite as the last (אחרון‎) or as Maphtir on Sabbaths or Festivals and he is not present they can call up another by name.

5. If there were no Priest in Synagogue, or if he happened to be there and they did not know it, and they called in his stead an Israelite who went to the Torah and said ברכו את ה' המברך‎ but did not say the benediction אשר בחר בנו‎; if the Priest came in or they remembered that he was there they call up the Priest and he goes to the Torah and he also says ברכו וכו'‎. The Israelite stands there until the Priest and the Levite have been called up and then he is called up, but if he had already said ברוך אתה ה'‎ the Priest cannot be called up. This is the rule also for a Levite who has been called up in the place of the Priest or vice-versa.

6. It is a rule not to call up a Priest or Levite (after their turn) among the fixed number to be called up. It is not the custom to call

either except as the last (אחרון) or as Maphtir. On a public fast day
neither may be called up even as Maphtir for this is one of the obligatory number to be called to the Law.

7. In cases of emergency, e.g. if the "Israelites" are not
sufficient for the necessary number, a Cohen or a Levite may be called
up in their stead, even two Cohanim or Levites provided an Israelite
be called up between each of them and then they are called up by name.

8. The following are entitled to be called to the Torah in the
following order of precedence : (1) A bridegroom on the day of his
wedding or on the Sabbath before his wedding. (2) A godfather on the
day of the circumcision. (3) The husband of a woman confined with a
daughter and on the Sabbath when his wife goes to Synagogue for prayers after the confinement. (4) The husband of a woman visiting the
Synagogue after being confined with a son. (5) One who has Jahrzeit on
that day. (6) The father of a son on the day of the circumcision.
(7) One who has Jahrzeit in the coming week. (8) The circumciser on
the day of the circumcision. (9) The godfather and then the circumciser on the Sabbath before the circumcision. If two people have
equal rights to be called up the decision rests with the "Segan." If
a person be not a member of the Synagogue, he must not take precedence before any member who has a right to be called up. It is a
custom to call up one who is starting on a journey after the Sabbath, or
one who has returned from a journey. We also are wont to call up
a respectable stranger for the sake of paying honour to him, but he
must not infringe on any one's rights who is entitled to be called up.

9. If a person has been called up in one Synagogue and came
to another where he is called up, even to the same section to which he
had already been called, nevertheless he goes up to the Law and says
the benedictions.

10. Two brothers are not called up consecutively, it matters not
whether they have the same father or mother. We do not call up
father and son or grandson consecutively, even though they declare
they do not mind this. When a separate Scroll is taken out for the
Maphtir, we may call one (of these relatives) as the last in one Scroll
and the other as Maphtir. In all these cases if he had been called up
and had already gone up he should not return. In cases of necessity
it may be permitted to deliberately call them up consecutively.

11. A child is not to be called up unless it be as Maphtir, except
for the "Four Special Sabbaths " (before Passover).

12. A blind man may be called up, for the prohibition to do so

could only refer to " words which are written in the Scroll which must not be said by heart," but nowadays the one who goes to the Law does not read as was the custom in olden days.

13. When a Bar Mitzvah is called up, it is the custom in many places that he reads the section; but if he be blind, he is prohibited to recite it by heart.

14. On a public fast day when ויחל (Ex. xxxii. 11) is read, only those who fast may be called up. If there be only one Cohen present who does not fast at all or who does not complete the fast, then a Levite or Israelite is called up in his stead, and it is right for the Cohen to leave the Synagogue.

15. If one's father became an apostate, and if he be grown up and had been accustomed to be called up by his father's name (N son of N) he is to be called up in this wise, but if he was not thus accustomed then he should be called up by his grandfather's name. If one's father be unknown he is called up by the name of his mother's father. It would, however, be better to call him up as the " Son of Abraham " just as we call up a proselyte.

16. He who is called up to the Torah, ascends to the Reading Desk by the nearest way from his seat and he descends and takes the longest way back; if both ways be equal he ascends by the right and descends in the opposite direction.

17. The Scroll is opened and the Reader finds the place where he has to read and the one called up takes hold of the handles when it is thus open and says aloud : ברכו את ה' המברך the congregation respond ברוך ה' המברך לעולם ועד and after the congregation has said this, the one called up repeats it and continues the benediction אשר בחר בנו and the congregation respond אמן. He then removes from the Scroll his left hand and takes hold of the Scroll with his right hand only during the reading. He also reads silently the portion and after the reading, he again takes hold of the Scroll with both hands and rolls it up and says the benediction אשר נתן לנו and whilst saying the benedictions he must not look into the Scroll so that the people should not be misled and think that they are written in the Scroll. Whilst saying the benediction and hearing the reading one must stand erect and one must not lean on anything unless he be very feeble. One waits until the person called up next has said the benedictions and then he descends from the Reading Desk.

18. He who lifts up the Torah opens it so that three columns of

34

the script are visible, and whilst it is open it must be shown on his right and on his left, in front and behind him, for it is the duty of everyone to see the script. The Scroll must be rolled up so that the sewing is in the centre. The handle attached to the beginning of the Scripture must be above the other handle. He who lifts up and he who rolls up the Scroll must avoid touching the parchment with their hands and, if necessary, they may touch it with the Tallis or Mantle.

THE RULES FOR THE READER OF THE TORAH.

1. A minor must not read the Torah in public.

2. The Reader must only read out of the Scroll, it is not permissible to read a single word from a book. All the time he reads he must stand erect and must not lean on anything.

3. The Reader must take care to pronounce the words correctly and to join them properly. He must prepare himself by reading the portion two or three times prior to the public recital, even though he be an expert.

4. If the Reader be inexperienced and another person stands near to read in advance, the latter must read quietly so that the public do not hear him, for "two voices are not able to be understood" and the congregation would not perform their duty of hearing the Law.

5. If the Reader made a mistake in such wise as to alter the meaning of the word, then he must repeat and correct it, but he need not do so if he made a mistake in the intonation. If he skipped a single word only and if he became aware of this after he had completed the entire portion, he must repeat and read that verse and the two following ones. All this refers to the Sabbath Morning reading, but at the Sabbath Afternoon service and on Monday and Thursday he does not repeat in case he skipped a single word.

6. The Reader may not begin until he has said אמן.

7. When they divide the Portion in order to increase the number of those to be called up, the Reader must not stop if he does not leave over at least three verses before the end of the portion or fixed points of conclusion (Pethuca or Sethuma where פ or ס is printed in the text). If the one called up had already said the benediction after the Reader had concluded, leaving less than three verses before the next portion, it is not necessary to commence the reading for the one called up next from the preceding verse; he commences only

35

from the place where the previous reading concluded and the **Reader** must read a further three verses of the next section. He must begin and end with a context dealing with a pleasant subject.

8. It is necessary to read at least three verses to every one called up. On Monday and Thursday and at Sabbath Afternoon service it is necessary to read to all called up at least ten verses in all, and to the third person at least four verses should be read. But if only nine verses have been read in all, three to each, this is valid. On Purim only nine verses are read in all and this is due to the fact that the lesson is contained in the nine verses.

9. On Sabbath when two portions are read, the second portion forms part of the fourth section.

10. The reproof in the portions בחקתי (Lev. xxvi. 3 ff.) and כי תבוא (Deut. xxvi. 1 ff.) must not be interrupted. One should begin from the preceding part, but so as not to begin a section with less than three verses, it is necessary to begin three verses before the reproof section and at the conclusion at least one verse after the end of the reproof section must be read; but he must not conclude with less than three verses from the beginning of the section. In the portion כי תשא (Ex. xxx. 11 ff.)we are accustomed to read in a subdued voice from ויתן אל משה ככלתו (ibid. xxxi. 18) up to ויחל משה (ibid. xxxii. 11) and when he begins ויהל he reads with a loud voice up to ויפן וירד משה (ibid. 15) and when he begins ויפן he again reads in a subdued voice up to ומשה יקח את האהל (ibid. xxxiii. 7) when he reads again in a loud voice to the end of the portion. Also the reproof in the portions בחקתי and כי תבוא is read in a subdued voice, but the verse וזכרתי את בריתי יעקב (Lev. xxvi. 42) is read in a loud voice and after that the verse והארץ תעזב (ibid. 43) in a subdued voice, but ואף גם זאת (ibid. xxvi. 44) in a loud voice to the end. In the portion כי תבוא the entire verse ליראה את השם הנכבד (Deut. xxviii. 58) is read in a loud voice, thereafter in a subdued voice up to ואין קנה (ibid. 68). In the portion בהעלתך (Nu. viii. 1 ff.) we are accustomed to read in a subdued voice from ויהי העם כמתאננים (ibid. xi. 1) up to והמן כזרע גד (ibid. 7). Whatever is read in a subdued voice must at least be audible to the congregation, otherwise they have not fulfilled their duty of hearing the Law. We must not interrupt the section of the "journeyings" in the portion מסעי (ibid. xxxiii. 1ff.).

11. When an extra Scroll is taken out, if it happen that they put upon the desk the Scroll set for another reading, even if they have opened the Scroll, they must change it and read out of the Scroll specially set.

LAWS AND CUSTOMS OF ISRAEL

ERRORS IN THE SCROLL.

1. If a defect be found in the Scroll whereby the form of the word is changed another Scroll must be taken out. If it be discovered between the calling up of two people, the Scroll is exchanged and we commence where the previous reading concluded and we complete the number of those to be called up. All who had been called up to the defective Scroll are reckoned among those to be called up. If it be Sabbath and it be possible to read in the exchanged Scroll seven people it should be done.

2. If the defect be found in the middle of the reading, diverse opinions and customs obtain. Where there is no fixed custom one must cease reading forthwith and another Scroll is taken out and we read where we stopped in the other Scroll. If this happened in the middle of a verse, the reading must start from the beginning of that verse and we finish the portion and the last benediction is to be said.

3. If the defect occur in the middle of the reading set for Maphtir and if this be a special one, e.g., on Holy Days or Sabbath New Moon or Shekalim, etc., when a special Scroll is taken out for the Maphtir then the rule is as in the preceding paragraph, but on an ordinary Sabbath when the Maphtir is a repetition of that read to the seventh person we do not take out another Scroll but conclude in the defective one omitting the last benediction. If the defect be discovered before the first blessing for the Maphtir section had been said, then we do not read this section, but the previous person (אחרון) says the Haphtora with its benedictions.

4. When we use more than one Scroll, if a defect be discovered so that another Scroll must be used, it is right to take out another one and not to read the section from the Scroll prepared for another reading, one should read from each Scroll that for which it is set.

5. What is meant by a serious mistake or defect? If, for instance, a superfluous or deficient letter or even if a single letter were changed so as to vary the reading, e.g., תומים (perfection) and תאומים (twins); מגרשיהן and מגרשיהם (their suburbs) although in this latter case the meaning is the same, nevertheless since the reading is not the same it is reckoned as a defect. If the mistake be of such a nature that it might be read in the same way as it would be if written properly, but it is so written that the meaning is changed thereby, e.g., in the portion תרומה (Ex. xxv. 1 ff.) ואמה וחצי רחבו (ibid. 10) if in place of רחבו we found רחבה although both words might be read alike, nevertheless as it is now written, it involves a doubt, it is reckoned a serious defect which changes the meaning.

6. If a single letter be split so as to appear like two, or if two letters be so near each other as to look like one, or if there be a superfluous word entirely out of place or a reduplication, or if there be a change in the form of the separate sections, e.g., a 'פ where a 'ס ought to be or vice-versa, or a division in a portion which is unnecessary or where a necessary division in the portion is wanting, all these cases constitute a defect involving the need of using another Scroll.

7. If one letter be joined to another, if it be clear that this arose after the Scroll had been written, it may be used providing the shape of the letters be not changed, but if it arose when it was being written then if the letters be joined before they are quite finished, e.g., if ז be connected with ה (thus חז) the Scroll is unfit for use then, but on a week day one can erase the letter where it is joined to the next. If the letters became joined after they had been written the Scroll may be used and another Scroll need not be taken out.

8. If a letter had lost its shape whether at the time when it was written or thereafter owing to the presence of an aperture then the Scroll is unfit for use, but if the aperture be in the middle of the letter or outside it so that the shape of the letter remains but it is not surrounded by parchment and it is evident that the aperture was made after the letter had been written then the Scroll is fit for use, because at the time of writing the letter, it was surrounded by parchment. If the ink had faded from any letter so that it is not black as is proper, the Scroll is unfit for use.

9. If there be any doubt as to whether any letter has its shape, it is shown to a child who is neither too clever nor too silly, and if he read it properly the Scroll may be used, otherwise not. If several children differ, the view of the majority is adopted. It is only when we are in doubt that we resort to the child, because then it is not merely a declaration of a mere fact for if we see that the letter is not as it should be and also if the upper part of ע and ש be missing or the lower part of ה and similar letters the Scroll may not be used, although a child might read the letter. In this case we see that the letter is not as it should be.

10. If the sewing between two skins of parchment of the Scroll be rent but the greater part thereof remains intact, we may read therein, if this be not the case we take out another Scroll, and if there be not another if the rent be in that book of the Pentateuch which has to be read, we do not read therein unless there remain over at least

38

five complete seams, but if the rent be in another book we read in the Scroll, although only two seams remain.

11. If wax or fat be found upon a letter or word and it be on a week-day it may be removed; but if it be on Sabbath or Holy Day and the letters be visible it may be read, but if the letters are so thickly covered so as to be invisible then if it be where the reading does not occur we may use that Scroll and say the benedictions. If it be where we have to read, and since it is prohibited to read even a letter other than from the written text, therefore if it be possible to remove the wax or fat there and then, i.e., if it were so thoroughly dry that by bending the parchment it would come off, let this be done otherwise we do not read therefrom. When they remove the wax or fat on week-days, if it cover the Divine Name care must be taken to avoid erasing the letters. One should warm the parchment on the reverse side so that the wax or fat fall off.

RULES CONCERNING ובא לציון AND אשרי.

1. We then say אשרי (Ps. cxlv.) and pay heed to the verse פותח then we say למנצח (Ps. xx.) which is omitted on the following days: New Moon, Chanucah, Minor Purim (two days), Purim and Shushan Purim, the day before Passover, Fast of Ab, the day before the Day of Atonement or in the house of a Mourner. When למנצח is omitted we do not say אל ארך אפים. The קדושה of ובא לציון with the Targum thereof is to be said with devotion, but the Targum is said silently. One must endeavour to say this קדושה with the Congregation and therefore if one should come into a Synagogue when the Congregation say this prayer he should join therein. This rule applies if he happened to say אשרי and the Congregation were about to say this קדושה, he should skip what he was saying and join them and afterwards he can say what he has omitted. One must not leave the Synagogue before this קדושה has been said. The Reader says full קדיש after this prayer.

2. We then say עלינו with devotion for it was instituted by Joshua, thereafter the Mourner's קדיש and the psalm for the day are recited, and when we leave the Synagogue we say the verse ה' נחני וכו' (Ps. v. 8) and we bow towards the Ark and depart, but we do not turn our back towards the Ark but we go out sideways. It is prohibited to run out of the Synagogue or to walk with great strides, but if one should go from the Synagogue to the House of Study it is a duty to hasten one's step.

The Rules as to The Mourner's Kaddish.

1. According to the Midrashim one's father and mother reap merit if their sons say prayers or Kaddish in public, therefore it is the custom to do this and to endeavour to be called up Maphtir during the entire eleven months from the day of the burial of father or mother. Thus if this took place on the 10th of Ellul, Kaddish and public prayers should be recited by the mourner until and including the 9th of Ab and at night he ceases to do this. In a leap year he ceases to say Kaddish at the evening of the 10th of Tamuz. A man should charge his sons to walk in the ways of the Torah, and especially should he urge them to cleave to this or that precept to do it faithfully and zealously and thereby to bring merit to his parents. This is a good rule. If perchance they are unable to pray regularly in public or to say Kaddish, at all events let them be careful to say the Evening Service especially at the termination of Sabbath, for this is a propitious time to pray for Divine Grace. Of course one must not say prayers in public unless one be acceptable to the Congregation and such a person who knows how to say the prayers should do so and let a child (who is a mourner also) say the Kaddish. If one's mother died, but the father be alive, then he should say Kaddish in memory of his mother and his father must not object. But if both his parents be alive, he must not say the Mourner's Kaddish in memory of other relatives, but to read Service and to say the various forms of Kaddish in the Service is permitted.

2. An adult in the first seven days of mourning (שבעה) who goes to Synagogue on Sabbath, even if he had a proper Service in his own house, is nevertheless entitled to all the Kaddêshim and takes precedence in this matter before one in the first 30 days of mourning as well as before one who has Jahrzeit. A child, in the first seven days of mourning, who goes daily to the Synagogue, is also entitled to all the Kaddêshim even though one in the first 30 days of mourning be present. But one who has Jahrzeit must have one Kaddish. If there be several people who have Jahrzeit they have all the Kaddêshim and the child is debarred. As regards Kaddish in the first seven days of mourning there is no difference between a stranger or a member. We do not apply the rule " part of the day equals the entire day " with reference to Kaddish, so that even on the seventh day at the afternoon service the rule for one in the first seven days of mourning applies.

3. If one's mourning of the שבעה be annulled owing to a festival, nevertheless during all the first seven days after the day of burial the rules of a child keeping שבעה apply to him, e.g., when he goes to the Synagogue. Likewise if his father died on a festival, the rules of a child keeping שבעה apply to him with reference to Kaddish, and after the festival, even when he keeps the mourning, he has not nevertheless

with reference to Kaddish the right of one keeping שבעה, except for the first seven days from the day of burial. Thereafter he only has the rights of one in the first thirty days of mourning. Likewise if one only hear of the demise of his father or mother after many days, although he keeps the customs of mourning, he only has the rights of a person keeping שבעה during the first seven days (of his mourning).

4. A child and an adult keeping שבעה have the same privileges. If there be an adult and a child keeping שבעה and also one who has Jahrzeit, and Kaddish has to be said three times, then the Jahrzeit does not say Kaddish and the adult keeping שבעה says Kaddish twice and the child says it once ; for the adult says to the child, I have not taken the Kaddish from thee but from the Jahrzeit.

5. A Jahrzeit or one in the first thirty days of mourning must take precedence before mourners who are keeping the year of mourning with reference to all occasions for saying the obligatory Kaddish, for these latter mourners say the Kaddish constantly. If there be a person in the first thirty days of mourning and a Jahrzeit, the latter says one Kaddish at each service on that day. If there be several persons who have Jahrzeit corresponding to the number of Kaddêshim, the one observing the first thirty days of mourning is debarred from saying Kaddish (that day). In some Synagogues the rule obtains whereby the Kaddish de Rabbanan and the Kaddish after עלינו are allotted to the Jahrzeit or to the one in the first thirty days of mourning and the other Kaddêshim are distributed among the other mourners if their numbers correspond respectively, (e.g., three mourners to say three Kaddêshim).

6. If there be two mourners with equal rights, e.g., both in the שבעה or both mourners during the rest of the year, or both having Jahrzeit, then they cast lots for saying Kaddish. The one who is privileged to say the Kaddish at the Evening Service does not say it next morning, when it is said by the other mourner without casting lots. But for the third Kaddish (at the Afternoon Service) they cast lots, so also if there be many mourners. The one who says one Kaddish does not participate in the casting of lots until each mourner has said a Kaddish also.

THE RULES OF KADDISH WITH REFERENCE TO A MEMBER AND A STRANGER.

1. If a person have a seat in a Synagogue even though he does not dwell in its neighbourhood, or if a person dwelt in its neighbourhood and constantly prays in the Synagogue without renting a seat, they are reckoned as members with reference to Kaddish. But if neither of these be present, then everyone else is considered to be a stranger, e.g., if he dwelt in the neighbourhood, but always prayed in another Synagogue, then he is to be debarred from saying Kaddish even though he be in the שבעה, for he is accounted as being inferior to a stranger because the latter has no other Synagogue, whereas he has.

2. A member who has Jahrzeit entirely debars a stranger who also has Jahrzeit from saying Kaddish. A member who observes the first thirty days of mourning or the rest of the year of mourning yields one Kaddish to a stranger who has Jahrzeit. If there be a member having Jahrzeit and a member in the first thirty days of mourning and a stranger having Jahrzeit, then the last-named has one Kaddish, but the member who has Jahrzeit cannot deprive the stranger who has Jahrzeit of his Kaddish, for the latter can say, I have not deprived thee but only the one keeping the thirty days of mourning. The member with Jahrzeit says the first Kaddish, the stranger says the second Kaddish and the one in the thirty days says the third Kaddish.

3. A member in the rest of the year of mourning and a stranger in the first thirty days have equal rights and they share at each Service the Kaddêshim. In the case of a member having Jahrzeit and a stranger in the first thirty days, the former says Kaddish twice and the latter says it once. A stranger in the rest of his year of mourning is entitled to one Kaddish among the members if they also be in the rest of their year of mourning. If there be many mourners with equal rights the rule obtains in some places, so as to avoid strife, to let them all say Kaddish together. If one knew that his father and mother were evildoers, it is proper then to say Kaddish for twelve months.

4. If one have special rights in the matter of saying Kaddish, e.g. one in the שבעה or in the first thirty days of mourning or a Jahrzeit, he also enjoys the privilege of officiating. If two have equal rights and are both able to officiate and are both acceptable to the Congregation, then they cast lots for one to officiate; up to אשרי ובא לציון and the other one continues from אשרי ובא לציון. If only one of them be able to officiate, he still retains his rights as to Kaddish. If only one be acceptable to the Congregation then the rule in the preceding sentence obtains.

3. On Sabbath and Festivals a mourner does not officiate, but if he had been accustomed to do so on Sabbaths and Festivals before he became a mourner, then he may do so in spite of being in mourning.

6. If one be a mourner or have Jahrzeit for one's father as well as for one's mother, he does not enjoy any rights above those of any other mourner or Jahrzeit with reference to officiating or Kaddish, because in both instances the memorial is the same.

LAWS AND CUSTOMS OF ISRAEL

The Rules Concerning Jahrzeit.

1. It is a duty to fast every year on the day when one's father or mother died. In the Afternoon Service of the anniversary he says עננו as on a private fast day. If he fasted once without making any reservation then he must consider this fast as though he had vowed to keep it and he must always fast on the anniversary. If he be unable he must have his vow annulled. If he distincly declare that he does not accept the fast as a vow, annulment is unnecessary. If he cannot fast, he should strive at least to repent and should carefully examine his actions and regret his sins.

2. It is the custom to kindle a lamp for Jahrzeit on the eve of the anniversary and if this should fall on Sabbath and he forgot to kindle it whilst it was yet day, then he can request a non-Jew to kindle same before night. On Sabbath it may not be kindled even by a non-Jew. On a Festival a Jew may not kindle same. One must be particular in always having this lamp kindled in the House of Study so that people may pray and learn by its light. If we have the anniversary on one day for two dead relatives, one lamp suffices in this case.

3. The anniversary is always the day of death, even in the first year. If the death took place at the close of the day, after Mincha had been said, but if it be still day than that day is fixed as the Jahrzeit. If three days or more have elapsed between death and burial, the first Jahrzeit is observed on the anniversay of the burial and in subsequent years on the anniversary of the death. If one died in Adar in an ordinary year, two Jahrzeits are observed in a leap year, on the particular date in the first Adar and on the same date in the second Adar, but the one keeping Jahrzeit may not bar other mourners or a Jahrzeit from saying Kaddish. If the death took place in a leap year, then in that particular month in which death took place the Jahrzeit is observed. The day of Jahrzeit is always reckoned according to the date of the Hebrew month. The months of Marcheshvan, Kislev and Adar sometimes have the last day of their respective months counted as New Moon, so that sometimes the following months have one day New Moon and sometimes two days. If one's father or mother died on the first day of the New Moon, if in the next year when the Jahrzeit is observed there are also two days of the New Moon, the Jahrzeit is observed on the first day of the New Moon. Thereafter whether there be two days of the New Moon or one day, the Jahrzeit is observed on the New Moon, that is to say, where there are two days of the New Moon, the Jahrzeit is kept on the first day

43

of the New Moon, but if the New Moon be only one day the anniversary is on that day. If at the first anniversary the New Moon be only one day, then in any year thereafter when there are two days New Moon (of the month in question) the anniversary is observed on the first day of the New Moon, and in any year when the New Moon is only one day the anniversary is observed on the 29th day of the preceding month, i.e., the day before the New Moon. On the New Moon if there be no other people entitled to Kaddish, the one who kept the Jahrzeit on the preceding day may officiate and say Kaddish, but he must not infringe upon the rights of others.

4. One who has Jahrzeit does not fast on the anniversary if it fall on any day when תחנון is omitted. On a day when a circumcision takes place the following persons may not observe thereon the Jahrzeit fast: the father of the child circumcised, the godfather, the operator; likewise on the day when the first born son is redeemed neither the father nor the Priest concerned observe the Jahrzeit fast. The bridegroom during his week of marriage festivities does not keep the Jahrzeit fast. A person who has Jahrzeit may not partake of the repast held in connection with the conclusion of the reading of a Talmudic tractate. On the eve of one's Jahrzeit he must not eat at a bridal banquet because the wedding musicians are playing, but he may eat at a feast in connection with: (1) a circumcision or (2) a redemption of a first-born son or (3) the conclusion of the reading of a a Talmudic tractate.

5. If one be unaware of the day of his father's or mother's death, he should select a certain day to keep thereon the anniversary; but he must not encroach upon the rights of others with regard to Kaddish. If one had Jahrzeit but failed to say Kaddish on the anniversary owing to some cause or other, he should say Kaddish at the Evening Service following his day of anniversary.

6. If there be no mourner for father or mother in the Synagogue, anyone whose parents are both dead should say Kaddish in memory of all the departed in Israel. In some places the custom obtains that people say Kaddish for relatives when there are no mourners for parents present. Even though there should be mourners for their parents and if anyone desire to say Kaddish in memory of his son or daughter who died childless, the other mourners should allow him to say one Kaddish after each of them had said one Kaddish. In some places it is the custom to say Kaddish for any relative (apart from one's parents) even though there be present mourners for their father or mother. But a distinction is to be made by not allowing the former as many Kaddeshim as the mourners for parents say. In all this one follows the custom provided or fixed for that place.

RULES CONCERNING THE STUDY OF THE LAW AND THE SANCTITY OF SACRED BOOKS.

1. Every Israelite must fix a certain time by day and

study the Torah, at least after his prayers he should study the laws which are essential for every Israelite to know. If one cannot study through inability to learn or by reason of his many diversions, he should support others who devote themselves to study and this will be accounted unto him as though he himself had studied. When one studies and must interrupt his reading, he must not leave his book open. Whatsoever he studies he should read audibly and attentively.

2. It is an affirmative precept devolving upon every Israelite to write for himself a Scroll of the Law. If he inherited a Scroll from his father, he is in duty bound to write one for himself. If he bought one and found a mistake in the writing and corrected it, in this case it is accounted as though he had written it. A Scroll must not be sold, but if one be compelled to sell his property, he must consult the Ecclesiastical Authorities. It is the duty of every Israelite to purchase sacred books for study and lending purposes.

3. One must treat the Scroll with deepest respect and appoint for its custody a special place which must be beautifully adorned. One must not spit before a Scroll, nor take hold of the parchment without the cover. If one see a Scroll being carried before him, he must stand up until he can no longer see it. In the Synagogue when the Scroll is taken out or replaced, it is to be followed by the worshippers. If sacred books be placed on the bench it must not be used as a seat unless the books are put on something which is a hand-breadth in height. It is, of course, forbidden to put the books on the ground. A Scroll must not be put on one's knees resting his arms thereon. In an emergency one may sit on a chest containing sacred books, but it is forbidden to do so if a Scroll be therein. The Pentateuch may be placed upon the Prophetical Books or upon the Hagiographa, but neither of the latter two may be placed upon the Pentateuch. One must not do anything objectionable before these books nor should they be turned upside down and if they be thus found, they must be put in their proper position. If the Scroll or any sacred book or anything used for divine worship be worn out, it must be hidden away.

4. One must not use a sacred book for a personal benefit, e.g., to use it as a screen against the sun, unless he should do this for the purpose of study, when it is permitted to do so. One must not deliberately make coverings or mantles for the Scroll from material which has been used for ordinary purposes, but if it has been done we are permitted to use them. This does not apply in any case if the material had been used for idolatrous purposes. One must not destroy anything which has been used for a holy purpose.

45

LAWS AND CUSTOMS OF ISRAEL

5. When an Israelite sees a Scroll, Tephillin or Mezuzoth in the possession of a non-Jew he should try to buy them, but he should offer neither too little nor too much but he should give him their proper value.

6. If a Scroll fell out of one's hand, even in its mantle, he is obliged to fast and all who witness this should fast also. One must not write a verse of a sacred document without traced lines, one must not write profane words in the script used for the writing of the Scroll of the Law.

RULES CONCERNING THE PROHIBITION OF TALEBEARING, SLANDER AND OTHER ETHICAL PRINCIPLES.

1. It is written: "Thou shalt not go up and down as a tale-bearer among thy people" (Lev. xix. 16), this refers to a tell-tale who goes from one to another saying: "Thus spake so and so concerning thee. I have heard concerning so and so this and that which he did to thee." Although it might be true one must not do this. More blame-worthy than this is slander which means speaking unfavourably of one's fellow, even though it be the truth and if he utter false reports, he is guilty of defamation of his fellow's character. It is pro-hibited to curse anybody even when a rebuke is administered. One must not vex his fellow, even to grieve him by one's words is forbid-den. One must neither participate in quarrels nor associate with evil people. It is a duty to associate oneself with God-fearing people.

2. It is written: "Thou shalt not hate thy brother in thine heart" (ibid. 17), this means that even if he speak peacefully unto his fellow, he must not hate him in his heart. If one asked one's fellow to do him a favour but he refused, then the former must not bear a grudge against him. It is prohibited to take vengeance. One must judge one's fellow charitably unless he be known as an evildoer. If one saw him acting improperly, it is a duty to rebuke him. One should not put oneself in danger. Should a non-believer in a discus-sion utter incorrect statements concerning the Torah, he must be answered, but if his remarks refer to worldly matters he need not be answered. One should not suffer oneself to quarrel with an evildoer when fortune smiles on him. One should not show favour to a transgressor of the Law, unless he be afraid that the latter will kill him. One must not speak indecently or scoffingly and he should neither say any unbecoming word nor do anything disgusting in the presence of his fellow.

3. When a man hears evil reports concerning his fellow from one person they must not be believed unless they be substantiated, when they may be believed. When a man sees anyone doing evil, he

46

should rebuke him directly and, if necessarily, repeatedly. A pupil may rebuke his master if he think he will listen to him, and he should rebuke his fellow man even if he will not listen to him. It is prohibited to tell others what he has heard from his fellow without his consent. One must not speak too much of his fellow's goodness, for too much praise may lead to his disgrace. A visitor must not praise his host lest too many other visitors become a burden to him.

4. Every one is commanded to love all human beings as one loves oneself, provided they are good and upright, but one must hate an evil person who will not accept rebuke. One is obliged to love strangers and look after orphans and widows even though they be very wealthy. Anyone who vexes them or provokes them to anger or grieves them or domineers over them or wastes their fortune transgresses a negative precept ; this applies much more if one smite them or curse them. All this applies when one afflicts them for his own advantage, but if it be for their benefit, e.g., to teach the orphans the Torah or a trade or to train them in the right path, it is permitted. Nevertheless , one must lead them with love and mercy. They are considered to be orphans in this matter until they no longer need the assistance of another and are able to keep themselves. One must not put a stumbling-block in the way of a person who is ignorant of the good and righteous way, lest he transgress the Law.

5. The following are general moral rules : Not to talk about other people except for some good cause. Neither to utter nor to listen to idle words which serve no useful purpose. To cultivate a silent tongue and not to talk except to acquire wisdom or to satisfy the needs of one's physical life. To speak gently with one's fellow creatures. Not to talk of material things in the House of Study. To learn from every man and to accept the truth from all who speak it. To be anxious to promote the welfare of his fellow and to pursue peace. To remember the day of death and continually to have in one's mind the purpose of his creation in this world.

6. Men differ according to their natures : some are jocular and happy, others are sad and mournful ; some are gentle, others are hard-hearted ; some are boastful whose desires are never satisfied, others lack all desires even for the actual needs of life ; some constantly pursue material gain, whilst others are idle not even seeking their daily needs. Likewise is it with all ethical principles.

The right course for a man to accustom himself to pursue is the golden mean, and he should avoid any extreme. Nevertheless if he should accustom himself to some evil habit, so that he has gone to one extreme, the best counsel for this person is to go to the opposite extreme, until he can eradicate this vice from his nature ; thereafter he should pursue the golden mean. Pride is an extremely bad vice, and therefore the proud should pursue the opposite extreme and become humble in spirit. Likewise with anger, all those addicted thereto must strive to avoid becoming angry in any circumstance. But when one has to exercize his authority over his children, he may pretend to be angry in their presence, whilst in his heart he is quite composed.

7. A man must not pray to God to punish his fellow, and even though he cannot obtain redress on earth he should not adopt such a course without informing him of his intention.

8. A man must not accustom himself to indulge in flattery or deception, saying one thing with his tongue and thinking otherwise in his mind. The inner spirit must correspond with the actions of a man and what one has in one's heart must find expression in one's word. It is forbidden to deceive any human being, whether Jew or non-Jew. For instance, one must not sell meat which is ritually forbidden (נבלה) as though it were ritually allowed (שחוטה), nor shoes made from the leather of an animal which died of itself (מתה), as though it were the leather of an animal ritually slaughtered (and therefore superior in quality). One must not urge his fellow to be his guest, when he knows that he will not accept. A man must not offer gifts with importunity, knowing they will not be accepted. One must not pretend to open casks of wine with the intention of deceiving anyone as though it were done to show him honour, whereas he opens them in order to sell the wine. Any similar action is prohibited, even one word of dissimulation or deceit is forbidden. One's word must be true and one's spirit honest and one's heart free from all works of deceit. One must avoid doing anything which might lead others to suspect him of transgressing the Law. It is a rule of holiness not to accept a gift from any man, but only to trust in God.

RULES FOR PHYSICAL WELL-BEING.

1. Since it is God's will for man to keep his body healthy and sound, because it is impossible for a man, if he be ill, to understand anything concerning the Creator, it is necessary therefore to avoid aught what injures the body but rather to accustom oneself to such actions which promote physical well-being, namely : A man should eat only

48

4

when he is hungry, and drink only when he is thirsty. He should not neglect for a moment the calls of nature, but he should arise forthwith and attend thereto. One must not eat overmuch, but rather leave off eating before he has quite satisfied his appetite. He should drink only a little water mixed with wine during the meal. He may drink as much as he needs when his food has commenced to be digested and even when it has been digested he should not drink too much water. He must not begin his meal until he has attended to the calls of nature.

2. A man should not eat unless he has had exercise and made his body fairly warm, or unless he has done some work which has made him tired. As a general rule, one should take physical exercise every morning until the body becomes fairly warm, thereupon he should rest until he has regained his normal condition and then he should eat. It is good to take a warm bath when one is tired, then let him rest awhile and then eat.

3. When one has eaten one's meal, he should continue to be seated or recline on his left side, but he should neither go for a walk nor ride, nor weary himself, nor excite his body, nor move about until his food had been digested. If one should move about or weary oneself directly after eating, he renders himself liable to serious illnesses.

4. The day and night have 24 hours, it is enough for a man to sleep a third part thereof, i.e. 8 hours. These hours should be at the end of the night, so that from the beginning of his sleep until sunrise, eight hours should intervene, consequently he will get up just before sunrise.

5. A man should sleep neither on his face nor on his back but on his side; at the beginning of the night on his left side and at the end of the night on the right side. He should not go to sleep directly after eating, but he should let three or four hours elapse. He should not sleep by day.

6. Such things which possess laxative qualities, e.g., grapes, figs, mulberries, pears, melons and various kinds of cucumbers and other melons, should be eaten before the meal and must not be mixed with one's food. Therefore after partaking thereof he must wait awhile until they have been partly digested and then he should take his meal. Fruits with costive qualities, e.g., pomegranates, quinces, apples and pears may be eaten immediately after the meal, but in moderation.

7. Should one wish to partake of poultry and meat at the same meal, he should eat the poultry first; should he wish to eat eggs and poultry, he should eat the eggs first, so also with mutton or lamb and beef, he should eat the mutton or lamb first. As a general rule, one should always eat first such things which are more easily digested.

8. In summer he should eat cooling food, avoiding too much spice but rather using vinegar. In winter he should partake of heating food with plenty of spices and a little mustard and asafœtida. Let him observe similar rules according to the climate of the place where he lives.

9. Some food is extremely injurious and should be entirely avoided, e.g., large stale salted fish, stale salt cheese or mushrooms and truffles, old salt meat and wine from the press and cooked food which has lost its flavour or food with a very bitter taste, all these are to the body as a deadly poison. Again there are some kinds of food which are also injurious, although not to the same extent as the former; therefore one should partake but little of them and on rare occasions. He must neither use them for his daily food nor eat them continually with his meals. Again these kinds of food are injurious : large fish, cheese, milk which has stood for more than 24 hours after the milking, the meat of large oxen or big rams, beans, lentils, pulse, barley bread, un-leavened bread, cabbage, leek, onions, garlic, mustard and radish. One should partake thereof but very sparingly and only in winter. One should avoid them altogether in summer. A meal of beans or lentils only should not be eaten, either in summer or in winter. In summer cucumbers may be eaten.

10. There are other kinds of food which, although injurious, are not so bad as those last mentioned. They are as follows : water-fowl, little young pigeons, dates, bread dried in oil, fine flour which has been so thoroughly sifted so as not to leave a particle of bran, also fish-brine and pickle. One must not partake of these in excess. A prudent man, who can curb his appetite and does not suffer himself to be carried away by his desires, will abstain altogether from these things unless he needs them as medicine.

11.   One should abstain from fruits of the trees and should not
eat too much thereof, even dry fruit, much less fresh ; but before they
are quite ripe they are like swords to the body.   Carobs are always
injurious, also all sour fruits are bad, and should only be taken in
small quantities in summer time and in hot climates.   Figs, grapes and
almonds are always wholesome, whether fresh or dried.   One may
partake of them to his satisfaction.   Yet he must not use them as his
daily food, although they are more wholesome than all the other fruits
of the trees.

12.   Honey and wine are injurious to the young, but wholesome
to the old, especially in winter.   One should eat in summer two-thirds
only of the amount which one takes in winter.

13.   One should always see to it that his bowels are lax, even if
they be more than slightly relaxed, for this is a fundamental rule of
health.   As long as the bowels are constipated or act with difficulty,
serious diseases ensue.   How can one cause his bowels to become
relaxed if they be slightly inclined to be constipated ?   If he be an
adult he should take boiled salts and spices with olive oil and fish-hash
without bread every morning, or he should take any other effective
aperient.   If he be an old man he should take honey dissolved in warm
water in the early morning and then wait about four hours before
taking his breakfast, let this be done for a few days, if necessary, until
his bowels become relaxed.

14.   There is another rule to be observed regarding physical
health : as long as a person works and takes plenty of exercise, and
does not eat to satiety, and his bowels are regular, he is sure to escape
illness, and he will find his strength increasing, even if he should eat
unwholesome food.

15.   But any one who sits idle, taking no exercise whatever, or
who neglects the calls of nature, even if he take the most wholesome
food, and live strictly according to the laws of health, yet all his life
will he be ailing and find his strength failing.   Excessive eating is
like deadly poison to the body of man and is the cause of all diseases ;
indeed, most maladies which befall men arise either from unwholesome
food, or from excessive eating even of wholesome food.   To this
Solomon wisely alludes : " *Whosoever keepeth his* MOUTH *and his* TONGUE,
keepeth his life from troubles " (Prov. xxi. 23) referring to the one who
keeps his mouth from eating unhealthy food or from gluttony, and his
tongue from speaking except what is necessary for his daily needs.

16. The following are the rules for bathing : one should take a bath once a week, it must not be taken immediately after meals, nor when he is hungry, but when the food begins to digest. He should bathe the whole of his body in warm water, but not so hot as almost to scald the body, the head only in warmer water; afterwards he should bathe in tepid water, then some degrees cooler, and ultimately in cold water; the head, however, should not be washed either with tepid or cold water. In winter one should not bathe in cold water, nor take the bath until the whole body perspires and the blood thoroughly circulates. He should not stay long in the bath, but as soon as his body perspires, and his blood is in circulation, he should rinse himself and get out. He should take care to attend to the calls of nature before bathing or afterwards ; this also applies before meals or after meals, before or after exercise, as well as before or after sleep.

17. When he quits the bath he should dress and cover his head forthwith so as to avoid taking cold ; even in the summer time he must be careful. After leaving the bath he is to wait awhile till he has refreshed and rested himself, and the heat has subsided, and then he may take his meal. If he can sleep a little on leaving the bath, before he takes his meal, so much the better. He must not drink cold water when he comes out of the bath, much less in the bath ; but if he be thirsty on leaving the bath, so that he cannot resist drinking, then he may take water mixed with wine or honey. After one's bath in the winter it is beneficial to have the body rubbed with oil.

18. He who conducts himself according to the rules, which we have laid down, can be assured that he will not suffer illness all his days until he reaches a ripe old age and dies. He will not need a physician, and he will always enjoy good and perfect health, unless he had an unhealthy constitution from his birth, or had given way to evil habits from early youth, or owing to extraordinary calamities, such as an epidemic or famine.

19. All these rules, which we have mentioned, are for the guidance of the healthy only ; but a person who is ill, or who has led for many years an irregular life, must follow other rules and prescriptions according to the nature of his malady, as it is explained in the book on medicine ; change of the regular course of life is the root of all illness.

20. Where there is no physician, it behoves both the healthy and the sick not to depart from any of the rules mentioned in this chapter, inasmuch as each of them leads to a beneficial result.

21. In a town where the following are not to be found, a wise man ought not to reside, viz. :—a physician, a surgeon, baths, public convenience, water supply from the river or a spring, a Synagogue, a teacher, a scribe, an overseer of the poor and a court of law.

Rules for Preserving the Health of Body and Mind.

1. It is good to accustom oneself to take breakfast in the morning. A person should endeavour to dwell in a locality where the air is clear and pure, on elevated ground and in a house of ample proportions. If possible he should not reside in the summer in a place facing north or east, and it should be free from all decayed refuse. It is very beneficial to continually purify the air of the house with good disinfectants. One should see that the atmosphere of the house is maintained at an even temperature, neither too hot nor too cold, but so as neither to chill a person nor to make one too warm.

2. Our sages of blessed memory have said, that one should not eat the heart of an animal or fowl. One should not eat any food which had been partly eaten by a mouse, rat or any other animal.

3. To preserve the sense of sight one should note the following : not to go suddenly from a dark place to a well illuminated place, or vice-versa, for the sudden change is very injurious to the optic nerve, therefore the eyes should become accustomed gradually to the change. Light reflected by the sun is injurious to the eyes, i.e., the light reflected from a surface upon which the sun shines affects the eyesight. One should not strain his eyes in the dusk of twilight nor in the sunshine of mid-day nor at night by lamp light. He should neither gaze steadily at white or bright red colours nor at the glare of fire. Smoke and sulphureous odours are injurious to the eyes. Fine dust or strong wind or excessive walking or a rapid gait or excessive weeping, are all injurious to the eyes ; but "the precept of the Lord is pure, enlightening the eyes " (Ps. xix. 8).

The Rules of a Perfect Man.

1. Let a man be neither a glutton nor a drunkard, he should eat only in his own house but neither in a shop nor in a market-place,

except through great necessity, and one should not eat frequently at all sorts of places, nor should one partake of meals where there are large gatherings unless it be a feast for a religious purpose. One should not drink more wine than is necessary to dissolve his food. To become intoxicated is sinful and disgraceful, and causes his wisdom to diminish. It is forbidden to drink wine at noon, not even a little at the end of the meal, but it is allowed in the course of the meal.

2. A wise man acts as follows: first of all he establishes himself in a business or profession from which he derives a livelihood, he then buys a house as a residence, and then he marries. The business of a man learned in the Law must be honest, giving a liberal price when he buys from other people, not being too stringent with them and paying at once. He becomes neither a surety, nor a receiver, nor does he act in an authoritative spirit, nor does he assume business responsibilities which the תורה does not impose on him, so that his words are consistent without any alteration thereof. If others become liable to him by law, he is lenient with them and forgives them. He lends and is merciful, he does not interfere with the occupation of his neighbour, and never distresses anyone in securing a livelihood. As a general rule of conduct one should be of those who are persecuted rather than the persecutor, and of those who are reviled rather than the reviler.

3. The perfect man in all his deeds acts justly. Our sages have taught:—A man's outlay for food should be less then he can afford, he should dress according to his means, but for the happiness of his wife and children he may spend even a little more than his usual expenditure. A man must not dispose of his entire property, even for a sacred cause and thereby become a public charge. One should not sell his field for the sake of purchasing a house, nor sell his house in order to buy chattels or to invest the money in business.

THE LAWS OF REPENTANCE.
(FROM THE CODE OF MAIMONIDES).

1. If a man trespass against any of the precepts, either presumptuously or through ignorance, he is bound to confess before God when he repents and turns from his sin, as it is said: "When any man or woman shall commit any sin . . . Then they shall confess the sin which they have done" (Nu. v. 6, 7). By which is meant *verbal confession*. Now this confession is a *positive commandment*. The more amply one confesses and reflects on the matter the more praiseworthy is he. Even if a person had been wicked all his life and at last he repented, not the least part of his wickedness will be recorded against him. (See Ezek. xxxiii. 12.)

2. What constitutes perfect repentance? If an occasion in which a man had once transgressed occur again, and yet he shrinks from it, and does not sin, such a person is a true penitent, and this is what Solomon said : "Remember now thy Creator in the days of thy youth" (Eccl. xii. 1). However if one repent only in his old age, or when it is no longer in his power to do that which he was in the habit of doing : although this is certainly not genuine repentance, yet it still avai s, and he is said to be a penitent. Though he may have been a transgressor all his life, yet if he repent on the day of his death, so that he die a penitent, all his sins are pardoned.

3. Now what is the nature of repentance? It means that the sinner forsakes his sin, and removes it from his thoughts; and that he resolves in his heart never to do it again, as it is said : "Let the wicked forsake his way" (Is. lv. 7). He also ought to be sorry for the past, as it is said : "Surely after I repented, I was grieved" (Jer. xxxi. 19). And he ought also to call God to witness who knows all secrets, that he will never return to this sin again.

4. The penitent should cry continually to the Lord with weeping and supplication; he should give charity as much as he can ; he should remove very far from his transgression, and he should altogether alter his actions for the better, and in a direction conformable to the way of righteousness, and to become meek and lowly of spirit.

5. It is praiseworthy for the penitent to confess saying : Surely I have offended such and such a person, and I have done unto him so and so ; but I now repent, and deeply regret my conduct. But he who is proud, and does not acknowledge in public his transgressions, "shall not prosper" (Prov. xxviii. 13). This, however, refers only to transgressions between man and man ; but concerning transgressions between man and God, he need not make them public, as it would be a mark of arrogance if he were to do this. He need only repent before God, and specify his sins to Him alone, but in public his confession ought to be a general one, as it is said : "Blessed is he whose transgression is forgiven, whose sin is covered " (Ps. xxxi. 1).

6. Although repentance and supplication are at all times commendable, they are still more so during the ten days of penitence between the New Year and the Day of Atonement, as then the supplications of the penitent are accepted, as it is said : "Seek ye the Lord while he may be found" (Is. lv. 6). This applies only to an individual. As for a congregation, whenever they repent and make supplication with all their hearts, they are answered, as it is said :" As the Lord our God is in all things when we call upon Him " (Deut. iv. 7).

7. The Day of Atonement is the proper time for general repentance, both for the individual and the public, as being the definite time of pardon and forgiveness to Israel. Every one is therefore bound to repent and to confess on the Day of Atonement. The confession should actually begin on the day preceding the Fast and before taking the final meal before the Fast, lest death overtake him before

he had confessed. But although one had confessed before eating the final meal, he ought to confess again on the Day of Atonement.

8. Repentance and the Day of Atonement atone only for transgressions between man and God; for instance eating a thing which is forbidden, and similar transgressions; but with regard to offences between man and man, for instance, if one injure or curse his fellow man, or rob him, and the like offences, he is never pardoned until he restores to him that which he owes him, and until he appeases him. For although he restored to his fellow man the money which he owed him, it is necessary to appease him and ask his pardon. Should he however not be willing to pardon him, he ought to bring with him three of his friends, in order that these may diligently plead on his behalf; should the offended party still not be reconciled, he ought to bring his friends a second or even third time; but should the other still be unwilling to grant him pardon, he may leave him alone and depart, and then the one who refuses pardon becomes a sinner. However if the offended party happen to be his teacher, he must repeat his entreaties even a thousand times until he obtains his pardon.

9. It is not lawful for a man to be cruel and implacable; he should be easily moved to reconciliation, and with difficulty moved to anger. Even though the other had seriously oppressed or offended him, still he must not avenge himself, nor bear a grudge; this forbearance is the characteristic of the seed of Israel.

10. If one offended another and the latter died before the offender had sought his pardon, he ought to take with him ten men to the grave of his fellow and say before them these words: I have sinned against the Lord God of Israel, and also against this man, having done unto him so and so. Moreover if he owed him money, he ought to restore it to his heirs: if, so far as he knows, there be no heirs, he ought to deposit it in a court of justice and make his confession.

11. He who regrets having fulfilled the commandments, and deplores his good deeds, has altogether undone the merit of his previous good life, and no merit of his whatsoever will be remembered unto him, as it is said: "The righteousness of the righteous shall not deliver him on the day of his transgression" (Ezek. xxxiii. 12), which applies to anyone who regrets his former good deeds.

12. The following have no portion in the world to come: (1) he who denies God and Providence; (2) he who says that there is a Providence, but that this Providence consists of two or more Deities; (3) he who says that there is indeed only one God, but that He is corporeal and has a similitude; (4) he who says that He is not the only first being and the Rock of the whole universe; (5) he who worships besides Him some star or planet, that the same may become an intercessor between himself and the Lord of the universe; (6) he who says that there is neither prophecy, nor any kind of knowledge which, emanating from the Creator, enters into the minds of the sons of men; (7) he who denies the prophecy of Moses, our teacher; (8) he

who says that the Creator knows not the actions of the sons of men ;.
(9) he who says that the Law is not from the Lord ; even if he say of
one verse or of one word, that it was invented by Moses ; (10) he
who denies the interpretation thereof which constitutes the Oral Law ;.
(11) he who says that the Creator has changed one precept for another,
so that this law is already abolished, although it was originally from
the Lord ; (12) he who denies the resurrection, (13) and the coming
of the Redeemer ; (14) he who transgresses only one commandment
presumptuously, and habitually, becoming notorious thereby ; (15)
he who is a transgressor against the whole Law, e.g., who embraces
the creed of the idolators and adheres to them, saying : "Of what
benefit will it be to me to adhere to the Israelites who are humbled
and persecuted ? It will be better for me to adhere to these idolators
whose power is uppermost"; (16) those who cause the public to sin in.
important matters or in trivial matters or whether one force others to
sin or whether one delude others and thrust them away (from God);
(17) he who departs from the moral and religious life of the congregation, though he commit no real transgression but only separates
himself from Israel, so that he neither fulfils the commandments with
them, nor sympathizes with them in their distress, nor fasts with
them, but follows his own self-willed course, just as though he were a.
non-Jew and not one of them ; (18) he who transgresses presumptuously in public, whether trivial or important laws, moreover such a man
is said to be perverting and misinterpreting the Law, inasmuch as
he was impudent enough unblushingly to violate the Law ; (19) he
who by his information delivers up his fellow-man into the hands of a
tyrant who will slay or torture him ; (20) he who delivers up the
property of his fellow-man into the hands of a tyrant ; (21) he who
rules over a congregation by force, so that they fear him greatly,
whilst the object he has in view is to gratify his ambition, and not that
of delighting in the glory of Heaven ; (22) he who sheds man's blood ;.
(23) he who slanders ; (24) he who conceals the mark of circumcision.

(13). None of these twenty-four classes of men just enumerated,
although they be Israelites, will inherit the world to come. There
are, however, transgressions less serious than those mentioned above,
but according to the opinion of the sages, he who habituates himself to
these sins, has no share in the world to come. They must be shunned
and avoided. The following are the sins alluded to : He who gives
his fellow-man a degrading by-name, or calls him by a degrading by-
name given by others ; he who puts another to the blush in public
or glories in his disgrace ; he who despises scholars or teachers or
the festivals ; and he who profanes sacred things. What we have
said here, however, namely that these sinners have no share in the
world to come, holds good only when the sinner dies unrepentant ; but
if he turn from his wickedness and die penitent, then such a man

inherits the world to come, for there is nothing which cannot be atoned for by repentance ; even though one deny the fundamental religious principle all his life, still if he repent at the end, whether publicly or secretly, his repentance will be accepted and he will inherit the world to come.

14.   There are twenty-four causes which prevent man from repenting. Four of these being serious offences, God might not suffer him who commits any of them to become a penitent, because his offence is of too serious a nature. The following are the sins : (1) he who causes the public to sin, or prevents the public from fulfilling any of the precepts ; (2) he who causes his fellow to turn aside from the good to the wicked way, e.g., the seducer and enticer (cf. Deut. viii.) ; (3) he who sees his son falling into vice, and yet does not check him, whilst under his control. To this class he also belongs, who has it in his power to restrain others (not his children), whether an individual or a multitude, and yet does not do so but suffers them to stumble ; (4) he who says to himself : I will sin now but the Day of Atonement will atone for it. Again there are five causes which obstruct the ways of repentance before all who practice them. They are :—(1) he who separates from the congregation ; because he does not participate in their repentance and consequently he will not profit by their merits ; (2) he who gainsays the words of the sages, because such refutation causes him to separate from them, and he remains ignorant of the nature of repentance ; (3) he who scorns the precepts for he will neither seek after them nor fulfil them, and then how can he obtain merit ?; (4) he who despises his teachers, wherefore the teacher will discard and expel him, as Gehazi was expelled by his master. Thereafter he will not find a teacher to guide him in the way of truth. (5) He who hates rebuke, whereby he has left to himself no means of repentance, for rebuke gives rise to repentance. Again there are five sins which the transgressor cannot amend, because they consist of offences between man and man, in cases when the offender does not know enough of the person offended to be able to make amends to him or to entreat his pardon. They are the following :—(1) he who curses a multitude of men, without having specified any one in particular, of whom he might have asked forgiveness ; (2) he who shares in the plunder with the thief, because he does not know to whom the thing stolen belonged, it being the thief alone who stole the same and brought it to him, whereas he only bought it of the thief. Moreover by purchasing stolen goods he encourages the thief and consequently causes him to sin. (3) He who finds a thing which was lost, and has not advertised it so as to enable it to be restored to its owner, for should he after a lapse of time become a penitent, he will still not know to whom he ought to restore it ; (4) he who lives by the spoil of the poor, orphans, or widows. Now these are dejected and not well known, and are sometimes forced to wander from city to city. it may so happen that there will be no one who knows anything of them, and of

whom he (the spoiler) can learn to whom that spoil belongs and to whom he ought to restore it; (5) he who takes a bribe to pervert judgment, because he cannot know how far this perversion may extend, or what consequences it may have, so that he might make amends for it, moreover he gives his support to the one who has given the bribe and causes him to sin. Again there are five sins for which the offender is not likely ever to become a penitent because by the generality of men they are considered to be trifling matters, and consequently one may sin by committing the same, and yet imagine that it is no sin. They are the following: (1) he who partakes as a guest of a repast, which he knows is not sufficient even for his host alone; (2) he who uses for his own advantage the pledge of a poor man; (3) he who looks at women with a lustful eye; (4) he who glories in the disgrace of his fellow-men; (5) he who suspects an honest man. Again there are five sins of such a nature that he who commits the same will always be addicted to them, so that it will be difficult for him to renounce them. They are the following:—(1) tale-bearing; (2) slander; (3) passion; (4) evil thoughts, and (5) associating with the wicked. All these and the like sins, although they may retard a man from becoming a penitent, cannot altogether deprive him of that benefit, but on the contrary if one repent of the same, he becomes a penitent, and has a share in the world to come.

15.   Do not say that only such transgressions as are connected with an act require repentance; it is not so, but in the same way as one ought to turn from these transgressions, so ought he also to examine the wicked disposition he may have, and to turn from anger, hatred, jealousy, mockery, the pursuit after wealth and honour, or after dainty food and the like; from all these ought a man to turn with repentance. And indeed these sins are even more serious than those connected with some act, inasmuch as when man is plunged in these, it is very difficult for him to extricate himself from them. Moreover the penitent must not imagine that he is far below the degree of the righteous because of the iniquities and sins which he has committed. The matter is not so; but he is beloved and acceptable to the Creator as if he had never sinned; indeed his reward will be greater still; for he has tasted of sin, and yet has abandoned it, and subdued his wicked desires. Thus the sages say : The position which the penitent occupy, not even the perfectly righteous themselves can attain; meaning that the degree of the penitent is even higher than the degree of those who have never sinned, inasmuch as the former had to overcome their evil inclinations, far more than the latter.

Things Prohibited for the Sake of Body and Soul.

1.   The sages have prohibited many things because they are injurious to life. Whosoever transgresses and says : "Verily I injure myself, how does it concern others?" or, "I disregard this matter," truly he risks his life. The prohibitions are :—Not to put the mouth under

a tap from which the water is running and drink. He should neither drink water from rivers or ponds, nor should he drink at night in the dark lest he swallow something injurious, nor should he drink luke-warm water which had not been boiled, even though it be in a metal vessel provided he had not put tea leaves in it. It is, however, permissible to drink it out of an earthenware vessel, or if it had been boiled or if he had put tea leaves in it. It is forbidden to walk in a dangerous place, for instance near a bulging wall or on a broken bridge, nor should one go out alone at night, nor sleep in a house alone, nor should one utter an evil prognostication against an Israelite, even to say, If so and so were alive he would have come here, for "a covenant is made with the lips." One must not open one's mouth inauspiciously by invoking evil upon himself, nor should any one frighten a child by means of an unclean thing, by saying, "A cat or dog will fetch you."

2. It is forbidden to eat fish with meat, even with poultry fat. One should not bake in a small oven meat and fish unless one or the other be covered, and if one eat fish and immediately thereafter meat or vice-versa, he should eat some bread and drink some beverage between them, this will wash it down and rinse his mouth. It is also forbidden to partake of food and drink loathsome to a man's soul or out of unclean vessels, nor should one eat when one's hands are unclean. One should also be careful not to drink of any uncovered beverage.

3. One should guard against a person's perspiration, because it is like a deadly poison, with the exception of the perspiration of the face. Therefore, one should not allow any food to come into contact with any part of his body which is perspiring, nor should anyone put money in one's mouth, as some perspiration may cling to it, moreover since it has circulated through many hands, including people with infectious diseases. One should also avoid placing under a bed any kind of food or drink, even though it be covered.

4. It is forbidden to cut down a fruit-tree bearing fruit, for instance, an olive tree producing a quarter (Kab) measure of olives, and a date tree producing a measure of dates, because it is dangerous to do so, but if the tree adjoin other more valuable trees and cause them to waste away (through its proximity), or if he require the space it

occupies, or if it be more valuable for its timber than for its fruit, it is permissible to cut it down. One who is constipated is forbidden to employ the remedy recommended by some people, namely the application of a hot water bottle to his abdomen, as it is dangerous to do so without the instruction of a physician. It is also forbidden to cross a stream when the water is rising, so that it reaches above his loins, as he is in danger of the water carrying him away. If a beast and fowl were in danger, and were afterwards slaughtered, although it was lawful to slaughter them, still the scrupulous are most careful not to partake of them. One must also avoid everything that leads to danger, as it is even more important to guard against danger than against the infringement of a precept, and the risk of danger is to be apprehended even more than the risk of infringing a precept.

5. There is no one more wicked than he who commits suicide, as it is said : " And surely your blood, (the blood) of your lives, will I require " (Gen. ix. 5). The world was created for the sake of man as an individual, thus he who destroys one life in Israel is as though he had destroyed the entire world, and he who preserves one life in Israel is as if he had maintained the entire world.

LAWS REGARDING CHARITY.

1. It is a positive precept to give charity to the poor, as it is said : " Thou shalt surely open thine hand unto him " (Deut. xv. 8). It is also said : " That thy brother may live with thee " (Lev. xxv. 36) ; furthermore he who is deaf to the supplication of the poor and refuses him relief, transgresses a negative precept, as it is said : " Thou shalt not harden thine heart, nor shut thine hand from thy poor brother " (Deut. xv. 7). One must be careful not to infringe that law, lest by its violation he might be guilty of bloodshed in causing the death of the supplicant by not granting him immediate relief. One should remember that fortune's wheel is ever revolving, and that such a man may eventually have the same measure meted out unto himself, his son or his grandson.

2. No one ever becomes impoverished by giving charity, nor will any evil or harm result from its practice, as it is said : " And the work of charity shall be peace " (Is. xxxii. 17). To the merciful mercy is shown, as it is said : " And shew thee mercy, and have compassion on thee, and multiply thee " (Deut. xiii. 17). If one be cruel and merciless it may be assumed that his lineage is non Jewish, since cruelty is not a characteristic of the children of Israel. All Israel and those who are associated with them are like brethren, as it is said, " Ye are the children of the Lord your God " (ibid. xiv. 1) and if a brother should not be merciful to a brother, who shall shew compassion unto him ? To their brethren alone are the eyes of the poor uplifted.

3. He who is deaf to the appeals of charity is called Belial, as it is said, " Beware that there be not a thought in thy heart of a Belial " (Deut. xv. 9), he is also called " wicked," as it is said : " But the tender

mercies of the wicked are cruel" (Prov. xii. 12). He is also called "sinner," as it is said, "And he cry unto the Lord against thee, and it be sin unto thee" (Deut. xv. 9) for the Holy One, blessed be He, is nigh unto the cry of the poor, as we say, "Thou hearest the cry of the poor" (cf. Job xxxiv. 28), therefore one should beware lest they cry against him unto God who hath made a covenant with them, as it is said, "And it shall come to pass, when he crieth unto Me, that I will hear; for I am gracious" (Ex. xxii. 27).

4. He who gives alms to the poor with an unfriendly mien and downcast face, even if he give a thousand pieces of gold, has no merit owing to his manner of giving, but one should give joyfully with a cheerful mien, he should also sympathize with him in his distress, as it is said, "Did I not weep for him that was in trouble? Was not my soul grieved for the needy?" (Job. xxx. 25).

5. If a poor man ask your help and you have nothing to give him, then appease him with words. It is forbidden to rebuke a poor man, for his heart is broken and humble, as it is said "A broken and humble heart, O God, thou wilt not despise" (Ps. li. 17). Woe unto him who has put the poor to shame. One should be as a father unto them in tender mercy, as it is said, "I was a father to the needy" (Job xxix. 16).

6. He who urges others to give charity and causes them to practice it, earns a greater reward than he who gives, as it is said: "And the work of charity shall be peace" (Is. xxxii. 17). Concerning the almoners, and others like them, it is said, "And they that turn many to charity (shall shine) as the stars for ever and ever" (Dan. xii. 13).

7. There are eight degrees in the practice of charity, one higher than the other. The highest degree which cannot be excelled is attained by him who comes to the relief of an Israelite who has become poor, by making him a gift or a loan or by entering into partnership with him, or by obtaining employment for him, thus he relieves him from his poverty, so that he is not forced to seek support from his fellow creatures. Concerning him it is said, "Then thou shalt relieve him... he shall live with thee" (Lev. xxx. 35) that is, assist him so that he fall not into poverty.

8. A lower degree than the former is attained by one who gives charity to the poor without knowing who is the recipient thereof, the identity of the donor being likewise unknown to the poor, this is truly a duty performed for its own merit, for such a purpose was the private room in the Temple where the righteous were wont privately to make contributions. Similar to him is he who deposits his donation in a contribution box. However no man should place his donation in a contribution box unless he knows that the man in charge thereof is trustworthy and wise, one who is like Rabbi Chananiah Ben Teradion, and understands the proper dispensation of charity.

9. A still lower degree is obtained by one who knows to whom he gives but his identity is unknown to the poor, such was the practice of the great Sages who were wont to go secretly and throw the money

LAWS AND CUSTOMS OF ISRAEL

inside the homes of the poor. This is a proper mode of procedure and it is a good measure to adopt in case the officials of the charity do not act in a proper manner.

10. A degree inferior to the last is attained when the poor person knows from whom he receives although his identity is unknown to the donor. Such was the practice of the great Sages who had the money tied up in the mantles hanging over their shoulders in such a way that the poor could take the alms without being put to the blush.

11. A degree inferior to the last is attained by him who places the money in the poor man's hand before the latter asks for same.

12. An inferior degree is attained when one gives alms after he had been asked to give.

13. An inferior degree is attained by one who gives less than he ought, even if he give with a cheerful countenance.

14. The lowest degree in alms-giving is to give with a disagreeable mien.

15. The greatest of our Sages were wont to give a Peruta (a small coin) to the poor before prayer, then they would pray, because it is said, "As for me, I shall behold Thy face in charity" (Ps. xvii. 15).

16. He who supports his adult sons and daughters, whom he is not obliged to maintain, but he acts thus in order to teach his sons the Torah, and to lead his daughters in an upright way that they come not to shame, also he who maintains his father and mother, behold, they are accounted charitable. They thus perform great charity, as the nearest of kin are entitled to precedence. He who entertains the poor and the orphans at his table, behold, he calls unto the Lord, and He answers him, as it is said : "Then shalt thou call, and the Lord shall answer" (Is. lviii. 9).

17. The Sages have ordained that the members of one's household should be the poor and the orphans in the place of servants, it is well to make use of those so that the children of Abraham, Isaac and Jacob benefit thereby, and if the poor be the members of a man's household he is always adding to his meritorious deeds and to the fulfilment of the precepts.

18. A man should at all times suffer hardships rather than become a public charge or solicit the support of the community. Our Sages taught, "Make thy Sabbath as a week day (not to live better on that day) and do not need the aid of the public." If one were an honoured Sage and he became poor, he should find some occupation, even of a menial kind, rather than need the support of the community. It is better for him to flay a carcase, rather than to say to the people, "I am a great Sage, I am a priest, therefore support me." Some of the greatest of the Sages were hewers of wood and carriers of beams, they were also engaged in drawing water for gardens, they even toiled with iron and coal and they neither asked the community to support them, nor did they accept anything when offered to them.

19. One not needing alms, who deceives the people and takes, will not die of old age until he actually requires the help of the community and he is included amongst those of whom it is said: "Cursed is the man that trusteth in man" (Jer. xvii. 5). One who is in need of alms and cannot exist unless he would take help, e.g., an old man or a sick man or a suffering man, but he does not take through pride, behold he sheds blood and forfeits his own life, and he has nothing for his pains except sin and trespass. But he who is in need and rather suffers distress and constrains himself to live a life of hardship so that he shall not become a public charge, he will not die ot old age until he has supported others from his own means, and of him and such as he, it is said: "Blessed is the man that trusteth in the Lord" (*ibid.* 7).

(Quoted from Maimonides, "Gifts to the Poor" Chapter x.)

20. Every man must contribute to charity according to his means. Even a poor man who, having a little money of his own, is yet permitted to obtain support from the contributions of charity, as what he has is not sufficient to provide him with capital to invest in business and to support himself with the profits, nevertheless, as he has something to live upon, he is obliged to give charity from that which is given to him; even if it be only very little that he can give, yet should he not withold it, for the contribution of his mite is as esteemed as the largest of the rich.

21. How much shall a man contribute to charity? The first year the tithe of his capital, thereafter the tithe of his annual profits apart from his household expenses, this, however, is but charity of a modest kind, but the most approved manner of fulfilling this commandment is to give a fifth of the capital the first year, and thereafter a fifth of the annual profits. One should not devote more than one fifth, so that he may not eventually need the support of the community. This rule, however, is only applicable during a man's lifetime, but at the time of one's death, he can bequeath even a third of his fortune to charity. One should not apply the tithe-money to the fulfilment of any (other) commandment, it is to be given solely to the poor; however, when it happens that one has to fulfil a commandment, e.g., to become a בעל ברית (one who initiates a son into the covenant of Abraham), or to dower a bride and bridegroom who are poor, and thus enable them to enter into wedlock or commandments of a similar nature, also to purchase religious books wherein to learn and to lend them to others to learn therein; if he could not afford to spend his own money, and consequently, would not have fulfilled any of these commandments, he may use the tithe money for these purposes. One who buys religious books with the money set aside for tithes, must be careful to lend them to others, unless he needs them for his own use, when he takes precedence, he should also write on them that they were bought with the tithe-money, so that his children, after his death, shall not take possession of them.

64

22. How much should be given to a poor man? Sufficient for his needs, this applies, only to a poor man who receives charity privately, in his case the men of his city must supply all his wants, even to maintain him in the same style in which he was accustomed to live before he became poor. But for the beggar who goes begging from door to door a small sum is given, in proportion to one's means. In any case the least that is to be given him in each town is bread sufficient for two meals and a place where he may sleep. The poor of all other nations must be fed and clothed equally with the poor of Israel.

23. He who desires to prove himself worthy must suppress his evil passions and open his hand, and see that everything that he does for the glory of God shall be of the best, thus if he build a Synagogue it must be more beautiful than his own home. When he feeds the hungry he must feed them with the best food from his table; when he clothes the naked, he must clothe them with his best garments, when he consecrates a thing he should consecrate his best possession.

24. One's own maintenance takes precedence before that of any one else. One is, therefore, not obliged to give alms before he can maintain himself, thereafter he shall give to others in the following order of precedence: His parents, his children, his brother from the father's side, his brother from the mother's side, other relatives, his neighbours, the poor of his city, the poor of another city. More especially must care be taken in the treatment of a scholar who is poor, to give him in a manner according to his dignity, and if he be unwilling to accept charity, some goods should be obtained for him, and if he know how to conduct a business money should be lent to him wherewith to do business. Our Rabbis, of blessed memory, say: "He who supplies a scholar with goods whereby he may gain a livelihood, is worthy of the future life," they also said: "The predictions of all the Prophets apply to the one who establishes a scholar in business, and who gives him his daughter in marriage." The wife of a Sage must be assisted equally with the Sage himself. The inhabitants of the Holy Land must be assisted before the inhabitants of any other land. It is one's duty to feed the hungry before clothing the naked. A woman should be assisted before a man, both as regards food as well as with reference to raiment. One who is indebted to other people should not exceed in giving charity.

25. A promise to give charity is in the nature of a vow. If one say, This coin is to be for charity, it must be given to the poor at once, and if he delay in giving it he transgresses the precept: "Thou shalt not delay" (Deut. xxiii. 21), since he could have given it forthwith. However if the poor are not present, he should lay that money aside until he finds poor people (to whom to give it). When one makes an offering in Synagogue, where the money is given to the treasurer, he does not transgress the precept until the latter had asked for it, non-compliance with this demand makes him transgress that precept, unless he knows that the treasurer does not then

need the money for charitable purposes, but that he would only keep it in his possession. One who declares, "I will give this coin as charity to this poor man," then he does not transgress that precept until that poor man came and he refused to give. One may put aside a certain sum of money for charity which must be in his care, and he may make a gradual distribution thereof when he sees fit.

26. One who devotes anything to charity may inscribe his name thereon, so that he may perpetuate his memory.

Laws Concerning the Separation of the Dough (חלה).[1]

1. Dough of the following five species of grain, viz.: wheat, barley, spelt, rye and oats, must be separated. Previous to separating same he says : ברוך אתה ה' אלהינו מלך העולם אשר קדשנו במצותיו וצונו להפריש חלה. Then dough of the size of an olive is taken and burnt. The rule is to burn it in the (fire of the) same oven where the bread is being baked.

2. The quantity of dough which becomes liable to the Law of Challah is five quarters of flour, or the quantity of forty-three and one-fifth eggs.

3. If one prepare dough for cooking or frying purposes, he must separate the Challah portion without saying a benediction. If a part thereof, be it ever so little, be used for baking, the Challah portion must be separated and the benediction must be said.

4. If the dough be kneaded with eggs or with the juice of fruit, then a little water or milk or honey or wine or olive oil should be mingled therewith so that the Challah portion can be selected therefrom and the benediction said.

5. Two portions of dough which singly do not contain the requisite quantity for Challah, but together make up the required quantity for separating the Challah, or if one portion contain the requisite quantity and the other does not, if both belong to a person who is not particular about their being mixed together, and if the portions be connected in such a way that the separation of one portion would cause some of the other to be separated with it, then they count as one to make up the requisite quantity for separating the Challah, and even if they be not connected together but are in one vessel, then that vessel unites them so that Challah is obligatory.

6. The unleavened cakes baked for Passover, although each mass of dough does not contain the requisite quantity of flour for separating the Challah, nevertheless by being placed in one vessel it unites them and makes the separation of the Challah obligatory. Care should be taken to have all the unleavened cakes inside the vessel, yet if part be inside the vessel and part outside, nevertheless they count as one, but if

---

[1] See Num. xv. 20 for Laws as to Challah, the priests' share of the dough.

whole unleavened cakes be outside the vessel, they do not count as one (quantity), even if he covered them with a cloth it does not avail. If he had placed the unleavened cakes in a sheet it is considered as though it were a vessel to make them count as one even though some of the unleavened cakes in the middle be uncovered, care should be taken that whole unleavened cakes are not outside the sheet.

7. The leaven taken from the dough for causing fermentation in other dough should be removed before the Challah is separated. But the leaven taken for causing fermentation in liquids should be removed after the Challah has been separated.

8. The precept concerning the separation of the Challah applies especially to a woman, but if she be not at home, and it is to be feared that the dough may become spoiled before she returns, then the servant or some other person can separate the Challah.

9. If one forgot to separate the Challah on the Eve of Sabbath, in countries other than Palestine the bread can be eaten on the Sabbath, and a portion of it is left over and at the termination of Sabbath when the Challah is to be taken therefrom, that portion should be large enough for the Challah to be separated therefrom and still leave something over, as it is necessary to recognize by the remainder that its Challah has been separated.

10. People who buy bread of Jewish bakers who are suspected of not having separated the Challah from the dough, should separate Challah from the bread without saying a benediction. One who buys bread from a non-Jewish baker need not separate the Challah therefrom.

LAWS CONCERNING THE SALTING OF MEAT.

1. Before the meat is salted it must be thoroughly washed in water. All the meat should be soaked and entirely submerged in water for half an hour. Wherever a particle of blood is visible it should be thoroughly washed off. This applies also to fowls where the incision is made at the killing thereof, and also inside the fowls where any blood is visible. Sometimes in cattle and fowls lumps of coagulated blood due to a wound are to be found, these must be cut away and removed before the meat is soaked. When the water is very cold, it should be made luke-warm before the meat is soaked therein, because

on account of the cold in the water the meat becomes hardened and thereby the blood will not emerge when the meat is salted.

2. If one forgot and allowed the meat to soak in water for twenty-four hours, the meat as well as the vessel in which it was soaked must not be used, if this occurred with liver, then the ecclesiastical authorities should be consulted.

3. On the Eve of the Sabbath where there is no time to spare or on another occasion, when one is pressed for time, it is sufficient to thoroughly wash the meat and let it soak just a little in water and when the water is no longer coloured red (because of the blood) the meat may be salted.

4. If the meat were cut up after the soaking into two pieces, it must be thoroughly rinsed especially where it has been cut on account of the blood which is in that part.

5. Meat that was hardened by the frost must be softened but it must not be placed near a hot fire. In a case of emergency it may be soaked in tepid water.

6. The utensil used for soaking the meat must not be used in connection with any other kind of food.

7. After the meat has been soaked the water must be shaken off so that the salt should not dissolve and thereby the blood will not be drawn out. It is necessary to take care that the meat should not have become quite dry as otherwise the salt would fall off.

8. The salt should not be as fine-grained as flour, as it would forthwith become dissolved and would not properly absorb the blood. Very coarse grained salt is also not to be used for that purpose as it drops from the meat. It should be neither too fine nor too coarse, like the salt prepared by being boiled, but it must be dry so that it can be thoroughly sprinkled.

9. The meat must be well sprinkled on all sides with salt so that there is not a spot left unsalted. One should therefore take care to open poultry properly so that they can be salted from within.

10. The meat that has been salted must be placed where the blood can easily flow therefrom, therefore the drainer with the meat thereon must not be placed horizontally, as the flow of blood will be impeded thereby. Even though the meat remained in salt for the proper period of time (one hour) previous to cleansing it, yet it should not be placed where the blood cannot flow freely therefrom. The drainer on which the salted meat should be placed must be put in an oblique position in order that the blood may freely flow down. There

must also be no hollow part in the drainer where fatty matter can accumulate. When one salts poultry or the entire abdomen of an animal which contains a cavity, then the same must be turned downwards so that the blood may freely flow down.

11.   The meat should be salted for one hour, but in cases of emergency 24 minutes suffice.

12.   After the meat had remained in the salt the proper time, the salt should be entirely brushed off therefrom and the meat thoroughly washed three times. A God-fearing woman will personally supervise the washing of the meat, for her servant may sometimes stint with the water and thereby blood might be there contrary to the law. The meat before it had been washed must not be placed inside a vessel without water.

13.   Care must be taken to remove the heads of poultry before being soaked and if they were salted with the heads attached, the ecclesiastical authorities must be consulted. The same rule must be applied in respect to cattle.

14.   Meat which had not been salted must not be placed on a spot where salt is sometimes put. A special vessel for the meat must be set aside and one must not put therein vegetables or fruit or other articles of food which are consumed without being washed, for the blood from the meat clings to the vessel and thereby it may be communicated to the articles of food.

15.   The head must be split open and the brain must be removed and the membrane upon it must be rent before the soaking can take place. After the head has been soaked it is salted by itself within and also without, even though the hair be there.

16.   Bones containing marrow whilst they still adhere to the meat should be salted together with the meat just as they are; but if they be separated from the meat, they should be salted by themselves, and during the salting they should not be placed near the meat.

17.   The hoofs of animals must be cut round at their extremities before the soaking takes place so that the blood can flow out. It is permissible to salt them upon the hair and they must be put in such a position that the blood can flow out.

18.   It is necessary to rend the heart before the soaking takes place so that the blood may issue forth.

19.   It is also customary to cut the lung of the animal and to lay open the large tubes which it contains before soaking takes place.

20.   The liver which has a large quantity of blood is not made ready for cooking by the mere process of salting, but it must be broiled prior thereto.   It should be properly rent asunder and where the rent is, it must be placed on the fire in order to draw out all the blood thoroughly. It must be washed before it is placed on the fire and slightly besprinkled with salt as it is broiling over the fire.   It should be sufficiently broiled to make it fit to eat.   Then it must be thoroughly washed so that all the blood which has been discharged is rinsed off.   Care is to be taken that it should be washed three times and it can then be cooked.

21.   Care should be taken to broil the liver over the fire only and not in an oven cleansed of ashes.   It must also not be tied to a spit, even though it be a small one.   The liver, before it is broiled, should not be salted in the same manner as meat is salted, and more especially it must not be salted together with meat.

22.   The spleen is governed by the same laws as apply to meat, with the exception, however, that the membrane which surrounds it, which is forbidden because of the fat which it contains, should be removed before the soaking.   It should be porged as follows: the head of the vein (of the spleen) is taken out which draws along with it three cords contained therein, care should be taken not to sever any of these cords, for if they be severed it is necessary to remove them.

23.   The bowels and other entrails should be salted on their exterior surface where the fat adheres.

24.   The udder must not be salted together with meat, and it is customary not to cook it but to broil it over a coal fire; before it is broiled it should be rent cross-wise so that the milk issues forth; after it has been broiled it is permissible to cut it with a knife used for meat, but it is forbidden to broil the udder in a vessel, as this is termed cooking (בשׁול).

25.   The stomach of a calf containing milk must have the latter removed before the soaking and it is then treated like other meat.

26.   Eggs found inside poultry, it matters not whether the former be in the first stages of growth or whether they are found in a complete state even in their shells, require soaking, salting and washing off; but they should be salted separately from the meat, and be placed in such a position that the blood from the meat could not flow upon them.   Such eggs even though they be covered with a shell, are forbidden to be partaken of together with milk.

27.   Meat which had been put aside for 72 hours must not be cooked unless it had been soaked in the interval.

28. It is customary to singe fowls which have been plucked so as to remove the remaining feathers. Care should be taken that this should only be done over the flame of stubble or straw and that it be a small flame, and that the poultry be moved to and fro so that it should not become heated.

LAWS CONCERNING THE IMMERSION OF UTENSILS.

1. One who purchased of a non-Jew table utensils made of metal or glass must not use them, even if they be new or even if they be for cold viands, before he dips them in a spring or in a ritual immersion bath or in a stream, but in a time of excessive rain or during a thaw they must not be dipped in a stream. Previous to the immersion the following benediction should be said: בא״י אמ״ה אקב״ו על טבילת, כלי if one vessel be immersed, but if two or more be immersed he should conclude with the word כלים.

2. Wooden or earthenware utensils do not require immersion unless the wooden vessel have bands of iron, or if the earthenware vessels be glazed, they should be immersed without pronouncing the benediction. This is also the law in the case of an Israelite who gave a metal utensil or a broken and leaking vessel that could not contain a fourth of a Log (a quantity equal to the capacity of one and a half eggs) to a non-Jewish artisan to repair for him, he must immerse it without saying a benediction, also in the case of an Israelite who has a factory of glassware and employs non-Jews, the vessels manufactured require immersion but no benediction need be said. In the immersion of all the foregoing one should endeavour to have them immersed together with the vessels over which a benediction must be said.

3. If a non-Jew had used an old vessel in such a manner as to necessitate its being made Kosher (ritually fit for use) by the process of purification by boiling water or by making it white by heat, it should first be made Kosher and then immersed.

4. A glass vessel borrowed or hired of a non-Jew does not require immersion but if borrowed or hired of a Jewish dealer it requires immersion but no benediction need be said, and the dealer should inform the one who buys it in order that the latter should not again immerse it and pronounce a benediction.

5. There are three kinds of table utensils subject to different laws of immersion : (1) Vessels used for containing food fit to be eaten at once require immersion preceded by the benediction ; (2) vessels used for containing food that is not yet fit to be eaten, do not require any immersion whatsoever; (3) vessels used to hold food which

71

is not yet fit to be eaten, but if they be also able to hold food fit to be eaten, then they require immersion but without any benediction.

6. Before dipping the vessel in the water it must be examined as to its thorough cleanliness, it must be neither soiled nor rusty (but a particle of rust or a little black, usual on such a vessel and regarding which one is not particular, is not reckoned as a thing intervening). The entire vessel and its handle should be submerged both together in the water, and the one who holds the vessel during the immersion should first dip his hand in the water. The vessel should not be held tightly in one's hand, but it should be held with an ordinary grip. If the vessel be dipped by means of a string attached thereto, the string should be loosely knotted in order that the water may reach every part of the vessel. If the vessel have a narrow mouth, one should be careful to keep it in the water until it fills entirely so that the water should cover it both within and without.

7. A boy or girl may not be trusted with the immersion of vessels.

8. It is forbidden to immerse a vessel either on Sabbath or on a Holyday. If one had forgotten to immerse it before those days, he should give it to a non-Jew, and then borrow it of him. It it be a vessel proper to carry water therein (in a locality where carrying on the Sabbath is permissible) he should draw water therewith and bring the water to his house in order that it shall not appear as if he had immersed it, but he should not say the benediction over the same.

9. If the vessel had been used before it was immersed, the victuals that were in it do not become prohibited thereby, nevertheless it must be immersed, even if it had been used a hundred times.

Laws Concerning the Bread and Cooked Food of a Non-Jew.

1. In some places there are Jews who are not very stringent and purchase bread of a non-Jewish baker (if there be no suspicion of it containing anything contrary to the Jewish dietary laws). Where there is no Jewish baker, or where the bread of the Jewish baker is inferior to that of the non-Jewish baker, it is permissible to purchase the bread of the non-Jewish baker, but the bread of a private person specially baked for his own family should not be eaten, unless one be on a journey and it be impossible for him to obtain the bread of an Israelite, or if he be in a locality where a baker cannot be found, he is then permitted to partake of the bread of a private person. If an Israelite had thrown but one piece of wood in the furnace of the oven (of the non-Jew) at the time the fire was lit, it is permissible to partake of bread baked in that oven as it is no longer accounted as the bread of a non-Jew.

2. An article of food that is not eaten in its natural state, and is fit to be served at the table of kings, either as a relish eaten with

bread or as dessert, if cooked or roasted by a non-Jew even in the
utensils of an Israelite and in the house of an Israelite it is yet forbidden food, inasmuch as it is the cooking of a non-Jew; however an
article of food that is eaten when raw, or that is neither a delicacy nor
fit to be served at the table of kings, is not affected by the rules dealing with the cooking of a non-Jew, nor need any apprehension be felt
regarding utensils wherein it was cooked, as it may be assumed regarding vessels in general that no cooking has been done in them during
the past twenty-four hours.

3. A Jewish family employing a non-Jewess, who cooks for them
in their own house, may eat of her cooking, but they are forbidden to
partake of the cooking that she does for herself if it be of food coming
under the rules of the cooking of a non-Jew, but regarding the vessel
which she used for her own cooking the ecclesiastical authorities should
be consulted (as to whether it may be used again). Food cooked by a
non-Jew for a sick person on Sabbath is forbidden to be eaten at the
close of Sabbath, even by the sick person himself if it be possible to
cook other food for him, and the ecclesiastical authorities should be
consulted regarding the future use of the vessel in which the cooking
was done.

4. It is less becoming to eat the bread of an Israelite baked by a
non-Jew than to eat the bread belonging to a non-Jew previously
mentioned, as it is forbidden inasmuch as it comes under the rule of
the cooking of a non-Jew, therefore all who send their bread to be
baked by a non-Jewish baker, or by a Jewish baker who openly dese-
crates the Sabbath should see to it that an Israelite throws a piece of
wood into the furnace or that he should place the bread in the oven.

5. Fruits, not fully grown, which have been preserved by a non-
Jew, as well as boiled eggs and bread smeared over with egg when
cooked or baked by a non-Jew are forbidden food. It is also prohibited to drink coffee, chocolate, or tea at the house of a non-Jew if a
regular practice be made thereof.

6. Milk which has been milked by a non-Jew is prohibited to be
consumed, it is even forbidden to make cheese therefrom, for it is
necessary that an Israelite be present at the outset, when the milking
is about to take place, to see that the milk pail is clean. We avoid
using the milk pail which the non-Jew generally uses for milking purposes. Should a non-Jewess milk the cows on the premises of an Israelite
or in his barn, where the house of a non-Jew does not intervene, and
it is not feared that (the milk may be drawn) from an unclean animal,
the use of that milk is permitted. However, if the house of a non-Jew
should intervene, it is necessary for an Israelite to be present at the
milking, even a boy or girl aged nine years would suffice for that
purpose.

7. The cheese of a non-Jew is forbidden food, if, however, an
Israelite had witnessed the milking as well as the making of the cheese

73

and if during the process the cheese belonged to the Israelite, he is permitted to partake thereof, but if during the process it belonged to the non-Jew, it is forbidden food.

8. In some places people make a practice of eating the butter of a non-Jew, but there is no authority to support this practice, unless such people have reliable knowledge that the butter does not contain anything which makes it forbidden to be eaten.

The Law Concerning One Who Desires to Eat or Drink Prior to the Meal.

1. Before washing the hands one should avoid eating such things which will be served in the course of the meal. It matters not whether they be such things which require a separate benediction during the meal, e.g., fruit, or whether they do not require a benediction during the meal, e.g., different kinds of relish or peas or potatoes.

2. Before washing the hands one should avoid drinking. But if one will drink a glass of wine also after Grace at the conclusion of the meal so that its special grace will be said thereafter, then this will exempt from benediction that which he drank before washing the hands.

3. If, before washing the hands, one desire to partake of such kinds of food after which we say על המחיה (for the sustenance, etc.), and whether he intends to eat of the same during the meal or not, grace after meals exempts him from saying the benediction, since the grace after meals exempts one from saying the grace על המחיה. The foregoing, however, only applies to him who washes his hands after partaking of that food, without any undue interruption, but if he be compelled to allow a long interval to elapse, he should say the grace על המחיה on account of what he had eaten, even if he should intend to eat of the same kinds of food during the meal.

Laws Concerning the Washing of the Hands Before Meals.

1. It is not required to wash the hands (ritually) except before partaking of bread over which the benediction המוציא is said. Bread is the staff of life without which it is impossible to exist, but if one desire to partake of food upon which the benediction המוציא is not pronounced, e.g., if it be of the kind over which the benediction בורא מיני מזונות is pronounced, he is not obliged to wash his hands previous to partaking thereof, if he should not make a proper meal of it. If, however, he should make a proper meal of it, it is regarded as if it were bread, inasmuch as it is necessary to pronounce the benediction המוציא before eating it and it therefore requires also the (ritual) washing of the hands. Ablution is necessary only when one intends to eat bread of the size of an egg, he must then wash his hands and pronounce

the benediction, but if he wish to eat bread less than the size of an egg, he should wash his hands but should not say the benediction.

2. One should not wash one's hands otherwise than by means of a vessel, and all vessels may be used for that purpose providing they were made expressly to hold liquids, but if they were not made originally for the purpose of holding liquids, e.g., the covers of vessels and the like, it is forbidden to wash the hands therewith. A vessel that can stand only by the support of another, if it had been expressly made to be used thus, is considered a proper vessel as regards the law of washing the hands therewith.

3. The vessel must hold no less than a quarter (רביעית)[1] of a Log, it should also be intact, having neither hole nor an open crack therein, it should also have an even surface without any cavities or protruding parts. When one has a vessel with a spout through which the water is poured, then he must not let the water with which he washes his hands run through the spout, as the law applying to a vessel does not hold good in the case of a spout of the vessel, since it does not contain any liquid, he must therefore pour the water from the edge of the vessel which contains the liquid. A vessel which has a crack that can serve as an outlet for liquids, that is a very small hole through which, however, the water does not leak out drop by drop, and if one have no other vessel and if he be pressed for time, he may wash his hands therewith.

4. A vessel that has a tap, inasmuch as it was thus originally made for its improvement, is called a vessel (wherewith it is proper to wash the hands), however when washing therewith one should open and close the tap on every occasion of washing. This can be properly performed with a vessel in which there is a tap, but the taps with which our houses are supplied, which project from the wall and serve as an outlet for the water which flows through a water pipe, inasmuch as that is not a vessel one should not wash one's hands therefrom. In an emergency, however, it is permissible to wash therefrom, provided one place one's hands below the tap close to its mouth where the water flows, but care must be taken on every occasion of washing, to turn the tap and to have one's hands beneath the tap only when the water is flowing forth.

5. One should not wash his neighbour's hands with one's hands full of water, the same law applies to one who had washed one hand, he is forbidden to take water therein in order to wash the other hand, as the washing must be performed only by means of a vessel.

6. One who has no vessel is permitted to wash his hands by dipping them into a river, or into an immersion tank, and in an emergency when one cannot obtain water, he is permitted to dip his hands in snow which lies on the ground if its quantity, as it thus rests upon the ground, is equal to the capacity of forty Seahs[2] (i.e. approximately twenty-four cubic feet) of water, and it does not matter if it be close

---

[1] The Log equals the capacity contained by six eggs.
[2] A Seah also equals 10.656 qts. according to the Oxford Gesenius.

to the ground, he should pronounce the benediction על נטילת ידים, but it is forbidden to place snow into a vessel and to dip his hands therein ; if, however, he melted it, it is treated as water.

7. If one had immersed his hands into a vessel containing water and dabbled therein, he has not ritually performed the ablution, and he must again wash his hands without pronouncing a benediction.

8. Just as it is necessary that the water wherewith one performs the ablution should be poured from a vessel, so it is necessary to have it performed by human agency, that means, that it must be poured out by a person, and all persons are fit to pour out the water, even a deaf and dumb person, an insane person and a minor, with the following exceptions, a non-Jew or a menstruant ; one should also, if possible, be careful to avoid the help of a child less than six years old.

9. If the water's appearance had changed either through its situation or through something that fell therein, it is unfit for use in washing the hands, but if the change arose naturally it is fit. If the water resumed its former proper appearance, even if the change had been caused by some external means, it is fit for use. Salt, foul, bitter or turbid water, which is not fit for a dog to drink, is not fit for use in washing the hands. If its turbid state be due to mire and a dog could drink thereof, it is fit for use. Sea-water is only fit for use after it has been boiled.

10. Water which had been used, e.g., he had washed soiled utensils or had soaked vegetables therewith, or he had therein a vessel containing a liquid for the purpose of keeping it cool, or cracked vessels in order to repair same, or if he had tested (therewith) the capacity of measure or had soaked bread therein, even if he had intended to soak the bread in a different vessel and it fell into that vessel, inasmuch as it suits him to have it thus, such water is accounted as though it had been poured out, and is unfit for use. If, however, he did not at all desire to soak or wash anything, but it fell accidently into a vessel of water, such water is fit for use. Water which had become loathsome, e.g., whereof a dog or swine or the like had drunk, should not be used for washing the hands if other water can be obtained.

11. One who had not washed his hands, although he had touched the water, does not defile it thereby, but if he dabbled with his hands in it to cleanse them, or even if he only washed his little finger therein in order to cleanse it, all that water thereby becomes unfit (for the ritual washing) as it has been used for some other purpose.

12. If one have no water, he is permitted to wash his hands with beer or with other beverages or with warm water, even if the water be very warm. Water in which he had put an aromatic substance so as to scent it may be used for the ablution of the hands.

13. If water fit for use were mixed with water which was unfit, then the condition of the greater quantity determines that of the rest.

14. One should guard against anything intervening (between any part of the hand and the water) e.g., clay or dirt under the finger nails which protrude beyond the fleshy part of the finger, but what is under the surface of the nails next to the flesh is not an 'interposition,' as it is a small matter about which people in general are not particular, but all people are particular about that which is above the flesh, and even one who is not fastidious in that regard, must give way to the opinion of the majority. As regards the rest of the hand everything which clings to it is 'an interposition,' one should therefore remove the rings from one's fingers. If the rings were loose on his fingers and he had inadvertently washed his hands whilst wearing them, the ablution is counted as properly performed ; however, whenever possible one must remove them. If one has a bruise upon his hand and it be covered with a plaster which it would be painful to remove, the latter is considered to be an 'interposition.'

15. One whose hands are dyed, but without having any dye stuff upon them, this mere colouring is not counted 'an interposition,' but if the dye stuff be upon them even a small quantity, this is an 'interposition.' If, however, he be a dyer or one who is always engaged in writing and whose fingers are ink-stained, and he is accustomed thereto, and all of his craft are not particular in that respect, it is not counted as an 'interposition,' unless it cover the greater part of the hand.

16. It is difficult to exactly determine the quantity of water necessary for use in washing the hands, but it is necessary to pour plenty of water upon each hand. First the right hand should be washed, then the left, then the water should be poured on the entire hand as far as the arm. He should leave no part of his hand unwashed, for that reason he should slightly separate the fingers, and raise them slightly upward in order that the water should run down the entire length of his fingers, also upon the finger tips and around them. The entire hand should be thus washed by one act of pouring out the water. He should therefore not wash his hands out of a vessel with a narrow opening, for the water cannot flow freely by one act of pouring out. The water must be poured twice on each hand. This ablution can be performed either on a vessel or upon the ground.

17. After one had washed both hands, he should rub them together, then raise them upward, as it is written: "Lift up your hands :" (Ps. cxxxiv. 2) then before drying them he should say the benediction נטילת ידים על. If he did not say the benediction before drying his hands, then after having said the benediction המוציא, he cannot say the benediction על נטילת ידים. The hands should not be dried during the recital of the verses שאו ידיכם as this is contrary to the law. The hands should be dried while saying the benediction על נטילת ידים, care being taken that the benediction is completed before the hands are completely dry. The hands should be thoroughly dried, but one should not dry them on one's garments.

18. If, after having poured the water upon one hand, he had touched that hand with his other hand, or some one else had touched it, that contact defiled the water which was upon his hand and he must dry it and wash his hands again; if, however, that occurred after he had already said the benediction על נטילת ידים, he need not repeat the same.

19. All doubts in connection with the fulfilment of the law of washing the hands are decided leniently. E.g., if one be uncertain whether any work was done with the water or whether he had poured the proper quantity of water upon his hands or whether there was an 'interposition' during the washing, or whether the vessel was sound, or whether one who had not washed his hands had touched his own hand, even if he were in doubt of all of the above on one occasion, he is not obliged to wash his hands again because of the uncertainty. Likewise if one be in doubt about having said the benediction על נטילת ידים he need not repeat the same.

20. One is forbidden to eat without having previously washed his hands, this also applies if he desire to wrap his hands in a cloth. If one be upon a journey without water, but he knows that water can be obtained four miles ahead or one mile backwards, he must travel four miles ahead or one mile backwards in order to wash his hands before eating, but if water cannot be obtained there or if he travel with other people and he is afraid to separate himself from them, or if one be prevented from washing his hands through some other cause, he should wrap his hands in a cloth or put on gloves and then eat.

21. One who has discharged nature's call before a meal (and must therefore wash his hands and say the benediction אשר יצר) must also wash his hands before the meal, proceeding as follows: he should first wash his hands by pouring a little water in the palm of one hand and with that water rub both hands together and say the benediction אשר יצר. Since this washing does not fulfil the law concerning "the washing of the hands before a meal" he should therefore immediately wash his hands again according to the law of נטילת ידים and should say the benediction על נטילת ידים as is proper.

23. If, during the meal, one had touched any part of the body usually covered or had scratched his head or had discharged nature's call, he should again wash his hands without any benediction.

LAWS CONCERNING THE BREAKING OF BREAD AND ITS BENEDICTION (המוציא).

1. We say grace (המוציא) over a complete loaf made of one of the five kinds of grain and thereafter we say the grace after meals.

2. One must avoid any interruption between the washing of the hands and the benediction המוציא, but he may respond אמן after any benediction which he has heard. A pause lasting as long as it takes to walk twenty-two paces or walking from one house to another, be it only a short distance, or talking without reference to the meal

constitute an "interruption," however, if one had inadvertently made
an interruption it does not matter, unless he had done some task or had
engaged in a conversation, these constitute diverted attention and he
must wash his hands again.

3. It is proper to have salt set on the table before breaking the
bread, and the piece of bread over which the benediction המוציא was
said should be dipped into the salt, because the table represents the
altar and the food symbolizes the offerings, as it is said : "With all
thine oblations thou shalt offer salt" (Lev. ii. 13).

4. It is proper to break the choicest bread ; if he had before him
a part of a loaf and a whole loaf which are of the same kind of grain,
and he intends to partake in the course of the meal of both, even if
the latter one be smaller and of a coarse flour, he should nevertheless
break the whole one for it is nicer. If they are not of the same kind
of grain, the whole one being of an inferior kind, e.g., of spelt, and the
piece be of wheat and at the same time the smaller of the two, we say
the benediction over the bread made of wheat. If they be both whole
or both broken and both of the same kind of grain, he should say the
benediction over that which is purer, and if they be both equal in this
respect, then the benediction is said over the larger piece.

5. If he have before him bread baked by an Israelite and that
which was baked by a non-Jew and he does not mind eating bread
baked by the latter if they be both whole or both broken, also of the
same size and of the same kind of flour, he should say the benediction
over the bread baked by the Israelite, but if the bread of the Israelite
be not as pure as that of the non-Jew, he should say the benediction
over whichever he prefers, but if the master of the house be wont not
to eat bread baked by a non-Jew but this kind was bought for the sake
of a guest, it should be removed from the table until the benediction
המוציא has been said.

6. Previous to saying the benediction he should lay both hands
upon the bread. When he pronounces the Divine Name he should
raise the bread, on the Sabbath he should raise both loaves. He must
say the benediction devoutly and aspirate distinctly the ה of המוציא and
separate the words לחם and מן in order not to slur over the ם. After
he had said the benediction he should eat immediately, as it is forbidden to permit any interruption between the blessing and the
beginning of the meal, not even for the purpose of responding אמן. It
is proper to eat after the benediction bread which is the size of an
olive without any interruption.

7. The bread should be broken at its best part in honour of the
benediction. The crust of the bread is the best part, for that is where
it is baked best. Nevertheless, an old person for whom it is difficult
to eat hard bread should break the soft part. When he is about to
break a loaf which is not whole, he should not cut it entirely before
the benediction has been said, so that when he says the benediction the
loaf is as large as possible. On Sabbath, however, the loaf is not cut

at all until after the benediction, so that the loaves are whole, also on a week-day, if the bread be a wafer, one should say the benediction before it is broken for no pause is caused by breaking it.

8.   One should not break off a small portion of bread so that he should not appear to be mean, nor a portion larger than the size of an egg so that he should not appear to be a glutton, this holds good if one should be eating alone.   But if one eat in company with many people, and he has to give to each one a portion of the size of an olive, he may divide the bread in such a manner as is best suited for the occasion.   On Sabbath, even when he eats by himself, it is permitted to break off a portion large enough to last him the entire meal in honour of the Sabbath.

9.   It is proper to partake of the portion which he had broken off before partaking of any other bread.   It is not proper to give aught thereof either to a non-Jew, or (to feed) cattle or poultry (therewith).

10.   When one distributes the bread among those who are at the table, he should not throw it as it is forbidden to throw bread, neither should he give it into his hand but he should place it before him.

RULES CONCERNING A REPAST.

1.   If one possess cattle or poultry and had to feed them, he is forbidden to partake of any food until he has provided them with food, this applies only with respect to eating, since it is written: " Drink, and I will give thy camels drink also " (Gen. xxiv. 46), it is also written: " So thou shalt give the congregation and their cattle drink " (Num. xx. 8).

2.   One may make use of bread as long as it does not become loathsome, when the use of it is prohibited.   One is not permitted to use it to support a dish which is filled with food, because if the latter be spilled upon the bread, it makes it loathsome.   If one eat anything by means of a slice of bread which he uses instead of a spoon, he must eat some of the bread with every mouthful of the other food, and what remains over of the bread should also be eaten by him.

3.   It is forbidden to throw bread even where it will not become loathsome thereby, for the very act of throwing is a degradation to the bread, other articles of food however should not be thrown if they would become loathsome thereby, but it is permitted to throw them, if it would not make them loathsome, such as nuts and the like. One should not sit upon a bag containing fruit which would thereby become loathsome.   When one has water he should not wash his hands with wine or any other beverage on account of their being degraded thereby.   When one sees an article of food lying upon the

ground he must pick it up. Food proper for man should not be given as food to beasts on account of being thereby degraded.

4. One who is obliged to use bread or any other food as a medicament, (e.g., a poultice) is permitted to use it thus even if he make it loathsome thereby.

5. One should be careful not to throw crumbs about, but he should gather them together and give them to the fowls.

6. One should not eat or drink like a glutton, one should neither eat nor drink whilst standing, and even if one had but poor fare, still his table should be clean and nicely covered. One should neither grasp a portion which is as large as an egg and eat thereof, nor seize the food with one hand and tear therefrom with the other. One should not drink a glass of wine at one draught, for one who does so is a tippler. It is the correct thing to drink one's wine in two draughts, but one who finishes his wine in three draughts, behold he is haughty. If, however, the glass be extra large, one may finish it in several draughts ; likewise if it be very small, one may finish it in one draught.

7. One should not place upon the table the piece of bread which he had bitten, neither should he give it to his neighbour, nor should he put it in the dish, as his neighbour may find it loathsome. One should not hand a cup, the contents of which he has partly drunk, to one's neighbour, as the latter may through bashfulness drink against his will. The utmost care should be taken not to drink of the leavings of the cup of which one's neighbour had partaken. When drinking water, one should turn one's face aside, but in drinking other beverages one need not do so.

8. A man should not be hot tempered at his meal lest the guests and members of his household be ashamed to eat, thinking that he rages and is angry because they are eating. One should neither stare in the face of a person who is eating or drinking, nor look at the portion set before him, so that he put him not to shame.

9. We do not talk while partaking of a meal, not even to discuss the Torah, owing to the danger of choking arising from the simultaneous use of his windpipe and gullet. It is even forbidden to say "Good Health" (אסותה) to one who had sneezed, but when not engaged in eating, it is a duty to discourse at table upon matters relating to the Torah. It is the custom of God-fearing people after having eaten the morsel over which they had said the benediction המוציא, to read Psalm xxiii. מזמור לדוד וכו׳, which is a psalm of thanksgiving as well as a prayer for one's sustenance. At the conclusion of the meal it is the rule on week-days to say : על נהרות בבל וכו׳ (Ps. cxxxvii.) and on Sabbaths, Holydays and upon such days when supplication (תחנון) is not said it is customary to say שיר המעלות וכו׳ (ibid. cxxvi.).

10.   When two eat at one table, even if each one have his separate
plate before him or if they partake of fruit and each one have his portion before him, it is meet for the elder of the two to begin to eat
first and he who stretches forth his hand before his elder or superior is
a glutton.   When two eat out of one dish, and one had stopped eating
in order to drink, or for some other trivial matter, it is polite for the
other to wait until his companion resumes eating, but if they be three,
the other two need not wait for the sake of the one.

11.   It is the duty of one to whom odorous food and beverages,
which whet the appetite, are served to give immediately thereof to the
waiter, as it is injurious to the person who sees food for which he longs
if he cannot eat thereof.

12.   A woman should not drink wine during her husband's absence
even in her own home, and at any other place even in her husband's
presence she is forbidden to drink wine or any other intoxicating
beverage, if, however she be accustomed to drink wine in her husband's
presence, she is permitted to partake of a little thereof during his
absence.

13.   One should not give food to an Israelite unless he knows him
to be of those who wash their hands and say the appropriate benediction.   This, however, applies only to him who provides one with
food as a part of his pay, but if the recipient be a poor man, he should
provide him with food as an act of charity without making any inquiry
as to his piety.

14.   Guests must not give to the children of their host aught of
what had been set before them, as the host may have no more food
than that which was set before them.   Therefore if they do not leave
enough for themselves he will be ashamed on account of his poverty.
If the table were richly supplied it is permissible for them to do so.

15.   One who enters a house should not say, Give me to eat, but
he should wait until he is invited to eat.   It is forbidden to partake of
a repast which does not suffice for the host, for this would be akin to
robbery.   Moreover the host invites him to dine with him only as an
act of politeness.

16.   One must not leave his place at the table before he has said
the Grace after meals, even to go into another room in the midst of
his meal to finish it there, or with the intention of returning to his
original place and to finish it there.   Nevertheless one who has transgressed and left his place either to finish his meal in his present place
or to return to his original place and there to finish his meal, is not
required to repeat the benediction המוציא inasmuch as bread forms the
staple feature of his meal it is counted as though it were all one meal,
despite the fact that he had changed his place during its process.   He

LAWS AND CUSTOMS OF ISRAEL

must, however, eat bread at least the size of an olive in the place where
he says the Grace after meals.

17. If at the time of saying the benediction המוציא he had the
intention of going thereafter into another room to finish his meal
there and also to say the Grace after meals, he is permitted to do so,
but he should be careful to eat bread there the size of an olive, this
should be done only in an emergency, e.g., at a religious feast.

18. One whose attention was diverted from the meal during its
course, e.g., by praying or by dozing or by the interruption of other
matters which he is at liberty to attend to, or by nature's demands,
should again wash his hands but he need not repeat the benedictions
על נטילת ידים and המוציא.

19. One should be careful not to place upon the table a book
which he had not read for several days, as they often have numerous
bookworms, and he might thereby violate the precept (forbidding
worms in food) and injure his health. One should also exercise great
care in using fruits which are purchased of dealers who also sell
forbidden fat, as the latter may sometimes cling to the fruits, besides
they may be the medium of dangerous bacilli through the handling
thereof by sick people, one should therefore peel them or wash them
thoroughly.

20. If the master of the house had finished his meal and resolved
to say Grace after meals, and then he changed his mind and desired
to resume eating or drinking, there are divergent opinions as to the
laws concerning the benedictions applying thereto, therefore such an
action should be avoided, but immediately he has resolved to say the
Grace after the meals he should do so.

RULES CONCERNING THE BENEDICTIONS TO BE SAID BEFORE
SPECIAL COURSES DURING A MEAL.

1. All kinds of food which one is accustomed to eat to satisfy
one's hunger in the course of a meal, such as meat, fish, relish, crushed
grain soup, pancakes and the like, although they are eaten without
bread, yet they do not require a benediction to be said either before or
after partaking thereof, because one partakes of them to satisfy one's
hunger and they form part of the meal which is connected with the
bread which forms the staple food for human sustenance, therefore all
the other kinds of food are exempt from separate benedictions,
through the benediction המוציא said over the bread, also through the
Grace after meals. Thus even if the edibles were sent to him from other
houses he need not say a benediction upon them, it being assumed that
one is prepared to partake of whatever will be served. Likewise one
need not say a benediction over any beverage which he may drink in
the course of the meal, as drinking belongs to the meal ; wine, however,

83

forms an exception, owing to its importance (inasmuch as there are many occasions when one must say a benediction over wine, even if he have no need to drink it, e.g., at *Kiddush* and *Habdallah* and the like), one must therefore say a benediction over it when he drinks thereof in the course of the meal.

2. If one desire in the course of a meal to partake of fruits without bread, since they are not an essential part of the meal, therefore even if they were upon the table before he had said the benediction המוציא, they are, nevertheless, not exempt from their particular benediction through the benediction המוציא and one must say over them their benediction before eating same, but not the benediction which follows them as one is exempted from saying the latter by the Grace after meals. If he have no desire to eat the fruit without bread, he need not say a separate benediction, as the fruit then becomes an adjunct to the bread, but should he not intend to eat it solely with bread, he should take care to partake of some fruit without bread and say its benediction and then he can eat some with bread. Various kinds of food which are served in the course of a meal for the sole purpose of whetting the appetite, such as pickled or preserved fruits. are called " auxiliary to the meal " as they stimulate him to eat more they are therefore exempt from a separate benediction by that said over the bread, but whatever is served at the conclusion of the meal to help digestion, such as coffee or the like, are not auxiliary to the meal and a benediction must be said before they are consumed. If one eat cakes and pastries in the course of a meal in order to satisfy his hunger, he need not say a special benediction, but if he eat them to gratify his pleasure, it is a question whether he is not required to say a benediction, he should therefore, when he says המוציא, think of these dainties and they will thus be exempt from a separate benediction.

3. Fruits cooked with meat do not require a separate benediction if partaken of in the course of a meal, but if they be cooked without meat they require a separate benediction. If the principal part of his meal be fruit eaten with bread, it does not in any case need a separate benediction, as it is exempt by המוציא (pronounced over the bread) and it makes no difference even if they were brought later to the table, provided he first partook of the fruit together with bread. Thereafter he may eat it also without bread and without pronouncing a special benediction.

4. If one desire to partake of fruit or vegetables or to drink any beverage (except wine or brandy) before washing the hands, and he also intends to eat or drink of the same during the meal, then this will involve him in an uncertainty as to the necessity of saying the final benediction, as it is a question whether the Grace after meals exempts him from saying this final benediction over that which he had partaken of prior to the washing of the hands, he should therefore take care

LAWS AND CUSTOMS OF ISRAEL

when he has said the Grace after meals that he eats or drinks of that
food which requires the same benediction and says the benediction both
before and after partaking of the same, so that, when saying the final
benediction he should have the intention of also including the food of
which he had partaken before washing the hands. One who drinks
brandy before washing the hands is also involved in an uncertainty
regarding the necessity of saying the final benediction, he should therefore drink less than the measure of the size of an olive. One who eats
of food prepared from any of the " five species of grain " before he has
washed his hands, is exempt from saying the final benediction על
חמחיה, by saying the Grace after meals, even if he did not partake
thereof in the course of the meal. The foregoing, however, applies
only to one who washes his hands after partaking of that food, without
any undue interruption, but if he be forced to let a long interval elapse,
he should say the benediction על המחיה before washing the hands, even
if it be his intention to eat of the same food during the meal.

5. If he had said a benediction over wine before washing the
hands and it was his intention to partake of some also during the meal,
or if he be accustomed to drink wine in the course of the meal, it is not
necessary to repeat the benediction פרי הגפן. Brandy, however, involves
uncertainty as to the benediction therefore he should drink less than
the measure of the size of an olive before washing the hands, and have the
intention when saying the benediction that he also includes the brandy
which he will drink during the meal, or during the meal he may say
a benediction over a lump of sugar and thereby exempt the brandy
from a separate benediction

Laws Concerning the Washing of the Hands at the Conclusion of the Meal and at the Grace After Meals.

1. One should wash the hands before saying Grace after meals,
this ablution is called מים אחרונים and one need only wash the first two
joints of his fingers; he should hold his hands down before drying
them. The one who will say Grace takes precedence in washing the
hands; this, however, only applies if there be but five at the table but if
there be many, the ablution should be begun by a young member of
the company and followed by the others in rotation as they are seated
at the table. The honour of priority does not obtain in the use of מים
אחרונים, until the turn of the last five is reached, when the one who will
say Grace precedes the others in washing the hands. If water be lacking one may wash the hands with any kind of liquid even with that
which is unfit to use for ritual purposes at the beginning of the meal.
One should not however wash his hand with warm water. One should
not wash his hands upon the ground but in a vessel, and if he have no
vessel he should wash his hands where there are no people. He should
dry his hands before saying Grace after meals and there should not be
any interruption between the ablution and the saying of Grace.

2. The table cloth and the bread must not be removed until

85

Grace after meals has been said. But a whole loaf should not be brought to the table before the Grace after meals, but if it had been there for some time it need not be removed. Before saying the Grace after meals it is customary to remove the knives from the table or else to cover them, but this is not necessary on Sabbath or a Holiday.

3. It is proper to say Grace and to have for benediction thereafter a glass of wine, beer or brandy. The glass should be filled before the washing of the hands. If there be three at the table, the one who recites the Grace should take the glass with both hands, and when beginning to say Grace he should take it in his right hand, unaided by his left hand. One who is left-handed should take it in *his* right hand. It is lifted up a hand-breadth above the table, and he looks at it and says the Grace, but if he say the Grace for himself, he should not hold the glass in his hand while saying the Grace after meals but he should place it before him.

4. The beverage contained in the "glass of blessing" must not be defective, that is, no one should have partaken thereof. A defective glass can be rectified by adding a little of the beverage or water which had not become defective. If one had poured the contents of a defective glass into the decanter, the wine therein is fit for benediction if the quantity in the decanter be more than the defective beverage.

5. The glass used for benediction must be sound without any crack, for even the least defect, such as a notch in which one's nail might be caught, makes it unfit for ritual use, and if its base be broken it is also unfit. It also requires rinsing inside and washing outside, but if it be clean it does not require it, and if he wipe it with a cloth this suffices. The liquid should be poured from the decanter into the glass for the purpose of saying a benediction ; he should fill it to the brim, and at the conclusion of Grace he should pass it on to his wife that she may drink thereof, even if she did not join in the meal. Before saying the Grace after meals all empty vessels should be removed from the table. From the time when the glass was handed to the one who will say the Grace it is forbidden for the former as well as for those who are at the table to talk.

6. If one had eaten but a piece of bread no larger than the size of an olive and if it be of any of the five species of grain and made in such a manner that it is necessary to say the benediction המוציא before partaking thereof, he is obliged to say Grace after meals thereafter. The Grace after meals should be said neither standing nor walking, but only whilst sitting, therefore if one had walked to and fro in his house when eating, or if he had then stood or inclined, when he has to say Grace after meals he should sit down in order that he may say it with devotion. He should not assume a proud bearing by reclining on his seat, but he should put on his coat and place his hat upon his head in order that the fear of heaven be upon him, and his attention be concentrated upon saying the Grace with reverence and awe. Whilst saying Grace it is forbidden to interrupt it any way. He must not partake of any drink whilst Grace is being said. One who is on the

road and eats as he walks must also say Grace whilst walking as his mind is not quite at ease. If, however, he had eaten whilst sitting down, he must say Grace whilst sitting down, unless he be forced to do otherwise.

7. The master of the house who had eaten together with his young children who had arrived at the age when it is proper to train them to say Grace after meals, but who do not know how to say it, or if he dine with his wife who does not know how to say it, he must say the Grace aloud in order that they should hear him and thus do their duty. It is right for them to say each word with him, but they should hasten to conclude each benediction before the one who says the Grace does so, in order that they may respond אמן, which is also to be said after ומכל טוב תמיד אל יחסרנו for there the benediction הטוב והמטיב ends. It is also a proper custom to respond אמן after each הרחמן sentence in the Grace.

8. If one be prevented from saying Grace after meals at the place where he ate, he may go to another corner of the room to say it, and it matters not if it be a large room, even if he cannot see the place where he originally sat. For a very slight cause one is permitted to change his place and say the Grace within four cubits of the place where he ate, inasmuch as within four cubits it is considered as the same place.

9. If, when saying the benediction המוציא, one had the intention of saying the Grace in another room he is permitted to say it there even if he did not partake of anything in that room, however, one should not do this deliberately, unless, if for some cause, he will be prevented from saying the Grace in the room (where he had his meal).

10. If one desire to go to another house and had this intention when saying the benediction המוציא he is permitted to do so, provided he eats there a piece of bread the size of an olive, but he need not say a benediction over aught which he may eat or drink there. If he did not originally have this intention he may not go forth voluntarily, even if he desire to eat in that place, but he must say the Grace after meals before he goes forth. If, however he had transgressed the Law and had left the house (before saying Grace after meals) if he have bread even less than the size of an olive in the place where he arrives, he may eat it there without saying the benediction המוציא, no other benediction over anything else which he may eat and drink there is required but he must say Grace after meals. But if he have no bread he must return to his original place and say the Grace there because he had left the house deliberately, if, however he had left the house inadvertently, and if he be pressed for time he need not return to his former place, but he may say the Grace where he now is. If his present place be at such a distance from his original place, that it is to be feared that before reaching it he will have digested his food, in which case the saying of Grace is futile, he may quite properly say the Grace where he remembered the duty of doing so.

11. How long (after the meal) can one properly say Grace ? Until his food is digested. This period is estimated to be that interval after eating during which he has not become hungry. If one had eaten but little and owing to inability to determine whether the sensation of hunger he now feels is as intense as that which he felt before he ate, he should eat another piece of bread the size of an olive and say the Grace after meals, and thus include also what he had eaten previously. If his attention were diverted in the meantime, he should first say the benediction המוציא over the bread. Thus should he also do when he is in doubt whether he had said Grace after meals or not, he should wash his hands, say the benediction המוציא and eat a piece of bread of the size of an olive and then say Grace after meals.

12. If one erred on Sabbath and omitted רצה, or if one did not say יעלה ויבא on a Holyday he should proceed as follows : if he became aware of the omission before he had pronounced the Divine Name in the benediction ברוך אתה ה' בונה he should there insert רצה or יעלה ויבא and then say ובנה etc., but if he did not become aware of the omission until after he had pronounced the Divine Name he should conclude the benediction בונה ברחמיו ירושלים אמן and then if it be Sabbath say ברוך אתה ה' אלהינו מלך העולם אשר נתן שבתות למנוחה לעמו ישראל באהבה לאות ולברית, ברוך אתה ה' מקדש השבת and on a Holyday he should say ברוך אתה ה' אלהינו מלך העולם אשר נתן ימים טובים לעמו ישראל ולשמחה את יום חג (naming the Holyday) הזה, ברוך אתה ה' מקדש ישראל והזמנים. If the Holyday fell upon a Sabbath and he forgot to say רצה and יעלה ויבא, he should say ברוך אתה ה' אלהינו מלך העולם אשר נתן שבתות למנוחה לעמו ישראל באהבה לאות ולברית, וימים טובים לששון ולשמחה, את יום חג (naming the Holyday) הזה, ברוך אתה ה' מקדש השבת וישראל והזמנים instead ; and if he had said רצה but had omitted יעלה ויבא he should say that which is to be said on a Holyday alone, and if he had said יעלה ויבא but had omitted רצה he should say that which is to be said upon Sabbath.

13. If he did not become aware of the omission until after he had begun the benediction following, which is ברוך אתה ה' אלהינו מלך העולם האל אבינו וכו' he can no longer remedy the omission by saying the benediction אשר נתן therefore if this occur in the first two meals he should repeat the Grace after meals but if in the third meal, whether of a Sabbath or of a Holyday, he need not repeat it but should conclude the Grace. In spite of the above if one had become aware of the omission in a place where it is still possible for him to remedy it by saying the benediction אשר נתן it is his duty to do so even if it happen at several meals.

14. If one had erred on the New Moon by not saying יעלה ויבא he should say ברוך אתה ה' אל' מלך העולם אשר נתן ראשים חדשים לעמו ישראל לזכרון and he must not conclude this benediction. (In this connection it

makes no difference whether it be day or night). And during the Intermediate days of the Festivals he should say אשר נתן מועדים לעמו ישראל לששון ולשמחה, את יום חג (naming the Festival) הזה, ברוך אתה ה' מקדש ישראל והזמנים. On the New Year he should say אשר נתן ימים טובים לעמו ישראל את יום הזכרון הוא, ברוך אתה ה' מקדש ישראל ויום הזכרון. And if he did not become aware of the omission until after he had begun the benediction following, he need not repeat the previous benediction.

15. On Sabbath upon which any of the following days occur, viz. : New Moon, a Holyday, or an Intermediate day, רצה should be said before יעלה ויבא, and if on Sabbath which is New Moon one forgot to say רצה and יעלה ויבא he should mention both in the benediction אשר נתן and conclude with ברוך אתה ה' מקדש וכו'. For although that benediction would not be completed on a New Moon only, in the case mentioned since he concludes the benediction for the sake of the Sabbath, he also mentions the New Moon. If one had said רצה but had omitted יעלה ויבא and he did not become aware of the omission until after he had begun the benediction which follows it, he need not repeat the previous benediction.

16. If one had omitted על הנסים in Grace either on Chanucah or Purim and did not become aware of the omission until after he had pronounced the Divine Name at the conclusion of the benediction, that is, he had already said ברוך אתה ה' he need not repeat the benediction, he may, however, insert it whilst saying הרחמן and say הרחמן הוא יעשה לנו נסים ונפלאות וכו' and then add בימי וכו'.

17. One who had commenced a meal on Sabbath, and continued it until it grew dark should say רצה, inasmuch as he has not said the Evening Service. Likewise on a Festival, New Moon or Chanucah or Purim if he had begun his meal while it was yet day, he is required to say the special form of Grace for that day even if it were night when he said the Grace after meals, if, however, one had begun his meal before the New Moon set in and continued it also during the night when he ate bread of the size of an olive, he is required to say יעלה ויבא, this rule applies also with reference to taking meals before Chanucah and Purim had set in. One who had begun his meal on Sabbath that was also the eve of New Moon, and continued it during the night when he also partook of bread of the size of an olive, should say רצה and יעלה ויבא ; this rule also applies to the Sabbath upon which the Eve of Chanucah or Purim falls. It would, however, be preferable to avoid continuing the meal at such times.

18. If a non-Jew be present whilst the Grace after meals is being said, אותנו בני ברית כולנו יחד should be added.

19. It is necessary for one to hear the words he is uttering, nevertheless, if one had unwittingly said the Grace after meals without

89

having heard the words, provided he had uttered them with his lips, he has fulfilled his duty.

20. If one had said Grace after meals and then discovered that something filthy was in the room, he is required to repeat the Grace, repetition is unnecessary if this were in a liquid state.

Laws Concerning the Grace After Meals.

1. It is the duty of three men who ate together to unite in saying the Grace after meals and it is a duty to say the benediction over a glass of liquor after the meal. If possible a glass of wine should be used, otherwise beer or the common beverage of the land or brandy when this is the common beverage of the land, which is sometimes the case when vine culture does not obtain in that part, and consequently wine is dear and the people are wont to drink brandy instead of beer or the like.

2. The glass is filled before the hands are washed.

3. If the wine in the glass has been partly consumed, what remains renders the glass incomplete and unfit for use at the Grace after meals until it has been rendered fit for use by having a little wine or water added, neither of the latter being in an "unfit" condition. Since the glass must be filled for the special purpose of using it with a benediction ; therefore if the contents of the glass be deficient, he can remedy this by pouring its contents into the decanter and then again into the glass for the special purpose mentioned.

4. See *supra. p.* 86, *paragraph* 5.

5. If those who sit at table are all equal, and if there be a priest (כהן) in their midst, it is proper to honour him with the privilege of saying Grace after meals, as it is written :—"Thou shalt sanctify him" (Lev. xxi. 8), however, if there be a worthy and eminent man in their midst he should say Grace. It is customary to let a mourner say Grace, but only when they are all of equal rank. It is right to confer this honour of saying Grace upon one who is kind and hates covetousness, and who gives charity with his own money.

LAWS AND CUSTOMS OF ISRAEL

6. The one who recites the Grace after meals should begin by
saying הב לן ונברך (Let us say Grace), for every service of sanctification
requires definite appointment (הוזמנה) on behalf of those participating.
He might also employ the phrase used by German or Polish Jews
ועלען בענשען (or וויר), רבותי מיר, the rest of the company respond יהי שם
and ברשות וכו' נברך שאכלנו וכו' then he continues ה' מבורך מעתה ועד עולם.
the others reply : ברוך שאכלנו וכו' and he repeats this sentence.

7. The one reciting Grace should say it aloud, whilst the others
should say quietly every word with him, and at the conclusion of each
benediction they should hasten to finish the benediction first in order
that they may respond אמן.

8. Upon conclusion of the Grace after meals, the one who reads
it should pronounce the benediction over the glass over which he had
said Grace and drink a quantity equal to the capacity of one and a
half eggs, so that he may be enabled to say its Grace. If those at the
table have their glasses before them, but they are deficient, the one who
said Grace should, after having pronounced the benediction בורא פרי הגפן
and previous to drinking thereof, pour a little of his wine into their
glasses, in order that they may also pronounce a benediction over
glasses which are not deficient, likewise if their glasses be empty, he
should also pour therein a little of his wine, and they should not taste
thereof before the reciter had tasted his, but if they have each a glass
which is not deficient, he is not required to give them aught of his
wine, and they may partake of theirs before he partakes of his, thus it
is proper for each guest to have, if possible, a full glass.

9. If the one who said Grace after meals did not wish to drink,
some authorities say he can let one of the guests say the benediction
בורא פרי הגפן and this one should drink the proper quantity (רביעית) and
say its Grace. Other authorities say that this procedure is incorrect
and that only the one who had said Grace after meals with others participating (בזימון) can say the benediction over the glass of wine and
this is the correct custom.

10. It is proper for two people who had eaten together to request
a third person to join them so as to participate in saying Grace, even if
that third person had come after the two had already finished their
repast : yet, if something would have been brought to them as dessert
they would have been disposed to eat thereof ; it is proper to induce
the third person to join them so as to say the Grace, and they should
do this by giving him bread the size of an olive, which requires Grace
thereafter. Even if he should not eat, but he had a רביעית of any kind
of beverage excepting water, he is to respond ברוך שאכלנו. Although
he did not eat, he may yet say שאכלנו (that we ate) as drinking is also
included in the term " eating." After the one saying Grace had concluded the benedictions which terminate with הזן את הכל the newcomer
should say the ברכה אחרונה over what he had eaten or drunk. However

91

if the third person had arrived after the other two had washed their hands with מים אחרונים he is no longer to be reckoned with them.

11. Three who had partaken of a meal in company, inasmuch as they are obliged to unite for the saying of Grace after meals, are not permitted to separate. The same rule applies when four or five have eaten together, not one of them is permitted to say the Grace privately, for it is obligatory upon all of them to unite to say Grace. If the company consist of six or more up to ten, they may separate in such a manner that three, the requisite number for participating in the recital of Grace, remain for each group.

12. If there be ten (adults) present they must add in the Grace the Divine Name, i.e. the one saying Grace says נברך אלהינו שאכלנו משלו וכו' (he must not say נברך לאלהינו). The others respond ברוך אלהינו שאכלנו משלו וכו'. Since they must specially mention the Divine Name they must not separate into groups unless they be twenty or more, when they may divide into two groups (of at least ten persons in each) and then each group can unite for the saying of Grace with the Divine Name.

13. If a company of ten unite for Grace and the one who says it, as well as the others make a mistake by not mentioning the Divine Name, they cannot unite again if once Grace has been said, since they have fulfilled their duty as regards being united for saying Grace. Their omission refers to their failure to mention the Divine Name and since this is the case it cannot be rectified, unless the others (who were listeners) had not yet responded after the one who says Grace. In this case he should recommence and mention the Divine Name.

14. If seven had eaten bread and three had eaten fruit or had drunk a רביעית of liquor, which requires a Grace thereafter, they may unite to say Grace and mention the Divine Name. It is a special duty to seek after ten to say Grace and mention the Divine Name. But if only six had eaten bread they cannot unite to mention the Divine Name for we require in this matter a large majority of the ten easily recognized.

15. All who had eaten together, even if they did not eat the entire meal together, but had sat down to eat and had said the benediction המוציא and each one had subsequently eaten from his own loaf, inasmuch as they had united as one body, whether in a body of three or a body of ten, they are not permitted to separate, even if one of them desire to finish his meal before the rest of the company, they are still not allowed to separate, but if they did not unite as one body at the beginning of the meal, but after two people had eaten already, even if it were no more than a כזית that they had eaten and then the third one arrived and joined them, if he finished his meal with them they are obliged to unite to say Grace, however if he desired to finish his meal before them, in view of the fact that he did not begin the meal with

them, nor did he finish it with them, he is permitted to separate and
say the Grace privately, nevertheless, it is proper to wait and unite
to say Grace. If one be forced, or fear the possibility of loss, even if
he had originally joined them, he is permitted to finish his meal before
them and to say the Grace privately, however. if it be not an urgent
case it is proper to unite with others.

16.   If three had eaten in company and one of them had forgotten
about uniting to say Grace, and had said the Grace privately, his
companions may yet unite with him even after he had concluded his
Grace, and he may also respond ברוך שאכלנו וכו', however if he had been
united with two others to say Grace, he cannot be counted with the
former two. If two had said the Grace, even privately, they cannot
unite (with othres) to say Grace.

17.   If three had eaten in company and two had finished their
meal and wish to say Grace whilst the third one had not yet finished
his meal, the latter should interrupt his meal in order that they may
unite to say Grace, and he may respond with them, and thus discharge
the duty of uniting to say Grace, he should therefore wait until the one
saying Grace had concluded הזן את הכל, and he can then resume his
meal and after he had concluded the repast, he should say the Grace
privately, but he need not say the first paragraph of the Grace, as
when he heard it he had the intention to complete his meal. Two,
however, need not interrupt their meal for the sake of one unless they
wish to do him honour more than is actually demanded by the Law.
If ten eat together, four are obliged to interrupt their meal for the sake
of six, but they need only wait until ברוך אלהינו before resuming their
meal and after they have concluded their repast they should unite to
say Grace together but they should not mention the Divine Name in
the introduction.

18.   At large banquets where many guests are present, it is right
to choose someone to say Grace with a powerful voice, so that all
present can hear him, at least up to הזן את הכל. If this be impossible they should form groups of ten to say Grace.

19.   If a number of persons eating in one room were divided in
two separate groups, also if they ate in two separate rooms but some
of them could see each other, they count as one company and can unite
together to say Grace, however if they cannot see each other, each
group must unite separately, nevertheless, if one person wait upon
both groups he is the means of causing them to count as one company,
that is, provided they had originally separated themselves with the
intention of being counted as one company, but in whatever manner
they unite they count as one, and it is essential that they all hear the
one saying Grace at least up to הזן את הכל.

20.   One who hears others saying Grace and they had united for
this purpose whereas he had neither eaten nor drunk with them, when
he hears the one saying Grace say : נברך שאכלנו משלו he should respond
ברוך ומבורך שמו תמיד לעולם ועד whilst the others are responding ברוך

93

שאבלנו. If a party of ten had united to say Grace and the one leading says נברך וכו' he should respond ברוך אלהינו ומבורך שמו תמיד לעולם ועד, this pplies only to him who heard the leader say נברך וכו', but if he did t come until after the leader had already said נברך וכו' and he heard ose who responded ברוך וכו', he should not respond with them but should say אמן at the conclusion of their responses.

21. When three people eat together, each one having his own af, and one of them had bread baked by a non-Jew, whereas the other two avoid eating such bread, they nevertheless unite to say Grace after meals, and the one who ate the bread of a non-Jewish baker should recite the Grace because he could eat of the bread of the other two people. Likewise if one partook of milk diet and two persons (at the same time) partook of meat food, they unite to say Grace after meals, and the former recites the Grace, because he could partake of the food of the other two. If this person should not take wine or if fresh beer only be available and he avoids taking this, then it is better for one who has eaten and partaken of a beverage (wine or beer) to say the Grace and use therewith a glass for benediction. If one had eaten hard cheese and two people had partaken of meat, they may unite for Grace because they could all partake of one loaf of bread.

22. If women had partaken of a meal with men who were obliged to unite to say Grace, it also becomes obligatory upon the former to hear the recital of the Grace. A child does not participate in the privilege of saying Grace aloud until he is thirteen years and one day old.

23. One who does not read the שמע morning and evening, or who publicly transgresses the precepts is not counted in with those who unite to say the Grace. A proselyte may unite with those who say Grace, he is also permitted to recite the Grace and to say על שהנחלת לאבותינו (who hast caused our fathers to inherit).

LAWS & CUSTOMS OF ISRAEL.
Vol. 2.

THE
LAWS & CUSTOMS
OF ISRAEL.

VOL. 2.

LAWS CONCERNING FORBIDDEN FOOD.

1. The blood found in eggs is forbidden and occasionally it is prohibited to eat the entire egg on account thereof, therefore one must examine the egg before using it for cooking purposes.

2. The blood of fish is permitted, but if poured into a vessel its use is prohibited owing to its appearance (resembling blood which might be forbidden) but if it be evident that it is the blood of a fish, e.g., if it contain scales, then its use is permitted.

3. If one bite a piece of bread (or anything else) and if blood from his gums should come upon the bread, he must cut off the part where the blood is and throw it away. The blood from the gums may be pressed out on a week-day, if it had not discharged itself, but this does not apply on a Sabbath.

4. Blood is sometimes found in milk, because the blood comes from the animal's udder together with the milk, when that occurs the ecclesiastical authorities must be consulted.

5. Meat and milk are prohibited to be eaten or cooked together, nor may they be used together for one's benefit. If, therefore, in any dish they have been mixed together and are thereby prohibited, then the ecclesiastical authorities must be consulted as to whether one may have any benefit therefrom, as in some cases this might be sanctioned.

6. Two Jewish acquaintances, even though they be particular towards each other, one of whom desires to partake of animal food and the other of milk food, are forbidden to eat at one table unless they make a certain mark to distinguish between them, e.g., by having a separate cover laid for each, or by placing upon the table between

their respective food a certain article that does not properly belong there, they should also be careful that they should not both drink from one vessel as the food clings thereon.

7. One should be most particular not to eat bread of the same loaf with both meat and milk, and it is customary also to have separate salt-cellars, one for meat and another for milk food, for it happens that the food is dipped in the salt and part thereof may remain therein.

8. It is customary to mark the knife used for milk food and all other milk and butter utensils in order that they may not be exchanged (for those used for meat.)

9. One who had partaken of meat or even of a dish prepared with meat should not partake of milk food until an interval of six hours had elapsed, and one who had masticated the food for an infant is obliged also to wait that period. If, after having waited the proper period, one found meat between his teeth he must remove it but he need not wait thereafter, yet he should cleanse his mouth and rinse it, that is to say, he should eat a little bread and cleanse his mouth therewith and rinse his mouth with water or any other liquid.

10. If the [dish had neither meat nor meat fat therein but had been cooked in a pot used for meat, even if that pot were not thoroughly cleansed beforehand, it is yet permissible to partake of milk food after (partaking of this dish).

11. After cheese has been eaten, one may partake of meat thereafter at the next meal, but he should carefully examine his hands to see that no particle of cheese clings to them, he should also cleanse his teeth and rinse his mouth. If the cheese were stale and hard, that is to say, because it was curdled by rennet and was six months old or if it had worms and he desires to eat meat thereafter, he must allow an interval of six hours to elapse.

12. If he had eaten cheese and he desires to eat meat he must remove from the table the rest of the bread of which he had partaken whilst eating the cheese. Cheese should not be eaten upon a tablecloth whereon one had eaten meat or *vice-versa*, nor should one cut bread which he intends to eat with cheese with a knife used for meat or *vice-versa*, even if the knife be clean, however, in an emergency, e.g., when one is on a journey, he is permitted to cut the bread he wishes to eat with cheese with a knife that was used for meat, or *vice-versa*, if the knife were thoroughly clean.

13. If one had cut onions or any other pungent article of food with a meat knife and had put the same in food containing milk, or *vice-versa*, the ecclesiastical authorities should be consulted.

14. One who prepares a dish of meat and milk of almonds must put almonds therein on account of its resemblance to milk (and thereby allay any suspicion of having transgressed the Law).

15. It is customary that no utensil used for milk should be (ritually) purified by boiling water in order to make it fit for use for meat or *vice-versa*.

16. If one had given wine, meat or a piece of fish, all of which had no special mark (by which they might be recognised) into the care of an idolater or an Israelite, who is suspected of tampering therewith, to store or to forward, the same must have two seals (apiece), but for boiled wine or vinegar, milk, bread and cheese one seal suffices.

17. If one forwarded or gave on deposit anything in a sack, it is necessary that its stitches should be inside and it must be tied and sealed.

18. If it happened that one had forwarded through a non-Jew a ritually slaughtered beast or fowl or anything else without a seal, then the ecclesiastical authorities must be consulted.

19. Cheese or other articles of food which are in the hands of a non-Jew, although they be sealed or stamped stating that they are ritually fit for food (כשר), are nevertheless prohibited as we do not know who sealed them.

20. Care should be taken that two persons, one of them an Israelite and the other a non-Jew, should not cook or fry together in two pots next to one another, one pot containing food ritually fit for use (כשר) and the other containing food which is not fit (טרפה), nor should the pots be left in the care of servants (upon whom one cannot depend in the matter of כשר food) if a professing Israelite be not present to supervise it.

21. It is forbidden to purchase wine or food of which the כשרות (i.e. ritual fitness) is in doubt of one who has not an established reputation for כשרות (i.e. complying with the Jewish laws), however if one became that person's guest he may eat with him so long as no suspicion arose as to his כשרות.

22. Care should be taken not to allow one's culinary utensils to remain in the house of a non-Jew, lest he may make use thereof.

23. Sometimes people buy a fowl with its legs tied and they throw it upon the ground. Subsequently it is ritually killed and it is strictly forbidden to partake of it; because a beast or fowl which fell may not be declared as fit for food unless one saw it walk (after the fall) at least four cubits. It is therefore proper to be careful in this matter with lambs or calves also.

24. In the summer time slight swellings like warts are to be found upon the intestines of ducks and many become ritually unfit for food thereby, it is therefore proper to examine the intestines at that time and to consult the ecclesiastical authorities regarding them.

25.   One should not knead dough with milk, for it is to be feared that it may be eaten with meat, and therefore on that account it is forbidden to eat even the bread itself, if entirely prepared in that manner.   If, however, the bread were formed in a manner so that it would be easy for one to discern that it is not to be eaten with meat, it is then permitted to prepare it with milk.   The same law is applicable to the use of fat in the kneading of dough.   One should not bake bread with pancakes or pies in one oven, as it is to be feared that the butter or fat may flow under the bread.

26.   If bread had been baked in one oven with roasted meat and the oven had been closed whilst the meat was uncovered, it is forbidden to eat that bread with milk ; it is permitted, however, to eat the bread with milk if the roasted meat were covered or if the oven, which was as large as a regular baker's oven, were open.   Care should, however, be taken not to roast meat in an oven in which bread is being baked, as it may be feared that the grease will flow under the bread.

27.   If grease or milk flow upon the floor of an oven it should be purified by means of glowing heat in accordance with the Law, that is to say, glowing coals should be spread on it so that it is heated white.

28.   Castrated cocks may be eaten, but if any cause for doubt as to their ritual fitness should arise, (e.g.) if the entrails be not in their proper position, then they are forbidden to be eaten.

29.   It is customary in preserving fruit to place the same in a jar which is covered and tied down with a bladder skin over the opening In this way it is placed in a warm oven so that the fruit may be preserved.   The bladder skin must be from an animal ritually fit for food and it also needs salting and proper rinsing to make it fit for use.

30.   It is forbidden to drink the water of wells and rivers reputed to be infested with worms before the water has been strained, and if one had inadvertently cooked in such unfiltered water, the use (of that food) should be forbidden.   It is likewise forbidden to soak meat in such water or to wash therewith articles of food, because the worms cling to the food.

31.   The water should be filtered by means of a cloth which should make the passage of even the smallest worm an impossibility.

32.   Vinegar, which contains worms, is unfit for use if it had only been filtered.   For even the smallest worm in vinegar will pass

98

through any cloth, but when once the worms are dead owing to the boiling they will not pass through when the vinegar is strained.

33. Worms that grow in the fruit whilst attached to the tree are forbidden even if they did not move from place to place (in the fruit). A black spot is sometimes found in fruit as well as in beans and lentils ; this is where the worm takes its origin and this must be removed from the fruit and it is forbidden even as the worm itself.

34. All such fruits, that usually have worms when they are attached to the tree, may be partaken of without examination, provided twelve months had elapsed from the time they were taken off the tree, as no living creature without bones can exist longer than twelve months, and they have therefore become as dust, however as it may be apprehended that the fruit had become wormy since it was picked, they should be examined and cleansed from all worms and animalcula found upon the surface, after which they should be placed in cold water and thoroughly mixed together and as the worms and the worm eaten fruit will rise to the surface they should be thrown away, the rest should be placed in boiling water, so that if any worm remain it will perish immediately before becoming separated from its place.

35. All fruits requiring examination (because of having worms) should be opened one by one and the stones removed, in order that the examination may be thorough, great care should be observed therewith when preserving them in honey and sugar. One should not rely upon the examination of a portion of them, even the greater portion, but each fruit should be examined separately.

36. Flour and other cereals are sometimes found to contain large worms, it suffices therefore if they be sifted with a sieve through which the worms cannot pass, but if the flour contain mites sifting is useless. One who possesses wormy wheat should consult the ecclesiastical authorities as to the manner in which it should be ground.

37. It is forbidden to sell an article of food containing worms to a non-Jew, if it be of the kind not usually examined to ascertain if it be free from worms, for fear that the latter will, in turn, sell it to an Israelite, but one is permitted to distil brandy therefrom.

38. There are many vegetables that are infested with worms. There are housewives who say that if they singe them they will be destroyed, but that is useless. There are certain kinds of fruit and vegetables infested with worms to such an extent that it is well nigh impossible to examine them ; therefore a God-fearing man must not

partake of any of them. There are also certain kinds of fruit whose kernels are infested with worms and it is forbidden to eat them.

39. Sometimes one finds that fruits preserved in honey and sugar have mites on the surface at the edge of the vessel containing same. This part must be thoroughly cleansed and some of the fruit should be removed until it is quite clear that no mites are in the rest.

40. If, whilst cutting fruit or radish with a knife, one had also cut a worm that was therein he should wipe the knife well, and also peel a portion of the fruit or radish at the place where it was cut.

41. Worms are often found in the interior of fish, such as the brain, the liver, the intestines, the mouth or the ears, especially is this the case with the fish called pike, which contains long and thin worms, and such places where they are likely to be found must be examined. Thin worms are found in the fat of herring and it requires examination. In some localities the fish is found to be infested with very small insects, round as a lentil, which are upon its surface near its fins, also upon its fins, in its mouth and behind its ears, they should be examined there and well scraped off.

42. The mites found in cheese, if they be not loathsome, are permitted to be eaten (with the cheese) as long as they are not separated therefrom.

43. If one had consulted the ecclesiastical authorities who had prohibited the use of the thing in question, then he must not consult other ecclesiastical authorities unless he notify them that the previous ones consulted had prohibited the use of the same.

LAWS CONCERNING THE BENEDICTION OVER THE FIVE SPECIES OF GRAIN.

1. If one should eat bread of any of the five species of grain made for the purpose of serving as sweetmeats, but less than the fixed quantity which is reckoned as a meal (the size of an olive), he need neither wash his hands nor say המוציא, but only בורא מיני מזונות and thereafter על המחיה. If, however, he should eat thereof the fixed quantity reckoned as a meal, then the rule applies as in the case of a whole loaf of bread, and he must wash his hands and say המוציא and thereafter Grace after meals.

2. What is the meaning of פת הבאה בכיסנין ? Some authorities
say that it is bread which is prepared like pies filled with fruit, meat,
cheese and the like, also when it is prepared like pancakes. Some
authorities explain the expression as referring to bread kneaded with
oil, fat, honey, milk, eggs or cheese, or with fruit juice, even if a little
water were also added. We adopt both interpretations to facilitate
the practice of the Law and include both explanations in defining
פת הבאה בכיסנין.

3. The quantity of food constituting a meal is not to be reckoned
by one's own appetite but by the average amount usually considered
sufficient for the mid-day meal or for supper when one eats till one be
satisfied. If one had eaten this quantity and although he be not
satisfied, nevertheless it is governed by the same law as applies to
bread. If one eat such bread with a relish, we estimate the amount
according to that which would satisfy other people who would eat the
same with a relish. If he were to eat a small quantity without a
relish and he felt satisfied, whereas other people would not be satisfied
therewith but only with a relish would they be satisfied, then the law
which applies to bread holds good in this case also.

4. If it were originally his intention to eat only a little and he
said בורא מיני מזונות and then he changed his mind and resolved to eat
the quantity constituting a meal, if there be not a sufficient quantity
for a meal left of the food he desires to eat, unless he counts in that
which he had eaten before, he should eat and then say the Grace after
the meal. If the quantity be more than the amount which constitutes
a meal, he should wash his hands and say the benediction המוציא over
that which he desires to eat, but it is not necessary for him to say על
המחיה over that which he had eaten, as the Grace which he will subsequently say, exempts it from that benediction.

5. Dough that was kneaded with water, and loosely mingled
together, if it were baked in an oven or even in a pan, without any
liquor, even if the pan were besmeared with oil, in order that the
dough should not burn, this is not considered as a liquor, and is
governed by the law that applies to proper bread, and to eat even a
piece the size of an olive requires the washing of the hands, the saying
of המוציא and also Grace after meals, however if it were fried in any
liquid it is not counted as bread even if he ate thereof till he was
satisfied. Likewise such wafers which are very thin and which are
baked in a mould in a gridiron are exempt from the law applying to
bread, even if one had eaten thereof to satisfy his appetite, he need
only say בורא מ"מ and thereafter על המחיה. Sometimes the dough is
made so thin, that is to say, flour and water are put into a pot and after

being mixed together, it is poured over vegetables and baked in an oven (*i.e.* a pie crust), this dough is governed by the law which applies to פת הבא בכיסנין (see supra §2).

6. Dough, which has been boiled and afterwards baked as in the case of certain puddings, is considered to be bread proper provided it be well baked.

7. Regarding proper bread, cooked or fried in butter and the like, even if the appearance of bread had been taken therefrom, e.g., by being smeared with eggs, all the laws concerning bread relate t a portion thereof the size of an olive, but if there be not the amount equal to the size of an olive in each portion, although on account of the cooking the dough expanded so that each portion was the size of an olive, or if the cooking made it to cling together and it became a large mass, and even if it have the appearance of bread, yet the law concerning bread does not apply thereto, and only the benediction בורא מיני מזונות before eating and על המחיה after eating are to be said, even if he ate till he was satisfied, but if he did not cook it, but merely poured hot broth upon it, the benediction to be pronounced thereon is doubtful, because we are not sure whether the pouring out of the broth is considered in this manner to be cooking or not; it is best not to partake thereof in the course of a meal. If it were not cooked but soaked in some liquid or soup and the like, and the portions thereof were not the size of an olive, the law depends upon the following consideration : whether it possess the appearance of bread or not, in the former case the laws relating to bread apply, but if it have not the appearance of bread the laws relating to bread do not apply thereto, and he should say only the benediction בורא מיני מזונות before and על המחיה thereafter, even if he ate till he was satisfied. If the appearance of the liquid were changed by the portions of the food soaked therein, it is evident that is has lost the appearance of bread, likewise if it were soaked in red wine it has lost the appearance of bread.

8. Over dough that was cooked, after having been kneaded with water only, the benediction בורא מיני מזונות must be said before partaking thereof, and the benediction על המחיה thereafter, even if he had eaten till he was satisfied. Likewise barley, which belongs to the five species of grain, that was cooked, requires also, prior to being eaten, to be preceded by the benediction בורא מיני מזונות and followed by the benediction על המחיה, even if one had eaten till he was satisfied. If he had eaten this with soup, or farinaceous food which he had eaten with soup or milk in which it was cooked, he is not required to say a benediction over the soup or the milk, for they are secondary to the farinaceous food, and have lost their essential value, however if one had cooked but little of the farinaceous food or barley, and his main object was the preparation of the broth or milk, then the latter do not lose their essential value, and he should first say the benediction שהכל over the broth or the milk. Although he has partaken of the farinaceous food or barley, the broth or the milk must be considered as the

staple element of the dish. Nevertheless in order to do the proper
thing, it is right to say the benediction שהכל first over the broth or
milk alone and to drink a little thereof, and thereafter to say the
benediction ב' מ' מוזנות over the farinaceous food or barley, since
they also are not of secondary importance although the main object in
preparing the dish was not on their account, but as they belong to a
species of corn they are of value and do not become of secondary
importance so as to lose their appropriate and special benediction,
which would otherwise be the case when anything is used merely to
give a flavour to a dish.

9. Food prepared from ground מצה or pieces of bread mixed
with fat, eggs, or milk and which are kneaded, cooked or fried, are
subject to the benedictions בורא מיני, מוזנות and על המחיה before and
thereafter respectively.

10. If one had cooked certain kinds of corn-flour with flour of
different species as is the custom of cooking little pieces of dough with
bay-leaves or beans (or peas), and if the majority belong to one species,
since each species is distinct from the other, he must say two benedictions, preceding with the benediction בורא מיני מוזנות and partaking of
the dough, and then following with the benediction בפה"א over the
beans, etc. of which he should also partake, then he should eat these
together and the broth is held to be of secondary importance and
no benediction need be said on its account. If, however, they were
dissolved and merged in one, such as takes places with a dish consis-
ting of flour, eggs and cheese which is cooked or fried, even if the flour
be but little, nevertheless because it belongs to the five species of corn
it is esteemed and the benediction בורא מיני מוזנות must be said before
partaking thereof and על המחיה after partaking thereof, but this only
applies when the flour is required in order to flavour the dish, but if it
were used merely as a thickening ingredient, just as occurs when
different kinds of relish are prepared with a little flour or when
almonds, sugar and eggs are used for making pastries, it is then that
the flour loses its identity and over the principal component of the
dish alone should he say the benediction. Likewise over broth which
is cooked or prepared with a little flour which has been roasted or fried
in butter, we say only the benediction שהכל. But if he pick out the
pieces which have been fried and eat them he must say ב'מ'מ before
partaking thereof and if he have eaten thereof an amount equal to the
size of an olive he must say thereafter על המחיה.

LAWS CONCERNING THE BENEDICTION TO BE PRONOUNCED OVER
WINE, ALSO RELATING TO THE BENEDICTION הטוב והמטיב.

1. Over wine the benediction בפה"ג is said and thereafter על הגפן
and it makes no difference whether the wine were still bubbling, or

exuding by itself, or if it were prepared with spices, (i.e. it contained honey and spices) or if it were absinthe which is bitter, or if the wine gave forth the odour of vinegar, so long as it tastes like wine, it is considered to be wine with reference to a benediction. But if it turned sour to such a degree that there are some who would avoid drinking it on account of its acidity, the benediction to be pronounced thereon is a matter of doubt, he should therefore not partake thereof until he had pronounced a benediction over good wine.

2.   If he poured water upon kernels that yield wine upon a slight pressure and which were not yet squeezed in a wine press, although the wine he finds does not exceed the quantity of water which he had poured upon them, or even if the wine they yielded were less than the quantity of the water, nevertheless, if it taste like wine, the benediction בורא פרי הגפן must be said (before partaking thereof); however, if the kernels had been squeezed in a wine press, after which water had been poured upon them, or if water had been poured upon wine dregs, it is considered as water only.

3.   When wine has been mingled with water and if the wine were only a sixth part thereof, the wine is disregarded and it is considered to be merely water. If, however the wine be more (than a sixth part of the water) and if it be the custom in that place to mix wine in that proportion and to drink it in lieu of wine, then before partaking thereof the benediction בפה"ג must be said and thereafter על הגפן, but if this be not the case the wine therein may be disregarded.

4.   Just as bread when fixed as the staple food includes all kinds of food (in its benediction), so with wine, (if one resolve to partake of wine by way of refreshment) he may drink all other beverages provided they were set before him when he said the benediction over the wine, or if he intended to drink these beverages as well when he said the benediction, without being required to say the benediction that precede and follow their consumption. But if they were not before him nor did he intend to drink them, it is doubtful whether they require a benediction or not, one should therefore avoid partaking thereof until he has said the benediction after wine, or until he has said the benediction שהכל over some kind of food having then the intention of including the beverages.

5.   However if he drank the wine casually and had no intention of drinking other beverages, he is required to say the preceding benediction over the other beverages, but there is a doubt as to the necessity of saying the benediction thereafter owing to the possibility of it being exempt by saying the benediction על הגפן over the wine, therefore one should partake of some fruit that necessitates the saying of בורא נפשות thereafter, whereby the beverages may be exempt from the concluding benediction.

6. One who says the benediction of sanctification (Kiddush) over wine and intends to drink brandy or coffee thereafter, it is doubtful whether the latter are exempt or not from a separate benediction by that pronounced over the wine, he should resolve that he does not exempt them, and therefore he should say the benediction שהכל over some confectionery (requiring such a benediction) and thus exempt the beverages from a separate benediction.

7. When one is about to say the benediction over wine in the course of a repast and also in the presence of others, he should say סברי רבותי ("Give heed! O my friends") in order to direct attention so that they should interrupt their meal and hear the benediction.

8. If one had partaken of one kind of wine, whether in the course of the repast or not, and another kind of wine is brought to him, he does not say the benediction בורא פרי הגפן over the latter, since he has neither changed his mind on this matter nor has his attention been diverted from his wine, but he should say the benediction הטוב והמטיב. Likewise if they bring before him a third kind of wine, he also says over this the benediction הטוב והמטיב and so on.

9. If his mind were diverted therefrom in such wise that it is necessary to say the benediction בורא פרי הגפן, he should first say בפה"ג and thereafter הטוב והמטיב.

10. The benediction הטוב והמטיב is to be said only on the assumption that the one who partakes of the second kind of wine has no knowledge of it being inferior to the wine he previously drank although he is not certain that it is superior thereto, but if it be known that it is inferior to that already used, then no benediction is to be said but if it be also more wholesome than the former, although its taste be inferior, he should say over the same the benediction הטוב והמטיב.

11. Even if they had from the beginning of the repast two kinds of wine but they were not both on the table when the benediction בפה"ג was said, then over the second kind which happens to be superior the benediction הטו"מ is said. If the two kinds were on the table, the benediction הטו"מ is not to be said, but בפה"ג must be said over the wine of superior quality to exempt the inferior kind from any benediction.

12. The benediction הטו"מ is not said unless there be some more of the first kind of wine used, as the second sort is partaken of merely for the sake of varying the wine used. But if the second kind be provided because the first sort is exhausted the benediction הטו"מ is not said over the same.

13. The benediction הטו"מ is not said unless there be another person present who also drinks of the two kinds of wine,

implying that God is good (המוב) to him and that He dispenses good (והמטיב) to his companion. This is also the rule if one have his wife and sons with him at table, but if he be alone he does not say the benediction המוה"מ.

14. Guests who are at their host's table may indulge in as much wine as they wish, the host having placed on the table a decanter of wine, as is the custom at banquets, then the wine is considered to be their common property, and they should say the benediction המוב והמטיב. If the host had given a glass of wine to each guest, they should not say the benediction המוב והמטיב inasmuch as the wine is not their common property, even the host should not say that benediction.

15. One person may say the benediction and exempt all the rest of the company from their obligation of saying the same and he should first say סברי רבותי to direct their attention to the benediction and they should respond אמן implying that they are exempt by this benediction. This applies only if each one have his glass before him in order that he may immediately drink without interruption between the benediction and the drinking.

16. If he recite Grace after the meal over a glass of wine of a different kind (to that which he had drunk previously) he need not say the benediction המוב והמטיב thereafter, as he is exempt by the section המוב והמטיב which he says in the Grace after the meal.

RULES CONCERNING THE BENEDICTION TO BE SAID
BEFORE ENJOYING THE GIFTS OF GOD.

1. If one had inadvertently said the benediction שהכל over any article of food or drink, be it even bread and wine, his religions duty is done. But this must not be done intentionally. It is therefore a duty to learn how to distinguish the various benedictions and to say the appropriate one according to the kind to be enjoyed. But in the case of something of which he is in doubt as to which class it belongs or concerning which there are varying opinions held by the ecclesiastical authorities, and no definite decision is available as to the appropriate benediction, he should say שהכל, but it is preferable if he should exempt it from any benediction by partaking thereof in the course of the meal.

2. He should take the article, over which he is about to say the benediction before eating or drinking or smelling the same, in his right hand and think devoutly which benediction he ought to say, so that when mentioning the Divine Name, which is the principal part of the benediction, he may know how to conclude the same. If he had said the benediction over the article without having taken it in his hand, so long as it was before him (at that time) his duty is done, however if the article were not before him when he said the benediction but it was brought to him later, even if his mind were centred thereon whilst saying the benediction still his duty is not done and he must repeat the benediction.

3. If he took in his hand some fruit to eat and he said the
benediction and it fell out of his hand and was lost, or became too
loathsome to be partaken of, or, if he had said a benediction over a
glass of liquor and spilt it, if at that time there were more of the same
kind before him of which it was also his intention to consume
even more than was in his hand, consequently the benediction which he
had said referred also to what remained before him. he need not therefore repeat the benediction, but if this were not the case, then the
benediction applies only to that which is before him, and he should
repeat the benediction. Likewise, if he intended to partake of more
of the same article, but if it were not before him at the time he said the
benediction but was brought later, he must repeat the benediction
even if he would ordinarily have been exempt from repeating the
same over that which would be brought later had he partaken of the
first (quantity), in this case, however, it is different.

4. Between the benediction over food and its consumption he
should avoid a pause lasting as long as it takes to say a few words.
Even when masticating the first mouthful of food he must not pause
until he has swallowed it. If after saying the benediction, he interrupted himself before eating by speaking of something irrevelant to
the meal, he must repeat the benediction, but if he delayed in eating
by pausing silently, he need not repeat the benediction. Any delay
necessary for the purpose of the meal is not considered an interruption,
therefore should one desire to partake of a large fruit which he must
cut up before eating, he must say the benediction while it is whole, as
it is proper to say the benediction over an entire article, inasmuch
as the subsequent delay, caused by cutting up the fruit for the purpose
of eating it, is not considered an interruption. However, if one
desire to eat a fruit that might contain worms and therefore improper
to partake of, and if there be no more, he should open it and examine
it before saying the benediction.

5. If one were about to drink water, but before partaking thereof
he spilt a little fearing that the surface water might be unhealthy, he
should do this before saying the benediction and not thereafter, so as
to avoid any disrespect with regard to the benediction.

6. One who tastes food to ascertain if it need salt, or for similar
purposes, if he eject it instead of swallowing it, he is not required to
say a benediction, however, if he swallow it, there is a doubt as to his
obligation to say a benediction, inasmuch as he swallowed it, although
he did not intend to make a meal thereof, he should therefore bear in
mind, when he partakes thereof, that he relishes it as a meal, and he
should first say a benediction and then swallow the food.

7. One who partakes of food or drink as medicine, if it be something savoury which he relishes, even if it be forbidden food, he should
say the preceding and the concluding benedictions appropriate thereto,
since the Law permits him now to partake thereof, even if the article

be of a bitter taste and unpalatable, he should say a benediction over it, because he enjoys the nourishment it affords him.

8. One who drinks some beverage or eats a piece of bread or any other food which affords him some benefit, for the purpose of aiding him to swallow something that had lodged in his throat, should say its preceding and concluding benedictions, but if he drink water, not because of thirst, but for the purpose of aiding him to swallow what had lodged in his throat or for any other purpose, he is not obliged to say any benediction, for a man does not enjoy the drinking of water unless it be to allay his thirst.

9. If one had inadvertently taken food in his mouth without having said its benediction, he should act as follows : If it be an article that can be ejected without becoming loathsome, he should eject it into his hand and say the benediction over the same, but he should not say the benediction while it is yet in his mouth. But if it be an article, the ejectment thereof would make it loathsome, inasmuch as wasting food is prohibited, he should let it remain on one side of his mouth, while saying the benediction. However in the case of a beverage, which it is impossible to place on one side of the mouth (so as to say the benediction) if he have some more of the beverage besides, he should eject it and let it be wasted, but if he have no other and he is in pressing need of the little that he has in his mouth he should swallow it, and then say its preceding but not its concluding benediction.

10. If two kinds of food subject to the same benediction were before him, e.g., a nut and an apple, so that he can say a benediction over the one kind and exempt the other, then he should do this. He is forbidden to say the benediction over one kind with the intention of not having the other kind exempt so that he would have to say the benediction also over the other kind separately, since it is forbidden to give occasion for the saying of a benediction when it is unnecessary to do so. Therefore he should say the benediction over that which belongs to the superior kind and exempt the other kind, although he may not have the intention to exempt the latter. But if he said the benediction over the inferior kind, then the other kind is not exempt thereby unless he had the intention of doing this. If he therefore merely said the benediction over the inferior kind without any further intention, he must say the benediction again over the other kind which is superior, for it is not proper that the benediction over the inferior kind should unintentinally cause the superior kind to be exempt from its benediction.

11. If there be two kinds, e.g., fruit of a tree and fruit of the earth or if there be also a kind over which the benediction שהכל is said, he should say the benediction appropriate to each, in spite of the fact that he had inadvertently said שהכל over all of them, or if he had said the benediction ב'פ'ה when he would have done his duty, nevertheless, it is forbidden to act thus intentionally. When partaking of the three kinds aforementioned the order is as follows : the benediction ב'פ'ה takes

precedence over שהכל. If one had wine and grapes before him and he desired to drink the wine first, and he must say the benediction בפה"ג, although if he have the intention to exempt the grapes from a separate benediction by the prayer בורא פרי הגפן over the wine he may do so, nevertheless he should not intentionally act thus, but he should resolve not to exempt the grapes (by the benediction said over the wine) and should say its proper benediction בורא פרי העץ.

12. Whilst partaking of all kinds of food except bread, if one had changed his place although his thoughts were not diverted from the food he was consuming, nevertheless the change of place is reckoned as though he had diverted his thoughts from this food, consequently if one ate or drank in one room and then went into another room to conclude the eating or drinking, even if the food be of the kind he first consumed, and even if he held that food or beverage in his hand and carried it into another room, nevertheless he is obliged to repeat there the preceding benediction over that food, but he is not required to say a concluding benediction over that which he had first consumed as the concluding benediction will do for both.

13. Likewise if he went outside (his house) and thereafter returned to his former place to conclude his repast, he must say the preceding benediction again. The foregoing applies only to one who had eaten alone or to one who had eaten with others and all had left their place, however if one of the company had remained in his place whilst those who went away had the intention of returning to their companion in their former place to finish their repast, then on their return when they resume the meal the benediction need not be repeated, for inasmuch as one of the company had remained there, their gathering together did not cease since they all return to their original meeting place, and it is all reckoned as one meal.

14. Change of place is not involved when one goes from one corner to another in a room, no matter how large the room may be.

15. One who ate fruit in an orchard that was fenced around, and said a benediction over the fruit of one tree with the intention of partaking also of the fruit of other trees, even if they be not in view of each other, so long as he did not divert his thoughts from his intention he is not required to repeat the benediction; but if the orchard were not fenced around, and more especially if he went from one orchard to another, it does not avail him that his thoughts were not diverted therefrom (and he must repeat the benediction).

RULES CONCERNING THE CONCLUDING BENEDICTION (ברכה אחרונה).

1. After having partaken of the fruit of the tree (not of the seven species mentioned in Deut. viii. 8) and of the fruit of the earth,

and of vegetables and of any food that is not the direct produce of the earth, one should say בורא נ"ר, even if he ate and drank, for one benediction thereafter suffices for all that he had consumed.

2. The concluding benediction as well as the Grace after meals must not be said unless one had eaten the maximum quantity which is the amount equal to the size of an olive. After having partaken of food that is less than the quantity equal to the size of an olive, one is not required to say the concluding benediction. According to some authorities one is not bound to say the concluding benediction after having partaken of liquor unless it contained a רביעית. Other authorities hold that he is required to say that benediction after having partaken of liquor that contained a כזית. Therefore in order to avoid any doubt one should take care to drink less than the quantity equal to the size of an olive (כזית) or to the quantity רביעית. It makes no difference whether the beverage be brandy or any other liquid.

3. If a thing be exactly as it is produced by nature, e g., a nut or any other fruit, or even a bean, although its quantity does not equal the quantity of an olive, nevertheless since the article is whole we say thereafter the concluding benediction. The authorities, however, differ on this point. Therefore to avoid any doubt one should not eat unless there be the amount of an olive. If the article had been divided before it was eaten, it loses its special value (from the ritual standpoint) and according to all the authorities we do not say the concluding benediction if less than an olive measure had been consumed.

4. All articles of food can be combined together to make up the required quantity of a כזית (with reference to the concluding benediction), thus if one ate half of the required quantity of a כזית of a food after which בורא נפשות is said, and another half of a כזית of another food after which the benediction מעין שלש is said, or if it were half the required quantity of a כזית of bread after which בורא נפשות is said, and if he ate half the required quantity of a כזית of such kinds of fruit after which על העץ is said and half the quantity of a כזית of a kind of of food after which על המחיה is said, or if he ate half the quantity of a כזית of bread then in all the aforesaid cases בורא נפשות is the only benediction that is said ; however. if one ate half of the required quantity of a כזית of a kind after which the benediction על המחיה is said and another half of the required quantity of a כזית of bread—the benediction על המחיה should be said ; eating and drinking are not reckoned together in this respect.

5. If one ate half the required quantity of a כזית and also drank and then resumed eating the second half of the quantity of a כזית, if the interval between the two occasions of eating did not exceed the time taken to eat a piece of bread, then the two occasions of eating are considered to be one and thereafter the concluding benediction is said. If, however, the interval exceeded this limit then the two occasions of eating are reckoned as separate. With regard to drinking, if he made a pause of less time than the limit just mentioned the separate acts of drinking are not combined.

6. If one drink a hot beverage gradually, since he does not drink

כזית* lit. like an olive.

the minimum quantity (required for the benediction) although this is the usual way of drinking it, nevertheless the different quantities consumed are not combined and no concluding benediction is to be said.

7. The land of Israel is famous for the seven species which it produces. Moreover concerning bread the Torah is explicit in its precept: "And thou shalt eat and be satisfied, and thou shalt bless" (Deut. viii. 10); therefore one who had eaten bread of the five species of grain, viz., wheat and barley, (mentioned in Deut. viii. 8,) and also spelt, oats or rye, which are included as belonging to wheat and barley, must say the Grace thereafter. This consists of three complete benedictions, including also the benediction הטוב והמטיב. However after having partaken of food, which is not really bread but which is farinaceous, prepared from the five species of grain aforementioned, also after having partaken of the vine, in the form of wine or grapes, either fresh or dried, large or small, or of figs, pomegranates, olives or dates, the latter being the "honey" of which the Torah speaks, inasmuch as honey exudes therefrom, the grace known as ברכה אחת מעין שלש should be said. This Grace contains in a brief form the three benedictions as well as the benediction הטוב"מ of the Grace after meals.

8. The Grace מעין שלש which is said after various kinds of food, other than bread, prepared from any of the "five species of grain" begins thus: ב'א'י'א'מ'ה'ה' על המחיה ועל הכלכלה ("Blessed art Thou, O Lord our God, King of the Universe for the sustenance and the nourishment") and concludes thus: ונודה לך על הארץ ועל המחיה ב'א'י' על הארץ ועל המחיה ועל הכלכלה ("And we will give Thee thanks for the land and for the sustenance. Blessed art Thou, O Lord, for the land and for the sustenance."). The Grace after wine begins (after the usual introduction): על הגפן ועל פרי הגפן ("for the wine and the fruit of the vine.") and concludes thus: על הארץ ועל פרי הגפן ב'א'י' על הארץ ועל פרי הגפן ("for the land and for the fruit of the vine. Blessed art Thou, O Lord, for the land and for the fruit of the vine."). After fruit the Grace begins (after the usual introduction): על העץ ועל פרי העץ ("for the tree and the fruit of the tree") and concludes על הארץ ועל פרות ב'א'י' על הארץ ועל הפרות ("for the land and for the fruits. Blessed....for the land and for the fruits."). In Palestine and even elsewhere should we eat the fruit of the Holy Land we conclude the Grace thus: על הארץ ועל פרותיה ("for the land and for its fruit." If one ate various kinds of farinaceous food and drank wine also he should combine in one Grace the benedictions relating to both, so also with fruit and wine. So also after grapes, wine, fruit and farinaceous food or even after farinaceous food, and wine and spirits he should combine the three benedictions in one Grace, first mentioning על המחיה, then על הגפן and finally על העץ. When he combines על המחיה with any other formula he should not say at the conclusion ועל הכלכלה, but ב'א'י' על הארץ ועל המחיה ועל פרי הגפן (Blessed....for the land and for the sustenance.), or על המחיה ועל הפרות (for the sustenance and for the fruit) or ע'ה'י' וע'פ'ה ועל הפרות (for the sustenance and for the fruit of the vine and for the fruit").

9. On Sabbath or Holyday or New Moon, he should insert what relates especially to these days, but if he had forgotten it, he need not repeat the Grace.

10. One should be as particular with this Grace as with the Grace after meals.

11. In the Grace בורא נפשות some authorities decide that we should read שבראת ("that Thou hast created") and others decide שברא ("that He has created"). The latter seems to be more correct, for the meaning of the Grace is : "who has created many living beings with their wants," i.e., He has created the living beings and also their wants, meaning thereby all things needed for their wants, namely the things which are absolutely necessary for life's existence, such as bread and water and also all the other things which He has created, but which are not absolutely essential but are rather for purposes of enjoyment, e.g., fruit and the like—"for all we thank Thee." We must read חי העולמים (the letter ח with a Patach).

12. If one had partaken of fruit after which the Grace מעין שלש is said and had also eaten fruits after which בורא נפשות is said, he should say the Grace מעין שלש and as he mentions therein פרי העץ ("the fruit of the tree") he thereby exempts all the other fruits which he had eaten from the Grace בורא נפשות, but if what he had eaten requires thereafter the Grace בורא נפשות as it is a different kind of food, it is not exempt from its Grace by the formula מעין שלש. He should first say the Grace מעין שלש and then בורא נפשות.

13. One is forbidden to deliberately leave his place or to engage in any occupation before saying the concluding Grace, lest he forget to say it. But if he had left his place, and if בורא נפשות were the Grace he is obliged to say, he should say it where he is, but if it were מעין שלש he should return to his place and say it there, just as he would do if it were the Grace after meals.

14. If after eating or drinking he did not immediately say the concluding Grace he has time to do so until he has digested the food, which lasts so long as he has no desire to eat or drink, after such time he should no longer say it, but if one be unable to properly estimate that time, then if he remember that he had not said the Grace, he should say a benediction over some more of that food whereof he had partaken and eat thereof, after which he should say the concluding Grace and thus exempt that which he had eaten previously.

15, If one ate or drank and vomited, he should not say the concluding Grace as it is (with regard to the Grace) the same as though the food had been digested.

Rules Concerning the Benedictions בורא פרי העץ
ובורא פרי האדמה ושהכל

1. Before eating fruit which grows on trees one should say the benediction בורא פרי העץ ; before partaking of produce which grows

In or on the ground, such as turnips, vegetables, beans and herbs, one should say בורא פרי האדמה. A tree (for the purpose of this law) must have branches which remain in spite of the winter, and which produce leaves in the spring, even though the leaves be as thin as the capsules of flax. But a plant whose branches perish in the winter and whose root alone remains, is not called a "tree" and over its fruit we say בורא פרי האדמה.

2. Before partaking of food, which is not a product of the ground, such as meat, fish, milk and cheese, also on drinking any beverage except wine and olive-oil the benediction שהכל should be said. We read נהיה with a Kamez under the י.

3. Although mushrooms and truffles imbibe nutrition from the moisture of the earth, and their growth is not dependent on the soil but on the atmosphere, therefore they are not called "fruit of the ground," and the benediction שהכל should be said over the same.

4. The benedictions בורא פרי העץ or בורא פרי האדמה should be said only over an article fit to be eaten when raw, and which it is customary to eat in this state, but if it be not customary to eat it raw and it is eaten only when cooked, although it is also fit for food when raw, nevertheless, it is inferior food when raw, and its benediction should be said only when one eats it cooked, but if one ate it raw he should say the benediction שהכל. Pickled food is considered the same as cooked food, thus before partaking of pickled cabbage one should say the benediction בורא פרי האדמה. Salted food is also governed by the same law as cooked food in this respect.

5. Before partaking of radish one should say the benediction בורא פרי האדמה, likewise over garlic and onions that are soft and which are usually eaten raw; although they are generally eaten only with bread, nevertheless, if one ate them without bread the benediction בורא פרי האדמה should be said, but if through being old they became very pungent in taste and it is not usual to eat them raw, one who ate them raw should say the benediction שהכל.

6. Some articles are more proper for food when they are raw than when they are cooked, as the cooking spoils them; one who is about to partake of them when cooked, should say the benediction שהכל although if one cooked them with meat and its taste became improved

because of the meat, nevertheless, inasmuch as the meat is the principal article of food, only the benediction שהכל should be said over the
same, however, if one cooked them in such a manner that they became
the principal article of food and also improved them thereby, as for
instance, if he had fried them in fat or honey or the like, he should
say the proper benediction, as it makes no difference whether they
were cooked in water or in fat or in honey.

7.   The inferior kinds of fruit which grow on thorn-bushes and
briars, or on other shrubs which are of spontaneous growth and are
not planted by man, such as wild apples and the like which are not fit
to eat when raw, even if he cooked or fried them in honey or sugar,
thus making them fit for food, only the benediction שהכל should be
said, but hazel-nuts, although they grow in the woods, are considered
superior articles of food and the benediction בורא פרי העץ should be said.

8.   Herbs which grow spontaneously without cultivation,
and are fit to eat when raw, although he had cooked them so that they
are a proper dish, inasmuch as they were not planted they are not
considered as fruits, and the benediction שהכל should be said.   Over
lettuce, however, and similar vegetables that were planted, one should
say the benediction בורא פרי האדמה.   Over the herbs of spontaneous
growth if they include fruit of a superior kind, such as
gooseberries and raspberries, the benediction בורא פרי האדמה must be
said.

9.   That portion of the fruit which is not its principal part is not
esteemed as highly as the fruit itself but is slightly inferior, thus over
such inferior portion of a fruit tree one should say the benediction
בורא פרי האדמה or in the case of a fruit of the ground one should say
the benediction שהכל, therefore with the caper tree, the leaves of which
are fit for food, for they have fruit-like excrescenses (as on the leaves of
the myrtle) and are called caper-berries and they form the chief part of
the fruit.   But caper-flowers, which are the husks around the fruit,
like the shells of nuts, are also eatable, therefore over caper-berries
which are the essential fruit we say בפה"ע, over the leaves and berries
we say בפה"א.   Likewise over preserves made from rose leaves with
honey and sugar we say the benediction בורא פרי האדמה, over preserves
prepared from orange-peel and over preserves prepared from the rind of
melons one should say the benediction שהכל.   Over the pods of peas
that are cultivated in the field, although they are sweet in taste, still
if one eat them without the peas he should say the benediction שהכל.
If, however, they were cultivated in the garden for the purpose of eating

them raw while in their pods, he should say the benediction בורא פרי האדמה even if he should partake of the pods alone.

10. Before partaking of the seeds of fruit one should say the benediction בורא פרי האדמה providing they be sweet, if, however, they be bitter they are of no value whatever, and the one who partakes thereof need not say any benediction over the same, yet if he sweeten them by the fire or in a like manner, the benediction שהכל is to be said.

11. Over bitter almonds when small and whose husks are therefore not bitter, which are planted for the sake of the latter which are then eaten, the benediction בורא פרי העץ should be said, but if the almonds be large the kernel is then the principal part thereof, but as that is bitter he need not say any benediction on partaking of the same, however if he make them palatable by putting them over the fire or in any other way, inasmuch as they are fruits and are planted for that purpose, the benediction to be said over them is בורא פרי העץ. Sugared almonds, even if the sugar were profusely sprinkled on them, require the benediction בורא פרי העץ when one partakes thereof.

12. On partaking of fruits that are not yet ripe whilst on the tree, which one had cooked or fried in honey or the like, as this is the method of preserving unripe fruit in honey or sugar, one should say the benediction שהכל. On partaking of preserved citron one should say the benediction בורא פרי העץ.

13. Over spoiled fruit such as became withered through the heat, and fell from the tree before they were ripe, since they have deteriorated, one says only the benediction שהכל. Likewise over bread which is stale, or over a dish which became slightly spoiled, one should say the benediction שהכל, but if they were spoiled to such an extent as to make them unfit for food, no benediction should be said. Nor should a benediction be said over strong vinegar which ferments when poured out on the ground; however if one had mingled it with water until it became fit to drink, he should say the benediction שהכל.

14. Some fruits never become ripe whilst on the tree, but after being plucked from the tree they become ripe by being placed in stubble or straw or the like; e.g., certain kinds of small pears, inasmuch as that is their usual way, the benediction בורא פרי העץ should be said over them.

15. Some fruits which only contain juice stored up in their stones (or pips) which are not fit to be eaten, but after the juice has been extracted they are thrown away, over the juice the benediction שהכל should be said, and although one ate the fruit with their skins and seeds, still the only benediction to be said is שהכל.

16. We say neither the benediction בפה"ע nor the benediction בפה"א unless one can slightly recognize the fruit, but if they be crushed until they are unrecognizable, as with jam which has been boiled or small fruit which has been entirely crushed, the benediction to be said thereon is שהכל. Yet if he had inadvertently said the benediction originally appropriate thereto his duty is done, however if the fruit be generally eaten in a crushed form, the benediction originally appropriate thereto is the one that is now applicable.

17. Over rice and grit that were cooked in such a manner that they were not dissolved, we say the benediction בורא פרי האדמה, but if they were dissolved, or if one had made a paste of them like bread. there is a difference between rice and grit (in this respect). Because according to the strict law the benediction במ"מ should be said over rice, whereas שהכל should be said over grit and as we are not sure whether אורז be really rice or whether דוחן be grit or vice-versa there. fore a religiously minded person should only partake of these kinds when disssoved in the course of a meal. However in an emergency, if one have no bread (and thus he cannot make a meal wherein he might include them) he should say the benediction שהכל before partaking of them and after eating the same he should say the concluding Grace בורא נפשות. Before partaking of bread made of pulse, even where such bread is the staple food, one should say the benediction שהכל.

18. We say שהכל over sugar and likewise if one suck sugar-canes or cinnamon or liquorice which is chewed and only the taste thereof is enjoyed whilst the chief part is ejected, then the benediction is שהכל.

LAWS CONCERNING THE BENEDICTIONS TO BE SAID OVER SOUP ALSO OVER FRUIT AND VEGETABLE EXTRACTS.

1. Over liquors extracted from fruits and vegetables we say the benediction שהכל, this also applies to the honey extracted from date as the liquor is termed "fruit," except wine and olive-oil which are also highly esteemed, and if he enjoy the same in such a manner that he is obliged to say a benediction, he says בורא פרי העץ.

2. If one cooked fruits which it is not customary to cook, since they are usually eaten raw, he should say the benediction שהכל before partaking of their liquor, however if it be a kind of fruit which it is customary to dry and to cook and which are easily procurable and are also grown for that purpose, if one cooked them in order to partake of the fruit and its liquor, he should say בורא פרי העץ over the liquor, even if he should not eat the fruit therewith. Likewise if one cooked pulse or vegetables, according to the general method of preparing gruel food for consumption, he should say the benediction בורא פרי האדמה over their liquor even if he did not partake of the (rest of the) dish, however if the one who cooked them did so only for the sake of the fruit or vegetable, if he does not desire to eat them but only to drink the liquor he should previously say the benediction שהכל and if he cooked them with meat, although the cooking was done also for the sake of the liquor, in any case שהכל is the benediction to be said over the liquor, as the meat is the principal part of the dish.

3. Some fruits are soaked only for the sake of their liquor, the latter is subject to the benediction שהכל, hence over tea, coffee or beer, whether made from dates or from barley, the benediction to be said is שהכל.

4. If vegetables or fruits, such as cucumbers, beetroot, leeks, etc., preserved in water became sour, although that usually happens, nevertheless over their liquor one says only the benediction שהכל. Although the liquor has the taste of the vegetable or fruit, nevertheless since they were preserved, not on account of flavouring the liquor, but so that they might be prepared as preserves, therefore the benediction שהכל only is to be said. But if he first ate the vegetable and said the benediction בפה"א and then he wished also to drink some of the liquor, it is a doubtful point whether he must say a benediction over the same, for perhaps his obligation in this matter has been fulfilled by the recital of the benediction בפה"א. It is better not to act in the aforementioned manner.

5. The same is the case with fruits, vegetables or pulse and the like, which one had cooked in a liquor having a taste peculiar to itself, as for instance, in vinegar or in beetroot soup or in milk, the benediction שהכל should be pronounced over their liquor.

6. Raisins having so much juice that the latter will exude when they are pressed, if they have been beaten and then soaked in water for the purpose of making a beverage therefrom and not for the purpose of eating the raisins as food, if they were soaking thus for three days, and then began to ferment, and after three days he poured its liquor into another vessel that liquor is proper wine over which the benediction בורא פרי הגפן and thereafter מעין שלש should be said, and on all occasions where a glass of wine is required, one may fulfil his duty by using that as wine. It is necessary, however, to see that the raisins form more than a sixth part of the water, one should estimate the raisins just as though they were in a fresh state before they were dried; all the above-mentioned applies only to wine that was made by the soaking of raisins, but if he boiled the raisins in water, the boiling thereof does not cause it to become wine.

LAWS CONCERNING THAT WHICH IS IMPORTANT AND THAT WHICH IS ACCESSORY THERETO.

1. If one partake of two articles of food, or if he eat and drink, and one of these articles is important for him whilst the other is merely an accessory thereto, for his intention was not to eat the latter apart from the former and if he did not have that which was important he would not eat its accessory; e.g., if one felt faint and with a view of reviving himself, he partook of salt herring or radishes, but since they are pungent he also ate therewith a small piece of bread or something else to mitigate the pungency, likewise if he desire to drink some brandy and having done so, he partakes of a little bread to mitigate the pungency, or instead thereof he eats some fruit he is obliged to say a benediction only over that which is important and not over that which is accessory thereto—the latter requires neither a preceding nor a concluding benediction—because it is exempt by reason of the benediction over the important article of food, it does not require even the washing of the hands.

2. This applies only if he first ate the article which is important for him and then that which is accessory thereto, and also when he said the benediction over this article, he mentally included its accessory, or if he be accustomed to partake of them in such a manner, which is as though he had mentally included the latter (in his benediction over the former), furthermore if he partook of the accessory in the same place and did not go into another room before doing so, as otherwise he is obliged to say a separate benediction over the accessory.

3. Likewise the eating of the accessory before the important article raises a question as to its benediction; e.g., if one desire to drink wine or brandy and in order not to drink upon an empty stomach, he first eats a small piece of some food, then he should rather drink first of all a little of the wine or brandy and then its benediction will exempt the accessory from any further benediction.

4. If one's mind be equally intent upon two articles of food, e.g., if one desire to drink brandy, and also to eat honey-cake, preserves or the like, he should say a separate benediction over each, giving precedence to the benediction over the cake and preserves, because they count more, thereafter he should say the benediction over the brandy. Much more is this the case if he ate dessert (cakes) and also drank coffee, that he must say separate benedictions over both, first over the dessert (cakes) and then over the coffee, for his intention referred to both.

5. If one desire to partake of a dish composed of two different kinds of food which were cooked together, if each kind be separated, he should say over each kind the benediction appropriate to each, but if they be dissolved and cling together he should say the benediction over that kind which predominates, for that is the more important element, and it exempts its accessories (from a separate benediction), however, if one kind be of the five species (even if it be the least in quantity), the benediction should be said over it, as it is reckoned as the more important element.

6. A dish to which one had added milk or soup which he intended to consume together (is subject to the following conditions). if it were his primary object to eat the dish, he should say a benediction over that only, for then the milk or soup is but an accessory to that dish, but, if the soup or milk be what he desired principally to partake of, he should say a benediction over that, and the dish is accessory thereto ; if his mind were equally set upon partaking of both, but each is subject to a different benediction, he should first say the benediction over the dish and eat a little thereof, and then he should say the benediction שהכל over the soup or milk, the question of a greater quantity is of no consideration in the foregoing, and even if the food be of a species of grain, it is not (in this connection) reckoned as an essential article.

7. Before partaking of ground spices mixed with sugar a benediction should be said only over the spices which are considered to be the essential elements. Over a nutmeg one should say the benediction בורא פרי העץ, over cinnamon בורא פרי האדמה, and over ginger בורא פרי האדמה.

8. If one desire to drink olive-oil in its natural state, inasmuch as it is injurious to his health, he should not say any benediction, if, however, he mixed it with other ingredients it becomes a mere accessory, and he should say the benediction upon that which is paramount, however if he have some ailment and he must drink the oil medicinally, and he mixes it with other ingredients in order to avoid its injurious effect, inasmuch as the oil is the primary object for him, even if it be the least of the ingredients he should say the benediction בורא פרי העץ thereon and exempt the other ingredients. However, if one be thirsty and if he partake of a beverage to quench his thirst, and incidentally he also mixes therewith some olive-oil for a medical purpose, he should say a benediction only over the beverage. This law applies also when one puts muscatels or cinnamon or ginger in a beverage, in all such cases we always consider what his primary object was.

LAWS AND CUSTOMS OF ISRAEL

9. In all kinds of preserves, the honey and the sugar are mere accessories, and the benediction should be said only over the fruit, which is the essential element.

LAWS CONCERNING THE ORDER OF PRECEDENCE RELATING TO BENEDICTIONS.

1. If one have before him many varieties of fruit and if he desire to partake of all of them he should be guided by the following conditions : if they be all subject to the same benediction, he should say it over the kind which he likes best ; if he be equally fond of all and if there be amongst them one of the seven species with which the land of Israel was praised, he should say the benediction over this even if there be only a half of that fruit, whilst the others are whole ; but if there be none of the seven species amongst them, if some fruit be whole, and others be not whole, the benediction should preferably be said over the whole fruit, likewise when the benediction over each kind is the same. The same conditions apply to one who desires to partake of two kinds of fruit that are each subject to a different benediction, e.g., one kind is subject to the benediction בורא פרי העץ and the other to the benediction בורא פרי האדמה, thus requiring the recital of both. If he be fonder of one of the two kinds, he should give the precedence in saying the benediction to that of which he is fonder, and if he be equally fond of both, one of the seven species should have the precedence, even if it be not whole, but if there be none of the seven species amongst them, precedence should be given to the whole fruit, but if they be both the same, either whole or not, the benediction should be בורא פרי האדמה.

2. If all the fruit be of the seven species, and he is equally fond of them, he should give the precedence in pronouncing the benediction to that kind which is mentioned first in the Torah (Deut. xiii. 8). The second ארץ (a land) in the verse enumerating the seven species subdivides the narrative, therefore, dates take precedence over grapes, because dates are the second that are mentioned after the second ארץ whilst grapes are mentioned third after the first ארץ in that verse, that is only as far as grapes are concerned, but wine, being an important beverage, has its special benediction and therefore it takes precedence over all kinds of fruit.

3. The precedence given to one of the seven species is obligatory only if the fruit be ripe, but if the fruit be unripe it has no claim to precedence because the text is not concerned with anything which is not complete and proper. Likewise if he ate thereof in a manner so that he cannot enjoy it, e.g., the chewing of wheat, the law of precedence does not apply thereto.

4. If one had before him a kind of food over which the benediction בורא פרי העץ or בורא פרי האדמה is to be said, and another kind over which the benediction שהכל should be recited, even if he prefer to eat both kinds he should, nevertheless, give precedence by saying the

120

benediction בורא פרי העץ or בורא פרי האדמה for they are important since they do not refer to more than one kind apiece whereas שהכל is a comprehensive benediction. This applies even in the case where he prefers to partake of something over which he must say שהכל.

5. The benediction בורא מיני מזונות takes precedence over all others even over the benediction over wine, except the benediction המוציא which takes precedence over the benediction בורא מיני מזונות. Therefore on Sabbaths and on Holydays when saying the sanctification (קידוש) over wine, the bread should be covered, also on a Sabbath morning when he intends to partake of farinaceous food after קידוש he should have that food covered when pronouncing the קידוש over wine.

Laws Concerning Benedictions Pronounced Erroneously.

1. One who by error said the benediction בורא מיני מזונות over proper bread or the benediction המוציא over cake has fulfilled his obligation, if, however, he had said the benediction המוציא over food even if prepared from the five species of grain, his obligation is not discharged. If by error he had said the benediction בורא פרי הגפן over grapes his obligation is discharged, likewise, if he had erred in saying the concluding grace על הגפן, his obligation is fulfilled, as grapes are also fruit of the vine.

2. If by error one said the benediction בורא פרי האדמה over a fruit of the tree, or if both kinds were before him, and by error he had given precedence in saying the benediction over the fruit of the ground with the intention of including the fruit of the tree, his obligation is fulfilled, as the fruit of the tree also gets its sustenance from the ground, but if he said the benediction בורא פרי העץ over a fruit of the ground his obligation is not fulfilled. Consequently if one be in doubt as to which species a fruit belongs, whether to the tree or to the ground and it is impossible for him to ascertain the fact, he should say the benediction בורא פרי האדמה.

3. If by error he had said over wine the benediction בורא פרי העץ if he at once became aware of it, he should immediately add the words בורא פרי הגפן, but if he did not become aware of it immediately, and it happened unintentionally, his obligation is fulfilled.

4. If by error he had said the benediction שהכל over any article, even over bread or wine, his obligation is fulfilled.

5. At the outset one should know the purpose of the benediction he is about to say, nevertheless if he erred having unintentionally said the wrong benediction, e.g., he thought he was about to drink wine, and he began the benediction with the intention of concluding it with בורא פרי הגפן but before thus concluding it he had discovered that it was water or beer and concluded the benediction with the formula of שהכל וכו' it is unnecessary to repeat the benediction, since

it is not obligatory to repeat a benediction owing to an error in one's intention. Much more so is this the case if the above-mentioned example were reversed, and if he had mistaken wine for beer or water and said the benediction with the intention of concluding it with שהכל, but before saying שהכל he had become aware of his error and discovered that it was wine and he said בורא פרי הגפן his duty is fulfilled, for if he had said שהכל he would also have fulfilled his obligation.

6. Moreover even if he had concluded the benediction erroneously but instantly became aware of his error and rectified it, e.g., if he took a glass of water or beer, thinking that it was wine and said בפ"ג and then he found out immediately that it was water or beer and he concluded by reciting שהנ"ב saying thus בפה"ג—שהנ"ב his obligation is fulfilled.

7. If he did not instantly become aware, he must say again the benediction שהכל if he desire to drink this glass, and if he also intend to partake of wine, he should take wine and drink a little and it is not necessary to say a second benediction provided he had not interrupted by speaking, even though he first tasted the contents of the glass and discovered that it contained water or beer, nevertheless this is not considered an interruption if he acted in this manner.

LAW AS TO THE BENEDICTION OVER AN ARTICLE OF FOOD, WHERE MORE WAS TAKEN THAN WAS ORIGINALLY INTENDED.

1. If one had said a benediction over bread, having no intention of partaking of more than what he had prepared, e.g., he had purchased a loaf or a roll and he thought that this would suffice and then he desired to eat more of the same, and he sent and had some more bought and even if he had more of the same kind which he had originally prepared before him, he is nevertheless obliged to repeat the benediction המוציא over that which was brought to him, as he had changed his mind, however if one have bread in the house and he cut off a portion thinking it would be sufficient, and then he desired to partake of more of it and he cut off some more, although he had no more of the first piece, still he need not repeat the benediction, as that is not considered as though he had changed his mind, for this is the usual custom.

2. If one had said a benediction over fruit and he partook thereof, when more of it was brought to him, if at the time he said the benediction it was his purpose to include thereby all that would be brought to him, he is exempt from repeating the benediction over that which is subsequently brought to him, even if he have no more of the first fruit, and even if they be not of the same kind as the first fruit but, are subject to the same benediction, if, however, he changed his mind

in regard to what was brought later, that is to say, if it were his original intention to eat only what was before him, but he subsequently changed his mind and decided to eat more than that, even if that which was brought later be of the same kind as the first, and he also had some left of the first fruit, he is nevertheless obliged to repeat the benediction over that which was subsequently brought to him.

3. However if one had no thought, one way or the other, concerning anything that might be brought later, then the following distinction should be observed :- if none of that kind (first partaken of) were left at the time when more of it was brought to him, he must repeat the benediction, but if he had more left, there is a diversity of opinion whether there is any obligation to repeat the benediction over that which was brought later, one should therefore take the precaution, when saying the original benediction, to resolve to exempt thereby all things requiring the same benediction that might be brought later. If when saying the benediction he had no thought concerning what might be brought subsequently, he should abstain from eating thereof, owing to the doubt as to the necessity of repeating the benediction.

4. If fruit were brought to him and this happened to be of a superior kind and of which he was fonder than of the first (kind of which he had previously partaken) or if something of the seven species were brought to him, he is required to repeat the benediction, even if he had then more of the first left, for the benediction said over an inferior article cannot exempt a superior article, unless he clearly intended to exempt the same when he said the original benediction.

5. Having said the benediction שהכל over beer, with the intention of exempting all articles subject to the same benediction, if they brought fish to table, he is not required to repeat the benediction, if, however, he had no thought when saying the benediction concerning what might be brought subsequently, he is required to repeat שהכל over the fish that is brought, regardless of the fact that he still had some of the beer left at that time, as the law concerning the exemption of two kinds of fruits is not applicable in this case, e.g., if the first kind were apples and the other nuts, nevertheless they are both one class of food ; but beer and fish are entirely different kinds, one is an eatable and the other is a beverage, and the one kind cannot exempt the other, unless they be both before him at the time of saying the benediction, or if he intended to exempt the one by the other.

6. The above rules apply only to one who eats of his own provision, but one who eats at his neighbour's house exempts, by the benediction said over one kind, all that might be brought subsequently, even if there be no more of the first kind (on the table) as it all depends on the host's will. Yet if he had dismissed all thoughts concerning the article that was subsequently brought to him, he is obliged to repeat the benediction over the same. If the host had no intention of serving his guests with more of the same food, but served them solely

at their own request, then the latter are not obliged to repeat the benediction inasmuch as they rely upon their host to supply them with as much as they need.

7. One who came to a feast and had said a benediction over a glass (of wine) that was given to him, need not repeat the benediction over the glasses that will be given to him thereafter if it be usual to give more than one glass, as it is assumed when saying the benediction over the first glass that he intended to exempt all the others.

LAWS CONCERNING THE BENEDICTION TO BE SAID WHEN SMELLING FRAGRANT SPICES.

1. Just as one is forbidden to enjoy any article of food or drink before its benediction has been said, likewise is one forbidden to enjoy any fragrant odour before saying a benediction, however after having enjoyed the same, one is not required to say a concluding Grace, for as soon as he has ceased to inhale the fragrance his pleasure has ceased, therefore as regards the Grace it is to be compared with food which is digested (which requires no further prayer).

2. Under what circumstances do we say the benediction over a pleasant fragrance ? If it arise from fruit which is fit for food, whether it be fruit of the tree or of the ground, even if it be only made fit by being mixed together with other ingredients, such as the nutmeg, the lemon or the "Ethrog" inasmuch as they are principally used as food, he should say the benediction הנותן ריח טוב בפרות, provided he had intentionally inhaled their fragrance ; if, however, when partaking thereof the fragrance had reached him unintentionally he is not obliged to say a benediction over the same. If one inhale the scent of roasted coffee which is pleasant, he should say the benediction הנותן ריח טוב בפרות.

3. Before inhaling the fragrance of plants, which are unfit for food, but are chiefly esteemed for their fragrance, such as the myrtle or the rose, or frankincense and the like, one should say the benediction בורא עצי בשמים. One should not smell pepper or ginger, as a benediction is not said over the same.

4. Before inhaling the fragrance of herbs and vegetables, one should say the benediction בורא עשבות בשמים. A vegetable is distinguished from a tree in the following manner : if it possess a stem as

124

hard as the stalk of flax, and be perennial, and produce leaves, it is a tree, but if its stalk be always soft it is an odorous herb.

5. If it be neither a tree nor a herb, such as musk and the like, on inhaling its fragrance one should say the benediction בורא מיני בשמים, the same rule applies on smelling dried fungi when they have a pleasant odour.

6. Over balsam-oil which grows in the soil of the land of Israel, the special benediction בורא שמן ערב has been instituted, on account of its special worth as being associated with the land of Israel.

7. If on smelling fragrant woods one had in error said the benediction בורא עשבי בשמים or vice-versa, he has not fulfilled his obligation, if, however, he had said the benediction בורא מיני בשמים over any of the odorous species, his obligation is fulfilled, thus, if he be in doubt as to the benediction and he cannot distinguish the species he should say the benediction בורא מיני בשמים. If he said the benediction בורא עצי בשמים over fruit of a tree, he has done his duty. Over cloves and over the rind of bitter oranges and lemons he should say the benediction בורא עצי בשמים.

8. Oil or water that was scented with spices, or with fragrant wood, is subject to the benediction בורא עצי בשמים, but if scented with fragrant plants, to the benediction בורא עשבי בשמים, and if prepared with divers kinds of perfume due to bark and plants, it is subject to the benediction בורא מיני בשמים. Likewise in all cases where the fragrance is due to several articles being employed for this purpose. If the perfume were abstracted from the oil or water leaving none of that element therein except its perfume, it is a question whether a benediction is required on smelling it, one should therefore not smell this perfume.

9. If a fragrant fruit, odorous bark and plants and aromatic spices were set before a person, he should say the benediction appropriate to each, in the following order : first over the fruit, then over the bark, then over the plants, and then over the spices.

10. One who inhales incense, due to spices being burnt upon coals, should say a benediction as soon as the fumes ascend and before he inhales its fragrance, as obtains in all cases of saying the benediction over articles for human enjoyment. The benediction should not be said before the fumes ascend, since the benediction must precede the enjoyment without delay : if he burn fragrant bark he should say בורא עצי בשמים, if he burn plants בורא עשבי בשמים and if he burn other

kinds of spices בורא מיני בשמים. A benediction should be said as above only if he burn the spices specially to inhale their perfume, but if he burn them for the purpose of fumigating the room, as in the case of disinfectants used with a corpse, a benediction should not be said.

11. Likewise wherever the spices are not placed for the special purpose of smelling them, such as spices that are placed in a room as merchandise and also perfume used to scent utensils, which is not made for purposes of inhaling but only to scent the utensils, these spices and perfumes need no benediction, even when one smells them intentionally.

12. If, however, one entered a store where various spices are sold, or a chemist's shop, and intended to smell them, he should previously say the benediction בורא מיני בשמים as the spices are there for this purpose, for the shopkeeper is glad if people smell them and purchase thereof. If one had entered and left the place several times in succession, if when first saying the benediction he had in mind to exempt subsequent visits, he need not repeat the benediction, but if his attention were diverted therefrom or if he had remained a long time outside the shop, he is required to say the benediction whenever he returns there.

13. Scent without any substance, e.g. garments which have been perfumed, or spices which had been placed in a vessel and their scent had evaporated, likewise one who handled Ethrogim (citrons) or other fruit with a fragrant odour which remains on his fingers or garments, in all these cases no benediction is required.

LAWS CONCERNING THE BENEDICTIONS שהחינו AND הטוב והמטיב

1. On hearing good tidings from a reliable party, who was an eye-witness, one should say the benediction שהחינו. This applies if he had been an eye-witness to the matter in question and in which he alone is interested, but if it be good for him and others as well, he should say the benediction ברוך . . הטוב והמטיב implying that it is good for himself and that God dispenses good to his fellowmen. If at the time he beheld that which was good for himself or heard the good tidings he could not say the benediction on account of his physical condition or owing to the locality where he happened to be, he can say the benediction later. This applies also to the benediction דין האמת.

2. On hearing bad tidings one says the benediction ברוך . . דין האמת and if many reports reached him at one time, whether good or evil, one benediction is sufficient and one is bound to bless God also

for the misfortune with perfect confidence and a willing spirit just as he blesses God for the good.

3. One to whom a benefit had occurred or who had heard good tidings, although the good is of such a nature that evil will apparently ensue therefrom, e.g., if one found an object and the king will confiscate all his possessions if the matter be found out, he should, nevertheless, say the benediction הטוב והמטיב. Likewise if evil befell him, or if he hear evil reports, although these misfortunes will apparently have a good result, e.g., if a flood swept his field and injured its produce and thereafter it became beneficial because it watered his field, nevertheless one should say the benediction דין האמת since we bless only over the occurrences of the present, and not over the events of the future.

4. A man should be wont to say always כל מה דעביד רחמנא לטב עב יד ("Whatever the All-merciful does is for the best.")

5. If one's wife give birth to a son, both husband and wife should say the benediction הטוב והמטיב.

6. If one's father or relative died, or even a non-relative but a pious man, and much more so in the case of a scholar, whose death grieves him sorely, he should say the benediction ברוך אתה ה' אלהינו מלך העולם דין האמת. On the demise of one whose death does not cause him so much grief, one should say the benediction ברוך דין האמת omitting the Divine Name and Kingship.

7. If one had built or bought a house, or if he had purchased vessels or valuable garments, although he had previously acquired similar possessions, so long as he had never owned these previously and he rejoices in their acquisition, he should say the benediction שהחינו. The benediction should be said at the time the purchase is made or upon the completion of the building, although he had not yet made use of the same, as the benediction is on account of his joy of acquisition.

8. If one wear (for the first time) a new garment he should say the benediction מלביש ערמים, even if he had already said that benediction in the morning prayers he should repeat the same when putting on the new attire, if, however, he had dressed himself therein in the morning, the benediction of the morning prayer will exempt him from saying a separate benediction over the same. If he purchased a טלית he should say the benediction שהחינו after he has inserted the ציצת, but if he did not say the benediction at that time, he should say it when first enwrapping himself therein after having said the benediction להתעטף בציצת.

9. On purchasing articles for household use, one should say the benediction הטוב והמטיב.

10. If one were presented therewith he should say the benediction הטוב והמטיב as the recipient derives benefit from the gift and likewise this applies to the donor. If the recipient be a poor man then the donor is found worthy by God, who has enabled him to perform the precept concerning charity, and if the recipient be a rich man, the donor is gratified by the former's acceptance of the gift.

11. On purchasing new sacred books one should not say the benediction שהחיינו as the things wherewith the precepts are performed are not for sensual enjoyment.

12. On purchasing an article that is of slight value, such as a shirt, shoes or socks, one should not say a benediction, even if he be poor and its acquisition give him joy. If a rich man purchased new utensils whose acquisition would fill one of the middle class with joy, but which the rich man in comparison to his wealth esteems but lightly not finding joy therein, he should not say a benediction.

13. It is customary to say to one who puts on new apparel: "Mayest thou wear out this garment and acquire a new one." One should not say this to one who wears shoes or a new garment made of leather from an unclean animal, even if the leather be sewn beneath cloth.

14. If one partake for the first time of a fruit, which is reproduced each year, he should say the benediction שהחיינו, and then the benediction appropriate to the fruit; if, however, he forgot and first said the benediction over the fruit, he can say the benediction שהחיינו thereafter, without it being considered an interruption. One who omitted the benediction שהחיינו when first partaking of a new fruit, should not say it on subsequently partaking of the same. One who has before him several kinds of new fruit, should say the benediction שהחיינו over one kind and include all the rest. Two species of fruit, although they slightly resemble each other, such as a cherry and a damson, even if they bear a name in common and differ in taste, such as green figs and dried figs—if one had said the benediction שהחיינו over one of them, he is required to repeat it when subsequently partaking of the other, as the eating of each of these fruits constitutes a separate pleasure.

15. If one said the benediction שהחיינו over grapes, some authorities say that it is not necessary to say the benediction שהחיינו when partaking of new wine, because there is an additional pleasure in the latter. Therefore it is proper that if he had said the benediction שהחיינו over grapes, then if he should partake of new wine he should first say the benediction שהחיינו over some special kind of food and thereby exempt the wine from this benediction. If one had said the benediction שהחיינו over the new wine he is no longer required to repeat it over grapes, this applies only if it were new wine (תירוש) which can be recognized as such, but if he did not partake thereof until it was

(fermented) wine (יין), even if he did not say the benediction שהחינו over grapes, he should not say over it this benediction שהחיינו because one cannot distinguish between new and old (wine).

16. We do not say the benediction שהחיינו over half-ripe grapes unless the cluster of grapes had become ripe, likewise with all fruit unless they are fully grown.

17. The benediction שהחיינו should not be said over vegetables or turnips for the reason that they remain well preserved for a long time by being kept in the earth or in sand, and being very plentiful one does not take joy therein.

18. One should not say the benediction שהחיינו over a fragrant odour.

19. One who sees his fellow-man after an interval of thirty days from the time when he last saw him, if he be greatly attached to him, he should say the benediction שהחיינו. Especially when he is his superior, as for instance, his father or teacher, and he rejoices in seeing him, he should say the benediction שהחיינו, even if he had received a letter from him in the interval. On beholding him for the first time in twelve months, he should say the benediction ב'א'י'א'מ'ה' מחיה המתים but if he had received a letter from him at that time, or had heard of his welfare, he should not say מחיה המתים but he should say שהחיינו. The law is applicable to both male and female, for even if a man see his wife or mother or sister or daughter, or if a woman see her husband or brother or son the benediction שהחיינו is likewise to be said.

20. One who sees a friend whom he had never met before, but with whom he became friends as a result of having corresponded with one another, need not say a benediction when seeing him, for since they have never seen each other before, the love they mutually bear cannot be so great that he should be overjoyed at seeing him.

BENEDICTIONS CONCERNING SEEING.

1. On seeing fruit trees in blossom one should say the benediction ב'א'י'א'מ'ה' שלא חסר בעולמו כלום וברא בו בריות טובות ואילנות טובות להנות בהם בני אדם. ("Blessed art Thou, O Lord our God, King of the Universe, who hast made Thy world lacking in nought, but hast produced therein goodly creatures and goodly trees wherewith to give delight unto the children of men.") This benediction should be said only once a year. If he delayed the recital of this benediction until the fruit grew he must not say it subsequently.

2. On seeing shooting stars which dart across the sky from place to place with a transient light, or a comet or a meteor, or on witnessing an earthquake or a hurricane or lightning, one should say the benediction עשה מעשה בראשית ב׳א׳י׳א׳מ׳ה׳ (".. who hast made the creation"). This benediction should be said over a shooting-star but once during the night even if he saw another that night. Over a comet one should say a benediction but once in thirty days. On hearing thunder after the lightning has passed, one should say the benediction שכחו וגבורתו מלא עולם ("whose strength and might fill the world"). If one saw lightning and heard thunder simultaneously he should say only one benediction עשה מעשה בראשית ("who hast made the creation"). If one said the benediction עשה מעשה בראשית over the lightning and without any interval the thunder was heard immediately thereafter, it is not necessary to say a benediction on account thereof, for it is exempt by the benediction said over the lightning. The benedictions over lightning and thunder should be said directly they happen, and if an interruption occurred he should not say the benediction.

3. With the benediction which he says once over the lightning or thunder, he exempts the repetition of the same that he may see or hear subsequently so long as the clouds have not passed by, but if the clouds had disappeared and the sky had cleared up in the interval between one flash of lightning and the other, or between one peal of thunder and another he must repeat the benediction. A simple flash of lightning due to the heat and unaccompanied by thunder is not of the same nature as (storm) lightning and does not require the recital of a benediction.

4. On seeing the rainbow one should say the benediction ב׳א׳י׳א מ׳ה׳ זוכר הברית ונאמן בבריתו וקים במאמרו ("who rememberest the covenant, art faithful to Thy covenant, and keepest Thy promise").

5. At the sight of seas, or mountains famous for their great height one should say the benediction עשה מעשה בראשית.

6. On the appearance of the sun at the end of its cycle, i.e., after a period of twenty-eight years, when the vernal equinox of ניסן begins at the approach of night-fall on the eve of the fourth day one should say on the morning of the fourth day when the sun is shining ברוך . . . עשה מעשה בראשית. Before pronouncing the benediction one should say Psalm cxlviii. after which he should say the benediction, then he should say אל אדון until וחיות הקדש, then Psalm xix. and thereafter the קדיש and finally the עלינו לשבח should be recited.

7. This benediction should, if possible, be said in the morning immediately at the rising of the sun, for the zealous hasten to obey the commandments and it is proper to say the benediction in an assembly of the people, for " In the multitude of the people is the King's honour " (Prov. xiv. 28) (it is therefore proper to make a pub-

lic announcement of the occasion on the day preceding it, in order that. they may assemble). If it be impossible for them all to assemble in the morning they should not, for that reason, delay, but each one should say the benediction immediately he sees the sun shine. The rule concerning the "zealous who hasten to obey the commandments" takes precedence of the rule "In the multitude of the people is the King's honour." If it happened that one did not say the benediction in the morning, he may say it at any time till about 9 a.m., and if in the stress of circumstances (he delayed it still later) it may still be said until noon, consequently if the morning were cloudy so that the sun was obscured he should wait until it is near noon, as perhaps the sun will make its appearance, so that he may be able to say the benediction mentioning God as King of the Universe (שם ומלכות), but if it did not make its appearance, he should say the benediction and omit the Divine name and title of King.

8. If the Holy One, blessed be He, had wrought a miracle on behalf of someone, having helped him in a supernatural manner, on seeing the place where the miracle occurred, he should say the benediction ברוך . . שעשה לי נס במקום הזה ("Blessed .. who hast wrought a miracle for me in this place"). His son, his grandson, and even those who were born before the miracle happened, should also say the benediction. How should they say it? His son should say שעשה נס לאבי במקום הזה, ("who hast wrought a miracle for my father in this place,") and if there be many sons they should say לאבינו ("for our father.") His grandson should say לאבותי ("for my ancestors") and if there be many grandsons they should say לאבותינו ("for our ancestors"). One for whom many miracles were wrought, on arriving at one of the places where one of the miracles happened, should refer to all the other places and include them all in one benediction as follows : שעשה לי נס במקום הזה במקום פלוני ("who hast wrought a miracle for me in this place and in that place") mentioning the name of the other place. His sons and also his grandsons should also mention all the other places.

9. On seeing a Jewish scholar distinguished for his knowledge of the Torah, one should say the benediction ברוך . . . שחלק מחכמתו ליראיו ("who hast given of His wisdom to those who fear Him.") On seeing a sage of other nations, distinguished for secular knowledge, one should say the benediction ברוך . . . שחלק מחכמתו לבשר ודם ("who hast given of His wisdom to flesh and blood.")

10. On beholding a king or the ruler of a nation, one should say the benediction ברוך . . . שנתן מכבודו לבשר ודם, ("who hast given of His glory to flesh and blood"). Even if the king be invisible, but all the pomp of the royal state indicate his presence the benediction should be said. One who is blind should say the benediction but omit the Divine name and title of King. It is a duty for one to make an effort to behold the glory of kings. Having seen him once, one need not interrupt his study of the Torah in order to see him again, unless he appear this time with greater array and with more glory than previously.

11.   On seeing the graves of Israelites, one says the benediction
ברוך .. אשר יצר אתכם בדין וכו' (" who hast formed you in judgment," etc.)

12.   The benedictions which one had said on the occasions aforementioned should not be repeated on seeing the same within thirty
days.   On seeing different personages, however, i.e., another sage
or king, or other graves or the like, one should repeat the benedictio
even within thirty days.

13.   On seeing an Ethiopian or a red Indian or an Albino or a
living freak, e.g., a giant or a dwarf, or one who is wholly ulcerous,
or one whose entire hair is matted or an elephant or an ape, one
should say ברוך ... משנה הבריות (" who varies the forms of His creatures").
This benediction is to be said only on the first occasion of seeing these
freaks, for the first impression is very striking.

14.   On seeing for the first time a cripple or one without hands
or a blind person or one who is afflicted with leprosy or white leprosy
(which appears in white scabs), if they be thus afflicted from birth one
should say the formula משנה הבריות on the first occasion, but if
they were thus afflicted after birth and it grieves one to behold them,
he should say the benediction דין האמת (" Blessed be the true judge ").

15.   On seeing goodly trees, or beautiful creatures, human or
animal, ברוך ... שככה לו בעלמו (" who hast such as this in His world ")
should be said but once on seeing them for the first time, and should
not be repeated on seeing again the same or others of that kind,
unless the latter be more beautiful than the former.

LAWS CONCERNING THE BENEDICTION הגומל ALSO OTHER
BENEDICTIONS ON DIVERS OCCASIONS.

1.   Four classes of people must thank God for special mercy, such
as a person who has crossed the ocean and has reached the desired haven,
or on arriving safely at one's destination after having passed through
a desert or a dangerous road, or one who was in any peril whatsoever
and was saved therefrom, e.g.. if a wall fell upon him, or an ox
(attempted to) gore him, or robbers attacked him on a journey or
bandits by night and he was saved from them, or similar instances or
on recovering from a serious illness, or one who was imprisoned and
set free, even if his imprisonment were due to money matters, all of the
foregoing should say the benediction ברוך ... הגומל לחיבים טובות שגמלני
כל טוב "who bestows benefits upon the undeserving and who has
bestowed upon me all kinds of favours" to which the listeners should
respond : מי שגמלך כל טוב הוא יגמלך כל טוב סלה.   " May He who has
bestowed upon thee all favours continue thus to do."

2. The benediction הגומל should be said in the presence of ten (male adults) besides the one saying the benediction. Two of the ten should be scholars who are occupied with the Jewish Law, but the absence of the scholars does not disqualify the procedure. It is customary to say the benediction הגומל on being called to the Torah after having said the second benediction (ברכה אחרונה). One should not deliberately delay saying the benediction הגומל longer than three days, consequently, one who was preserved from danger on a Monday (after the Torah had been read) should immediately say the benediction הגומל without the Scroll of the Torah and he should not postpone the recital to the following Thursday. He must, however, say it standing before ten (male adults). Nevertheless, one who had inadvertently delayed the recital longer than three days may say it also after that time.

3. One to whom a miracle happened is in duty bound to set aside a certain sum of money for charity, as much as his means will allow, which he should divide amongst those who are occupied in the study of the Torah, and say " Behold, I give this money to charity, and may it be the Divine will to consider this as if I had brought a Thank Offering." It is also fitting that he should institute some public improvement in the city (where he resides) and every year on the anniversary he should set that day apart to thank God and to recall the miracle.

4. One who is about to undergo any operation or to try something as a remedy should first offer a brief prayer as follows, יהי רצון מלפניך ה' אלהי ואלהי אבותי שיהיה לי עסק זה לרפואה, כי רופא חולים אתה. and if the food or beverage, which he is about to partake of medicinally, require the recital of a benediction, he should first offer this prayer and then say the benediction. After the operation (e.g.) bleeding, he should say בא'י' א'מ'ה',רופא חולים (" who healest the sick ").

5. אסותא (" To your good health "), should be said to one who is sneezing, whereupon the latter should respond ברוך תהיה " Mayest thou be blessed." Thereafter he should say, לישועתך קויתי ה' " For Thy help I hope, O Lord " (Gen. xlix. 18); for the one, who prays on behalf of his fellow man, has his prayer answered.

6. One who prays concerning what has already happened, e.g., if one hear a cry in the town and he says : " May it be Thy will that this cry should not be in my house," is offering a vain prayer, for what has happened is a fact.

7. One who is about to measure his crops or the like, should say the following prayer : יהר"ם ה' אלהי שתשלח ברכה בכרי הזה (" to send a blessing on this my heap "), having begun the measurement he should say ברוך השולח ברכה בכרי הזה " who art sending a blessing on this my heap," omitting the Divine name and title. After he has measured, should he then offer prayer this is a vain petition, because God's blessing is to be sought only in such cases where the result is unknown or invisible.

LAWS AND CUSTOMS OF ISRAEL

8.   One whose son became בר מצוה (i.e. he is thirteen years and one day old) should say the benediction ("... ברוך ... שפטרני מעונשו של זה") who has released me from the responsibility for this child") when his son has been called to the Torah for the first time and after he had concluded the ברכה אחרונה over the reading in the Scroll of the Law. It is a religious duty for one to prepare a feast on the day on which his son became בר מצוה, that is, on the day when he has entered into his fourteenth year.   If the lad deliver a Talmudical discourse on that occasion, it becomes a religious feast even if celebrated on another day.

9.   If after a drought which caused general distress—although in our land the rain falls in its regular season and droughts are rare—there should be a rain-fall that descends with such force that it runs off in bubbling streams, it is necessary to say certain benedictions.

10.   What is to be said ?   One who is not the owner of a field should say מודים אנחנו לך ה' אלהינו על כל טפה וטפה שהורדת לנו, ואלו פינו מלא שירה כים, וכו' ("We thank Thee, O Lord our God, for every drop (of rain) which Thou hast brought down for us and if our mouths were full of songs as the sea," etc.) as far as ויקדישו וימליכו את שמך מלכנו, ב'א'ה', אל רוב ההודאות והתשבחות ("and hallow and assign kingship to Thy name, O our King.   Blessed art Thou, O Lord, God of many thanksgivings and praises.")   One who owns a field in partnership with another Israelite should say the benediction הטוב והמטיב, but if he have no Jewish partner, although he have a wife and children, he should say the benediction שהחינו.   One may say the benedictions הטוב והמטיב and שהחינו even if he should not see the rain but hears that it is raining, the benediction מודים should be said, however, only by the one who sees the rain descending.

LAWS OF BUYING AND SELLING.

1.   It is necessary to be most careful not to deceive one's neighbour, either in buying or selling, or with reference to hiring, contracts or exchange.   In any such case a negative precept would be transgressed (see Lev. xxv. 14.)

2.   Just as there is the prohibition of wrong doing (i.e. deception) with reference to buying and selling so also with regard to money changing.

3.   If a buyer or seller be honest in his dealings, and does not apprehend any deception, thus he says, "This article I bought at this price, and this is the amount of profit I wish to make out of it," although he had been cheated when buying that article, and since any-one who has been deceived is not permitted to deceive others on

134

that account, he is yet permitted to dispose of it, as (by his declaration) he makes it clear that the purchaser should not rely on (the price he asks to determine) the value of the article, (as he sells it) according to the price he paid for it.

4. If one have something to sell, he is forbidden to make it look better than what it really is in order to deceive thereby, e.g. to give an animal bran-water which helps to distend its bulk and makes its hair stand erect so that it seems to be fat and healthy. It is also forbidden to paint over old utensils so that they appear to be new, and all such devices are prohibited.

5. Likewise it is forbidden to mix a little bad fruit with plenty of good fruit to sell the same as though they were good, or to mix inferior liquor with superior liquor, but if the taste of the former predominate, the mixing is permitted for the purchaser will notice this.

6. A shopkeeper is permitted to give parched grain and nuts to children in order to accustom them to buy of him. He may also sell cheaper than the market price for the same reason, and the other tradesmen cannot prevent this.

7. He who gives short measure or weight to his companion or even to an idolater transgresses a negative precept of the Divine Law.

8. It is necessary to measure and to weigh with a generous eye, this means that he should give more than the exact quantity demanded, as it is said : " A perfect and just measure shalt thou have " (Deut. xxv. 15).

9. It is necessary to measure according to the laws of the country and no deviation therefrom is permitted. Where it is the custom to give " heaped " measure, one must not give " level " (or exact) measure even with the consent of the purchaser who pays him less money. Where it is the custom to give " level " measure, one must not give " heaped " measure even if the seller consent, as the buyer would pay more money, for the Torah has laid down strict rules prohibiting incorrect measures lest a stumbling-block for others arise therefrom, for an onlooker may notice that the measure is in this wise and he will think that this is the rule of the city, and in like manner will he give measure to another person, who is also ignorant of the law of the place, and thereby he deceives him.

10. It is obligatory upon the communal leaders to appoint supervisors whose duty it is to inspect the shops and all found to have deficient measures or weights or irregular scales should be punished as seems proper in their judgment.

11.   It is forbidden to keep in one's house or shop short measures although he does not use the same, even to keep them is to transgress a negative precept.   It is forbidden to use such an article even as a necessary bed-room utensil, lest someone might use it in ignorance to measure therewith.   If, however, it be the rule of the place that only marked measures (which are well-known) are used, and if this one be not marked, then it may be kept.

12.   One who seeks to buy or rent certain property, be it a piece of ground or chattels of a heathen or of an Israelite, if the bargain were struck although the sale was not yet completed, and some one else forestalled him and bought or rented it, the latter is called a wicked person.   But if they had not yet agreed upon the price, for the seller asks so much and the buyer offers less, then some one else may buy it.   One is forbidden to "remove his neighbour's landmark," i.e. to encroach upon his rights in the matter of hiring houses and the like.

13.   If one give money to his neighbour to purchase for him ground or chattels and the latter purchased the desired object for himself with his own money he is an imposter, but if he made the purchase with his neighbour's money, even if he intended it for himself, it is his duty to give it to his neighbour.

14.   If one had made a deposit on a purchase or had marked the article for identification in the seller's presence, or if the seller said to him :—"Mark your purchase," even though he did not thereby acquire proprietary rights in that article, nevertheless, be he the buyer or seller, he does not act as becomes an Israelite, and he incurs Divine punishment, i.e., he is accursed of the Beth Din who say :—"He who dealt out retribution to the men of the generation of the flood, and to the men of the generation of the dispersion, and to the men of Sodom and Gomorrah, and to the Egyptians who sank in the sea, may He deal out retribution to the one who does not keep his word."

15.   It is proper to keep one's word even though he neither paid anything on account nor did he put a mark upon the article, nor was the purchase completed but they merely agreed upon a price, neither of them may retract his agreement, and he who retracts, be he the buyer or the seller, is considered to be one of "little faith" (i.e. unreliable) and the spirit of our Sages finds no pleasure in him.

16.   Likewise if one promised a small gift to his neighbour, who depended upon it, being sure that he would give it to him, if he retract his promise and fail to give it, he is of those who are of "little faith"; if, however, he promised a large gift (and retracted) he is not of those who are of "little faith," as his neighbour did not depend upon it; nevertheless at the time when he said he would give it to

him it should have been his genuine intention to do so, and it should not have been his wish to alter his intention, all this refers to a promise made to a rich man, but if he made the promise to a poor man, be the promise of a small gift or a large gift, he is not at liberty to retract his promise for it is as though he made a vow, thus even if he did not utter the promise but he only determined in his heart that he would give, he must fulfil his intention.

17. If one desire to sell some ground or a house and two men come to buy, each one saying, "I am willing to pay the price demanded," it devolves upon the seller to know the law of precedence, the following rules appertain thereto : If neither be the immediate neighbour (of the seller) and if the one be a fellow townsman and the other man come from another place, the fellow townsman has the preference. If they were both fellow townsmen, the one being his neighbour, then he has the preference. If the other person were his friend who visited him whereas the neighbour did not, then the friend has the preference. If one were a friend and the other a relative, then the friend has the preference, but this does not apply with reference to all other people except to a scholar who enjoys a preference, even with regard to one's neighbour or a friend who is on visiting terms. If one of the two in question happened to be the immediate neighbour (occupying the adjacent property), he takes precedence before all others and even after he had already sold it to another, the immediate neighbour can refund the money to the buyer and make him relinquish that property, even if this buyer were a learned man or a neighbour or a relation of the seller, whereas the immediate neighbour might be an illiterate person and not related to the seller, nevertheless he enjoys the preference and can make the purchaser relinquish the property.

LAWS PROHIBITING VERBAL OPPRESSION AND DECEPTION OF ONE'S FELLOW CREATURES.

1. Just as oppression is forbidden with reference to buying and selling, likewise is it forbidden with regard to words, as it is said : " Ye shall not wrong one another ; but thou shalt fear thy God " (Lev. xxv. 17) this refers to the " oppression through words." More serious is this than the sin of pecuniary imposition, for the latter can be settled by calculation, not so the former. Again the latter refers to one's money but the former to one's person and he who cries to God on account of oppression through words, is answered forthwith. One must be most careful not to wound his wife's feelings through words.

2. What is the meaning of " oppression through words " ? Thus a man should not say to his neighbour : " At what price will you sell this article ?" when he has no intention of buying it. If he sought to buy produce, one should not direct him to go to a certain person, when he knows he has not got it to sell him. If his neighbour were a penitent he should not say to him : " Remember thy former deeds !" If afflictions befell his neighbour, he should not speak to him like the

comforters of Job who said, "Is not thy fear (of God) thy confidence ?
. . . Remember, I pray thee, who ever perished, being innocent ?"
(Job iv. 6, 7). If they asked him regarding some learned discussion,
he should not say to one who is ignorant thereof : " What is your
opinion ? " Likewise in all such similar forms of speech, which might
hurt the person addressed.

3. If one have an opprobrious nickname, although he be accustomed thereto and is not put to shame thereby, if another person
intend to insult him thereby it is forbidden to call him by the nickname on account of " oppression through words."

4. It is forbidden to deceive[1] any human being, even an idolater,
therefore it is forbidden to sell meat of an animal which is not ritually
slaughtered as though it had been lawfully killed. If one sell an
article possessing some imperfection, although it be worth the purchase-
price, it is nevertheless obligatory upon him to notify the purchaser of
its imperfection. In the case of a gift no question of deception can
arise.

5. One should not ask his neighbour to dine with him knowing
that he will not do so, nor should he make a present knowing that he
will not accept it. And in all such similar cases where one says something with the tongue and means something else in the heart, e.g., if
one seem to be paying honour to his neighbour, which is far from his
real intention, this conduct is forbidden. One should always let the
mouth and heart correspond, cultivating truth, uprightness and purity
of the heart.

LAWS DEALING WITH THE PROHIBITION OF TRADING IN
FORBIDDEN THINGS.

1. Any article the eating whereof the *Torah* has forbidden while
one is permitted to enjoy its use, if it be an article used solely for food
it is forbidden to deal therein or to lend thereon or even to buy
thereof in order to feed heathen labourers therewith. If it be something not designed for food, such as horses and asses, it is permitted
to deal in the same. To deal in the fat (of the beast not ritually
slaughtered) is allowed, as it is said concerning the same : "it may be
used for any other service " (Lev. vii. 24).

2. If one happened to acquire a forbidden article (of food) e.g., if,
when fishing, he caught a ritually unclean fish in his net, or if he had
found in his house a beast that died of itself or which was torn of
beasts,[2] he is permitted to sell them, since it was not his intention to
have it thus, but he should sell them immediately, and he should not
wait till they become more valuable for selling, he may also sell them

[1] Lit. : " to steal the mind."   [2] Cf. Lev. vii. 24.

through an agent although the latter will profit thereby, but the agent may not buy them on his own behalf as this would be traffic for his own benefit.

3. It is also permitted to levy on unclean things for one's claim, but he should sell them at once and not wait to derive profit therefrom, he is, however, permitted to keep them sufficiently long in order to protect himself against loss on his capital.

4. It is permitted to traffic with an article (the consumption of) which is forbidden by the Oral Law only, e.g., the cheese of gentiles.

THE LAWS CONCERNING INTEREST.

1. He who lends on interest transgresses six negative precepts, as it is said : "He hath given forth upon usury, and hath taken interest : shall he then live ? he shall not live" (Ezek. xviii. 13).[1] The borrower transgresses three negative precepts; the scribe, the witnesses, and the broker who negotiated the loan, all these transgress one negative precept. He who has transgressed and has taken interest is bound to return it, even though at the time of lending the money he did not fix the rate of interest, (as) he lent the money free of charge until a fixed point of time. Likewise if he sold to another person certain wares on credit for a certain time, or if he, in some other way, make another person responsible for the payment of the debt, be it what it may, and when the fixed period for payment arrives the debtor stipulates to give to the borrower something for forbearance, this is also interest.

2. Even if the borrower, of his own free will, give to the lender extra payment when the loan becomes due, which had not been arranged and without saying that he gives it as interest, this is also forbidden.

3. Even if the borrower, when paying the interest, declare it to be a gift, it is still forbidden to accept the same. But if he had accepted from him the interest and if the lender repented and wished to make restitution but the borrower refused it, the former is permitted to retain it.

4. It is forbidden to give interest either in advance or at the expiration of the loan, as for instance, if Reuben desire to borrow money from Simeon. Previous to negotiating the loan he sent to Simeon a present with the explanation that he does this in order that he should make him a loan, or if he made him a handsome present without explanation, it is quite evident that he did so in order that he should make him a loan, this is "interest in advance," (or) if he borrowed from him and repaid the loan and made him a present, as compensation for the time during which the money was in his possession, and therefore useless (to the lender), this is "postponed interest."

[1] See T. B. Baba Mezi'a 61b.

5. If one lend his neighbour a certain amount for a certain time, in order that the latter should afterwards reciprocate by lending him for the same period a larger amount or the same amount for a longer time, this is unqualified interest. If one lend his neighbour a certain amount for a time to cause him to reciprocate that favour, this is to be avoided. But if no agreement had been made to that effect and the former borrower of his own free-will lends the former lender, which is, however, on account of the previous loan, this may be permitted.

6. The lender should be careful not to derive any benefit through the borrower without his knowledge during the entire time of the loan, even if it be something that the borrower would have him enjoy even though no loan had been made. If he derived some benefit without the sanction of the borrower, it appears as though he relies on the fact that the borrower has his money and therefore he will not mind. However, with the borrower's knowledge, the lender may enjoy that which the borrower would have him enjoy had the loan not been made, provided it be not of a public nature.

7. If the borrower had not been accustomed to greet the lender in the past, he must not do so now. He must not show him any special honour in the synagogue or elsewhere if he had not been accustomed to do so, likewise all kinds of attention, even by word of mouth on account of a loan, are forbidden. Likewise the lender must avoid gaining any benefit even through mere words, e.g., if he say to the borrower : "Let me know if so and so should come from such and such a place." Even though he does not trouble him more than to speak a few words, if he had not been accustomed to request such a favour previously and now he bids him do this or do that on account of the loan and the obligation he is under, such conduct is in the nature of interest and is forbidden.

8. The lender is forbidden to derive any advantage, even though it be not of a pecuniary nature, from the borrower, e.g., if the lender be a workman and the borrower is not accustomed to give him work, only now because of the loan he desires to do so, this is forbidden.

9. It is forbidden to lend another a measure of grain on the condition of having the loan repaid thereafter with a measure of grain, even if both be of the same kind, for perchance, in the meantime, the price may have advanced and he consequently gives him more than he borrowed. A money valuation should therefore be placed upon it, so that even if there be an advance in the price of the grain, he must repay him only that amount of money at which it was originally valued.

If the borrower possess only a small amount of a particular kind he is permitted to borrow many bushels of the same kind, also if a certain kind have a fixed market-price one is permitted to borrow even if he have none of it ; all this relates to a thing of the same kind, but it is forbidden under any circumstance to lend a measure of wheat and to receive in return a measure of millet, although they both cost the same price and the lender has some millet. It is, however, under all circumstances permissible to lend a small article, the price of which, whether advancing or decreasing, people do not usually consider ; a woman is therefore allowed to lend a loaf of bread to her neighbour.

10.   If one lend money on the mortgage of a house or a field or a seat in a Synagogue, and if the lender have also the usufruct of that mortgage, this income should effect the liquidation of that debt, that means a fixed amount should be deducted yearly from his debt which should count as the rent paid by the lender, and they are permitted to stipulate the payment of a smaller amount than the actual rental value. The lender, however, should not reverse the arrangement and rent it to the borrower.

11.   One must not sell an article which has a fixed price above its value because it is sold on credit ; but if it have no standard price, although if bought for cash he would sell it cheaper, or if he sold it on credit it would cost a little more, this is allowed provided he does not advance the price to such an extent that it is evident to everybody that this increase is on account of being sold on credit. Nevertheless, if he should not advance the price very much, but he distinctly says, "If you pay me ready cash it costs ten coins, but if on credit it costs eleven," this is forbidden. Likewise it is forbidden for the purchaser to buy the merchandise above the market price in order to sell it immediately at a loss so as to have ready cash for some time (at his disposal).

12.   One is permitted to sell to another person a note which he holds against his neighbour at less than its value even before the date of payment, and the seller should write to the buyer : " I hereby sell and transfer to you this note and all that it implies," the note is accepted at the risk of the buyer, with the exception of such risk for which the seller is responsible, e.g., if the note were cancelled or the like, whereupon the seller is responsible. Just as one can sell such a note at less than its value to another, likewise can he sell it to the actual borrower.

13.   In this way one can avoid the peril of taking interest, e.g., Reuben, who requires a loan in Nisan, goes to Simeon who gives him a bond whereby (Simeon) undertakes to pay Reuben 100 gold coins in the month of Tishri, (and in consideration thereof Reuben gave Simon a note to the effect that he holds himself bound to repay 100

gold coins in Tishri so as to cover Simeon against loss). Reuben may now sell to Levi the note given by Simeon for 90 gold coins. Much more so may this course be pursued if Simeon have a bond, whereby Judah is responsible to repay him at a fixed period at some future date, which he can sell to Reuben on credit till that period and Reuben can give a bill to this effect. Then Reuben can sell the afore-mentioned bond for as much as he can get. Reuben is not allowed to write a deed, whereby he becomes responsible, in order to sell it to Simeon even through an agent.

14. It is forbidden to buy produce or any other object by paying the money in advance and agreeing for the produce to be delivered at some date thereafter, as we are afraid that in the meanwhile the price of the produce may advance and when later he has to deliver the pro-duce the purchaser will receive more than the value of his money owing to his having paid in advance. If, however, the seller should have all the produce which he is selling (at the time of the sale) although he will not deliver same to the buyer until some time has elapsed, this is permitted ; for what a man has in his possession he can sell, even at a very cheap price as it pleases him, and even if the produce were not quite in perfect condition as it ought to be, but it still requires one or two processes of labour, nevertheless it is held to be in perfect condition and this sale is permitted, but if it still require three processes of labour it is forbidden (to sell it in that condition).

15. If the market-price of produce were fixed, one may buy according to this rate by paying in advance, although the seller has none in stock, for even if the produce became dearer thereafter the buyer does not derive any profit by having paid in advance, since he could buy the produce then with his money at this price. And since he had fixed the bargain under conditions fixed by the law, although thereafter the produce became dearer when it had to be delivered and the seller does not wish to give it to him at the fixed price, he can take instead some other merchandise which the seller may offer him or the seller can give him the money value at the present price of the produce.

16. If one have merchandise which can be sold at a cheap price at one place and at a dearer price at another place, and his companion says to him : "Give it to me and I will take it to that place (to obtain the better price) and I will sell it there and I will use the money for my own purpose until such a date when I will refund the same to thee according to its (former) value after we have allowed for the expenses incurred in connection with the goods," and if the risk in transit were undertaken by the companion, the transaction is prohibited,

but it is permitted if the (owner and) seller take this risk and he can then give the companion some reward for his trouble.

17. One is permitted to lend his fellow 100 Dinars (or coins) to buy goods therewith in the market, and after they have been taken home the lender may give him 120 Dinars for the same, provided the lender received the goods and took them to his home and the risk in transit be undertaken by the lender; for it is as though he had a share in the profit of the transaction and consequently he takes the risk.

18. Simeon can say to Reuben who is going to a place where they sell goods cheaply, "Bring me goods from that place and I will give thee so much profit"; this is permitted provided the risk in connection with the goods be undertaken by Reuben until he has delivered the same to Simeon.

19. It is permitted to increase the rent of ground. How? If one let a court on hire to another saying to him before he took possession: "If thou wilt pay me the rent immediately it will be ten gold coins per annum and if monthly thou wilt pay me one gold coin," this is allowed. The reason is as follows: Because according to strict law rent is only due at the conclusion of the period of tenancy and since he is receiving a gold coin every month, he will receive 12 coins, this is not an extra consideration on account of waiting for the money for the tenant is not obliged to pay in advance, and as regards the proposal: "If thou wilt pay me the rent immediately it will be ten gold coins," he gives him the benefit of two gold coins because he pays in advance before payment falls due, this is allowed.

20. Only in hiring ground is it permitted to increase (and vary) the rent in this manner, because the ground is transferred to the buyer forthwith, but to increase the wages of a workman in this manner is forbidden, i.e., if one engage a workman to do some work for him after a certain time and if he gave him his wages in advance the day before he begins his work, and on this account he is willing to do the work at a cheaper rate than is right and proper, this is forbidden since the workman is not employed then and it is as though his labour then is in the nature of a loan, nevertheless if the workman had to begin his work immediately there and then, although he will not complete the work until many days have elapsed, it is permitted to pay his wages in advance in order that he may work at a cheaper rate, as it is wages proper since he has commenced his work immediately and it is not in the nature of a loan.

21. It is permitted to increase the dowry of the bridegroom, thus if one fixed a certain sum for his daughter's dowry and made an arrangement with his son-in-law that he would give him so much income yearly as long as he had possession of the dowry, this is permitted, for this is merely like an addition to the dowry, and if he say to him: "I will give thee a present of so and so much at such and such a time, and if I fail to do so I will add to the dowry so and so much," this is permitted. All this is valid provided they agreed thereto at the time of writing the marriage settlement, for until that time there was no obligation to pay anything and therefore it is all accounted as one liability. But if at the time of writing the marriage setlement he became liable for a certain sum as dowry and later at the wedding ceremony they agree to come to a different settlement, namely, to give the son-in-law something in consideration of forbearance (in paying the dowry), this is prohibited.

22. If an Israelite borrow from a heathen on interest and another Israelite became surety, if it be of such a nature and circumstance that the heathen can only claim the debt in the first instance from the borrower and if it be impossible to obtain the money from him, then he will be able to claim it from the surety, this case is permitted. But if the circumstances be such that the heathen could claim it in the first instance from the surety so that it would appear as though the surety had been the borrower and then he had lent it to the other Israelite, this case is forbidden. Likewise if a heathen borrow from one Israelite on interest and another Israelite is surety, if the circumstances be such that the lender can only claim the debt in the first instance from the heathen who is the borrower and then if the money cannot be obtained from him it can be taken from the surety, such a case is permitted. But if the circumstances be such that the lender could also in the first instance claim the debt from the surety so that the latter is as though he had been the borrower, this case is forbidden. If the Israelite be surety only as regards the capital and not for the interest, in this case it is permitted.

23. If a heathen say to an Israelite: "Borrow money on my behalf on interest from an Israelite on this security," or even if he should not give him any security except a bond (acknowledging the debt) and the lender is satisfied with the security or the bond of the heathen and no risk is attached to the intermediary, such a transaction is allowed. Even if the Israelite who was the intermediary should transmit the interest to the lender, the latter is permitted to accept it; provided the lender had definitely understood that all the risk connected with the security and the money, whether in transmission to the borrower or vice-versa, is his own, and the intermediary incurs no risks of any kind in the transaction.

24. Likewise an Israelite who has given security or a bond to his companion, who is an Israelite, that he should borrow on this for his

use money on interest from a heathen, and if the latter should
rely only on the security or bond without making the intermediary in
any way responsible, it is permitted. Likewise if the Israelite, who
in the first instance lends to another Israelite, his friend, upon the
security of a pledge should say to the lender, "Borrow money
from a heathen on interest on this pledge and I will be responsible for
the payment of the capital and interest," if the heathen be satisfied
with the pledge alone as security, this is permitted.

25. An Israelite who lent money on interest to a heathen on a
pledge at so and so much a month, and thereafter the Israelite came to
his friend so that he might lend him money on this pledge and thereby
receive the interest which will accrue from that day until repayment,
this is permitted. But if the first (mentioned) Israelite had already
converted the capital with the interest for the whole period of the loan,
then the entire sum forms part of the capital of the Israelite and it is
forbidden to borrow on this pledge from a fellow Israelite on interest,
for it is as though he gave the interest from his own pocket.

26. If the money of an Israelite were on deposit with a heathen
and the latter lends the same to an Israelite on interest, if the heathen
were responsible so that if the debt became a loss he would be
bound to pay with his own money, this transaction is then permitted, but if he accept no responsibility it is not permitted.

27. Partners who require to borrow money on interest from a
heathen should consult the Ecclesiastical Authorities how to act.

28. It is prohibited to borrow on interest from an apostate, and
to lend him money on interest should also be avoided.

Rules Concerning Business Partnership.

1. If one advance money to his neighbour to do business there
with, provided the profits be shared and also the loss be shared equally,
this is termed עסקא and is forbidden; because half the money is like
a loan in the hand of the receiver for it is entrusted to him on his own
responsibility and he also receives any profit, likewise he is (partly)
responsible for any loss, and half (thereof) is (in the nature of) a deposit
in his hands for the risk attached thereto is undertaken by the lender,
who has the profit arising from this half as well as the loss therefrom,
and the receiver who does the business with this half (i.e. the deposit)

145

which belongs to the lender for this (deposit) is lent on account of the fact that he has lent him the one half as a loan, this transaction is considered to be of the nature of interest and is forbidden. There is a method of legalizing the transaction as follows : if the lender give the receiver some remuneration on account of his work and trouble in connection with his (the lender's) half and this remuneration is stipulated or it is paid at the time when he gives him the money (or loan), then even a small remuneration suffices.

2. They can agree that the receiver should not be entitled to be believed should he say that he has lost part of the capital unless there be trustworthy witnesses, nor is he to be trusted as regards the profit except he take an oath.

3. They can agree that it is optional for the receiver, should he desire it, to receive so and so much in lieu of the profit due to him and that any surplus should also be his (the receiver's). This method is proper. Indeed it is to be assumed that the receiver does not wish to take an oath and to give to the lender according to the amount stipulated by them, this is the (so-called) "permit to do business" (היתר עיסקא) in vogue among us. Even if there be a loss, he can still give the lender his capital together with the profit agreed upon by them and no prohibition arises here, as owing to the fact that he is liable to take an oath, he can release himself therefrom by paying the money.

4. The receiver is forbidden to purchase the share of the lender's profit at so and so much, so that he would be obliged to give that amount in due course, under all circumstances the borrower must have the option (referred to in the previous section).

5. If one give money to another for business for a certain time and the money was returned after the time limit, then the receiver must give the lender a profit for the extra period. It is assumed that the money remained in his possession on the terms originally arranged. The best plan is to immediately write in the " business permit" that if the money remain in the hands of the receiver after the time limit, the condition set forth should continue to hold good thereafter.

6. The text of the business permit is as follows: " I, the undersigned, admit that I have received from N.N. the amount of 100 gold coins to do business therewith for half a year from the date mentioned below and I hold myself liable to purchase for so and so much mentioned above all such genuine merchandise as should seem to me to be especially suitable for the purpose of profit. This money takes precedence before my own money as regards all the profit which Providence may give to me in connection with that merchandise, half thereof shall be mine and half shall belong to N.N. and so with the loss in equal shares. As soon as the half year, from the date below, expires I am bound to return to N.N. aforementioned the capital and half the profit. I shall not be entitled to be believed if I

say I have had a loss unless it be corroborated by two trustworthy witnesses and as regards the profit I am only entitled to credence on oath. It is moreover on condition that if I desire to give N.N. ten gold coins for his share of the profit, then he can have no further claim against me and the balance of the profits shall belong to me only, even if it be evident that there is considerable profit. All the terms of the agreement in favour of the one on whose behalf it is drawn apply also after the term of the expiry mentioned therein and as long as I have not returned the aforementioned coins they remain in my hand for the purpose of the business in the manner aforementioned. I have received the remuneration for my trouble.

.................(Signature)

Place and date.   Signed in our presence.

.... (Signatures of witnesses)

7.   If there be not time to write the "business permit" it is permitted to agree orally to all the aformentioned conditions.

8.   If one pay in advance for merchandise, the business permit is to be written in the following manner : " I, the undersigned, acknowledge that I have received from N.N. of.........the sum of 100 gold coins to trade therewith with reference to the goods which I hold in ....until the 1st of Nisan next and the profit accruing to the account of the money after deducting all expenses shall be divided, half thereof for me and the other half for N.N., likewise if there be a loss, the same shall be shared. On the 1st of Nisan next I shall be bound to promptly restore to N.N. aforementioned the capital and interest belonging to him. I shall not be entitled to credence if I say I have suffered a loss until it be clearly corroborated by two trustworthy witnesses and with reference to the profit I shall not be entitled to be believed except on oath. Further this is also herewith agreed between us that if I desire on the 1st of Nisan next to give to N.N. aforementioned in consideration of his capital and his share of interest five measures of spirit, then he shall have no further claim against me. All the terms of the agreement in favour of the one on whose behalf it is drawn apply also after the term of expiry mentioned thererein and I acknowledge having received the remuneration for my labour.

... .(Signature)

Place and date.   Signed in our presence.

.... (Signatures of witnesses)

147

9. If the lender desire that the borrower should give him a deed of his indebtedness, simple and binding, according to the law of the land in order that if the receiver declined to pay when the term expires or if he should die, it would be easy for him to secure repayment of his money (by being recorded) in the municipal offices, but they agree orally that this money is subject to the " business permit;" even if the deed refer to the capital only, since the lender can collect all the money by means of the deed of indebtedness which he holds, even if there be a clear loss, such a transaction is forbidden. Even if the receiver be trustworthy to the lender, being a respectable person, nevertheless this is of no avail. Further, if the receiver give the lender also a " business permit " wherein it is written that the afore-mentioned bill of indebtedness is subject to the " business permit," this likewise is of no avail, for one can be afraid lest the lender or his heirs should thereafter conceal or annul the " business permit " and collect the money by means of the bill of indebtedness. The only permissible course of action is to triplicate the " business permit " and to deposit a copy with a third party (or trustee) or for the lender to sign this permit and for the borrower to keep the same, and for both of them to write upon the bill of indebtedness that it is subject to the conditions set forth in the " business permit," or at least they should have witnesses to the effect that the bill of indebtedness is subject to the " business permit." In all these cases it is immaterial if the capital with the interest be included in the deed of indebtedness.

10. A " business permit " is useless as a means of enabling a transaction to take place unless it is a fact that the borrower receives the money to do business therewith, but if he take the money merely to pay off a debt or the like than the " business permit " is useless since it is not genuine. The transaction can be carried through in this manner: thus A, who needs the money, has certain goods in another locality, he can sell the same to B at a very cheap price on the condition that the option lies with A that if he had not delivered the goods to B by such and such a date, he can pay him so much instead thereof (so that B will have the usual profit), then B can give the money required to A and they should make a symbolical agreement so as to make the transaction binding, that is to say, B the buyer should offer a portion of his garment to A to take hold of the same and by this symbolical act he purchases the goods of A, even though no witnesses be present and the goods are at the risk of B the buyer.

11. Likewise A who owes money to B and when the time of re-payment arrives A has no money and he assumes that B will wait a little longer, in this case a " business permit " is of no use, but A should sell to B some goods which he has in the aforementioned circum-stances, and B should restore to him the bill of indebtedness which

he formerly held, and A should give him a deed with reference to the goods which B has bought of him in the manner aforementioned.

12. If an Israelite give to his companion a beast to rear on the condition of their subsequently sharing the profit, the rule applies as in the case of lending money by a "business permit."

Laws Concerning Loans.

1. It is an affirmative precept to lend to a poor Israelite, as it is said: "If thou lend money to any of my people with thee that is poor, thou shalt not be to him as a creditor; neither shall ye lay upon him usury" (Ex. xxii. 25). Although the word "if" is written in the text, our sages, of blessed memory, have the tradition that this "if" is not to be interpreted as giving one the option to obey or disobey the precept but as being obligatory. Thus they say in the Mekhilta: "'If thou lend money to any of my people' this is a duty (to be observed). Dost thou say it is a duty, perhaps it is optional, therefore the verse teaches thee: 'Thou shalt surely lend him' (Deut. xv. 8). It is obligatory and not optional." A poor man who is a relative takes precedence before other poor people and the poor in one's city take precedence before the poor of another city. The religious act of lending to the poor is greater than the act of giving charity to the poor. The Torah stigmatizes one who refuses to lend to the poor, as it is said: "And thine eye be evil against thy poor brother" (ibid. 9). Concerning the one who lends to the poor in the time of his distress the text says: "Then shalt thou call, and the Lord shall answer" (Is. lviii. 9.) Even if a rich man be in need of a loan, it is a religious duty to lend to him and also to give him pleasure by means of kind speech and to advise him with advantage to his position.

2. It is forbidden to lend money even to a scholar without having witnesses, unless a pledge be forthcoming. The best course is to have a deed drawn up referring to the loan.

3. It is forbidden to exact payment from the borrower when it is known that he is unable to pay, even to confront him is prohibited lest he be put to shame since he cannot repay, and with reference to this it is said: "Thou shalt not be to him as a creditor" (Ex. xxii. 25). Just as the lender is forbidden to oppress the borrower, so is the latter forbidden to withhold his neighbour's money which he has in hand by telling him to come again when he has it, as it is said: "Say not to thy neighbour, Go, and come again"[1] (Prov. iii. 28).

4. A borrower is forbidden to take the loan and to lay it out unnecessarily so that it might be lost whereby the lender may not have anything from which he can exact repayment, even if the lender be very wealthy. He who acts in this manner is called an evil-doer, as

[1] The verse continues: "And to-morrow I will give: when thou hast it by thee.'

149

it is said : "The wicked borroweth, and payeth not again " (Ps. xxxvii. 21). The sages have commanded (us): "Let the money of thy fellow be as precious to thee as thine own" (Aboth ii. 17). And if the lender know that the borrower is a man of this type having no consideration for the money of others, it is better not to lend him money rather than to do so and to be compelled thereafter to exact repayment, and consequently he will transgress on each such occasion the precept : "Thou shalt not be to him as a creditor" (Ex. xxii. 25).

5. He who lends on a pledge must avoid using the same, as it might be considered to be interest, but if he lend to a poor man on the security of a ploughshare or an axe or the like which can be hired out at a good price and will only be slightly worn by use, he may let it out on hire without asking the owner's permission and he can deduct from the debt the proceeds, as it can be assumed that the borrower would agree to this. Some authorities hold that this applies only with reference to other people hiring the article, but not to the lender of the money lest he be suspected of using the article free of charge merely because of the loan.

6. If the lender wish to take a pledge from the borrower, not at the time of lending but thereafter, he must not do so except with the consent of the Jewish Court of Law (בית דין).

9. One should always avoid as much as possible becoming a surety or receiving trusts. If one have a note of indebtedness against his neighbour, which was becoming worn away and the script thereof was likely to be erased, he should go to the Jewish Court of Law to have it certified. One must not keep a cancelled note in one's house, as it is said: "And let not unrighteousness dwell in thy tents" (Job xi. 14).

8. Just as it is necessary to be careful in looking after a deposit so also must one be very particular in taking charge of a pledge, since he (the lender) becomes like a paid trustee with reference to the pledge. Just as the one entrusted therewith is not permitted to hand over the deposit to another person to take charge of same, so the lender is permitted neither to deposit the pledge with another nor to pawn it without the consent of the owner.

9. He who lends his neighbour on a pledge with the condition that if he should not repay the loan at a certain time, he shall forfeit the pledge, then the lender must take care to tell the borrower when the loan is made : "If you do not redeem the pledge by such and such a time, I am entitled thereto from the present time."

10. If one be aware of his indebtedness to his neighbour, but the latter says to him : "I am convinced that you do not owe me anything" he is exempt thereby from repayment, for the lender forgoes his claim

LAWS AND CUSTOMS OF ISRAEL

11. When a borrower repays the lender through a messenger, the latter acquires full title to the money on behalf of the lender immediately it is handed to him, and should the borrower regret having paid and desire again to borrow the money from the messenger (stipulating) to repay him after a while, he is forbidden to do this transaction as it is borrowing without the owner's knowledge and the messenger is also forbidden to return the money to the borrower.

LAWS OF RELEASE.

1. The majority of the authorities on Jewish Law agree that the cancellation of cash debts obtains in these days also, even outside Palestine, but the general rule has been to ignore this law and the great teachers in Israel have protested against this, but a few of them have endeavoured to find an excuse for the non-observance of the Law, based on the interpretation of a few authorities who are not stringent in this matter. If, however, anyone should wish to be particular in observing the precepts he is indeed obliged to follow the teaching of the majority of the authorities. In a particular instance one can evade the difficulty by means of the Prosbul[1] document and thereby he will escape a monetary loss. The Shemitah (7th) year was in 5635 (1875-6) and again in 5671 (1911-2).

2. The seventh year causes every lender to release his debtor, it makes no difference whether the loan were arranged orally or by deed or on mortgage. If one gave to his neighbour money by means of a "business permit" according to which half the money is considered to be a loan and the other half a deposit, the former half which is a loan is released (by the 7th year) and the other half which is a deposit is not released.

3. If one lend to his neighbour on a pledge, the loan is not released (by the 7th year) and if he lent on the security of a land mortgage, a diversity of opinion as to the law obtains in this case.

4. A surety who had paid to the lender but before the borrower had paid the surety the year of release had intervened, then the debt is cancelled.

5. One who has to take an oath concerning the money he owes his neighbour, if he were to admit his liability the year of release would cancel the debt, then it cancels also the oath.

6. One who owes money to his neighbour and denies his liability and they come to law and he is adjudged guilty; the judges write their judgment and hand it to the lender, then the year of release does not cancel this debt.

[1] See Jewish Encyclopedia, x. 219f.

7. If one lend money to his neighbour and make an agreement with him saying, "The year of release must not release my loan," even so the loan is released, but if he agreed with him that he would not release him with regard to this debt, even if it happened to be the year of release, it does not cause the debtor to be released. Likewise if he wrote in a deed the term "deposit," the year of release does not cancel the transaction.

8. If one lend money to his neighbour for a period of years and if the time of repayment occur after the year of release the debt is not cancelled thereby, because the lender was unable to claim the same earlier.

9. One who delivers his deeds to the Court of Law saying to the judges : "Collect my debt," the same are not cancelled by the year of release.

10. One who sells to his neighbour on credit, is considered as though he had lent him money and the debt is cancelled by the year of release, but the shopkeeper who sells to other people on credit and it is not his custom to claim payment until a certain amount has accumulated, the same is not cancelled; but if he had calculated the interest and entered this with the amounts due as a sum total, that is to say, he reckons all these items together and enters the sum total in his ledger, then he is like a lender and the debt is cancelled by the year of release.

11. The wages of a hired man are not cancelled, but if the same with interest had been entered as a sum total the year of release cancels same.

12. Whatever is derived from a heathen is treated as though it were identified with the heathen, therefore if one should purchase from a heathen a note of indebtedness due by an Israelite, the year of release does not cancel the note because the heathen can collect the debt of his note under all circumstances. Likewise if one went surety to a heathen on behalf of an Israelite and the latter failed to pay his debt, so that it becomes necessary for the other Israelite, who was surety, to pay the heathen from whom he takes the note referring to the borrower, then the same is not cancelled by the year of release. If there were no deed, but he sues his neighbour and says that the latter is obliged to pay the heathen on his behalf, then this neighbour need not pay.

13. The year of release cancels money debts only at its close, therefore the one who lends his neighbour in the year of release, may collect the debt during the whole of the year, but at sunset on the eve of the (following) New Year the debt is cancelled.

14. A borrower who comes to pay a debt to the lender after a year of release has elapsed (since it was borrowed) and the lender says to him : "I cancel the debt and you are already released as far as I am concerned." If the borrower say to him, "Nevertheless, I wish you to accept the money from me" the lender may do so, but the borrower must not say to him : "I pay you this money on account of

my debt" but he should say: "The money is mine and I give you the same as a gift." The lender may even make an effort to persuade the borrower to say that he is giving the money as a gift, and if this can not be done he must not accept the same.

15. The document called Prosbul relieves one from granting a release (in the seventh year). A Prosbul is obtained as follows, a man goes to three men, learned in the *Torah*, who form themselves into a Jewish Court of Law. He says to them: "Ye are judges, I deliver over to you all claims that I have against so and so, so that I can collect them when I so desire," they then write for him a Prosbul as follows : "In a session of three judges (where) we were together, so and so the lender came and said in our presence, I hand over, etc." The three of them sign at the foot of the document in the capacity of judges or as witnesses. They can do this also at the close of the year, that is to say on the day before the (ensuing) New Year before sunset. Some authorities say that it is not even necessary to write the Prosbul, but it suffices by reason of what he has stated in their presence. If there be no Jewish Court ot Law in his town he can say "I hand over my deeds to a Beth Din which is in such and such a place."

16. The Prosbul is of no avail unless the borrower has a piece of ground, be it ever so small it will suffice, even if he have only a flower pot which is perforated and even if the borrower have nothing at all except some one to be surety for him or someone who is indebted to him (the borrower), this is also sufficient, but if these latter persons have nothing and the lender have a piece of ground, be it ever so little, he can transfer it to the borrower even through a third party and even in his absence and this is sufficient to make the Prosbul valid.

LAW CONCERNING A CLAIMANT AND RESPONDENT ALSO REGARDING TESTIMONY.

1. When something has occurred between two persons to oppose one against the other, they should agree peacefully to compromise, each making the other some allowance in order to avoid as much as possible the humiliation of a legal process, but if it be impossible for them to agree to compromise, and they are forced to go to law, they should have recourse to a Jewish tribunal (Beth Din). In case of *force majeure* or if the respondent be hard and unyielding, the claimant should first summon him to appear before a Jewish tribunal and on his refusal to comply with the summons, the claimant should obtain the consent of the Beth Bin and protect himself by a civil process in a public Court of Law.

2. One who is sued for money, which he has in his possession, is forbidden to seek underhand means to escape from the demands of the claimant, thus forcing the latter to agree to a compromise whereby a part of the claim will be remitted. If he transgressed the commandment and did this, he has not fulfilled his obligation before heaven, until he gives the claimant what is due to him.

3. It is forbidden for one of the litigants to present his case before the judge in the absence of his fellow-litigant, for that reason he should not precede his fellow-litigant in appearing before the judge, in order that he should not be suspected of hastening to present his case in the absence of his opponent.

4. Just as the judge who takes a bribe, even to acquit the innocent, transgresses a negative precept, likewise he who gives the bribe transgresses also a negative precept, for "thou shalt not put a stumbling-block before the blind" (Lev. xix. 14).

5. One is also forbidden (under any circumstance) to put in a false plea even though he knows that although he is innocent, yet if he plead truthfully, judgment will be given against him, despite that, he must not plead falsely. Thus it is stated in the Talmud: "Our Rabbis have taught us: Whence do we know that he who is entitled to demand one Maneh[1] from his neighbour, should not say I will claim two so that if he admit owing the one Maneh he will be obliged to take an oath (with regard to the matter in dispute) and I will compel him to take the oath with regard to some other matter?—therefore the verse says: "Keep thee far from a false matter" (Ex. xxiii. 7). Whence do we know that he who is entitled to demand one Maneh from his neighbour and he demands two, then the borrower should not say, I will deny the entire transaction in the Court of Law, but outside the same I will admit to him (that I owe him one Maneh) so as to avoid the necessity of taking an oath and thereby he will be unable to make me swear with reference to some other matter?—therefore the verse says: "Keep thee far from a false matter" (ibid.) Whence do we know that if three people be entitled to demand one Maneh from one person, that one of them must not be prosecutor and the other two as witnesses in order to obtain the Maneh and divide among themselves?—therefore the verse says: 'Keep thee far from a false matter'" (ibid.) (T.B. Shebu'oth 31a.)

6. Occasionally the litigants choose men to arbitrate between them jointly with the Beth Din (Court of Law) or apart from the Beth Din; this is a proper course to pursue, for each one advocates the merits of the one who had selected him and the compromise will be properly effected, provided the arbitration be conducted in a just manner, but, heaven forbid that the compromise should be effected in a perverse way? For just as they are warned not to wrest a judgment so are they warned not to wrest a compromise.

7. When the men of a town appoint a Beth Din for themselves, they must know whether each one (composing the tribunal) possesses

[1] One hundred common Shekels.

the following seven qualifications :—wisdom in the Torah, humility, reverence, the hate of money even of their own, the love of truth, their fellow-creature's love towards them, the possession of a good reputation because of their conduct. Whosoever appoints a judge unfit for his position transgresses a negative precept, as it is said : " Ye shall not respect persons in judgment " (Deut. i. 17), meaning " Ye shall not favour anyone " by saying " so and so is so wealthy, he is my relative, I will cause him to sit on the bench." It is forbidden to stand up in the presence of any judge who is appointed by means of silver and gold and it is likewise prohibited to show him any mark of respect and with reference to such a person the Rabbis apply the text: " Ye shall not make with me judges of silver nor judges of gold " (Ex. xx. 23).

8. In towns where there are no wise men fit to be judges, they appoint the best and wisest of the townsmen in the opinion of the latter and they shall act as judges (although they are not properly qualified to act as judges) in order that the people should not appear before the tribunals of the heathens. As soon as the townsmen have accepted them (as judges) they cannot be removed from office and all their deeds should be done for the glory of heaven.

9. One who can testify on behalf of his neighbour, if it be proper to testify on his behalf and his neighbour would derive some benefit from his testimony, if the latter summon him to testify on his behalf at the Beth Din he is obliged to testify for him, whether there be another witness besides or whether he be alone, and if he suppress his testimony he is guilty according to the Divine laws. One is forbidden to testify concerning a matter unknown to him, although a reliable person should say to him that he would not lie by testifying in this manner, and even if the litigant said unto him, " Come and stand near the one witness whom I have and do not testify, only (do this in order) that my opponent (lit. debtor) shall be frightened, thereby imagining that I have two witnesses and he will admit his obligation to me " ; he must not hearken unto him, as it is said :—" Keep thee far from a false matter " (ibid. xxiii. 7).

10. A witness cannot testify alone, except when a money transaction is involved, when his single testimony is available in a matter requiring the administration of an oath. He can also testify regarding a forbidden matter with the object of preventing the violation of that prohibition, if it were not already violated, but if his neighbour had already violated the prohibition, one witness should not testify, for his single evidence is not believed and it is only as though he spread an evil report concerning his neighbour.

11. The testimony of one who is rewarded to testify is null and void, this, however, relates only to one who had already witnessed the facts in evidence, upon whom it, therefore, devolves to testify gratuitously. One is, however, permitted to take a compensation which should be no more than proportionate to the trouble involved in going

LAWS AND CUSTOMS OF ISRAEL

to witness a transaction regarding which he will subsequently be required to testify. Also if it be a trouble for him to go before the Beth Din he can take a proper compensation for the trouble he has, but no more. Any witness who derives any benefit or who has any interest, no matter how remotely, in the affair of his testimony is unfit to testify.

12. One should be most careful not to take an oath, even a true one, under any circumstance. If one's neighbour be obliged to testify on oath on his behalf, but he knows that he will swear falsely, he should come to terms in the best way possible, so as not to let him swear falsely, as it is said : "The oath of the Lord shall be between them *both*" (*ibid.* xxii. 11), and we infer from the text that the oath applies to both of them.

13. An Israelite who knows evidence concerning a heathen who has a law suit with another Israelite before the heathen tribunal, if the former by his evidence will cause his fellow Israelite to become liable more than would be the case according to strict Jewish law, then he may not testify, but if this result will not ensue he may give evidence. If the heathen had agreed originally with the Israelite that the latter should testify on his behalf, and if he should not do so the name of God would be desecrated (by the Israelite breaking faith) in failing to testify, under any circumstance he must give his evidence.

14. A person can testify as long as he remembers the facts and need have no fear that because it happened long ago his recollection thereof will not be clear, even if he cannot recollect his evidence unless he refers to the record (which they will hand him) and which he wrote in his own book to remind himself concerning the affair (which he might forget and which he would only recall by reference to the record). Likewise if he recall (the facts) by being reminded thereof through another person he can testify, even if the person be the second witness ; but if the litigant remind him and he can recollect the facts he must not give evidence. The litigant can lay the facts before another person who in turn can remind the other party (who had forgotten the facts) for this would be a case of being reminded by another person (and the evidence is allowed to be given).

15. A witness who is related to one of the litigants or to one of the judges, or if the witnesses be related to one another even though the relationship be on the wife's side, they are on certain occasions unfit to testify, and even if they be related only to the surety and not to the borrower, they are also unfit to bear witness on behalf of the borrower. The fact that the Torah has decreed that the testimony of relations shall not be valid, is not because of the love they bear to each other, for whether they testify to the innocence or the guilt of their relative, they are still unfit, it is simply a decree of the Torah, so that it were not proper even for Moses and Aaron to testify one for the other, therefore any witness who is related to any of the other parties or witnesses, or even if the relationship were dissolved, the judges not being aware of that fact, he must inform them thereof, and they will

tell him according to the Torah, whether it be right for him to testify or not.

16. If there be two witnesses, one of whom knows that the other is wicked and unfit to give evidence according to the Laws of the Torah and the Judges are not aware of his wickedness, he is forbidden to testify with him, although the testimony is true, as it is said: "Put not thine hand with the wicked to be an unrighteous witness" (ibid. xxiii. 1), as it is an implication of the text that the testimony of all is invalid even if the witnesses be many and one among them is unfit to testify. Who is considered by the Torah to be an evil-doer, who is unfit to testify? Anyone who transgresses in a matter which is recognized in Israel as a transgression and which is a negative precept of the Torah, provided he transgressed intentionally and did not repent. If it can be assumed that he acted unintentionally and in ignorance, not being aware of the prohibition, he is not disqualified as a witness.

LAWS CONCERNING THEFT AND ROBBERY.

1. It is forbidden to rob or steal even a trifle from an Israelite or from a Gentile. If it be a thing of such little value that no one would bother about it, e.g., a chip from a bundle for a tooth-pick, it is permitted. It is pious conduct to avoid doing even this. It is also forbidden to steal from one's neighbour even with the intention of returning it, it being done merely to annoy him somewhat or by way of a joke. It is also forbidden to oppress one's neighbour in the slightest degree, as it is said: "Thou shalt not oppress thy neighbour" (Lev. xix. 13). Who is an oppressor? One who has come into possession of his neighbour's money with the consent of the latter, e.g., he has in his possession a loan or rent and does not wish to refund it or he puts him off by saying, "Come again."

2. If one covet his neighbour's house or utensils or any article which the latter has no intention of selling and he uses the influence of many friends or by his own insistence urges him to sell it to him, he transgresses the precept "Thou shalt not desire" (Deut. v. 21) from the very moment that his heart was enticed, and he thought by what means he could buy it, for "desire" is only of the heart. Desire leads to covetousness. The one who buys the things which he has desired transgresses both negative precepts, it is therefore said: "Thou shalt not covet" and "Thou shalt not desire."

3. It is a positive precept for the robber to return the very thing that was stolen, if it be in its original state and had not been altered, as it is said, "He shall restore that which he took by robbery" (Lev. vi. 4). The same law applies to a thief, he does not do his duty by making restitution in money, even if the owner had given up hope of recovering his property. If the article, which had been stolen, were lost or altered in such a way that it cannot be restored to its original

state, or if it were sunk in a building and can only be recovered by tearing down the building which would be a great loss to him, he does his duty by refunding an amount of money equivalent to the value of the stolen article at the time of the robbery. If the victim of the robbery be in another town, he should notify him to come and he will pay him, but he need not send the money to him in his town, but if the one who had been robbed had died, he should make restitution to his heirs.

4. One who robs the public, e.g., a shopkeeper who measured with a short measure or weighed with short weight or if a public functionary were lenient towards his relatives and exacting towards others, also one who took usury from the public, for any of these it is a difficult matter to repent effectively, therefore he should supply a public need in order that those whom he robbed should also enjoy thereof. If, however, the identity of the robbed ones be known to him, he is obliged to make restitution to them, as his duty is not accomplished by supplying a public need.

5. It is forbidden to buy from a thief or a robber the article which has been robbed, this applies to Jew and Gentile, for the latter is bound by the commandment prohibiting theft and robbery. This applies also to one's neighbour who is a Gentile, since this commandment is one of the seven precepts given to the sons of Noah. It is a serious transgression to buy from the thief or robber for this only encourages the wrong-doer and with reference thereto it is said : "Whoso is partner with a thief hateth his own soul " (Prov. xxix. 24), causing the thief to steal again, for he will desist if he find no purchaser. Although the thief could take the stolen article to a place where he would not be known, still this course is not a likely one. If the purchaser act in order to benefit those robbed by restoring their property to them on payment of his outlay, then the purchase may be permitted. This is only permitted if the people robbed could not possibly protect themselves. It is forbidden to accept in trust a thing which has apparently been stolen or robbed.

6. It is forbidden to derive even the slightest benefit from the property that was stolen or robbed as long as it remains in the hands of the thief or robber, even if the theft be insignificant so that the owner would not be concerned at his loss, e.g., to change currency for the money that was stolen or robbed, it is forbidden to do this, it is also forbidden to enter a house, on account of the heat or rain or to pass through a field, which was acquired by robbery. The poor are forbidden to accept a thief's money as charity. If one offer to sell an

158

article, and it is apparent that that article was stolen by him, it is forbidden to buy of him. E g., fruit watchmen who sell fruit in a secluded spot or a seller who carries secretly the thing to be sold or he says to the buyer, "Hide it," in all these cases one must not buy. It is even forbidden to buy of a woman an article which, it may be apprehended, she is selling without the knowledge of her husband. It is likewise forbidden to buy of a man any of a woman's ornaments or apparel which, it may be apprehended, he is selling without the knowledge of his wife.

7. If one's vessels were exchanged at a feast or the like for those of another person, he should not make use of the property which is not his, and when the owner of the property applies for it, he must restore it to him even if his own were lost. If an article that does not belong to him were returned to him from the laundry, he must not make use of it but restore it to its owner, although his own property were lost, if, however, the article remained in his possession for a long time, so that it would be impossible for the owner in the meantime not to have inquired after his own property, then he can make use of it, for he may assume that the laundry proprietor had settled with the owner and paid him for this article.

8. It is forbidden to derive enjoyment from anything belonging to one's neighbour without his knowledge, even if he be definitely aware of the fact that when the neighbour learns thereof, the latter will rejoice and be glad because of the love he bears towards him, still even in this case the prohibition holds good. If one enter the orchard or garden of a neighbour, it is forbidden to gather fruit without the owner's knowledge, even though the latter loved and esteemed him as himself, and even though he would undoubtedly rejoice and be glad when he learns that the former had enjoyed his fruit, nevertheless since at the moment he is not aware of the circumstance, the former would be deriving benefit in an unlawful manner. It is necessary to warn the people generally who err in this manner owing to the lack of knowledge. Nevertheless it is lawful for a member of a person's household to give a piece of bread to the poor or to some of the friends of the master of the house without his cognizance, for thus is the custom of householders, and to do this is not considered as an action which is done without the cognizance of the owner, since it is a custom so to do, and the owners are aware thereof. For this reason it is permitted to accept charity from women, if it be a small amount, even without their husbands' knowledge, owing to the fact that it is customary for them (to give charity) and the husbands are aware of this custom. Likewise if one be accustomed to eat fruit in the garden of another with the owner's cognizance, it is permitted to do so on any occasion. This rule applies to any similar case.

9. If one find fruit on the road which fell from a tree which projects above the road, if they be fruits that usually fall, and become spoiled by falling, or even if they be not spoiled and most of those

who pass that place are heathens, or if the cattle usually eat (the fruit) while passing by, so that the owner has given up his rights thereto, then (anyone who finds them) may eat thereof. But if they be fruits which do not get spoiled by falling and if most of those who pass by are Israelites, it is forbidden to take them because of the law concerning robbery, and if the fruit, etc., be the property of little orphans it is forbidden to take thereof under any circumstances, for as regards orphans their waiving of rights is of no avail at all.

10. The law of the land is equally binding on the Jew.

LAWS CONCERNING FINANCIAL DAMAGES.

1. It is forbidden to injure one's neighbour financially, even with the intention of making reparation, just as it is forbidden to steal and to rob even with the intention of making restitution. One is even forbidden, either by action or speech, to cause his neighbour to sustain damage. Thus if Reuben sold goods to a heathen and Simeon informed the latter that they are not worth the price paid, even if this be a fact, still it is forbidden for Simeon to act thus since it is allowed to take advantageous profit in this case. He who causes his neighbour to sustain damage, although according to human laws he is exempt from punishment, yet is he guilty according to Divine law until he conciliates him.

2. One who incurred an injury may not rid himself thereof, if by so doing he should cause his neighbour to incur the same, for it is forbidden to save oneself by causing even financial injury to his neighbour. But before the harm happened to him it is permitted to escape therefrom, even though by this course harm will befall his fellowman, e.g., a bucket of water which is about to be thrown across his field, prior to the same entering his land, it is permitted to take steps to prevent this happening, even though this should involve the water falling on the field of his neighbour. As soon, however, as it had come into his field it is forbidden to get rid of it in such a manner as to touch his neighbour's field because now that the damage has befallen him, he is not allowed to rid himself thereof at his neighbour's hurt. Again if the king's army should come to a town and the townsmen are obliged to billet the soldiers, it is forbidden for one of the townsmen to bribe the captain to exempt him for thereby he is causing damage to another Israelite townsman. So also in all cases of taxes it is forbidden to influence the officer so as to exempt him, if by so doing, he makes the burden heavier for others and one who acts in this manner is called מסור (traitor).

160

3. An Israelite is forbidden to slander or betray secrets and whoever acts as an informer will have no portion in the world to come. It is even forbidden to lay information against an evildoer who transgresses the religious law, it matters not whether he will suffer in his person or in his wealth, and even if he were his enemy who constantly annoyed him by his words. But if one had been betrayed, and there is no possibility of escape unless he lay information against the betrayer, this course is permitted.

4. One must not stand in a neighbour's field to look at it when the crops are at their best to prevent harm because of the belief in the "evil eye." It is forbidden to gaze at one's neighbour in such a manner as to lead one to suppose that he wishes him harm, even with regard to his business and occupation where there is no thought at all of the influence of the "evil eye," if he be working in his own house and on his own property, it is nevertheless forbidden to stare at him without his consent, for it may be that he does not wish other people to know his business. It is a sign of good manners when one sees his fellow man engaged at his work to bless him by saying, "prosper in thy task."

5 One is forbidden to do anything, even on his own premises, whereby his neighbour will sustain damage, for that reason one must not place in his court near his neighbour's wall anything possessing warmth and emitting heat, such as manure and the like, thus damaging the wall, except at a distance of three hand-breadths, likewise the water that he pours out and also the drain-pipe that carries off the water from the roof must be at a distance of three hand-breadths from his neighbour's wall. Under no circumstance may one pour out the contents of a chamber in the vicinity of the wall of one's neighbour.

THE LAWS CONCERNING PHYSICAL INJURY.

1. One is forbidden to smite his fellow man, and if he did so he has transgressed a negative precept, as it is said : "If the wicked man be worthy to be beaten . . . forty stripes he may give him, and not exceed," (Deut. xxv. 2, 3). Since the Torah is particular with reference to the beating of the wicked, ordaining that he is not to be beaten for his fault beyond the limit laid down, how much more does this apply to the beating of the righteous. The one who raises his hand against his neighbour to smite him, even if he did not strike him, is called "wrong-doer," as it is said : "And he said to the wrong-doer, wherefore wilt thou smite thy fellow ?" (Ex. ii. 13). "Wherefore hast thou smitten" is not the reading in the verse, but "wherefore wilt thou smite," although he has not yet struck his fellow he is called "wrong-doer." Anyone who smites his fellow is excommunicated by the ban of the ancients, debarring him from participation in the public performance of any sacred duty until the Beth Din release him.

therefrom when he is willing to accept their decision. If someone strike him or another Israelite, and it is impossible for him to save himself or his neighbour from the hands of the striker except by striking him back, then it is permitted to do so. It is forbidden to strike even a servant who refuses to obey. It is, however, permissible for one to chastise his small children or an orphan whom he is bringing up in his house, in order to lead them in the upright way, as that is for their own benefit.

2. One must take care not to throw pieces of broken glass or the like in any place where they can cause harm to anybody. If one's neighbour have, for instance, a head-ache which would be aggravated by the noise of hammering, then it is forbidden even in one's own house to knock anything whereby the noise of hammering will reach his neighbour's house and annoy him.

3. There are many other things relating to damages to one's neighbour or to the general public, but the general rule is this, it is forbidden to do anything, even on one's own premises and especially on a public thoroughfare, that may cause any damage to one's neighbour or to the wayfarer on the public highway, unless it be a thing that has become a general custom, and anyone is at liberty to do it, which is equal to anyone being excused (for so doing) by all the inhabitants of the city, so that each of them is priviliged to do that certain thing whenever he or his son after him should find it necessary so to do.

4. One who frightens his neighbour, e.g., by screaming at him when behind him, or appearing before him in the dark or the like, is guilty according to Divine law.

5. The one who injures his neighbour, even though he give him the money due to him as compensation for the injury done, so also a thief or robber, even though the thing stolen had been returned or paid for, nevertheless those wrong-doers cannot obtain forgiveness until they ask pardon of the injured party or the one whose property was stolen on account of the pain caused. The latter should be ready to forgive and must not be cruel in this respect.

6. When one sees his neighbour in distress and it is in his power to save him or he can employ others to save him, it is his own duty to make strenuous efforts or to employ others in order to save him, and, if the latter can afford it he must refund him his money, as he can demand it from him, but if he cannot afford to do so, he should not shirk his duty on that account, but he should save him at his own expense. If he refrain from doing so he transgresses the precept: "Thou shalt not stand against the blood of thy neighbour" (Lev. xix. 16). Likewise when one overhears the wicked hatching a plot against one's neighbour or setting a trap for him, and he has not revealed it to him, or if he could satisfy them through money for the sake of saving his neighbour and thereby prevent their intention being realized, and he failed to do so, or by any similar means in a like case, he transgresses

the precept: "Thou shall not stand against the blood of thy neighbour" (*ibid.*) for he who preserves life in Israel is as though he had maintained the entire world.

7. One who counterfeits, and it is feared that thereby he will involve many in danger, is like a persecutor, and he must be warned not to continue his practices. If, however, he heed not, it is permissible to denounce him to the government with the declaration that no one else is implicated in that crime. If an individual be falsely accused of being an accomplice, he may likewise assert his innocence by saying : "I did not participate in that crime, he is the sole criminal."

8. According to the custom the seven elders of the community judge in the adjudication of fines, e.g., with reference to injuries, insults and the like, but they must not act independently of the Beth Din, since there are many varieties of legal points and it is not permitted to inflict a penalty more than the law requires, so that the honour of one's fellow creatures should not be treated as a trivial matter.

9. When a woman is in parturition with great travail, the doctor is permitted (in a critical case) prior to the birth to extract the embryo in a severed state, for if it had not come forth it is not accounted as a living soul and it is permissible to save the mother by sacrificing the embryo, for it is a matter of self-preservation. But if it protrude its head then one living soul must not be sacrificed for another, and this is the way of nature.

Laws Concerning Borrowing and Hiring.

1. One who borrows or hires from his neighbour an animal or moveables may neither lend nor hire out the same without the owner's consent. Even in the case of books where it is a religious duty to lend them, we do not say that we can take it for granted that the owner would approve of a religious duty being done at his expense, for may be he would not wish his property to be in the possession of a certain person whom he considered to be untrustworthy. It is, however, permitted for the borrower of a book to allow in his own house another person to study therein, on the condition that he studies alone, but not two people together. If it be known that it is the custom of the owner to trust the second party in such matters, then the borrower may lend to this party and the one who hires may hire out in turn to the same party.

2. It is a religious duty to pay the wages of a hired workman at the proper time and if one delay the same he transgresses a negative precept, as it is said : " At his day thou shalt give him his hire, neither shall the sun go down upon it " (Deut. xxiv. 15). Likewise it is a religious duty to pay for the hire of an animal or of utensils at the proper time and if one delay the same he transgresses a negative precept, as it is said : "Thou shall not oppress an hired servant that is poor and needy . . . at his day thou shalt give him his hire " (*ibid.* 14f.) What is the proper time ? If he finished the work during the day, his time for payment is all the day, and if the day had passed without paying the wages the (master) has transgressed the law, " At his *day* thou shalt give him his hire, neither shall the sun go down on it" (*ibid.*) If he finished the work after the end of the day and night had commenced, his time for payment is all night, and if the night had passed without paying the wages the (master) has transgressed the law : "The wages of him that is hired shall not abide with thee all night until the morning " (Lev. xix. 13). So also with one hired by the week, month or year. If one had finished his work during the day, the payment of his wages is valid during the whole day ; if he had finished his work during the night, the payment of his wages is valid during the whole night but not later. If one gave a garment to a tailor to repair for a sum agreed by contract and the latter brings it to him during the day, he can pay any time during that day only, and if he bought it at night, he can pay any time during that night only ; but as long as the garment is in the hands of the tailor although the work has been done, the owner does not transgress the law (by not paying), even if it be with the tailor for several days, and even if the latter had notified him that he should bring the money and fetch his property.

3. There is no transgression of the laws quoted (Lev. xix. 13 and Deut. xxiv. 14-15) unless the one who was hired asked for his wages and he had the money to pay same. If the wages were not demanded, or if the one hired had asked for his wages but the master had no money, then there is no violation of the law. Nevertheless, it is pious conduct to borrow so as to pay the wages at the right time, for the workman is poor and sets his heart upon his pay. In such cases where the masters are accustomed not to pay the workmen until the complete account (for all work to be done) has been delivered, even if they asked for a small sum, which they had undoubtedly earned, nevertheless (if this be refused) there is no violation of the law since the custom is known and on this condition the workmen were engaged.

4. A hired workman who had done some work for the master and had spoiled it, even by his own negligence, in such a manner that he is legally bound to make it good, it is a religious duty for the master to waive his legal right and forgive him, as it is said : "That thou mayest walk in the way of good men " (Prov. ii. 20). If the workman be poor and without food, it is a duty to give him his hire, as it is

said : "And keep the path of the righteous" (*ibid.*) Which is the "path of the righteous ?" To keep the way of the Lord, to practice charity and justice even more strictly than the actual law demands.

5. Just as the master is exhorted neither to rob the wages of the hired servant nor to delay the payment, likewise the poor (one who is hired) is warned not to neglect the work of the master and he is bound to work with all his might, as our father Jacob (peace be unto him) said : "For with all my power have I served your father" (Gen. xxxi. 6). Therefore a workman is not permitted to work all night and to hire himself out by day (for he is unfit owing to the night work) ; likewise he is not allowed to work his animal by night and to hire it out by day. The workman is also forbidden to starve himself or to stint himself with regard to his food for thereby he weakens his strength and he will not be able to do the work for his master in a proper manner. This law applies also to a teacher.

LAWS RELATING TO THE COMMANDMENT "THOU SHALT NOT MUZZLE."

1. Whosoever prevents a domestic animal from eating when working is punished, as it is said : "Thou shalt not muzzle the ox when he treadeth out the corn" (Deut. xxv. 4). This applies to an ox or to any animal or beast whether it be unclean or clean, whether it be engaged in treading out the corn or in any other work of the field, and only by way of example does the Torah say, "the ox when he treadeth out the corn." Included in this prohibition is even one who "muzzled the beast by his voice," that is to say, he shouted at it and it therefore did not eat, and he incurs punishment. If an Israelite thresh corn even with the cow of a heathen (when muzzled) he transgresses the law : "Thou shalt not muzzle." If the beast cannot eat through being thirsty, he must give it to drink. If the beast were at work on a field, the product whereof would be injurious to its system, it is permissible to muzzle the beast, for the Torah insists on its obtaining only that which it can enjoy, whereas in this case it would have no enjoyment.

LAWS CONCERNING A LOST THING AND THE FINDING THEREOF.

1. If one see a thing that an Israelite had lost, he is bound to attend thereto and to restore it to its owner, as it is said : "Thou shalt surely bring them again" (*ibid.* xxii. 1). Likewise when he can save his neighbour from loss of money it is his duty to do so, as this is also included in the law of restoring a lost thing, although legally (if it were found) in a place where the majority of the inhabitants are heathens and even if the Israelite had put a special mark thereon, there is no obligation to restore it, since there is the presumption that its owner had despaired of its recovery, it is good and right, nevertheless, to do more than the law requires and to return it to the Israelite upon identification of the article which he had marked, and he can be forced to restore it in this case. If the finder of the lost article be

poor and the owner be rich, the former need not do more than the law requires, but where one is required by the law of the land to restore a lost thing, he is obliged under all circumstances to restore it.

2. Any one who finds a lost thing, whether the thing be marked (or not) is immaterial, after it had been put there temporarily (by the owner), e.g., a garment or an axe by the side of the fence, and even if there be a doubt whether the owner had left the article there intentionally or whether he had lost it, then it is forbidden in such a case to touch the same.

3. If a man, who is aged and respected, found a thing which had been lost and that thing was a common article, i.e., of such a nature that even were it his own he would not take it up and bring it to his house because it would be undignified for him to do so, he is not bound to attend thereto, he should, nevertheless, do more than the law requires and concern himself therewith even if it be beneath his dignity.

4. If one found an article and he does not know who lost it, whether it be marked or not is immaterial, as there are many different laws concerning the same, he should consult the ecclesiastical authorities before acting in this matter.

Laws Concerning Deposits.

1. He who deposits money with his neighbour, in these times when we are all engaged in commercial affairs and money is in demand, we must take it for granted that the depositor tacitly consents to the use of that money by the receiver in the requirements of his business, the latter is therefore allowed thus to use it, and that (money) assumes the character of a loan, if, however, the money consigned be sealed up, or tied up with a peculiar knot, it is an indication of the depositor's objection to the use of that money by the receiver and the latter is not permitted to use it.

2. One to whom a neighbour had consigned any article is forbidden to make personal use of it, even to put it to such uses whereby the article is in nowise spoiled, he is nevertheless as one who borrows without the owner's knowledge, and he is classed as a robber. If it be well known that the depositor would not interpose any objection to his use thereof, it is permitted to use it. Some authorities forbid this on account of it being a deposit, and also in the case of a thing which people do not trouble about. The prohibition is due to the fact that the receiver is also in this manner making use of a trust or deposit and it is best to follow the stricter opinion and not to use the deposit.

3. It is the duty of the receiver to guard the article deposited with him in the best manner possible for such an article to be kept, even if the depositor did not usually take pains in guarding his own property, he must nevertheless be particularly vigilant in the keeping

of property deposited with him, and he is forbidden to deliver an article deposited with him into the hands of others, even if they be proper people and of greater integrity than himself, unless the depositor is accustomed to deposit such property with them. On returning an article which was deposited with him he should not return it to any of the members of the depositor's household without the latter's knowledge, this law also applies when returning a thing that he had borrowed, or when repaying a debt he may, however, return it to the depositor's wife, as it may be assumed, by virtue of her being the manageress of the house, he (the husband) consigns all he has into her charge.

Laws Concerning Unloading and Loading.

1. If one meet his neighbour on the road with his beast lying beneath its load, it is immaterial whether it be a fit and proper load or one too heavy to carry, he is required to assist him unloading the animal, as it is said : "Thou shalt surely help with him" (Ex. xxiii. 5), and after he had raised the load he should not depart, leaving his neighbour in distress, but he must help him to replace the load upon it, as it is said : "Thou shalt surely help him to lift them up again" (Deut. xxii. 4). If he left his neighbour neither helping to unload nor to reload, he has neglected an affirmative precept and transgressed a negative precept, as it is said, "Thou shalt not see thy brother's ass or his ox fallen down by the way, and hide thyself from them" (ibid.) If after he had unloaded and reloaded, it fell off again, he is obliged to assist him again in unloading and reloading, even a hundred times, as it is said : "Thou shalt surely help with him" (Ex. xxiii. 5), "Thou shalt surely help him to lift them up again" (Deut. xxii. 4) and for that reason he must accompany him the distance of a parasang,[1] as he may perhaps need him, unless the owner of the load tell him, "I do not need you." The commandment (of unloading is to be done gratuitously, but one is not obliged to load otherwise than for compensation, he should also be paid for accompanying him.

2. If a party travel together and an accident occurred to one of the party's asses through breaking its leg, the companions are not permitted to separate with their asses from him and to leave him alone on the road, but if the accident that occurred to the ass be of a serious nature and one that will prevent it from continuing the journey, they need not, for his sake, tarry any longer than a reasonable time and can separate from him. Likewise in a company who are travelling together in vehicles, and if an accident happened to one of the latter so that it is necessary to delay a little to repair the damage, the companions are not permitted to separate unless the delay be prolonged beyond a reasonable time.

*The Parasang = 4 mils=the distance walked by the average pedestrian in 1 hour 12 minutes.

LAWS RELATING TO PHYSICAL PRESERVATION AND TO THE PRECEPT "NOT TO DESTROY."

1. It is a positive commandment for one to make a battlement for his roof, as it is said : "And thou shalt make a battlement for thy roof" (*ibid.* 8). The height of the battlement should not be less than ten hand-breadths and it should be strongly constructed, in order that it may not give way when one leans upon it. The roofs of our houses are exempt from this precept because we do not use them as in the East. The precept applies not only to the roof, if used, but also to any place where danger might arise through a person meeting with an accident there and entailing a possibility of fatal consequences. Proper safeguards are required in all such cases and anyone who neglects this precaution violates an affirmative precept and transgresses a negative precept, as it is said : "Thou shalt not bring blood upon thine house" (*ibid.*) E.g., if one have a wall in his court, he is obliged to put around it an entrenchment ten hand-breadths high or to cover it to prevent anyone falling therein. So also with regard to any stumbling-block which might prove a danger to life, it is a religious duty to remove it or to beware thereof and to warn others in a kind manner, as it is said : "Take heed to thyself, and keep thy life diligently" (*ibid.* iv. 9). If one left these dangerous obstacles thereby not removing them, he has violated an affirmative precept and transgressed the law, "Thou shalt not bring blood upon thine house" (*ibid.* xxii. 8). E.g., if a broken ladder stand in his house or in his court, or if one bring up a vicious dog (it is his duty to remove the same).

2. Just as a man must guard his body against all injury or harm, as it is said : "Take heed to thyself, and keep thy life diligently (*ibid.* iv. 9), likewise has he been enjoined to guard his money against all loss, therefore one who breaks any utensil, or who tears a garment, or destroys food or drink, or befouls them, or who throws away money or spoils anything that is proper for man's enjoyment, transgresses a negative precept, as it is said : "Thou shalt not destroy the trees thereof" (*ibid.* xx. 19).

LAWS CONCERNING CRUELTY TO ANIMALS AND CASTRATION.

1. It is forbidden, according to the Torah, to hurt any living creature. It is, on the contrary, one's duty to save any living creatures from pain, it is immaterial whether the creature be ownerless or if it belong to a non-Jew. Nevertheless if they be injurious to man or if they be required for medicinial purposes or for any other human need, it is permitted to kill them and we do not hesitate to cause them pain thereby (of course, only the minimum pain) since the Torah has permitted Shechitah (ritual slaughter).

2. When horses which are drawing a cart come to a rough place or to a high hill and they cannot draw the cart without help, it is a religious duty to help even the horses of a non-Jew, because of the precept forbidding cruelty to animals, lest the owner smite them to make them draw more than their strength permits.

3. It is forbidden to bind together the feet of a beast, animal or bird in any way that might cause them to suffer pain.

4. It is forbidden to make a bird sit on eggs which are not of her own species, for this is cruelty to the creatures.

5. It is forbidden to castrate either a man, beast, an animal or a bird, clean or unclean, in Palestine or elsewhere. Anyone who transgresses deserves punishment by stripes. It is also forbidden to give a man or any other male living being anything to cause sterility.

6. It is forbidden to tell a heathen to castrate one of our animals. Some authorities say that it is forbidden even to sell it to a heathen or to give it to him on terms of half the profits if one be aware that he will castrate it, because the heathen is also forbidden to castrate. Therefore, in acting thus the Israelite would cause the heathen to transgress the law. If, however, the heathen who is the buyer would not himself castrate, but would give it to another heathen to castrate, this procedure is, according to all authorities, permitted, since the possible indirect cause of transgression is not operative in this case.

LAWS REGARDING VOWS AND OATHS.

1. One should not become accustomed to making vows. Every one who makes a vow is as though he had built a high place when it is forbidden to do so; and any one who fulfils such a vow is as though he had offered an offering upon the high place and thereby incurred guilt for offering a sacrifice outside the Temple. This applies to ordinary vows, but one is commanded to keep vows of consecration and one should not consult the wise concerning them, except in a case of necessity.

2. One should likewise keep aloof from taking an oath, but if one had transgressed and did take an oath concerning any matter, he should not consult the wise regarding its annulment as he is obliged to fulfil it, even if it cause him distress. One should not consult the wise regarding the annulment of an oath except in case of necessity.

3. It is necessary to avoid making a vow with regard to any matter. It is not good to vow, even for charity, but if one desire to give something which he has in his possession, he should give it forthwith, otherwise he should wait until he has it and then he should give it without any vow. If a call be made for charity and one is obliged to contribute in common with others, he should, when offering, expressly stipulate that he is not making a vow. At a memorial service, where it is usual to make charitable offerings, one should say, "I am not making any vow." When one is in distress he is permitted to make a vow.

4. If one resolve to fix a certain time for the study of the Torah or to observe a certain commandment and he is afraid that he will thereafter relax in his exertions in this matter, or if he fear lest, incited by passion, he might do something which is forbidden or he might be prevented thereby from observing one of the commandments he is permitted to fortify his soul by making a vow or taking an oath. Even if, when making a resolution, one merely make a simple declaration not in the formula of a vow or an oath, it is nevertheless a vow, and he is obliged to keep it. One should therefore take care, when he resolves to do a good deed or to adopt a certain good practice, to say that he does so without making a vow. This is likewise a good rule for a person to observe even when saying that he will do something which is optional, so as to obviate transgressing the sin of violating one's vow.

5. One who made a vow in order to improve his conduct is zealous and praiseworthy, e.g., if one be a glutton, and he vows that he will not eat meat for a certain time, or if he be intemperate and declares that he will not touch wine or other intoxicating spirits, likewise one who allowed himself to be conceited and proud on account of his good looks and to correct this folly he takes upon himself to be a Nazarite or the like, in all these cases these vows are for the worship of God. Nevertheless one should not accustom oneself to take even such vows, but one must strive to conquer one's passion even without a vow.

6. A vow is not effective unless the lips and heart (of the speaker) are in harmony, but if one made a vow in error, that is, he uttered with his lips a vow that he had no intention of making, or he thought of making a vow but he did not utter it with his lips, it is not accounted a vow.

7. If one had accustomed himself to strictly observe certain practices, from which he is exempt by law, but which he has voluntarily assumed that they should serve him as a barrier and a fence for self-control, e.g., fasting during the Ten days of Penitence, or abstaining from meat and wine from the 17th day of Tammuz to the 9th of Ab, and practices similar to these, even if he thus conducted himself but once, but he had it in his mind to make a rule thereof, or if he had thus conducted himself three times, although he did not

170

resolve to make a rule thereof, if he had not stipulated that he was
doing so without making a vow, and he desires to change his custom
owing to his ill-health, he requires absolution of his vow, and he should
make the opening remark (to those who will absolve him) by declaring
that he regrets that he had acted as though he had made a vow;
therefore one who desires to adopt a very strict observance of some
law, that should serve him as a fence for self-control he should first say
that he does not adopt it by a vow, he should furthermore say that it
is only for this occasion or for any other time when he will desire thus
to act and that he has no intention of making a regular practice
thereof.

8. How are vows or oaths to be annulled? The one, who had
made the vow or had taken the oath, goes to three men who are learned
in the Torah, and (at least) one of them is to be an expert in the laws
concerning vows in order that he may know what kind of a vow may
be annulled and what kind may not and in what manner they may
be annulled, these three absolve him. One who makes a vow in a
dream should be absolved thereof, preferably by a body of ten men
who are learned in the Torah.

9. Although with reference to all the precepts in the Torah a
son is not considered of age (and liable to perform same) until he is 13
years old and shows signs of puberty, and with regard to a daughter
the age is 12 years, but with reference to a vow or an oath they both
become responsible a year earlier (than the aforementioned ages). Thus
a son who had reached the age of twelve years and one day and a
daughter of eleven years and one day, even though they lack the signs
of puberty, and who furthermore understood in whose Name they
made the vow or took the oath, their vows are of no account. They
should, nevertheless, be reprimanded, and taught not to accustom
themselves to make vows or to take oaths. But if the vow be of a
trivial nature, not entailing (by its fulfilment) any physical suffering,
they should be compelled to keep it.

10. The father may annul the vows of his daughter until she
arrives at the age of twelve years and six months if she be unmarried.
The husband may annul the vows of his wife. How are the vows
annulled? He says three times "It is invalid" (מופר) or "nul and
void" or he uses some other expression which indicates that he has
entirely abrogated the vow, it being immaterial whether he said so in
her presence or not. But the expression (התרה) i.e., declaring that to
be permitted (which the one who took the oath had stated to be forbidden) does not apply to a father or a husband; moreover they can
only declare the vow void during the day they heard it declared. Thus
if they heard the vow pronounced at the beginning of the night they
can declare it void during the whole night as well as the day following.
If they heard it by day just before the time when the stars become
visible, they can declare it void only until the appearance of the stars,
thereafter they cannot annul the vow. On Sabbath he must not say

to her (מוּפָר) "it is invalid for thee" as on week days, but he should
annul it in his heart and say to her: "Take, eat" or similar expres-
sions. If the father or the husband first say that he is satisfied with
reference to the vow, although he had not explicitly said this but he
uses such language which indicated that he was satisfied, or even if he
only thought that he was satisfied with her vow, he cannot then annul
the same.

11. What vows can the father or husband annul? Only such
as involve physical suffering, e.g, to abstain from washing or toilet
(perfume) or cosmetics or rouge and such like. The husband can annul
even such vows which do not involve physical suffering if they refer to
private matters between husband and wife and might provoke jealousy
between them. These vows can only be disallowed as long as she lives
with him, but if she became a widow or divorced she is bound by the
vows.

THE LAW REGARDING THE PRAYER FOR A JOURNEY AND OTHER MATTERS TO BE NOTED WHEN TRAVELLING.

1. One who goes on a journey, whether from his house or from
the place where he lodged over night on his journey, as soon as he has
gone beyond the outskirts of the city, i.e. 70⅔ cubits beyond the
last house, should say the prayer for a journey, namely, יהר"מ ה'
אר"ש שתוליבנו לשלום וכו'.[1] The prayer is said in the plural except in the
phrase ותחנני לחן. It is proper to say the prayer after one had tra-
velled 2,000 cubits (i.e., a mil) beyond the outskirts of the city and
when he is travelling and has lodged over night in any place he can
say it in the morning before he resumes his journey.

2. The prayer is to be said if he travel at least a parasang (4
mils) and one should take care to say it during the first parasang, if he
should forget to do this, he can say it as long as he is travelling provided he had not yet reached the last parasang on his road to the city
where he intends to spend the night.

3. This prayer should be recited immediately after a benediction.
Therefore if one go forth on a journey in the morning and he says on
the road the morning prayers or if he had lodged over night when on
his journey in a certain place, he can say this prayer before he resumes
the journey. In the morning prayers he should say it after the benediction גומל חסדים טובים לעמו ישראל[2]. If he set forth from his house after
he had said his morning prayer, he should eat or drink something on
the road and say the concluding benediction (or Grace) and then say
the prayer for the journey.

4. It should be said whilst standing, if he be riding or travelling in a conveyance and if it be possible to let the animal drawing the same stand still he should do so, because one riding an animal is considered to be like one who walks. If it be not possible to let the animal stand still, he should say it whilst travelling in the conveyance.

5. It should be said only once daily whilst travelling, but if he rest in a certain place for the purpose of staying there overnight and then he changed his mind and went away thence to reach another place or to return to his home, he should say it again. If he travel by day and by night or if he spent the night in an uninhabited place, on the first occasion he should say the prayer to the end, but on the other occasions he should say it without the concluding benediction (בְרוּךְ . . . שׁוֹמֵעַ תְּפִלָּה) for as long as he does not spend the night in an inhabited place, his journey is reckoned as one uninterrupted way.

6. Before going on a journey one should give charity and also bid farewell to the leaders of the community so that they may bless him, wishing him a prosperous journey and if possible he should get some of them to accompany him a little way. One who accompanies his companion must stand still when the latter departs from him until he disappears from his view. The people who bless a person going on a journey should not say to him: "Go in peace," but "Go towards peace." When travelling he should meditate on the Torah, as it is said: "And when thou walkest by the way" (Deut. vi. 7). He should say devoutly and humbly a few psalms daily. He must be careful to take bread with him even if he be going to a place in his vicinity, he should also take fringes (צִיצִית) lest one of his fringes become unfit for use and then he would be unable to obtain another and he would be interrupted in the performance of a religious duty. A person should always enter a place whilst it is still day[1] and also go forth during day time, i.e., when he wishes to come to an inn for the night, he should go in whilst the sun is still shining and on the morrow he should wait for sunrise and then set out on his journey which will be prosperous. He should not eat much whilst travelling.

7. It may be necessary to make inquiries concerning his lodging to ascertain if the owner and his staff be trustworthy. If he desire to eat meat in a place which is unknown to him, it is necessary to investigate carefully the reputation of the slaughterer and to inquire concerning the ecclesiastical authority and the one who superintends the Shechitah (ritual slaughter).

8. When saying the morning prayers whilst on a journey he must enwrap himself in a large Tallis just as he would do when praying in the Synagogue, for the Arba' Kanfos lacks the proper size of a Tallis. If he were walking when he says the verse שְׁמַע "Hear, O Israel," etc., (ibid. 4) and the words בְּשִׁבְתְּךָ, he must stand still in

---

[1]Cf. T. B. Pesachim 2a. The expression means lit. "that it was good," see Gen. i. 4.

order to pray with devotion. If he ride or sit in a vehicle he can say this prayer as he is situated. He must stand still to say the Shemoneh 'Esreh. If he be pressed for time to complete his journey, he should, if possible, stand still at least for the recital of the first three benedictions and the last three benedictions If not, he should pray whilst sitting in the conveyance and thus perform the customary rights of bowing. Nevertheless it would be preferable to say the Shemoneh 'Esreh immediately after dawn and to say the afternoon prayer directly after 12.30 p m., in order to pray standing and in the proper manner.

9. If one ate whilst walking on a journey he may say Grace after meals whilst continuing the journey because he would feel uneasy if he were compelled to delay (to say the Grace whilst sitting down). If he ate whilst sitting then he must say the Grace in a like position.

10. The custom obtains among a few people that if they eat in the house of a heathen whilst travelling they do not unite to say the Grace after the meal, since they had not made an appointment here for this purpose. If, however, they had agreed to unite to eat together there, it would not be right to ignore the duty of uniting for saying Grace. They should say the following extra הרחמן: הרחמן הוא ישלח לנו ברכה מרובה במקום הליכתנו ובמקום ישיבתנו עד עולם. If they partake of the food of an individual they can say the special הרחמן: הרחמן הוא יברך את בעה"ב הזה, referring to their host, otherwise they should say הרחמן הוא יברך אותנו.

11. According to the strict interpretation of the law, it is forbidden to go on Friday more than three parasangs either to his house or to any other place. so that his household can prepare the Sabbath meals as is proper. In these lands we are not particular in this matter because the majority of people prepare in ease. Nevertheless it is necessary for everybody to enter his home whilst it is day, for frequently the Sabbath is desecrated by people delaying in this matter.

12. If one were in a lodging whilst on a journey on the Sabbath and he had money with him, if he can deposit it or put it away in safety it is well, as he must not keep it in his pocket for the money is מוקצה (i.e. that which is forbidden to be handled or used on Sabbath or Holyday). If he fear that the money will be stolen from him, he may sew it in his garment on Friday and he should remain indoors and not go out on the Sabbath wearing this garment in a place where there is no 'Erub (i.e the symbolical act whereby the legal fiction of community or continuity is established).[1] But if there be cause to fear that by reason of his refraining from going out the entire day, the people will imagine that he has money and that they might rob him, he can then go out with the money sewed in his garment but he may not go out under any circumstance if the money be in his pocket.

THE LAWS CONCERNING THE AFTERNOON SERVICE (מנחה).

1. The right time for the Afternoon Service is at $9\frac{1}{2}$ hours of the day and that is called the short period for Minchah (small Minchah.)

[1]See Jastrow, Targum Dictionary, p. 1075 b.

In a case of emergency, e.g., if he had to go on a journey or to take a meal he can say the afternoon service immediately after 6½ hours of the day (= 12.30 p.m.) and this is called (the beginning of) the "large Minchah." Actually its limit is extended to one hour and a quarter before night but not later. This is called פלג המנחה (half of the small Minchah, but if the day be exactly 12 hours long, this point of time is at 4.45 p.m), for two hours and a half intervene between the beginning of the small Minchah and nightfall, and half of this period is one hour and a quarter. If there were no option or in a case of necessity one can say the afternoon service until the stars appear. Likewise we are now accustomed in many congregations to say this service shortly before night. The hours referred to are proportionate to the length of the day from sunrise to sunset divided by twelve, and if the day be long containing 18 hours then every "hour" is really one hour and a half.

2. It is forbidden to begin even a little meal shortly before the "small Minchah." The term "shortly before" means half an hour. If he did not resolve to take a regular meal, but he was only eating or drinking momentarily, e.g., he partook of fruit or a dish of even one of the five special kinds of corn, to do so is permitted by some authorities. Others are stringent and forbid even this. It is also forbidden to begin even shortly before the "large Minchah," i.e. at noon, an elaborate banquet, such as a wedding banquet or a feast to celebrate a circumcision or the like, but he should wait until half an hour after noon had elapsed, and they should then say the afternoon prayer before the feast. In a place where people are summoned to attend Synagogue and if he be accustomed to go there to say his prayers with the congregation, he is permitted to begin a little meal shortly before the "small Minchah" and also thereafter, provided he will cease eating immediately when they call him to Synagogue to pray. It is forbidden to begin an elaborate banquet shortly before the "small Minchah," even in a place where they summon people to come to Synagogue.

3. Prior to beginning the Afternoon Service it is necessary to wash the hands up to the wrists as at the Morning Service. If on concluding the Afternoon Service he made an interruption before saying the Evening Service, or if upon terminating the Morning Service he made an interruption before saying the Additional Service, the ablution must be repeated.

4. אשרי (Ps. cxlv.) which inaugurates the Afternoon Service should not be said before there are ten male adults in the Synagogue in order that the Reader can say Kaddish after this psalm has been said in the presence of the Minyan. But if אשרי were said with less than a Minyan present, and in the meantime ten adults had assembled, another psalm should be said after which the Reader should say קדיש. The Reader should enwrap himself in the Tallis before reciting אשרי in order to avoid an interruption between אשרי and קדיש.

175

but if he only obtained a Tallis after he had already said אשרי, he should enwrap himself therein and say some verses of the Psalms, after which he should say קדיש.

5. If the time proper for Minchah be limited and night be approaching, immediately after the Kaddish the Reader should say the Shemoneh 'Esreh aloud whilst the Congregation should only listen and make the responses until the Reader has said האל הקדוש ("the Holy God") to which they should respond אמן, and then they should silently say their prayer, if, however, they be very much pressed for time, and it is to be feared that by waiting until the conclusion of האל הקדוש (by the Reader) they would be unable to conclude their prayer while it is yet day, they can immediately pray with the Reader saying silently word by word with him until האל הקדוש, it is nevertheless proper that there be at least one who can respond אמן to the Reader's benedictions.

6. One who arrives at the Synagogue whilst the Congregation say the Shemoneh 'Esreh should also say it with them and on concluding the same he can say אשרי. If, however, he will be unable to conclude the Shemoneh 'Esreh in time to say the Keddushah in the Reader's repetition and if he wait until the Reader has concluded the entire Shemoneh 'Esreh with the Kaddish, when the time proper for saying Minchah will then be passed, he should wait for the Reader's repetition and say with him silently word by word, he should even say the Reader's version of the Keddushah including לדור ודור וכו', and terminate the benedictions האל הקדוש and שומע תפלה with the Reader, he should also say מודים together with the Reader in order that he may then bow with the Congregation. On a fast day, however, he should not say עננו together with the Reader, but he should insert it in שומע תפלה as is proper for a private worshipper. Likewise if he desire to say the Evening Service with the congregation and if he should postpone saying the Minchah prayer until the conclusion of the Reader's repetition of the Shemoneh 'Esreh, he would be compelled to say the Evening Prayer privately, he should say the Minchah Shemoneh 'Esreh when it is repeated by the Reader. If he came into the Synagogue just before the Keddushah he should wait until the Reader has concluded the words האל הקדוש and then after responding אמן he should say the Shemoneh 'Esreh. And although he will miss the response אמן after the benediction שומע תפלה and also the response מודים ("We give thanks") which are obligatory, nevertheless it is better to miss these responses rather than to lose the opportunity of saying the Evening prayer with the Congregation. Much more so is this the case if the time for saying Minchah be on the point of passing by.

7. If the Minchah Service were prolonged until night Tachanun should not be said for this prayer of supplication may not be said at night. The utmost care should be taken not to delay the Minchah service until it is actually night, as then קדיש תתקבל cannot be said after prayers which were recited during the previous day, since the night belongs to the following day.

8. One who came to the Synagogue on a Friday afternoon and found that the Congregation had already inaugurated the Sabbath or Festival, that is to say on Sabbath they had said מזמור שיר ליום השבת or on the Eve of a Festival they had said ברכו, then he should not say the Minchah Service in that Synagogue, but he should withdraw and say his prayer. If he hear the Reader say ברכו he should not respond with the Congregation, for by responding to ברכו he forfeits his right to say the Minchah prayer of a week-day and if he made a mistake by doing so, he should say the Shemoneh 'Esreh of the Evening Service twice. If, however, he arrived at the Synagogue shortly before the Sabbath or Festival had been inaugurated and although he could not complete the Minchah prayer before the Congregation had inaugurated the Sabbath or Festival, he may conclude the same in the Synagogue as he began it there when it was permissible for him to do so.

Laws Concerning the Evening Service.

1. The time for reading the Shema' of the Evening Service is when three small stars are visible. On the day when the sky is overcast with clouds one should wait and not pray until he knows beyond a doubt that it is night. Nevertheless, the God-fearing man who had participated in the congregational Evening Service before night, should wait and not partake of any meal before night set in. Immediately after the stars are visible he should read the first three sections of the Shema.' One who does not join in the Synagogue service is not allowed to say the Evening Service before the stars have appeared.

2. The proper time for holding Evening Service is exactly when the stars appear. It is forbidden to begin a meal or to engage in any work or even to study (the Torah) half an hour before the stars appear, just as applies shortly before the "small Minchah." If, however, one had no spare time, e.g., he was engaged in public teaching he should at least not delay the recital of the Evening Service longer than midnight, although if one had inadvertently allowed that time to elapse without praying, he is permitted to say the prayers until dawn.

3. If one came to the Synagogue for Evening Service and found the congregation saying the Shemoneh 'Esreh, he should say it with them even if it should not be night, although it is less than one hour and a quarter before night. Later when night had set in he should

read the Shema' with its proper benedictions. If the Congregation were reading the middle of the Shema' with its benedictions and he will have time to read the Shema' with its benedictions as far as שומר עמו ישראל לעד before the Congregation say the Shemoneh 'Esreh, he should do so and omit ברוך ה' לעולם וכו' and he need not say this prayer after the Shemoneh 'Esreh. If, (when he found the Congregation saying the Shema') he had not yet said the Minchah Shemoneh 'Esreh he should say this prayer whilst the Congregation say the Shema' with its benedictions, after which he should wait for a short time, at least as long as it would take to walk four cubits, and he should then say the Shemoneh 'Esreh of the Evening Service with the Congregation, and after nightfall he can read the Shema' with its benedictions.

4. One should say the prayer, ברוך ה' לעולם up to יראו עינינו whilst sitting.[1] One is forbidden to interrupt oneself when saying the prayers from והוא רחום until after the Shemoneh 'Esreh, but the announcement by the beadle of יעלה ויבא or טל ומטר is not considered an interruption, inasmuch as it appertains to the requirements of the service.

5. If one would be left by himself whilst praying in Synagogue at night his companion is obliged to wait (for him) until he has completed his prayer so that his mind should not be disturbed. If, however, he began to say his prayers at such a time when he could not finish with the Congregation, the companion is not obliged to wait for him, for truly in this case it is evident that if one come thus (late), he will not be afraid (to conclude his prayers alone.)

RULES FOR THE NIGHT.

1. It is proper for a man of average health to take a frugal supper at night and it should be lighter than the meals of the day. It is sufficient for a healthy man to sleep six hours. One should neither sleep alone in a room nor in a place excessively hot or cold.

2. Every one who fears God will examine his deeds of the past day before he goes to sleep. If he find that he has transgressed he will feel remorse and repent and resolve with a perfect heart not to repeat this sin.

3. If one had not read the three sections of the Shema' when it was night, he should say them when he says the Shema' before retiring to rest at night. If he had said the three sections when it was night, he need not repeat them when saying his prayers in bed, he should say only the first section of the Shema.' Nevertheless the most desirable way of discharging this duty is to say the three sections. Then he

---

[1] Some authorities say that this prayer must be recited whilst standing.

should say psalms and Biblical verses referring to God's mercy, such as we find in the Prayer Books.[1] But in the majority of Prayer Books the benediction המפיל ("who makest to fall") is printed before the Shema', it would be better to say this benediction at the end of the prayers so that it should immediately preceed sleep. One should therefore read the Shema' and the psalms before getting into bed, and when in bed one should say the benediction המפיל and thereafter one should neither eat nor drink nor speak.

4. One must take off one's clothes and not sleep therein. When taking off the shoes and garments one should remove those on the left first. One must not place the clothes under the pillow and one must take great care to accustom oneself to sleep on one's side. It is strictly prohibited to sleep on one's back or in the reverse position.

Laws Concerning Honour due to Parents.

1. It is written, "*Honour* thy father and thy mother" (Ex. xx. 12) also "*Honour* the Lord with thy substance" (Prov. iii. 9). Again it is written, "Ye shall *fear* every man his mother, and his father" (Lev. xix. 3) also "Thou shalt *fear* the Lord thy God" (Deut. vi. 13). We thus see that in the same manner in which He commanded us to honour His great Name and to fear Him, He also commands us to honour and to fear our parents. Three partners have a share in man's creation, namely, the Holy One, blessed be He, one's father and mother.[2] When a man honours his father and his mother, the Holy One, blessed be He, says, "I regard them as though I dwelt among them and they honoured Me."

2. What is the fear due to parents ? One must neither stand in the place appointed for one's father according to his rank, nor in the place reserved for him to pray. One should not sit in the place of one's father's seat in his house. One must neither contradict one's father nor corroborate his words in his presence even by saying, "It is obvious that father is right." To what degree shall parents be feared ? If the son were attired in costly dress and presided over a meeting when his parents came and rent his garments, and struck his head, and spat in his face, he should neither insult them nor feel aggrieved in their presence, nor display anger towards them, but he should remain silent and fear the King who is the King of kings, the Holy One, blessed be He, who had thus decreed. He may, however, seek legal redress for the damage they have caused him.

[1] See Authorised Daily Prayer Book, pp. 294 ff.   [2] See T. B. Kiddushin, 30 b.

179

3. What is the honour due to parents ? To provide them with food and drink, with garments and clothing. He should bring them home and take them out. He should give them with a cheerful countenance, for even if one should feed them with crammed birds but show them an angry face, he incurs thereby Divine punishment. If his father or mother should be asleep, he should not arouse them, even if through their sleep he will lose much profit, but if the father would profit by being aroused, and if he should not be awakened he would be grieved for the loss of the profit, it is a duty to arouse him as that will make him happy. It is also a duty to awaken one's father to call him to go to synagogue or for the performance of any other commandment, as all are equally bound to honour the Omnipresent.

4. If the son were in need of something which his fellow-townsmen could do for him, and he knows that they would gratify his desire for his father's sake, even though he also knows they would do it for his own sake as well, he should not say : " Do this for my sake " but rather let him say : " Do it for the sake of my father," in order that it should redound to his father's honour. If his mother told him to do a certain thing which he did, and his father subsequently asked him, " Who told you to do this ? " If he perceive that by telling him that his mother asked him to do so, his father's anger would be kindled against his mother, he should not tell him, even if he himself thereby incur his father's wrath.

5. A son is bound to stand at his full height in the presence of his father and his mother if they be virtuous, and even if they be wicked and sinners it is proper for him, nevertheless, to honour and to fear them. Naturally it is forbidden to cause them pain. If he saw his father transgressing any of the commandments of the Torah, he should not say to him, " Thou hast transgressed the commands of the Torah," but he should rather say, " Father, is it not written thus and thus in the Torah?" as though asking for information, and not as though he admonished him, the father will thus take the hint without being put to shame. Whoever puts his father or mother to shame, even if only by words or only by a hint, is included among those whom the Almighty has cursed, as it is said, " Cursed be he that setteth light by his father or by his mother " (Deut. xxvii. 16).

6. To honour one's parents is the duty of both man and woman, with the exception of a married woman, who by virtue of her marriage is responsible to her husband. Therefore she is exempt from the duty of honouring her parents. Yet it is incumbent on her to do all she can towards fulfilling that commandment if her husband be not particular with her in this matter.

7. One is forbidden to place a heavy yoke upon his children and to be too exacting with them in matters relating to his honour, so that he should not thereby cause them to stumble. He should rather overlook their shortcomings and forgive them, as a father can allow his son to neglect the acts of honour due to him, and the son may avail himself of this permission.[1] One is forbidden to chastise his son when he has reason to apprehend that the latter will defend himself by opposing him either in speech or action, but he should rebuke him in words. He who beats his grown up son transgresses the commandment, "Thou shalt not put a stumbling-block before the blind" (Lev. xix. 14).

8. It is incumbent upon a man to honour the following persons : his grand-father, his elder brother whether from his father's or mother's side, his father-in-law, his mother-in-law, his step-mother during his father's life-time, his step-father during his mother's life time. It is highly proper to honour his step-mother or step-father, even after the death of his own parents.

9. It is one's duty to honour his parents also after their death, thus if he mentioned their name, either in speech or in writing, he should add "may his (or her) memory be a blessing." He who truly desires to honour his father or mother, should occupy himself with the study of the Torah and with good deeds, for this is a great honour to his parents, of whom people will say : "Happy are the parents who brought up such a son," but if the son go not in the right way his parents bear a reproach on his account, and he disgraces them in the most infamous manner possible. Likewise a father who is compassionate will go in a good upright way for his children to learn from him, and they also are honoured through him. But the offspring of one who perverts uprightness and chooses evil will take after him and will also choose the evil way, and will die in the sins of their fathers, as it is written, "visiting the iniquity of the fathers upon the children" (Ex. xx. 5). There is no cruelty more atrocious than this.

10. One should not hearken unto his father when he tells him to transgress a commandment of the Torah, whether it be a positive or a negative commandment or a Rabbinic injunction. Thus, if his father tell him that he should neither speak to, nor forgive a certain person to whom the son wishes to be reconciled, he should not pay heed to his father's command, as it is forbidden to hate any human being, unless he saw him transgressing a commandment, or if he be one who is notoriously wicked, in which case it is forbidden to associate with him. Likewise, if the son desire to go and study the Torah or to marry, and his father or mother oppose him doing so without giving good and sufficient reasons, then the son is not bound to obey them.

11. A proselyte is forbidden to curse or to despise his non-Jewish father, but he should treat him with some degree of respect.

[1] Lit. ; "his honour is remitted," see T.B. Kiddushin, 32 a.

LAWS CONCERNING THE HONOUR DUE TO ONE'S TEACHER, TO THE AGED, TO A SCHOLAR, AND TO A PRIEST.

1. It is written, "Thou shalt rise up before the hoary head, and honour the face of the old man" (Lev. xix 32). This has been explained by our Sages, of blessed memory, as implying that one is commanded to rise up before the hoary head, i.e., a septuagenarian, even if he be an ignoramus as long as he is not wicked. One should honour an old man, even if he be of any nationality, by speaking politely to him and giving him a hand for support.

2. The honour and reverence due to one's teacher is more obligatory than that due to one's father. It is a great sin to despise or to hate the scholars. It is forbidden to make servile use of a student of Halakhoth (Rabbinic Law). All the above applies only to a scholar who follows the ways of the Torah and Religion, but if he slight the commandments he is like the most worthless fellow in the congregation.

3. When three go together on the way and one of them is a Rabbi, he should walk in the centre whilst the other two should each fall back and walk on each side of him, the elder on his right, and the younger (or the less important person) on his left.

4. It is one of the positive precepts of the Torah to give a Priest the prerogative of being the first called to the reading of the Torah, also to be the first speaker at every public gathering. At a feast he should also be the first to say the benediction over the bread and to say Grace after the meal. In the absence of a Priest, a Levite should have the precedence over an Israelite in all the aforementioned cases.

5. It is forbidden to make servile use of a Priest, it is, however, permitted if he does not stand on his dignity, and the latter may, at any rate, bestow honour upon an Israelite, by giving him the precedence in all things aforementioned.

CONDITIONS TO BE OBSERVED FOR THE FULFILMENT OF EVERY COMMANDMENT.

1. One should be eager and anxious for an opportunity of fulfilling a commandment, he should eagerly desire to observe it with rejoicing and with intense love, and he should exercise the utmost care to do it in all its details; if possible, he should perform it with the congregation, as it is written, "In the multitude of people

is the King's glory " (Prov. xiv. 28). The fulfilment of the precepts requires the intention (of complying with the law), so that one should resolve to discharge his duty with regard to the commandment one is performing, which God has commanded us. He who begins to observe a precept should fulfil it in its entirety. It is better for one to accomplish a precept himself than to have it done through his agent.

2. The zealous hasten to fulfil the precepts, hence, one should rise early to perform a precept which must be accomplished during the day, and likewise one should begin early in the evening to fulfil that precept which is to be observed at night. To perform one precept by transgressing another is invalid.

3. One should not perform two precepts simultaneously lest he will not be able to give the necessary attention to both, therefore, one who is engaged in the performance of one precept is exempt (then) from the fulfilment of another. The precept which comes first to one's hand should be observed at once, and it should not be postponed on account of another precept which he desires to perform, even if he intend to carry out the former precept immediately thereafter. Much more so is it forbidden to neglect one precept for the sake of fulfilling another. One is forbidden to be needlessly dilatory in observing a precept, (intending) to fulfil it later on. All the aforementioned rules are applicable when it is possible to fulfil both precepts, but if only one of them can be fulfilled, then if one be more important, and the other less important, he should rather fulfil the former. If the observance of one of the precepts be of frequent recurrence whilst the other is fulfilled on rare occasions, he should preferably perform the former. If the time appointed for the observance of one of the precepts be passing by, whilst the other has no fixed time for its fulfilment, he should preferably perform the former. One should beware never to perform any precept in a spirit of levity or in a contemptuous manner. He should show more honour to the precepts than to his own personal honour. It is forbidden to derive any material benefit through the fulfilment of a precept during the time set for its observance.

4. It is written : " This is my God and I will glorify Him " (Ex. xv. 2), it is therefore necessary in the performance of every precept to do it so that it becomes glorious and beautiful. Our sages say : " One should spend for the sake of beautifying a precept as much as one-third more of the cost required for its ordinary fulfilment."

LAWS OF CIRCUMCISION.

1. It is a positive precept for a father to circumcise his son or to appoint another Israelite to act as his agent who knows the Laws of Circumcision, and is careful and zealous in the performance of this precept and qualified for performing the act of circumcision. If the father be incompetent to circumcise, and if the operator in attendance refuse to circumcise gratuitously, but only for remuneration, such a person should be censured by the ecclesiastical authorities. The

father should place his son upon the knees of the God-father[1] and hand
the knife to the operator and stand near him during the circumcision
to indicate that the former is his agent.

2. The circumcision shall not be performed until sunrise of the
eighth day after his birth, that entire day being the proper time for its
performance, but the zealous hasten to fulfil the precepts, wherefore
the circumcision is to be performed forthwith in the morning. The
circumcision, which (for certain reasons) is not performed at the appointed time (on the eighth day), can only be performed in the daytime.

3. The operator before performing the circumcision should stand
and say the benediction א״י ק ב״ו על המילה and he should not circumcise
before he had concluded the benediction, unlike the operators who,
eager to display their skill, perform the circumcision immediately they
begin the benediction, whereby they betray their ignorance. The
father of the child whilst standing should say, in the interval between
the circumcision of the foreskin and its uncovering, the benediction:
א״ק ב״ו להכניסו בבריתו של אברהם אבינו, those present should respond אמן
כשם שנכנס לברית כן יכנס לתורה ולחופה ולמעשים טובים. If the father be not
present at the circumcision, or know not how to say the benediction,
the God-father, who may remain seated, can say the benediction
להכניסו, וכו'.

4. One should be particular in his choice of an operator and a
God-father who should be the best and most righteous men possible to
select. It is customary for a father not to select as God-father one
who had already officiated as such at the circumcision of another of his
sons, unless this son had died. One who gave his word to an operator
that he should circumcise his son, is forbidden to retract his word and
bestow the honour upon another. If the one, to whom the assurance
was given, had in the meantime left the city, whereupon the father,
thinking that he would not be in attendance at the time of the circumcision, appointed another, and in the meantime the former returned,
then the former should perform the circumcision.

5. It is customary for those present at the circumcision to remain
standing with the exception of the God-father who holds the child,
and therefore he remains seated. It is also customary to prepare a
seat for Elijah, who is called the "Angel of the covenant,"[2] and when
he places the child upon the seat, he should say plainly זה הכסא של
אליהו. The father of the child and those present should say previous
to the performance of the circumcision, אשרי תבחר ותקרב, ישכון חצריך (Ps.
lxv. 4). The ceremony should be performed, if possible, in the
presence of ten adult male Israelites, but where that is impossible the
circumcision may be performed when less than ten are present.

6. After the circumcision is accomplished, a benediction should
be said over a cup of wine; if the child's parents be alive the benediction should be said as follows: או״א קים את הילד הזה לאביו ולאמו, if the

father were dead, the mother alone is mentioned (לאמו) and the reference to the father (לאביו) omitted. If the mother were dead, the father alone is mentioned and the reference to the mother is omitted, and if both were dead, the following should be said : קים את הילד הזה ויקרא וכו'. If the child be illegitimate, although all the benedictions said at the circumcision of a lawfully born Israelite are also said at his circumcision, yet the following benediction should be omitted : קים את הילד הזה, וכו', as well as the following response : כשם שנכנס לברית וכו', only אמן should be responded, and it should be publicly announced at the circumcision that the child is illegitimate.

7. If a child were born circumcised and requires only to undergo the operation causing a few drops of the " blood of the covenant " to flow, no benediction should be said but only the following : או"א קים וכו'. If two children have to be circumcised, even if they be twins, yet they should be brought one after another to the place where the circumcision is to take place and all the benedictions should be said for each child separately, and the one born first should be the first to enter into the covenant.

8. The one who says the benediction or the God-father should drink at least a mouthful of the cup of benediction, but if the circumcision take place on a fast day, even on the 9th of Ab, the cup of benediction may be drunk by the children, but on the Day of Atonement children should not be given to drink thereof, but it should be given to " the tender infant who is circumcised " in addition to that which is given to him when saying בדמיך וכו' (Ezek. xvi. 6).[1]

9. At the conclusion of the circumcision עלינו לשבח is said, if the circumcision took place in the Synagogue the Tephillin should not be taken off until after the circumcision, as they are both signs (of acknowledgment of the sovereignty of God). It is customary to prepare a banquet on the day of circumcision[2], and one who is invited is forbidden to refuse to attend, when the people who are present are respectable. He who can afford to prepare a proper banquet, but fulfils the duty in a niggardly manner by merely providing cakes, is acting wrongly and deserves censure.

10. It is the duty of the operator to thoroughly examine the infant previous to the circumcision to ascertain if he be ailing, as the fulfilment of all precepts must be postponed if there be danger to life. Moreover the circumcision can be performed later than the time appointed by the Law, but the soul of an Israelite once sacrificed cannot be restored. An infant who had been ailing but became convalescent, should not be circumcised before the doctor has been consulted as to when it is proper to perform the circumcision. Immediately the time for the child's circumcision has arrived, whether it be the appointed time or not, it is forbidden to delay the performance of this precept for any reason, e.g., to gain time for providing for the circumcision-feast, or the like. Therefore those who postpone the circumcision to celebrate it on Sunday are destined to render an account for their deeds.

[1] *Ibid.*   [2] *Ibid.*

LAWS AND CUSTOMS OF ISRAEL

11. If a woman lost two sons presumably from the effects of circumcision, as it was apparent that their constitutions were so weak that the circumcision had caused their exhaustion, her third son should not be circumcised until he had grown up and his constitution became strong. Likewise if the sons of two sisters had both died from the effects of circumcision, they should not circumcise the sons of the other sisters until they are grown up and have a strong constitution.

12. An infant born in the twilight or immediately preceding it, should not be circumcised before the ecclesiastical authorities have been consulted.

13. An infant who had died previous to his circumcision, should be circumcised at the grave with a flint-stone or a reed, so that he be not buried with the foreskin attached but no benediction should be said on this occasion. But a name should be given to perpetuate his memory. If through forgetfulness he was buried uncircumcised and they became aware thereof at a time when it would not be apprehended that the body had decomposed, his grave must be opened and he must be circumcised, if, however, it be surmised that decomposition had already set in, the grave should not be opened.

14. The one who causes the infant to enter into the covenant should make an effort to be called to the Torah upon the day of the circumcision, likewise the God-father and the operator should also be called to the Torah if possible.

Laws Concerning the Redemption of the First-Born.

1. It is a positive precept devolving upon every Israelite to redeem his son, who is the mother's first-born, from the Priest by giving him five Sela'im or their equivalent in silver or gold, or any other article, the value of which should equal two and two-thirds ounces of refined silver,[1] the father as well as the priest being fully agreed upon the latter's absolute right and title to that money as the price of his son's redemption, and if the priest should subsequently return that money or property as a gift to the father, the latter is permitted to accept it.

2. The first-born should not be redeemed before the 31st day after his birth, but if that day fall upon a Sabbath or Holyday, or if it be impossible for him to redeem his son on the 31st day through some hindrance, he is permitted to postpone the redemption to the day following.

3. If he had promised a certain friend that he should officiate at the redemption ceremony, he is forbidden to retract, nevertheless, if he had changed his mind and another priest had redeemed his son, the redemption is valid.

[1] Fifteen shillings.

LAWS AND CUSTOMS OF ISRAEL

4. A father who is not with his child may, nevertheless wherever he may be, redeem his son through a priest by saying to the latter, "I have a first-born son to redeem," whereupon the priest inquires, "Which wouldst thou rather, etc." The first-born of his mother, who became aware that he had not been redeemed, is obliged to have himself redeemed as soon as he is grown up, at which time he should say the benediction אקב"ו על פדיון הבן also שהחינו.

5. Priests and Levites are exempt from the redemption of their first-born sons. Even the daughter of a priest or Levite married to an Israelite is also exempt from the redemption of the first-born son.

6. In the case of a woman who had miscarried and subsequently gave birth to a healthy son, the ecclesiastical authorities should be consulted (regarding his redemption).

7. It is customary to hold a feast in honour of the redemption of the first-born son, and he who performs the commands of his Creator with joyfulness and gladness of heart on account of the abundance of all things is blessed by the Almighty, as it is written "and they shall put my name upon the children of Israel, and I will bless them" (Num. vi. 27).

LAWS CONCERNING FORBIDDEN IMAGES.

1. It is forbidden to draw pictures,[1] representing the faces of an ox, a man, a lion, and an eagle in one group. It is also forbidden to draw pictures of the sun, moon, and the stars, even if the figures be not in relief. It is likewise forbidden to draw them for the sake of a heathen. If the figures are not in relief one is permitted to keep them in the house. One should not, however, ask a non-Jew to draw them for him, for whatever an Israelite is forbidden to make, it is likewise forbidden to ask a heathen to make the same.

2. It is forbidden to make the graven image of a man or to make in relief even the mere outlines of a man's face, moreover one is forbidden to keep it in the house, unless he had slightly disfigured it. The foregoing prohibition applies only to the image of a full face, having the complete features of two eyes and a nose, but if the image be incomplete, it is not forbidden. One is forbidden to gaze at the graven image of a person as by doing so he transgresses the precept, "Turn ye not unto idols" (Lev. xix. 4). One is, however, permitted to gaze at the images on coins, since we are accustomed to see them continually. (See Tosaphoth to 'Abodah Zarah 50a).

3. One should not make a house after the pattern of the Temple, commensurate with its height, length and breadth, nor a gallery similar to the porch (of the Temple), nor a court similar to the court of the Temple, nor a table similar to the table which stood in the

[1] For idolatrous purposes, see Ex. xx. 23 and cf. Ezek. i. 10.

187

Temple, nor a lampstand similar to that which stood in the Temple, but he should make it of five or six or eight branches, and not of seven branches, even if he make it of any metal other than gold, and even if he make it without bowls, knops and flowers, and even if it be not eighteen handbreadths high, inasmuch as all of the foregoing were not indispensable adjuncts to the lampstand of the Temple. The lampstands which are made for the Synagogue must not be made with seven branches; it is forbidden even to make them with six branches in a circle and one in the centre.

Laws Concerning Fruit which is Counted as Uncircumcision.

1. The enjoyment of the fruit, seeds and skins of all kinds of trees (planted) for food, whether they belong to a Jew or to a heathen, even if they grow in pots without an orifice, during the first three years from the time they were planted, is entirely forbidden. These three years are not reckoned in full from one date to the other, but if one had planted the seed before the 16th day of Ab, inasmuch as there are yet 44 days to ראש השנה (New Year) of which 14 days are the period in which the plant takes root, and the 30 days that remain of that year are counted as a full year, so that two years are subsequently counted from תשרי. If, however, one planted at any time on or after the 16th day of Ab that (part of the) year is not counted at all, and he must count three years from Tishri.

2. One who had planted a seed, or branch, or who had transplanted a tree, is obliged to count the fruit of all these as uncircumcision. If one grafted a branch upon a different tree, likewise one who had bent the branch of a tree and had inserted it in a hollow in the earth (which he had prepared for it) in such a manner that the middle of the branch is buried in the ground while its end protrudes from the opposite side, even if he had severed it from the trunk of the tree, the laws concerning fruits counted as uncircumcision are not applicable thereto in countries apart from the Holy Land.

3. A tree which was cut down until its stump remained, being a handbreadth from the ground in height, if that stump should subsequently grow, one is not obliged to count its fruit as uncircumcision, but if the stump were less than a handbreadth high, he is obliged to count whatever grows subsequently as uncircumcision, and its years should be counted from the time the tree was cut down. A tree which was uprooted and had some of its roots left in the ground, no matter how few, if there be enough left to sustain their life without requiring additional earth, their produce is exempt from being counted as uncircumcision.

Laws Forbidding the Grafting of Diverse Kinds.

1. It is forbidden to graft[1] a tree of one kind upon that of another kind, e.g., to graft the branch of an apple-tree upon an Ethrog-tree or vice-versa, or even if the species be similar, such as the branch of an (ordinary) apple-tree upon an apple-tree that grows in the woods or the like, inasmuch as they are two different kinds it is forbidden to graft them. An Israelite must not allow a heathen to graft for him two diverse kinds of trees. It is forbidden to preserve a tree that is grafted with a diverse kind, but it is permitted to enjoy the fruit thereof. It is permitted to transplant the branch of a tree grafted with a diverse kind.

2. The mingled seeds of the vineyard and the mingled seeds of grain are not forbidden in countries outside the Holy Land, unless one had sown two kinds of grain or two kinds of vegetables together with the seed of the vineyard.

Laws Concerning Diverse Kinds of Cattle.

1. It is forbidden to let one's cattle gender with a diverse kind. This also applies to beast and fowl, as it is forbidden even to cause them to gender together.

2. It is forbidden to have work done by animals of diverse kinds, e.g., to plough with them or to let them draw a vehicle. It is forbidden even to lead them by one's voice by calling to them when they are harnessed together. Therefore it is forbidden for an Israelite to walk at the side of the cart of a heathen drawn by heterogeneous animals and having the load of the Israelite therein, as it may be feared that the Israelite will cry after them to hasten their pace, and that is forbidden on account of leading heterogeneous animals.

3. One is forbidden to sit in a vehicle drawn by heterogeneous animals even if he should not drive them. One should not attach to a vehicle drawn by beasts of one kind, a beast of a diverse kind, neither at the side of the vehicle, nor behind it. One is forbidden to tie together two heterogeneous animals, even for the purpose of guarding them so that they should not run away.

4. A mule is bred by a horse and an ass, and consists of two species. One species is bred by a horse and a she ass, and the other by a mare and an ass. They are considered as heterogeneous beasts, therefore one who wishes to tie two mules together should first examine their characteristic features, such as the ear, tail and voice, if there be a

[1] See Lev. xix. 19; and Deut. xxii. 9.

LAWS AND CUSTOMS OF ISRAEL

similarity in these, it is obvious that the female parent of both belongs to the same species, and it is permissible to tie them together. Some authorities are of the opinion that the use of even one mule as being "of a diverse kind," having been bred by heterogeneous species, is forbidden for the purpose of doing any work with it or for riding thereon.[1]

Laws Concerning Garments made of Linen and Wool.

1. It is forbidden to mix the wool of lambs and goats with linen because of the precept forbidding (the mixture of) "two things of diverse kinds."[2] Whether the woollen garment were sewn to the linen garment, even if it were sewn with silk thread or hemp thread or whether the woollen garment were sewn with linen thread or vice-versa, or whether linen thread were tied to woollen thread or braided together, all of the above are forbidden because of the precept forbidding "Kilayim." If one fastened two pieces (of material) with only one stitch and tied it or fastened the same with two stitches without tying them, both cases are considered to be connected (or woven) as far as Kilayim is concerned, therefore it is forbidden to connect a woollen and a linen garment even with a needle without thread.

2. It is permitted to sew garments made of lambs' skins with linen thread and there is no occasion to apprehend the possible connection of the woollen hairs with the linen thread, as these woollen hairs, not being threads, are of no account and are ignored.

3. Even if ten mattresses lie one upon another and the bottom one be a mixture of wool and linen (i.e. Kilayim) one is forbidden to sit on the top mattress. If a garment contain Kilayim at one end, it is forbidden to cover one's self with the other end, even if the former be resting upon the ground.

4. One who is sewing for a heathen, a garment made of Kilayim may sew it in the regular way, even if the garment rest upon his knees. he should not, however, intentionally derive pleasure from the garment being upon his knees. Likewise sellers of clothes who carry the clothing upon their shoulders in order to sell them, are permitted to do so, they should not, however, intentionally cover themselves therewith in order to protect themselves from the cold or rain.

5. Handkerchiefs, towels, table-cloths, and the like, also the covering of the reading desk in the Synagogue upon which the scroll of the Torah is read, if they contain Kilayim their use is forbidden, it is also forbidden to make a curtain of Kilayim but the curtain before the Holy Ark may be made thereof.

[1] See Tosephta Kilayim, v. 6. [2] See Lev. loc. cit. and Deut. xxii. 11.

190

13

LAWS AND CUSTOMS OF ISRAEL

The Prohibition of Tattooing and Making Bald for the Dead.

1. It is written in the Torah : "Ye shall not print any marks upon you " (Lev. xix. 28). What is the meaning of כתובת קעקע ? A mark which is etched in and submerged in the skin so that it can never be erased. One who scratches his skin and inserts in the incision stibium or ink or any other colouring matter which leaves a mark, likewise one who first dyes his skin and then scratches it there, transgresses a negative precept. Nevertheless it is permitted to put ashes and other things upon a wound for medical purposes even if a mark remain ; for this would also ensue as a result of the wound and this would show that it was not done for the sake of tattooing.

2. It is written : " Ye shall not make any cuttings in your flesh for the dead " (*ibid.*) and it is also written : " Ye shall not cut yourselves, nor make any baldness between your eyes for the dead " (Deut. xiv. 1). Scraping and incision are alike prohibited whether on account of the dead or not. Even to smite one's flesh with the hand so that blood flows is prohibited and any other form of self-mutiliation is also prohibited.

2. Baldness due to the plucking out of the hair of the head on account of the dead, even (the plucking out of) a single hair, is prohibited. Women likewise are to be cautioned against transgressing the precept, " Ye shall not make any baldness " (*ibid.*) and much more so with regard to, " Ye shall not make any cuttings " (Lev. xix. 28).

Laws Forbidding the Shaving of the Hair of the Temples and the Beard.

1. It is forbidden to shave off the hair of the temples on both sides of the head at their juncture with the hairs upon both cheeks and before the ears, or to cut the same even with scissors like a razor very close to the skin so that no hairs remain. Therefore if it be necessary to shave off the " corners " for the sake of health (e.g. in the case of an operation) one must take care not to shave them off quite close to the skin. The length of the hair of the temples is estimated to be from the hair of the forehead as far as the hair below the ear where it is divided by the chin.

2. The Torah has forbidden the shaving of the " corners " of the beard with a razor only. There are five " corners " of the beard and one's constitution increases with their growth, therefore, one who fears God should not use a razor on any part of his beard, even on his upper lip or under the chin. There is no difference (in the law) between a razor and a sharp stone which cuts the hair, e.g., pumice-

stone, they are both forbidden. All who remove their beard by means of a lapideous salve should be careful not to scrape off the salve with a knife which might cut the hair but they should use instead a piece of wood.

PROHIBITION OF A MALE PUTTING ON A WOMAN'S GARMENT.[1]

1. A man is forbidden to put on even a single garment of a woman even though he would be recognised as a male by his other garments. A woman is likewise forbidden to put on a single garment of a man. Not only are the garments forbidden, but also the ornaments and the various toilet utensils used by women for adorning themselves in that locality are forbidden to be used by a man in a similar manner and for a similar purpose. Likewise what is specifically intended for men must not be used by a woman.

LAWS CONCERNING ONE WHO IS SICK, THE DOCTOR, AND REMEDIES.

1. Our Sages of blessed memory have said, "One should always entreat God to preserve him from sickness. If he fall sick, he is told to produce his meritorious deeds and obtain relief." They have also said, "If he have headache, it should seem to him as if he were put in chains. If he became so ill that he had to be in bed, it should seem to him as if he were brought up to a scaffold to be punished. One who ascends the scaffold, if he have advocates to plead his cause may be saved, but if he have none he cannot escape." What do we mean by the advocates of a man ? Repentance and good deeds. Even if nine hundred and ninety-nine (accusers) show up his faults, and one (advocate) shows his merits, he is saved, as it is said : "If there be with him a messenger, an interpreter, one among a thousand, to show unto man his uprightness ; then He is gracious unto him, and saith, Deliver him from going down to the pit, . . ." (Job xxxiii. 23, 24).[2]

2. Rabbi Phineas, the son of Chama, preached saying : "Whoever has anyone sick in his house should go to a wise man and ask him to plead for mercy on his behalf, as it is said : "The wrath of a King is as messengers of death, but a wise man will pacify it" (Prov. xvi. 14). It is customary to give alms to the poor on behalf of the sick person for "Repentance, Prayer, and Charity avert the evil decree." It is also customary to bless the sick person in the Synagogue, and if he be

---

[1] See Deut. xxii. 5.   [2] The rest of the context up to verse 30 should be read.

dangerously ill, he is blessed even on a Sabbath and a Holyday. At times the name of the sick person is changed, as this may avert the judgment decreed against him.

3. The Torah has granted the doctor the privilege of healing, as it is said "and he shall cause him to be thoroughly healed" (Ex. xxi. 19). Therefore the sick person should not rely upon a miracle, but he is in duty bound to act according to the custom of the world and call in a doctor to heal him. He who avoids calling in the doctor is guilty of two evils : in the first instance of transgressing the rule forbidding one who is in danger to rely upon a miracle, the other evil is that he manifests presumption and pride in depending upon his righteousness to cause him to be healed in a miraculous manner. One should call in the most competent doctor and in spite of this, his heart should hope for the help of heaven and he should plead for the mercy of the Faithful Healer, blessed be His name, and his heart should trust in God only.

4. It is a religious duty for the competent doctor to heal. This duty is included in the general rule of saving a life in danger, and if he avoid doing so he is guilty of bloodshed, even if the sick person have another doctor : for the sick person does not enjoy the merit of being cured by every body, perchance he is the one appointed by Heaven to effect the cure. One should not, however, practice medicine unless he be competent to do so, and if there be nobody there more competent than he, otherwise he is guilty of bloodshed. One who has medicines, and his neighbour is sick and requires them, is forbidden to advance their price above their proper value.

5. One who is not seriously ill, whose cure might be effected by means of an article permitted to be used even if there be some delay in obtaining the same, should not be permitted to use a forbidden article, but if he especially require an article whereof it is forbidden to eat in the way in which the article is usually eaten, he is forbidden to eat thereof, because he is not seriously ill. He is, however, permitted to partake of it in such a manner so that it does not give him pleasure, for instance by mingling a bitter substance therewith, or to make a plaster thereof, or the like, even if it be an article whereof enjoyment is forbidden, with the exception of the mixed seeds (Kilayim) in the vineyard, and meat cooked in milk, the use of which is forbidden even in such a manner so as not to give him pleasure, so long as the illness is not serious. All the foregoing applies only when the article is forbidden by the Torah, but if the article be forbidden by the laws of the Rabbis, one may cure himself therewith, also a person who is not dangerously ill is permitted to partake thereof, even if taken in a manner so that pleasure is derived therefrom, but he should not eat or drink that which is forbidden.

6. One who is seriously ill may use for his cure any article that is forbidden, as nothing (forbidden by ritual law) must be insisted upon

LAWS AND CUSTOMS OF ISRAEL

in a case of saving a life in danger with the exception of idolatry, immorality and murder, concerning which one must give up his life rather than transgress any of them, consequently one should not cure himself by transgressing any of these three sins.[1]

7. A doctor may practise in the case of a woman, even a married woman, inasmuch as he does not do so in a sensual and an immoral spirit, but he is merely following his profession. In the case of his wife during menstruation, if she be not seriously ill and if there be another doctor available, who is as competent as he is, he must avoid attending her case.

LAWS CONCERNING VISITING THE SICK.

1. It is a religious duty to visit the sick. Relatives and friends should visit immediately, but strangers should not call until three days (of the illness) have elapsed, in order not to spoil his chance of recovery by casting upon him the designation of an invalid. If, however, one became suddenly seriously ill, even strangers should visit him immediately, and even a great man should visit a less important person than he is, and visit him even many times a day. He who visits the sick frequently is praiseworthy, but his calls must not trouble the invalid.

2. The essential feature in the religious duty of visiting the sick is to pay attention to the needs of the invalid, to see what is necessary to be done for his benefit, and to give him the pleasure of one's company, also to consider his condition and to pray for mercy on his behalf. If one visited a sick person and did not pray for mercy for him, he did not do his religious duty, therefore one should not visit a sick person during the first three hours of the day, since the sickness then assumes a milder form, the visitor will not be sufficiently impressed to pray for mercy for the sick person, nor should one visit him during the three closing hours of the day, as the sickness then takes a turn for the worse, and the visitor will despair of his recovery and will not pray for mercy on his behalf.

3. One should not visit an enemy in his sickness, nor comfort him when mourning, that the latter may not think that he is rejoicing on account of his misfortune, and that he came only to vex him. He is, however permitted to follow the dead to the grave, as that is the end of man. In the foregoing one must consider what sort of men the enemies are and what is the nature of the enmity that exists between them. The sick person should not rise up even in the presence of a great sage, but should he desire to do so, he should not be told to sit down or to lie down.

4. If the sick person lie upon the ground, the visitor should not sit upon a chair or a bench higher than the former, if, however, the sick person be in bed, the visitor is permitted to sit on a chair or bench.

[1] See T. B. Synhedrin 57b.

194

LAWS AND CUSTOMS OF ISRAEL

5. One who prays for the sick may say his prayers in any language he desires in his presence, if, however, he pray in the absence of the sick person, he should do so in Hebrew, and include him amongst all the sick of Israel, for by thus including him with the others, his prayer will be more readily heard for the sake of the many. The visitor should say to the sick person, המקום ירחם עליך בתוך כל חולי ישראל, and on Sabbath he should add שבת היא מלזעוק ורפואה קרובה לבוא, ורחמיו מרובים, ושבתו בשלום.

6. All who visit the sick person should speak to him with judgment and tact, they should speak in such a manner so as neither to revive him (with false hopes) nor to depress him (by words of despair), but they should tell him to concern himself with his affairs, indicating that if he had granted a loan to others, or had deposited anything with others or others with him (he should mention the fact). The sick person should not fear on this account that he will die.

7. One should visit neither a person who is suffering from abdomen troubles so as not to put him to shame, nor one who is troubled with his eyes, nor one who has headache, nor any person who is very ill and to whom conversation is difficult ; one should not visit any of the foregoing, but should call at the door of the house to make inquiries regarding his condition, and to ascertain if he be in need of anything ; he should also pay heed to his distress and pray for mercy on his behalf.

8. One who can discharge two religious duties, namely, visiting the sick and comforting the mourners, and it is possible for him to fulfil both, he should first visit the sick in order that he may pray for mercy on his behalf. But if he find it impossible to fulfil both duties he should rather fulfil that of comforting the mourners, as this is an act of loving service towards the living and the dead.

9. The spirit of the Sages takes no delight in one who bequeathes his property to strangers and disinherits his natural heirs, although the latter do not act properly towards him. Nevertheless the strangers are entitled to receive all that was bequeathed to them. The pious will refuse to witness a will in which the natural heirs are disinherited, even in the case of a son who does not act properly. If one desire to consecrate some of his possessions to religious purposes, he should consult the ecclesiastical authorities.

10. If one have young children, or both young and grown up children, or if his wife be pregnant, he should appoint a guardian to act on behalf of the little children until they grow up. A sick person who desires to make a transfer of his property by the symbolical ceremony of acquiring possession (קבלת קנין) in order to confirm his will, may do so even on the Sabbath ; likewise if he desire to send for his relatives, he may hire a heathen on the Sabbath and send him.

11. If a member of the family of the invalid had died he should **not be** informed thereof that it may not worry him, and even if he **became** aware thereof he should not be told to rend his garment, lest **it increase** his distress. One should neither weep nor mourn in the presence of the sick person, whether the dead be a member of the sick person's family or a stranger, lest he fear that he also will die. All who comfort mourners in the presence of the sick person should be compelled to remain silent.

12. The great exponents of the Law have written, that it is proper to institute in any city whenever one is sick the custom for the Treasurer of the Holy Association (חברה קדישה) or other people to visit him on the third day of his illness and to say to him : "Thou art aware that it is customary to remind all sick people to write their wills as they desire, therefore tell us and we will write your will, mentioning what you owe and what others owe you." He is furthermore told to confess his sins, for whosoever confesses, his sins are forgiven. This course is to be followed only where this is the usual custom familiar to all, where, however, this custom does not obtain, the sick person should not be spoken to in that manner, lest he become anxious that he is about to die, for it is characteristic of the people generally to be very nervous when told to confess. Nevertheless if the visitors perceive that he is dying they should tactfully turn the conversation so that they are led to tell him to confess and they should add : "Do not fear that evil will ensue, for many have confessed and did not die. On the contrary, as a reward for having confessed, thy life will be prolonged. Moreover all who confess have a share in the world to come." If he be unable to confess verbally, he should make a mental confession, and if he know not how to confess he should be told to say יהי רצון שתהא מיתתי כפרה על כל עונותי ("May my death atone for all my sins.") These words should be spoken neither in the presence of ignorant people nor before women and children for it may cause them to cry and thus make the sick person broken hearted but they should be excluded from the room. The sick person should also be reminded to ask the pardon of all against whom he had sinned, whether in money or by words.

13. A brief form of confession is as follows : "I acknowledge unto Thee, O Lord, my God and the God of my fathers, that my healing and my dying are in Thy hands. May it be Thy will to heal me with a perfect healing, and if I should die, may my death be an atonement for all the sins, iniquities and transgressions which I have sinned and perversely committed and transgressed before Thee, and grant my portion in Paradise and cause me to merit the life of the world to come, which it stored up for the righteous." If he desire to prolong the confession in a similar manner to the confession on the Day of Atonement, he is permitted to do so.

Laws Concerning One Who is Dying.

1. One who is dying is to be considered as a living being[1] in all

[1] See Semachoth 1.

matters, and it is forbidden to touch him (for fear of accelerating the end) for anyone who touches him is like one who sheds blood. With what is this comparable ? With the lamp's flickering flame, which becomes extinguished as soon as a person touches it. Likewise if he be a long time in a dying condition, and it causes great distress to himself and his relatives, it is, nevertheless, forbidden to hasten his end either by natural means or otherwise, still if there be a cause that prevents the flight of the soul, such as the noise of knocking, it is permitted to remove that cause, inasmuch as that is not a direct deed which hastens the end, but the mere removal of an obstacle whereby no one touches the dying person. Although it is forbidden to touch a dying person, nevertheless if the house caught fire, he should not be allowed to remain there, but should be carried out of the house, in which case he takes precedence over the preservation of sacred books.

2. From the moment that one is in the grip of death, it is forbidden to leave him, in order that his soul may not leave him while he is all alone. It is a religious duty to stand near the person at the time his soul is about to depart from him. It is indeed proper to gather ten persons (male adults) who should be present at the departure of the soul, these should not engage in frivolous conversation, but they should occupy themselves in words of the Torah and Psalms, also in prayers and supplications, as arranged in the book called מעבר יבק. It is customary to kindle lamps (or candles) in the presence of the dying. Those present should be careful to see that no part of his body (usually covered) projects out of the bed, they should therefore place chairs at the side of the bed in order that he should be unable to stretch a hand or foot outside thereof, nevertheless, if this were not done and he did project one of his limbs, it is forbidden to touch him for the purpose of placing the same back in the bed.

3. One should not prepare anything necessary for the dead before the soul has departed, such as bringing a coffin or shrouds, or digging a grave. It is forbidden to dig a grave and let it remain open until the following day. One should neither rend the garments nor lament before the soul has departed.

4. After the soul had departed those present should wait a few minutes and then place a feather near his nostrils, if it should not move it is a clear indication of his death, whereupon the windows of that house should be opened, and the mourners should say צדוק הדין and when the benediction ברוך דין האמת is about to be said by them, they add the Divine Name and title of King, they should then rend their garments in the manner described in the following section. All who are present during the departure of the soul are required to rend their garments. With what is death comparable ? With the burning of a Scroll of the Torah, as there is none so worthless in Israel who neither possessed some degree of knowledge, nor had fulfilled some of its commandments. The garments must be rent also at the death of a child who had learned the Bible, likewise at the death of a woman. Even if

the dead person had sometimes committed a transgression when misled by passion, still the garment must be rent for him, but if he were an habitual sinner, even if he only sinned through passion, he is yet reckoned among those who depart from the ways of the congregation, at whose death the garment should not be rent. The rending of the garments of those who are required to do so merely because they were present during the departure of the soul, but who are not mourners, may be discharged by rending the garment slightly, even at its side or hem.

5. The eyes of the dead person should be closed. If one had left sons it is the duty of one of the sons to do this, and if there be a first born son he should do it. In bearing the dead person from his bed in order to place him on the ground, care should be taken to keep him covered, as the laws of decency, which must not be infringed by the living, apply also to the dead.

6. It is customary to pour out all water contained in vessels in the vicinity of the dead, which means, the three houses including the one in which the dead lies; even if a child had died within thirty days of its birth, and even if a heathen had died within one's court, one must be careful to pour out the water. If an Israelite died on a Sabbath, the water must be poured out at the termination of Sabbath.

7. One who watches the dead, even if there be no kinship between them, is exempt from the reading of the Shema' and the Shemoneh 'Esreh and from the observance of all the precepts of the Torah. If, however, there be two watchers, one watches while the other reads the Shema' and recites his prayers. It is forbidden to pronounce any benediction in the room where the dead is lying.

LAWS CONCERNING THE RENDING OF GARMENTS FOR THE DEAD.

1. One who had lost a relative for whom he is required to mourn, e.g., his father, mother, also his son, daughter, brother or sister, being older than thirty days, for if the death occur on the 30th day the mourning need not be observed; it is immaterial whether the relationship be on the fathers's or the mother's side. even if they be disqualified by birth, but are not the issue of a non-Jewess and even if his sister had been married. and the husband mourns for his wife or the wife for her husband, all the aforementioned mourners are required whilst standing to rend their garments for their dead. If they were rent whilst sitting they must be rent again when standing. If possible one must rend his garments before the coffin is closed, when one's sorrow is still intense. For the dead enumerated above the relative must rend his garment near his neck in the front thereof. It must be rent lengthwise and not crosswise, also in the cloth of the garment and not at its seam.

2. The mode of rending the garments for one's father or mother differs in many respects from the mode obtaining for other relatives. For the latter it is sufficient to rend the external garment only a hand-breadth, and it must not be rent more than that, in order not to transgress the precept "Thou shalt not destroy" (Deut. xx. 19) but for a father or mother one must rend all one's garments opposite one's heart, with the exception of his shirt, and one need not rend the upper garment that one wears only occasionally, i.e. the overcoat. If one did not rend all the garments that he is required to rend, he did not fulfil his religious obligation. A woman should first rend her undergarment privately in accordance with the dictates of modesty, and place the torn part on one side, she should then rend her external garment, so as not to expose herself, for even if she were covered by her underlinen it would still be a breach of modesty to expose herself even thus. It is customary to rend the right side of the garment for all relatives other than one's father or mother, for whom the left side of the garment must be rent, nevertheless, if this were overlooked, it does not invalidate the fulfilment of the duty. For all other relatives one may rend his garment privately, but for one's father and mother they must be rent publicly.

3. For all relatives one may either rend his garment with his hand or with an instrument, but for one's father or mother it is with the hand only that one must rend it. It is customary for one of the brotherhood (חברה קדישה) to cut the garment slightly with a knife, whereupon the mourner takes hold of the garment where it was cut and rends it, those present must see to it that he makes the rent lengthwise and not crosswise. If he had not yet recited the benediction בא"י אמ"ה דין האמת ("Blessed . . . the true Judge") he should say it whilst rending his garment.

4. In the seven days of mourning for all relatives, one who changes his garments need not rend those he is putting on, if, however one who mourns for a father or mother, change his garments on a week-day during the seven days, he must rend them. But in honour of the Sabbath one should change one's garments, and not wear torn garments on the Sabbath day, if he have no other garments to change, he should hide the rent part of the garment. Changing one's garments for the Sabbath in this connection means putting on other garments which one wears on the week-days, and not such as are worn on the Sabbath.

5. Garments rent for all relatives should not be repaired at all by connecting the torn parts until after thirty days, after which period it is permitted to sew the torn parts together in a proper manner, but one should not connect the torn parts of garments rent for one's father or mother until after thirty days and one should never sew them together properly, (i.e. in such a manner that the seam should not be visible). One is forbidden, should he desire to do so, to mend the

torn part with another piece of cloth, but a woman out of modesty is permitted immediately to connect the edges of the torn parts. All the rent garments which one is forbidden to sew together, should not be mended even by one to whom they were sold. It is therefore necessary for the one who sells them, to inform the buyer thereof. If one sold them without giving this information with full particulars, then the one who bought them, not knowing for whom they had been rent, is forbidden ever to sew them, for perchance they were rent for a father or mother. It is forbidden to sell such a garment to a heathen. One is forbidden to rend a garment that he had borrowed unconditionally, as that is equal to robbery, and if he rend that garment, he did not fulfil his duty.

6. For all relatives, if one did not hear of their death until after thirty days, he need not rend his garments, but for a father or mother one must rend the garment he is wearing at the time when he hears of their death. He need not, however, rend the garment which he may change thereafter.

7. The intervention of a Holyday cancels the customs obligatory during the (first) thirty days (of mourning), also the rule concerning the rending of garments. If, therefore, after the death of any relative a Holyday occurred during the thirty days, one may sew the garment together completely on the eve of the Holyday after the afternoon service, and after the death of a father or mother one may then connect the edges of the rent.

8. If one had rent his garment for a dead relative and another death had occurred with the first seven days of mourning, he should either rend his garment anew, beginning at a distance of three fingers from the first rent, and rending it the length of a hand-breadth, or he should rend the original rent another hand-breadth, but if the second death occurred after the seven days, so long as he is wearing the rent garment, he may tear it asunder a little more and his duty is fulfilled. If, however, one had rent his garment for any other relative and his father or mother died thereafter, he must leave a space of three fingers' breadth from the first rent, and he must rend his garment anew in accordance with the rule, even if the death of his parent took place after the seven days of the first mourning, as the loss of a parent is not considered merely as an additional sorrow. The same law applies in the case of one who had first lost his father and then his mother, or vice versa, when he is required to rend his garments anew.

9. One whose father and mother had both died at the same time, or one who had simultaneously heard of the death of both, or of the death of two other relatives, should rend his garments once for his double loss. But for his father or mother and another relative (under like circumstances) he should first rend his garments for his father or mother, then leave a space of three fingers' breadth, and rend his garment the length of a hand-breadth for the other relative.

10. If a sick person had lost a relative, and he is unable to rend his garment owing to the serious nature of his sickness, but his mind is clear (so as to realize his loss), he is afterwards (when he has recovered) exempt from rending his garment, unless his recovery took place within the seven days of mourning, when it is natural for his grief to be intense. If, however, he could not rend his garments because his mind was not clear, he should rend his garments as soon as he regains his mental composure, for it is only when he realizes his loss that his sorrow is intense, he is therefore required to rend his garments for relatives if it be within the first thirty days of mourning, but for his father or mother there is no time limit.

11. If a child, under the age when he has to be trained in the precepts, had lost a relative, his garment should be slightly rent for him to manifest his grief and to mark his mourning. But if he had arrived at the age for training, it is a duty that he should rend his garment in the manner prescribed for an adult.

12. On one of the Intermediate days of a Festival, whether the burial had occurred thereon, or whether one had learned of the death at that time, the garments should not be rent, except for a father or mother, for the latter one must rend his garments even if he were not informed thereof until thirty days after the day of death had elapsed. But if one's father or mother had died on a Holyday, inasmuch as rending the garment must be postponed, he should not rend it during the Intermediate days of the Festival, but should wait until the Festival is over when his mourning begins. For other relatives the garments should not be rent during the Intermediate days of a Festival, unless one be informed of the death during the thirty days, and if by waiting until after the Holyday, the delay will cause that time to pass, he should rend his garment during the Intermediate days.

LAWS OF A MOURNER.[1]

1. One who had lost by death one of the relatives aforementioned is termed אונן (Onan) until after the interment; he must avoid levity and indicate by his conduct that he realizes his loss and that he is preoccupied in attending to the interment. He should not eat in the room where the dead is lying, but in another room, and if he have no other room, he should eat at a friend's house, and if he have no friend at whose house he can eat, he should erect a partition (or screen) which should be ten hand-breadths high, without a space of three hand breadths below, and of sufficient solidarity to resist the wind. If he cannot make a partition, he should turn his face aside and eat. Even if he be in another city (at such a time) he should not partake of an elaborate meal, but only of a simple meal. He should neither eat meat nor drink wine.

2. An Onan is exempt from the observance of all the precepts, even if he himself be not required to attend to the dead, having others who attend thereto in his stead. Even if he desire to be scrupulous

[1] Lit :" One who feels grieved."

(and fulfil the precepts) he must not do so, because of the honour due to the dead. He should not say any benediction, nor even respond אמן after the benedictions said by others, nor should he be included among those who make an appointment to say Grace, nor to a Minyan of ten male adults. Also a negative precept, even according to the Rabbis, is applicable to him, thus, if he desire to partake of bread, he must wash his hands, but he should not say the benediction על נטילת ידים, likewise on arising in the morning he should wash each hand three times according to the law, but he should not say the benediction.

3.   If he had eaten prior to the burial of the dead, and after the interment the food was not yet digested, he should say the Grace after meals.

4.   If the Onan be in another city and there are also relatives in the place where the dead lies who are required to mourn, the former is exempt from the obligations devolving upon an Onan. But if there be no relatives at the place where the dead lies, he is subject to all the laws relating to an Onan.

5.   After the relatives had come to terms with the Holy Brotherhood they are not legally subject to the laws of an Onan and are obliged to observe the duty of reading the Shema' and saying the Shemoneh 'Esreh and all the other precepts, still it is customary for an Onan not to pray until after the interment, nevertheless he may say Kaddish if he does not encroach thereby upon the rights of other mourners.

6.   As long as the dead is not buried the mourner should not take off his boots, for he may leave his house, but to bathe, or to participate in a joyous celebration, friendly greeting, and the study of the Torah all are prohibited. He is also forbidden to work, or even to allow others to work for him, even where a loss is entailed, but where the loss would be very great, he should consult the ecclesiastical authorities.

7.   One who is an Onan at the time when the Shema' and Shemoneh 'Esreh should be read, and when the interment was over a quarter of the day had passed, (which was the time for reading the Shema') he should, nevertheless, read it and its benedictions (without wearing Tephillin) until the third of the day, but if a third of the day had passed, he should read the Shema' without the benedictions. Until the hour of noon it is still permissible to say the Shemoneh 'Esreh and the additional service (Musaph) for New Moon can be said all day. Of the benedictions in the early morning service only the following three should be said : שלא עשני וי, שלא עשני עבד, שלא עשני אשה also the benediction of the Torah, as the entire day is the proper time for saying the same, if, however, the interment took place before a third of the day had passed, and if he should wait until he returns home, he would delay later than that time, his house being far from the cemetery, it is best for him to enter a house near the cemetery to read the Shema' and to pray at the proper time or even to do so in the open air where the

place is clean. As soon as they have begun to throw earth over the dead, he is permitted to read the Shema' and to say the Shemoneh 'Esreh although his period of mourning had not commenced then.

8. An Onan who continued in that condition of mourning until the proper time for praying had passed, need not make amends by saying the Shemoneh 'Esreh twice in the next service. If, however, he became an Onan after the time for prayer had begun, and he continued in that state of mourning until that time had passed, he should consult the ecclesiastical authorities.

9. If the dead were not buried because of the Sabbath, the mourner is not subject to the laws of an Onan. He is permitted to partake of meat and wine, he is also obliged to observe all the precepts, but cohabitation is prohibited, he is also forbidden to study the Torah. If he be a Reader in a Synagogue, and if there be another person to read the service he should not officiate, but if there be no other person he may officiate.

10. On the Sabbath, shortly before evening, he should read the Shema' without the benedictions, he should neither read the Evening Service nor perform the Habdallah ceremony at the termination of the Sabbath, and he is permitted to eat without having performed the Habdallah. After the interment he should perform the Habdallah over a cup (of wine). Even if the burial should take place on the morrow he can perform the Habdallah over a cup (of wine) [without candle and the spices] as he is permitted to perform the Habdallah until Tuesday. If he say the morning prayer before the time for (the Habdalah) had passed he should not say אתה חוננתנו. If it be necessary for him to attend to matters concerning the funeral on Sabbath towards evening, he becomes an Onan as soon as he begins to attend to the arrangements for the burial of the dead.

11. If one died on Friday afternoon at such a time as to make it impossible to bury before Sabbath, the mourner is permitted to say the Afternoon Service on that day.

12. If one died on the first day of a Festival, and the mourner desires to have the burial carried out on that day by a gentile, he is immediately subject to the laws relating to an Onan. This is more especially the case on the second day of a Festival when he is permitted to bury the dead on that day. And even if he should not desire to bury the dead on that day, nevertheless on the nights of the Festival, he should say the Sanctification (Kiddush) and all prayers, and he is not subject to the laws of an Onan.

13. One who had been an Onan at the termination of a Festival, should perform the Habdallah on the following day but not thereafter, as the proper time for Habdallah after a Festival, is only until the end of that day (following the Festival).

14. An Onan who has a son to be circumcised, if it be possible for him to bury the dead before the worshippers leave the Synagogue in the morning, the Holy Brotherhood should pray first and then bury

the dead, and thereafter the child should be circumcised. If that be impossible, the circumcision should, nevertheless, take place in the morning, and it is permissible for the Onan to be present at the circumcision but he should not pronounce any benediction, but the Godfather should say the benediction להכניסו inasmuch as where both duties, the interment of the dead and a circumcision have to be performed, the circumcision takes precedence.

15. On the eve of the 14th of Nisan, an Onan should employ an agent to search for the unleavened bread, but he should say כל חמירא.

16. During the counting of the 'Omer (one who was an Onan at night) should count the 'Omer on the following day without a benediction, but the rest of the nights he can say a benediction on counting the 'Omer. If he were an Onan by day and by night, he should count the rest of the 'Omer nights without reciting the benediction.

17. On the night of Purim an Onan should hear the Megillah (Book of Esther) read by another, and he should neither eat meat nor drink wine as he is not obliged to partake of a Feast (in honour of Purim) in the evening, and the interment should take place during the day after the worshippers had left the Synagogue. After the burial he should read the prayers and recite the Megillah or hear it read by another. If he had heard the reading of the Megillah before the interment, it is proper for him to read it again (after the interment) without the benediction, but he should not put on Tephillin even after the interment had taken place, inasmuch as it is the first day of his mourning. On Purim day an Onan is allowed to partake of meat and wine.

18. One, who had not yet prayed, in whose family a death had occurred, if he be unaware of the death and there is no one else to attend to the burial, it is necessary that he should be informed at once, but if there be other people who are attending to the funeral arrangements, he should not be told until he had said his prayers. If a wife had lost a relative, but she is not aware of her loss, then her husband must abstain from cohabitation.

19. One who had lost a relative whose interment is unavoidably postponed for several days, should consult the ecclesiastical authorities as to the proper course to pursue regarding the laws relating to an Onan (in his case).

LAWS RELATING TO PURIFICATION (TAHARAH) AND THE SHROUDS ALSO THE PROHIBITION TO ENJOY ANYTHING BELONGING TO THE DEAD.

1. The purification is as follows : The entire body, including the head, should be washed with warm water. The fingers and toes should be thoroughly cleansed, also everywhere else, and the (hair of the) head should be combed, the nails of the hands and feet should be cleaned, the body should not be placed face downwards, as that is a degrading posture, but it should be inclined, first on one side and then

on the other. After the body has been thoroughly cleansed, it should be washed with nine Kabbin (measures) of water[1], this should be done as follows : the corpse should be placed in a standing position on the ground or upon straw, and the water should be poured over the head and it should run down over the entire body.

2. The capacity of nine Kabbin (measures) is about twenty-four quarts, and it is not necessary for it to be poured out of one vessel, as two or even three vessels may be combined to make up that quantity, they should however, begin to pour out of the second vessel before they had finished pouring out the contents of the first vessel, also from the third vessel before they had finished with the second vessel, even when pouring all out of one vessel the flow of water should be uninterrupted ; four vessels, however, cannot be combined to count as one, even if the water be poured out simultaneously.

3. Then they beat an egg in its shell with some wine, and wash the head of the dead therewith. Care must be taken that the fingers of the dead man's hands are not shut. After being cleansed, the corpse should not be allowed to remain in the place where the rites of purification took place, he should be placed towards the door, inside the house. The board upon which he was placed during the purification, should not be turned over, as it is improper so to do.

4. One must not kiss one's children who died as it is unhealthy to do so, and one is warned not to grasp the hand of the dead saying that the dead should take him along. When the dead is being carried from the house nobody should go out before the body. The bearers, however, who are obliged to leave the house first in order to carry the body, need not be particular in this matter.

5. We must be careful that the shrouds should be prepared from fine white linen, but they should not be too costly, they should a so be sewed with linen thread only. Neither a hem nor a knot of any sort should be made in the shrouds, neither in the thread with which it is sewed, nor when dressing (the dead) therein. A dead male should be wrapped in a woollen Tallis with fringes, one of which, however, should be made unfit for religious use, but it would be more proper when the body is in the grave to put one fringe in the corner of the Tallis. If the deceased had a beautiful Tallis in which he had prayed during his life, it is not proper to wrap him, at his death, in an inferior Tallis instead, as it is becoming for one to be buried in the Tallis in which he had prayed during his life. When dressing the dead, they should devoutly think that just as they are dressing his body so may his soul be adorned in spiritual garments in the Garden of Eden. They should be careful not to alter the prevalent custom in the manner of dressing the dead. If they had forgotten to put on anything belonging to the shrouds, they should place it upon the coffin.

6. One who fell and died instantly, if his body were bruised and blood flowed from the wound, he should not be cleansed, but they should inter him in his garments and boots, but above his garments they should wrap a sheet which is called סובב. It is customary to dig the earth at the spot where he fell, if blood be there or near by, and all that earth upon which there is blood should be buried with him. He should be buried in those garments only which he wore when he fell, but if there were blood stains on other garments which he was not wearing, likewise if he were placed upon pillows and sheets whilst the blood was flowing these need not be buried, but they should be thoroughly washed until no trace of blood remains, and the water should be poured into his grave. If, however, the one who fell and died did not bleed, they should remove his garments and cleanse him, and dress him in shrouds, as in the case of other dead people. He who was drowned should (if his corpse were recovered) also be treated like other dead people.

7. Even if blood flowed from his body but it had ceased, and they had undressed him, after which he revived and lived for a few days and then died, whereupon he should be cleansed and shrouds should be prepared for him, although he be stained by his blood still he should be cleansed, for the blood which he had lost in his life time does not matter as we are only concerned with the blood which one loses at death.

8. One who was assassinated, although he did not bleed, should be buried in the clothes which he then wore. In the case of a woman who died while giving birth to a child, the ecclesiastical authorities should be consulted, this also applies in the case of one who had been executed by the government authorities.

9. It is forbidden to enjoy anything belonging to the dead, whether he be a Jew or non-Jew, neither his shrouds nor such things which are attached to his body, e.g., his wig or artificial teeth, these should be buried with him. But such articles which are not attached to his body one is permitted to use, i.e., such things which are not reckoned as part of the body, such as ornaments and garments.

Laws Concerning the Removal of the Dead, The Funeral, and the Burial Service.

1. If there be a death in the city, all the inhabitants are forbidden to work, if, however, the city have a society who appoint attendants for the funeral, then all those whose services are not required are permitted to work.

2. If there be a death in a small village there should be no greeting between the inhabitants, this is especially to be avoided on a cemetery if the dead be there, even if it be in a large city, but when there is no dead person (awaiting burial) on the cemetery, one may greet other people at a distance of four paces from the graves.

3. It is written : " His body shall not remain all night . . . but thou shalt in any wise bury him that day " (Deut. xxi. 23), hence our Rabbis have inferred that it is forbidden to let the body of the dead remain (unburied) over night. If, however, one let the body remain over night for the sake of honouring the dead, e.g. to procure a coffin, shrouds, or to await the arrival of relatives or others who will deliver the funeral orations, in these circumstances it is permitted, as the Torah forbade only that delay in burial which leads to contempt of the dead. If a dead man were found whose identity is not established, it is permitted to let him remain unburied all night until witnesses can make their appearance to identify the corpse or until his wife can come to identify him.

4. As far as dead relatives are concerned one who hastens to have them brought to their rest is praiseworthy, but when one's parents are dead, he who hastens to have them buried is despicable, unless it were on the Eve of Sabbath or a Holy-day, or if the rain descended upon the bier.

5. If two individuals died, he who died first should be taken out first '(for burial). After the interment of the first deceased, those present at the burial should not stand by the grave in a line, so as not to delay the burial of the second deceased. If they desire to let the first deceased remain (unburied) over night in order to honour him, they should not delay the burial of the second deceased on that account, but they should bury him at once.

6. If one of them were a learned man and the other an ignorant person, the former should be taken out first, even if the latter had died first. If one of them be a man and the other a woman, the woman should be taken out first, even if the man had died first.

7. If one weep on account of the death of a virtuous man, the Holy One, blessed be He, counts those tears and stores them up in His treasury. The merit of such conduct is great, for the children of this person will not die young.

8. He who beholds a funeral and does not accompany it is guilty of a great transgression, he should accompany the dead at least the distance of four cubits. Although he be prevented by some accident from accompanying the dead, he is nevertheless obliged to stand when he sees those who carry the dead pass by, for whenever a man sees others passing by who are engaged in the performance of a precept, he must stand up before them.

LAWS AND CUSTOMS OF ISRAEL

9. In our days it is assumed that every Israelite has studied the Bible and the Mishnah, therefore if one die, even the study of the Torah should be discontinued, in order to follow his funeral. For the sake, however, of a woman or a child this custom is not so strictly enforced, therefore one need not interrupt his study of the Torah in order to follow them. Children who attend school should at no time be forced to interrupt their studies.

10. On the way to the cemetery and also on returning therefrom, the men should keep apart from the women.

11. When those who accompany the dead have arrived within thirty paces from the grave, they should halt with the dead every four cubits, so that they will halt seven times. They should tarry awhile each time. On a day when ¡Prayers of Supplications (Tachanun) are not said they need not halt.

12. On reaching the cemetery, one who had not seen any graves for thirty days is required to say the benediction 'וכו ,אשר יצר אתכם בדין then להחיות מתים up to אתה גבור.

13. When the grave is filled צדוק הדין i.e., הצור תמים פעלו is said. This prayer should be commenced by one of the mourners, but if no mourner be present, the most important among those present should recite same. On the days when Tachanun is not said צדוק הדין should not be said, therefore it should not be said on Friday afternoon, nor on the eve of a Festival, but on the eve of a New Moon, and on the eve of Chanukah, and on the eve of Purim, it should be said even in the afternoon. If the deceased were a learned man it should be said even on ל"ג בעומר. On the days after the New Moon of Sivan until Pentecost, on the Ninth of Ab, and on the Eve of New Year, it should be said before noon. At night neither צדוק הדין nor קדיש should be said at the cemetery; צדוק הדין should not be said for a deceased infant less than 30 days old.

LAWS CONCERNING THE INTERMENT AND THE CEMETERY.

1. The burial mentioned in the Torah is the interment of the body of the dead in the earth itself. In many places, however, it is customary to place the dead in a coffin made of boards and to inter him thus, and as it is unlikely that there should not be a hole in the coffin, this suffices. The pious bore holes in the coffin. In some

208

places the dead are buried without a coffin, the corpse being placed in the ground without any board underneath, only one board on each side, or instead thereof, two rows of stones, and above these another board is placed or a heap of stones to prevent the earth falling down upon the dead body which would be a degradation. In other places the dead are generally buried in this way without being placed in a coffin, but the priests (כהנים) and the first-born, who are esteemed, are placed in coffins. One should be careful not to use the remnants of the wood whereof the coffin was made, they may be used only as fuel to heat the water to be used for the purification of the corpse. The generous people who had fed the poor at their table should be buried in a coffin made of the boards of that table, as it is said "And thy charity shall go before thee" (Is. lviii. 8).

2. The corpse is laid upon its back, with face upward, like one who is asleep. He who has earth from Palestine, should have some of it spread under him, and some of it upon him, as it is said : "And his land will atone for his people" (Deut. xxxii. 43). It is right to place some of it where the holy covenant is marked, also on his mouth, eyes and hands.

3. The graves should not be made close to each other, but they must be separated by a partition of at least six fingers' width, and if possible care must be taken of having a space of six hand-breadths between them. A man or woman, however, may be buried together with their son or daughter, or with their grandson or grand-daughter. As a rule, a child who had slept with the deceased in life, may be buried with the deceased at death, but an adult son should not be buried with his father, nor an adult daughter with her mother. Even the burial of children with their parents is only permitted when they are both buried at the same time, but if one had already been buried, it is forbidden to inter the other in the same grave.

4. If a male uncircumcised infant died, he should be circumcised at his grave, and a name given to him ; a female infant should also be given a name.

5. One coffin should not be placed upon another unless six hand-breadths of earth intervene between them.

6. A wicked man should not be buried next to a righteous man, for it is said, "Gather not thy soul with sinners" (Ps. xxvi. 9). One should not even inter an extremely wicked man next to one who was less wicked nor should a righteous man and more especially a man

209

of average piety be buried next to a man who was esteemed for his piety. Two who were enemies, should not be buried next to one another.

7. One should be careful not to take a hoe or pick-axe from the hand of one's neighbour at a burial, but one should lay it down and the other should take it up. After the deceased had been placed in the grave, the bier should be turned over three times, but this need not be done on a day when Tachanun is not said.

8. When about to return from the cemetery they should pluck up some grass and throw it behind their back saying, "He remembereth that we are dust" (*ibid.* ciii. 14). This custom is symbolical of the resurrection of the dead, as it is said, " And they of the city shall flourish like grass of the earth " (*ibid.* lxxii. 16). This is also permitted during the Intermediate days of a Festival. They should then wash their hands, for this ablution the use of a vessel is required. One should not take the vessel from one who had washed his hands, but the latter should put it down and then the former should take it. They should then sit down seven or three times (according to the custom) and say ויהי נועם וכו'.[1] Likewise if the burial took place on a Holyday they should sit down in the same manner as on a week day. It is usual to insist on the observance of the customs of washing the hands and sitting down in the case of a person (who had been with the dead) prior to entering the house.

9. The dead should not be removed (for burial) from a city where there is a cemetery to another city, unless it be from any country to Palestine, or if he had to be removed to the burial ground of his fathers, likewise if he had commanded that his remains should be conveyed from one place to another, it is permitted.

10. It is forbidden to open a grave after it had been closed, that is after the earth had been heaped upon the lid of the coffin, but as long as the earth had not been piled thereon, it is permitted to open the coffin, if there were occasion for it. If, because of a very urgent reason, a grave be required to be opened or the body of the dead to be removed therefrom, an eminent Rabbi should be consulted.

11. A grave that was dug should not be left open over night, as it is a dangerous practice, and if the dead could not be buried until the following day, the grave should be filled up with earth.

12. It is forbidden to tread upon the graves, nevertheless if one have occasion to visit a certain grave, and he had no other way of reaching it except by treading upon the graves, he is permitted to do so.

13. One should neither visit a cemetery nor go within four cubits of the dead, nor in a room where the dead is lying, when wearing תפלין upon his head or having the ציצת on his garment. If, however, they were covered, he may wear them. One should not pray there, but he may say the Psalms in honour of the dead.

[1] See Authorised Daily Prayer Book, pp. 320, 231.

14. One should neither eat nor drink in a cemetery nor should one gather the vegetation that grows there. It is permitted, however, to pick the fruits from trees, which, although planted in the cemetery, do not grow over the graves.

15. It is the custom in some places not to erect a tombstone until twelve months after death, but there are other places where the people are not particular in this matter.

Laws Concerning Burial on a Festival.

1. On the first day of a Festival[1] an Israelite should not be engaged in the burial of the dead, but if it be possible for a non-Jew to dig the grave and cut the boards, or make a coffin, and also sew the shrouds if necessary, then an Israelite is permitted to dress the body, also to warm water and cleanse the body, also to carry it out and place it in the grave, but filling in the grave with earth should be done by a non-Jew. If possible care should be taken to cleanse the dead without the use of a garment, in order that they should not violate the law by wringing the water out of the garment. If, however, one died on the first day of a Festival and it is possible to keep the body until the following day without injury to health, it is far preferable to let it remain unburied until the second day of the Festival.

2. On the second day of a Festival or even of Rosh Hashanah, if it be possible to have all the aforementioned duties performed by a non-Jew without causing any delay, a non-Jew should carry out the same, while all the other preparations aforementioned can be performed by Israelites. It is also permitted to use garments and sheets in performing the purification, care should, however, be taken not to wring out the water with the hands. If it be impossible to have the aforementioned duties done by a non-Jew, an Israelite is permitted to make all the preparations for the burial, as though it were a week-day, inasmuch as the Rabbis have compared the second day of a Festival with a week-day in the matter of preparing the dead for burial. If, however, it be possible to obtain ready-made shrouds, it is preferable (to use them) in order to avoid the necessity of sewing the same. It is permissible to attend to all matters relating to the dead only if the burial take place that day, but if not, it is forbidden to make the slightest preparation for the burial. It is even forbidden to handle the body.

3. On a Festival it is forbidden to fix the price of the shrouds, unless it be impossible to obtain them otherwise. Grave-diggers are forbidden to take any remuneration for their work on a Festival, but if they refuse to work without pay, they should be paid, but they will

---

[1]The text might be rendered: "An Israelite should not be engaged with one who died on the first day of a Festival."

211

have to render an account of their conduct in the future. The Holy Brotherhood should not take any money, but they can accept pledges without stipulating any amount.

4. Where there is no Jewish cemetery, although there is a place where that dead person may be buried, it is nevertheless permitted to convey him on the first day of a Festival, through a non-Jew, and on the second day of a Festival even through a Jew, to a place where he can be buried in a Jewish cemetery, but if it were not intended to bury him that day, an Israelite is forbidden to convey the body on a Festival in order to have it buried after the Festival.

5. On the first day of a Festival all who attend the funeral are forbidden to go beyond the Techum[1] but on the second day of a Festival they are permitted to go even beyond the Techum, they may also return to their homes on the same day. But it is forbidden to ride on an animal in order to accompany the dead on a Festival, even on the second day of a Festival. This rule also applies to the mourners. The gravediggers, however, are permitted to ride on the second day of a Festival, if it be impossible for them to walk, nevertheless they should not ride in the city.

6. If one is to be buried on a Festival, ten men should rise at an early hour and bury him whilst the Reader is reciting the (פיוטים) hymns, but if the deceased were a distinguished man so that a multitude would follow his funeral, he should be buried after the service is concluded but before the meal is eaten. If it be impossible to make all the necessary preparations for the burial by that time, he should be buried after the meal had been taken.

7. With regard to a dead child of thirty days old the same laws apply as to any other dead person, but if it be a male child whose circumcision had for some reason been postponed, he should not be buried on the first day of a Festival, even in spite of the decay, for it is necessary to remove his foreskin, which should not be done by a non-Jew, the body should therefore be kept until the second day of a Festival, when his foreskin should be removed and he should be buried.

8. A child who died before it was thirty days old should not be buried on the first day of a Festival even by a non-Jew, but should be kept until the second day of the Festival when it should be buried by a non-Jew but not by an Israelite, the foregoing applies if the body were not decaying, but otherwise it should be buried by a non-Jew on the first day of the Festival. If the child died on the second day of the Festival, it should be buried that very day by a non-Jew but not by an Israelite, but if it were a male child not yet circumcised, in spite of decay setting in he should not be buried even

---

[1] i.e. Two thousand cubits beyond the marked-off area around the town or place.

on the second day of the Festival by a non-Jew, but he should be kept until after the Festival when his foreskin should be removed and he should then be buried.

9. On Sabbaths and the Day of Atonement no one should be occupied in attending to the dead even through the agency of a non-Jew.

10. On Intermediate days of Festivals the dead should not be conveyed to the cemetery before the grave was prepared, so that it should not be necessary to let the bier remain standing.

Laws Concerning a Suicide and a Wicked Person's Death.

1. There is none more wicked than one who has committed suicide, as it is said : " And surely your blood of your lives will I require " (Gen. ix. 5). Also for the sake of an individual was the world created, thus he who destroys one soul is as though he had destroyed the whole world, therefore one should neither rend the garment nor mourn for him who had destroyed himself, nor should a funeral oration be pronounced on his behalf. He should, however be cleansed, dressed in shrouds and buried, and with regard to the saying of Kaddish the ecclesiastical authorities should be consulted.

2. When one who had been killed was discovered, as far as possible the act of killing should be regarded as the deed of another person and not as his own deed.

3. If a child committed suicide, it is considered that he had done the deed unwittingly. Likewise if an adult had killed himself and it is evident that the act was prompted by madness or through fear of terrible torture, he should be treated as an ordinary deceased person.

4. People who had cast off the yoke of the precepts and had led a life of libertinage also apostates, informers and heretics should not be mourned for (Onan) immediately after their demise before burial, nor should a period of mourning thereafter be observed for them.

5. One who had been executed, whether by the sentence of the Government or otherwise, even if he had been an apostate, should be mourned for as Onan and a period of mourning should be kept for him, inasmuch as he had suffered an unusual death, it is an atonement for his sins.

6. One who was an inveterate sinner, even if his transgressions were the result of his passions, still if he died without confession, he

should not be mourned for, but if he had confessed he should be mourned for, even if he had been a thief or a robber.

7. One should not mourn for a child of one or two years who had been converted with his father or mother, and had died.

LAWS CONCERNING THE DEFILEMENT OF A PRIEST.

1. The priest is warned against defiling himself by (coming into) contact with the dead. This includes an abortive whose limbs are undeveloped, if, however, the abortion occurred within forty days from conception, it is considered as only a fluid. The contact that defiles need not necessarily be with the dead body in its entirety, for there is pollution even in the touch of that which is separated therefrom, such as its blood and the like. He is likewise forbidden to defile himself by contact with the severed limb of a living person if there be much flesh thereon, so that it would be proper to have it healed if it were still connected with the body, even if that be his own limb he is forbidden to defile himself therewith. He is forbidden to enter the house of a dying person, although one in that state does not defile him, nevertheless he violates the precept " Neither shall he profane " (Lev. xxi. 12), for he is warned to preserve his priesthood so as not to profane it, and here he exposes it to profanation as death may occur at any moment.

2. A priest is forbidden to enter a house if a dead body be therein, even if the house be large, and even if there be two rooms in one of which the body is lying, and there is a wall that separates them but there is an aperture in that wall the size of a square hand-breadth, he is forbidden to enter the adjoining room, and even if there be a third room adjoining, but the wall separating it contains also an aperture as large as a square hand-breadth, he is forbidden to enter the third room also and thus *ad infinitum*. If the aperture were made to admit light even if it be very small, it still transmits the impurity.

3. Houses which are close together, with roofs projecting with the space of a hand-breadth, are conductors of the pollution of the corpse, which may be in any of them by means of the window or door of that house, which transmits it to the other houses through their open windows or doors, all counting as one on account of the roofs which project over them all, the priest is therefore forbidden to enter into any of the other houses, even if the roofs be not level, but one is higher

than the other, even if the roof of the house containing the corpse be much higher than the other roofs, or vice-versa, so long as there is no intervention between them, be it ever so slight, the impurity spreads from one house to another, but if there be a barrier between them, be it ever so slight, the impurity is not transmitted. Likewise if a beam lie across a court entrance, which is (sometimes) done for an 'Erub[1], which is a hand-breadth wide, and is covered by the roofs which project above it a hand-breadth from each side, the impurity is transmitted from beneath the roof to the space beneath the beam, and penetrates to the house on the opposite side, it also spreads in every direction where there is a portion of a house of the size of a hand-breadth until it is stopped by some barrier.

4. It is a Sinaitic tradition from Moses that the door through which the dead is to be carried from the house (inasmuch as the removal of the corpse makes that house clean again) should be considered (with regard to ritual impurity) as open even when closed, and a priest is forbidden to stand there under the lintel even if the door be locked from within. Likewise if there were a roof above which projected a hand-breadth over the door, it communicates the impurity to every place possible as though the door were open, but if there were another open door or window of four square hand-breadths on another side, the closed door is considered as open and a priest is permitted to stand there provided the impurity cannot reach him through the open door or window.

5. A priest who is in a room where the door and windows are closed in such a manner that there is neither an opening in the door of even a hand-breadth's space nor even a small aperture in the window, if he hear that there is a corpse lying in another room which is situated so that the opening of a door or window will cause the impurity to reach him it is forbidden to open either, but he should remain where he is until the corpse has been removed.

6. The priest is forbidden to approach within four cubits of a corpse, even though it be neither in a house nor in a grave, provided the body lie in a permanent place, if, however, it lie in a temporary place during the funeral procession or during the halts that are made at the cemetery, then he need not keep aloof more than four hand-breadths.

7. A priest who is asleep in a house containing a corpse, or in a house to which the impurity of the dead penetrates, and it is impossible to shut it in order to prevent the access of the impurity, must be awakened so that he should go out, but if he be undressed, he should

---

[1] On the "'Erub" see Jewish Encyclopedia, v. pp. 203 ff.

not be told of the impurity, but merely told to go out, so that he may first dress himself, for "great is the honour of humanity"; nevertheless, having become aware of the impurity, he is forbidden to stay there until he has dressed himself, but he must go out immediately.

8. A priest is permitted to become defiled in the case of the following relatives and to do so is a religious duty, namely: his wife whom he rightfully married (not one whom he is forbidden to marry), his father and mother, son and daughter, brother and sister from the father's side, if they had lived thirty days, but he should not defile himself for an abortion nor should he defile himself for his married sister. There are some authorities who say that the priest being allowed to defile himself by contact with relatives refers only to the needs of burial, or to the bringing of a coffin, shrouds, and the like, and that consequently on the Sabbath when burial is impossible on that day, he is forbidden to defile himself for the sake of guarding the corpse. It is right to be scrupulous in accordance with that opinion. But concerning all things necessary for burial he is in duty bound to defile himself for their sake. Even if all the burial preparations were made by the Holy Brotherhood and he does not attend to it at all, he is permitted to be in the room, for perchance he may be wanted to obtain something that they may need. He can defile himself by contact with these relatives only until the grave is closed.

9. The priest is not permitted to defile himself for any relative, for whom it is forbidden to mourn, such as one who had committed suicide, or one who had separated himself from the ways of Israel, nor should he defile himself by contact with a dead relative who lacked any of his limbs, and there are some authorities who are stringent and do not allow a priest to defile himself by coming into contact with one who was killed.

10. The elder priests are warned against deliberately defiling the young priests by putting them in contact with a dead body, but if one of the latter defiled himself, it is not obligatory upon them to remove him from being in contact with the corpse, this, however, is only applicable to a child who had not yet arrived at the proper age for practising the precepts, but if he had arrived at that age he should be removed from defilement. The wife of a priest, even though she be in pregnancy, is permitted to enter the house of the dead.

11. If the priest were sick and unable to leave the house, it is incumbent upon the relatives of the dead to remove the corpse in order that they should not cause the invalid to transgress a prohibition of the Law, but if he be well, it is not incumbent upon them to do so. If, however, the dead were an abortion, it is obligatory upon the relatives to remove it, even if the priest were well, and even on the Sabbath, through a non-Jew.

216

LAWS AND CUSTOMS OF ISRAEL

Laws Concerning those for whom One Must Mourn.

1. The following are the relatives for whom one must mourn: one's father, mother, son, daughter, brother and sister, whether from the father's or mother's side, even for a married sister. A husband must mourn for his wife, a wife for her husband. For all the aforementioned mourning must be kept the entire seven days, for other relatives, however, it is the custom to keep only partial mourning, during the first week of the death until after the Sabbath. Thus they do not bathe in hot water nor do they change all their clothes for that Sabbath as on other Sabbaths. There are degress in mourning relative to the closeness of relationship, thus for the demise of a relation in the second degree, e.g., a grandson, whether descended from a son or a daughter, one should manifest his grief by not wearing his outer garments for the Sabbath, (he is, however, permitted to change his under garments.) For a father-in-law, or a mother-in law, whether from the father's or mother's side, one must manifest sorrow by not changing one's clothes, with the exception of the under garments. All who mourn for the above should also observe the custom of neither bathing, nor combing their hair, nor eating out of their house, neither at a religious feast, nor at any festive gathering, until after the first Sabbath following the death.

2. For a child who had died within thirty days from its birth, even on the thirtieth day, even if its hair and nails were grown, one need neither rend one's garments, nor mourn as an Onan, nor keep a period of mourning, for it is regarded as an abortion. If, however, it died after the 30th day, (say) on the 31st day, even at an earlier hour than that on which it was born, the garment should be rent, and one should mourn as an Onan, and also keep a period of mourning, unless it were clearly known, that the child was born in the eighth month (as such a child cannot survive), but if it were clearly known that it was born in the ninth month, as for instance, the father had separated after cohabitation for nine full months when the child was born, even if it died on the day it was born, the garment should be rent, and one should mourn as an Onan, and a period of mourning should be kept.

3. If one of twin children had died within thirty days from birth whilst the other survived after thirty days, the ecclesiastical authorities should be consulted as to the necessity of observing mourning for the former. Male and female proselytes who were converted together with their children, should not mourn for one another, for every proselyte when converted is considered as a new born babe, and they are no longer considered as being related to one another.

217

LAWS AND CUSTOMS OF ISRAEL

Laws Governing the Time when Mourning Should Begin.

1. Mourning begins as soon as the grave has been filled up with earth when the mourner should remove his boots at the cemetery, but. if he be obliged to go home, and it is not possible for him to go without boots, he should place a little earth in them.

2. If the cemetery be near the city and the mourner did not go there, but after having accompanied the dead, he returned to his home, his period of mourning does not begin until he is told that the grave has been filled up. Nevertheless if night were approaching and he desired that day to count in the total of the seven days of mourning, he may begin to mourn from the time when he assumes that the grave had been filled up, and if he be afterwards told that the grave had been filled up before night-fall, he may count that day (as one of the days of mourning.) If the mourning began on the eve of a Festival, the latter abrogrates the observance of the seven days of mourning.

3. In places where the dead are conveyed to another city for burial, and consequently such mourners who are left in the city do not know when the burial takes place, they should therefore begin to mourn immediately when the people return from the funeral, and from that time they may also count the period of seven days and thirty days, but the people who accompany the dead to the place of his interment, should count from the time when the burial took place. If the head of a family accompany the dead, the members of the family who remain at home should consult the ecclesiastical authorities as to how they should act, also as to the time when their mourning begins.

4. One who was drowned or killed, and they searched for him but did not find him, as long as they did not abandon the search,. the relatives are neither amenable to the laws of mourning as Onan, nor do they need to begin a period of mourning. As soon as they have abandoned the search, they should begin to mourn, and if after the days of mourning are over, the corpse were found and buried, they do not need to mourn for him again, but if the deceased were a father or mother, one is required to rend one's garments. If the lost person had a wife and the proof of his death is not so clearly established that she can be permitted to marry again, no mourning should be kept for him, nor should Kaddish be said for him, they should nevertheless give pleasure to his soul by occasionally reading the prayers in public, by reading the Haphtorah, by uniting with others to say Grace, by giving charity, and by learning or hiring somebody to study in his memory.

5. If relatives had learned of the death of a kinsman, each should begin to count the seven days of mourning from the day whereon each.

had heard thereof, and they should cease mourning on the seventh day from the day on which each one had begun. Still there are occasions when the mourning may be uniformly observed by them all following the lead of the head of the family, (that is to say if they have in their midst a man or a woman, whom they respect in such a degree that were it a question of dividing the estate of the deceased, all matters would be left to his or her decision, and they would all follow his or her advice, even should such a one be young in years, that one is called the head of the family, and even if the same one be not the heir, e.g. if a widow be the manageress of the house, or one who lives with his father-in-law, and his wife had died, all these are termed the head of the family). This custom is only applicable under the following conditions : (1) that when the burial took place the mourners were not more than thirty miles therefrom ; (2) that the relatives with the head of the family were in the place where their relative had died or had been buried ; (3) if they did not know of the death until they came to the head of the family. If all these conditions obtain, even if he[1] arrived on the seventh day before they arose from their mourning, he should observe with them a partial mourning and he should count that in lieu of the seven days, and he keeps the thirty days with them, and even if he afterwards returned to his home, he should follow their lead and count with them. If, however, any of the above conditions be lacking, he should observe for himself seven days and thirty days.

6. If, when one heard of the death of one's relative, the congregation had already recited the evening prayers but it was yet day, and he had not yet prayed, he does not follow the congregation inasmuch as he can count that as one day, but if he had said the evening prayers, he cannot reckon that as one day, and he should count the seven days and the thirty days from the following day. This interpretation of the law is for the rigid observance thereof, and not to exempt thereby, thus if he had heard of the death on the thirtieth day after having said the evening prayers, we do not say that it is already night, and that the news was received after the time (of the thirty days) had passed, thereby exempting him in some measure, but we consider it as day and consequently he heard of the death in due time, so that he can count that day in the total of seven days. With regard to Tephillin, if he had heard of the death of a relative on any day except the thirtieth, after he had said the evening prayers but whilst it was yet day, he should lay them on the following day without saying a benediction, and he should keep them covered, but if that had occurred on the thirtieth day, he should put them on on the following day and say a benediction over them. If a woman had heard of the death of a relative after the congregation had already said the evening prayers though it be still day, if she be not accustomed to say the evening prayers, she is governed by the action of the congregation, and it enforces the law (requiring her to mourn), but that day she cannot count as one of the days of mourning.

7. When a plague breaks out, it is customary not to mourn, for

[1] *i.e.* The mourner.

all are in panic, but when the visitation has passed, and it is yet within thirty days from the demise of one's relative, he is required to mourn, if, however, it were not over until the thirty days had passed, or if a Festival had intervened in the meantime, one is not required to mourn thereafter.

LAWS CONCERNING THE MEAL OF CONDOLENCE.

1. What is the rule concerning the meal of condolence? On the first day of mourning the mourner is forbidden to eat the first meal of own food, therefore it is a religious duty for his neighbours to send him the first meal, this is called סעודת הבראה (the meal of condolence), which should begin with the eating of eggs or lentils, but these can be followed by all manner of food even meat. The mourner is also permitted to drink a little wine during that meal, if, however, he should not desire to eat until nightfall inasmuch as the first day has passed, he is permitted to eat of his own food. It is therefore proper for one who has no one who will send him the meal of condolence to fast until nightfall, nevertheless if he cannot fast, since he is not obliged to distress himself, he is permitted to eat of his own food.

2. To a woman in mourning the meal of condolence should not be supplied by men but by women. It is forbidden for a married woman to take the first meal of her husband's food, for inasmuch as it devolves upon him to support her it is her own food. Likewise a hired man who has also board as part of his hire, who became a mourner, should not eat the first meal of his employer's food. He who supports an orphan or his grown-up son or daughter whom he need not support, if the latter become mourners they may eat the first meal of his food.

3. If the burial took place at night and the mourner desired to eat at night, he is forbidden to eat of his own food, but he should be provided with a meal of condolence, and if he should not desire to eat at night, he is forbidden to eat the first meal of his own food in the day-time, for the day is counted with the preceding night, and it is therefore his first day of mourning.

4. On a Friday afternoon after 3 p.m. when it is forbidden to partake of a regular meal, the mourner should not be served with a meal of condolence out of honour for the Sabbath, and if on the Sabbath he had heard of the death within thirty days of its occurrence, the meal of condolence should not be served to him but he should eat of his own food nor should he be provided with that meal on the day following, inasmuch as the day when he heard the news had passed. Likewise one who must count seven days and thirty days after a Festival should not be provided with the meal of condolence on the day when he begins to observe mourning.

5. The meal of condolence should be given to one who had heard of the death (of a near relative) within thirty days of its occurrence, but not to one who had heard of it thereafter.

Laws Concerning the Comforting of Mourners.

1. It is taught in a Baraitha that Rabbi Meir said: "It is better to go to the house of mourning, than to go to the house of feasting for that is the end of all men; and the living will lay it to his heart" (Eccl. vii. 2). The text refers to death. It is an important religious duty to comfort the mourners, for by the fulfilment of this duty we perform an act of love toward the living and also give joy of spirit to the dead. It is a religious duty to teach the mourner that the ways of the Lord are upright, and that he should not question His dispensation, for He is just and righteous, and that he should accept in love Heaven's judgment.

2. It is written: "Weep ye not for the dead, neither bemoan him" (Jer. xxii. 10) this means "weep ye not for the dead" excessively, "neither bemoan him" inordinately, but three days should be allowed for weeping, seven days for bemoaning, and thirty days for wearing unwashed garments and abstaining from cutting the hair, thereafter, says the Holy One, blessed be He, "Ye do not feel more compassion for him than I do."

3. One must not say to the mourner: "What canst thou do. it is impossible to alter the decree of the Creator, blessed be He?" for that is akin to blasphemy, inferring that were it possible for him to change it, he would have done so. One must not say: "I was not punished as much as I deserve for my evil deeds," nor other words of a similar kind, for "a covenant is made with the lips" and the curse he has thus invoked upon himself might, Heaven forfend, be fulfilled!

4. The comforters are not permitted to say anything until the mourner had first commenced to speak, and if the comforters perceive that the mourner wishes them to withdraw, it is not permitted to sit by him (any longer).

5. A mourner or a sick person is not required to rise even before a man who is eminent in Israel. Although it is polite to say to one who desires to confer an honour upon the other by rising, "Keep your seat"; one should not say to a mourner: "Sit" or to a sick person, "Lie down" for it suggests "sit and remain in your mourning," or, "lie down and continue in your sickness."

6. The mourners should mourn in the place where the relative died. It is a religious duty to pray there with ten male adults (Minyan) both in the morning and in the evening, and if there be no mourner present, it is incumbent upon the neighbours and friends of the deceased to constitute a Minyan who should hold morning and evening service, and also study (the Torah) there.

7. Hallel should not be said in a house where one had died during the seven days if a mourner be there. If, however, there be another room, the mourner may go to that room while the worshippers say Hallel, but if there be no other room the worshippers should not say Hallel on a New Moon, but on Chanucah they should say it, even if the mourner be there. If they pray within the seven days in a house where one had died, but if the mourner be not there, or if he be there but the death did not occur in that house, then they should say Hallel even on a New Moon, but the mourner should not say Hallel. On a New Moon, which fell on the Sabbath, Hallel should be said by the congregation even in the mourner's house, for mourning is not observed on the Sabbath.

LAWS CONCERNING THE "TIMELY" AND "DELAYED" NEWS

OF A RELATIVE'S DEATH.

1. If one had heard of the death of his relative, for whom he is required to mourn, within thirty days of his burial, even on the thirtieth day the tidings are "timely" and he should rend his garments, and he is obliged to observe the seven days of mourning, counting them from the day on which he heard the news, he should also observe the thirty days of mourning counting them from the same day. The day when the news reached him is governed by the same laws as obtain on the day of burial.

2. If the news reached him after thirty days had elapsed from the day of burial, the tidings are "delayed" and he need not observe mourning for more than one hour, and it makes no difference whether he received the tidings by day or by night, one hour's mourning is sufficient even for one's parents, with the exception that it is his duty to observe the usual mourning of twelve months for one's parents, even if the tidings of the death were "delayed." The twelve months of mourning should be counted from the day of the death, and if the tidings reached him after the twelve months had passed, he should not observe mourning for more than one hour, even with reference to the observance relating to the entire twelve months.

3. One who receives "delayed" tidings need not observe the entire laws of mourning, it being sufficient for him to take off his boots, and he is permitted to work, to bathe, to anoint himself, to cohabit, and to study the Torah, if, however, he did not wear boots when the news reached him, he must do something else whereby it will be recognized that he mourns, e.g, to sit on the ground for one hour.

222

4. One who heard "timely" tidings on Sabbath, should count the Sabbath as one day, and at the termination of Sabbath he should rend his garments and count six more days of mourning thereafter.

5. If one had heard "timely" tidings on a Sabbath or Festival, but which at the termination of the Sabbath or Festival become "delayed," tidings, he is forbidden to transact thereon the private matters (from which a mourner must abstain) but at the termination of the Sabbath or the Festival, he should observe one hour's mourning as though the tidings were "delayed."

6. If one heard "timely" tidings on a Sabbath which is the eve of a Festival, inasmuch as he must then abstain from those private matters that are forbidden, the Festival annuls the seven days of mourning.

7. One who receives "delayed" tidings on a Sabbath or Festival should not observe mourning even with regard to private matters, but at the termination of the Sabbath or Festival he should observe one hour's mourning and that is sufficient.

8. If after a Festival one heard that his relative had died before the Festival, although the intervention of the Festival served to annul the mourning for those who had observed mourning prior thereto, nevertheless it does not affect his case, inasmuch as he did not observe any mourning at all before the Festival. Therefore if it were on the thirtieth day after the burial when the tidings reached him, they are "timely" and he is required to observe the seven days and also the thirty days of mourning.

9. One whose relative had died and he is not aware of it, should not be informed thereof, and concerning him who informs him thereof it is said : "He that uttereth a report is a fool" (Prov. x. 18). It is allowed to invite him to any joyful gathering, for so long as he is ignorant of his loss, he is not subject to the laws of mourning.

10. If a person be asked by a relative of one who had died if the latter be alive, he should not lie and tell him that he is alive, for it is said : "Keep thee far from a false matter" (Ex. xxiii. 7) but he should answer him ambiguously.

11. It is customary to inform sons of the death of their parents in order that they should say Kaddish.

Laws Prohibiting Work or Business During the Seven Days of Mourning.

1. During the seven days of mourning the mourner is forbidden to do any work, to bathe or anoint himself, to wear boots, to cohabit, to read the Torah, to greet friends, to wear freshly washed garments,

to cut his hair, or to be present at any festivity. On the first day he is also forbidden to lay Tephillin.

2. What is the law concerning work? During the first three days he is forbidden to work, even if he be so poor as to live through charity, but on and after the fourth day, if he be poor and have nothing to eat, he may work privately in his home, a woman also may work privately in her own home to earn enough for her sustenance. The Sages say: "May poverty overtake his neighbours, who force him to work," for it is their duty to provide for the poor, especially in his days of mourning.

3. He is even forbidden to have his work done by others, even through a non-Jew. If, however, the work be very urgent, and he might sustain a loss (by not doing it) he should consult the ecclesiastical authorities.

4. The mourner is forbidden to buy and sell, if, however, he possess merchandise, which will cause him to sustain a loss in his capital if not sold now, he should consult the ecclesiastical authorities in regard thereto. Likewise if merchandise had arrived by road or water, which is now to be sold cheaply, but which he will not be able to obtain later, likewise if he be at a market-place (or exchange) when he received timely tidings of the death of a relative he may buy and sell through others. If he have regular customers, and he is afraid they will accustom themselves to trade elsewhere, he may be permitted to sell to them through others. He is likewise permitted to send to collect money due to him, when he has cause to fear that the delay may spoil the recovery of the same.

5. Such writing that is allowed during the Intermediate days of a Festival is also permitted to a mourner, if it be impossible for him to have it done through another.

6. A mourner whose field is in other hands, either through a tenant (whereby the latter obtains a third or fourth of the produce) or through a holder (so that the latter pays the owner of the field a fixed amount of the produce), or on a lease (for which he is paid a certain sum of money), these tenants can attend to their work in the field as usual, when the owner is in mourning, for inasmuch as they derive the profit of their labour, they need not suffer a loss on account of his mourning. But if the mourner hire a day labourer to work in his field, he is forbidden to let him work, even if the field be in another city, since the work is done for the benefit of the mourner and is done publicly.

7. If the mourner be a tenant of the field of another person, he is forbidden to work in it himself but he is permitted to employ others to work therein, for it is not called the work of the mourner, but the

work of the owner of the field. If, however, there be different work for others which he has to do, he should not do it even by employing other people to do same, unless it be something that must be done or there will be a loss, this he may do through others.

8. If a mourner had let out animals on hire to another, the latter is permitted to do work therewith, inasmuch as he hired them before the former became a mourner, for he who hires anything acquires (for the time being) a proprietary right therein, but at the end of the time for which they were hired he is forbidden to use them.

9. It is permissible for a mourner to accept work to do after his period of mourning will expire, provided he neither weigh nor measure the same (then) as he would do at other times.

10. If a mourner had given out work to another on a contract and the latter had received it before the former became a mourner, and the work is done privataly at the house of the worker, it is permitted to be done by him.

11. A mourner is forbidden to carry on the construction of his building on a contract, even through heathens, and in a distant locality where no Israelites reside. If he had contracted with others to work on his farm and he pays them a stipulated amount for all the field-work, such as ploughing, sowing and reaping and the like, if possible he should be strict and prevent them working thereon.

12. Domestic occupations are not included in the work which a mourner is forbidden to do, thus it is permissible for a woman in mourning to bake and cook, and to attend to all her domestic duties, she is, however, forbidden to do work that is not necessary. A domestic servant in mourning is also permitted to do all the necessary housework, although she gets paid for it, but she should not do unnecessary work merely for the sake of gain; moreover she should not leave the house, as she is like other mourners in this respect.

13. If two kept a store in partnership and one of them became a mourner, the shop should be closed in order that the other should not do business publicly. He is permitted, however, to do business privately in his house, even to engage in such matters in which both partners are involved, this is, however, forbidden where the mourner is an eminent man, and the business is carried on in his name, except where a great loss may be entailed, in which case the ecclesiastical authorities should be consulted.

LAWS AND CUSTOMS OF ISRAEL

Laws Concerning the Prohibition to Bathe, to Anoint, to Wear Boots and to Cohabit.

1. The mourner is forbidden to bathe his entire body, even in cold water, moreover washing the face, hands and feet with warm water is prohibited, but with cold water it is permitted. Bathing in warm water is forbidden the entire thirty days. Bathing the entire body even in cold water is forbidden in the thirty days, if done (only) for the sake of pleasure. A woman who must bathe before immersion (טבילה) is permitted to bathe in warm water after her seven days of mourning.

2. If a woman who gave birth to a child became a mourner, if it be necessary for her to bathe, it is permissible for her to do so even during the seven days of mourning, but on the first day (of mourning) she should not bathe unless it be absolutely necessary. A person of delicate constitution who would be very distressed and indisposed by abstaining from bathing, is permitted to bathe. To preserve bodily cleanliness one is also permitted to cleanse one's hair even with warm water. One who went into mourning immediately after he had finished a period of mourning, is permitted to bathe in cold water. One is forbidden to anoint oneself in the slightest degree for the sake of pleasure, to do so, however, for hygienic purposes is permitted and it is certainly permitted to use ointment as a remedy.

3. The prohibition concerning the wearing of boots is applicable only to boots made of leather, as it is permissible to wear shoes made of cloth, rubber, hair, or wood, the terms "boots" refers only to those made of leather. A wooden shoe covered with leather is also forbidden to be worn. Although the mourner is forbidden to wear boots, he should nevertheless say the benediction שעשה לי כל צרכי in the morning service.

4. A woman within thirty days of giving birth to a child, also one who is suffering with sore feet, and a mourner who walks out of doors, are permitted to wear boots, they should, however, sprinkle a litle earth therein.

5. Cohabitation and kissing are forbidden, but other acts of attention, such as offering drink or making the bed and the like, are permitted to the husband and wife when either is in mourning.

LAWS AND CUSTOMS OF ISRAEL

Laws Prohibiting the Study of the Torah and Greeting.

1. The mourner is forbidden to study the Bible, the Mishnah, the Talmud, the Halakhoth and Haggadoth, but he is permitted to read Job, Lamentations, the mournful parts of Jeremiah, and all the distressing themes found in the Bible. One is permitted to study the laws of mourning in the Jewish codes. One is forbidden to consider too critically the aforementioned subjects which are permitted to be read.

2. A teacher who is in mourning is allowed after three days to teach his pupils all their lessons, their studies should not be discontinued. Likewise the young children of a mourner should not cease their studies, as mourning is not incumbent upon them.

3. Even if the mourner be the only priest in the Synagogue, he is forbidden to go to the reading of the Law.

4. During the seven days of mourning, the mourner should not say פטום הקטרת nor the סדר מעמדות, nor יהי רצון כאלו הקריבתי in איזהו מקומן and when saying the Habdallah benediction, he should omit the verses of joy that precede it, and begin only with the benedictions.

5. A mourner within the seven days of mourning should not officiate as Reader of the prayers for the Congregation unless there be no other person present capable of acting as such, if he, however, be a mourner for his parents, we are accustomed to permit him to act as Reader, even though another person, who is capable, is present. It is customary that a mourner should not act as Reader on Sabbaths and Festivals during the entire year, unless there be no other Reader or if he were accustomed to act as Reader before he became a mourner, in which event it is permissible for him to continue to do so under all circumstances.

6. What is the rule concerning greetings? During the first three days of mourning, he should neither salute any one, nor respond to another's salutation; but, he should inform them that he is a mourner; after three days until the seventh day he should not salute, but he may respond to another's salutation. From the seventh until the thirtieth day, he may salute another, inasmuch as the other may receive greetings of peace but others should not salute him, as he

227

Is not in a state of contentment, if, however, they saluted him, he should respond to their greeting. After thirty days (of mourning) he is like other people in regard to salutation. All the foregoing is applicable only to week-days, on the Sabbath, however, the mourner is permitted to salute others, and to respond to the salutations of others even during the (first) seven days of mourning.

7. In the seven days a mourner should not take a child in his arms, in order that it may not lead him to levity. He is likewise forbidden to hold much conversation with people, unless he should do so to honour them, e.g., he is permitted to say on the departure of many people who came to comfort him, "Go to your homes and fare ye well," this being permissible in honour of the majority.

8. It is permissible for him to say שהחיינו even during the seven days, when the occasion requires it, e.g., on Chanucah or on partaking of a new fruit and the like.

LAWS CONCERNING THINGS WHICH ARE FORBIDDEN TO A MOURNER.

1. He is forbidden to sit upon cushions and pillows during the seven days, he should sit only on the ground; in the case, however, of an invalid or of an old man, to whom sitting on the ground is painful, it is permissible for them to sit on a small cushion. The mourner may walk and stand, and he is not required to sit, except in the presence of comforters, when it is obligatory to sit.

2. On the first day of mourning, the mourner is forbidden to wear Tephillin, it matters not whether it be the day of death and burial, or of burial only. If the burial took place at night, it is forbidden to wear Tephillin the following day, and it is only permitted to wear them the day thereafter, after day-break. The day one receives "timely" tidings of a death of a relative is counted as the day of death and burial in regard to wearing Tephillin. But if the death occurred on a Festival, or if he heard "timely" tidings on that day, he may wear Tephillin on the first day after the Festival.

3. One is forbidden to wear a washed garment, even a shirt, during the seven days of mourning even in honour of the Sabbath. It is even prohibited to use freshly washed sheets or bed-spreads or (freshly washed) towels. In honour of the Sabbath, however, it is permissible to use the table-cloths that had been washed prior to the period of mourning.

4. One is forbidden to wash his garments, or even to put them aside, until after the seven days because it is work. If, however, his garments were in the hands of others, they are permitted to wash them, just as though it were any other work which they had contracted to do for him. One who became a mourner immediately after having finished a period of mourning, is permitted to wash his garment (but with water only, not with soap or the like) and to wear it.

5. After the first seven days until the thirtieth day, he should not wear a washed garment even if it be unbleached, unless another person had previously worn it for a short time, if, however, it were merely washed with water, it is unnecessary for another person to have worn it first.

6. If he did not change his garments for pleasure, but out of necessity, e.g., if the garments which he wears be soiled, or if it be necessary for the sake of cleanliness, he is permitted to do so even during the first seven days and on a week-day, provided the clean garments were first worn by another.

7. One is permitted to wash and bleach a garment after seven days, and to wear the same after thirty days and even within the thirty days, if another had worn it first.

8. During the thirty days of mourning one is forbidden to wear his Sabbath garments even on the Sabbath. It is forbidden likewise to wear new garments. One who mourns for a parent is forbidden to wear new garments the entire twelve months. If, however, he be in need of them, he should let another person wear them first, for two or three days.

9. A woman who had given birth to a child, and who wished to go to the Synagogue on a Sabbath during the thirty days of mourning, or even during the first seven days of her mourning, as it is customary for her to consider that Sabbath as a day of rejoicing and to wear her best garments and jewels, she is permitted on the Sabbath also to wear her Sabbath-garments, but not the best ones reserved for a Festival. It is not necessary for her to change her place (in the Synagogue).

10. One is forbidden to cut his hair during the thirty days of mourning, this refers not only to the hair on the head. If he mourn for a parent he is forbidden to cut his hair the entire twelve months, unless it be necessary, e.g., if his hair were a burden to him, or if he go amongst people of different beliefs, and he would be looked upon with disdain on account of his hair, which alters his appearance so that he is unlike other people to such an extent as to arouse comment, under such circumstances he is allowed to cut his hair, but only after the thirty days of mourning.

11. One is forbidden to pare his nails with an instrument, it is, however, permissible to do so with one's hands or teeth even during the first seven days of mourning. Even a Mohel is forbidden to shape his nails as is required for uncovering the foreskin, unless there be no other Mohel available to perform the circumcision, he is then permitted to do so even during the first seven days of his mourning. A woman who requires a ritual bath after the first seven days of mourning and during the thirty days of mourning, should ask another person to pare her nails. Combing the hair is allowed even during the first seven days of mourning.

12. It is customary for a mourner to change his place in the Synagogue during the entire thirty days. If he mourn for his parents he should change his place during the entire year. The changed place should be at least four cubits from his accustomed seat, and further removed from the Holy Ark.

LAW CONCERNING REJOICING FORBIDDEN TO A MOURNER

EVEN AFTER THE FIRST SEVEN DAYS OF MOURNING.

1. A mourner is forbidden to join in the circumcision feast or in the feast to celebrate the redemption of the first-born, or on the occasion of the conclusion of the reading of a tractate of Mishnah or Talmud, and more especially a wedding feast, during the thirty days of his mourning for one's relatives, and during the year for one's parents (even in a leap-year twelve months are sufficient). If a religious feast take place at his house, he is permitted to partake thereof, he should abstain from joining in a wedding feast, even if it take place at his house, unless one of the couple be an orphan whom he has given in marriage, and his abstaining from eating might cause the match to break off, he is then permitted to eat even if the feast be in another house; he is also permitted to wear the Sabbath garments (if it occurred) after thirty days even if he were in mourning for his parents, and for other relatives even during the thirty days.

2. He is not permitted to join with others to say Grace, or to say Grace with those who have united to do so. He should neither send gifts to others, nor should others send gifts to him during the thirty days of mourning, nor during the twelve months of mourning for one's parents.

3. If after thirty days a mourner (even for one's parents) officiate as Godfather or circumciser he is permitted to wear his Sabbath garments until after the circumcision and he may also join in the feast.

4. During the thirty days of mourning for other relatives, or during the twelve months of mourning for one's parents, the mourner is forbidden to enter a house where a wedding feast is being celebrated, even to hear only the benedictions that are recited on that occasion.

LAWS AND CUSTOMS OF ISRAEL

During the ceremony of marriage, however, when the benedictions of the marriage service are being said, he is allowed to stay and to listen to the benedictions, if it be after the thirty days of mourning even for a parent. He is even permitted to say the benedictions, and to act as best man escorting the bridegroom under the nuptial canopy, he is then also permitted to wear his Sabbath garments, but only if it be after the thirty days. A mourner is permitted to attend a wedding feast if he act as waiter, and he may eat in his own home what is sent to him from the feast.

Laws Prohibiting a Mourner to Marry During the Thirty Days of Mourning.

1. A mourner is forbidden to marry during the thirty days of mourning. A woman in mourning is likewise forbidden to be married until after the thirty days, thereafter, however, it is permissible, even if one mourn for a parent. It is, however, permitted to arrange a betrothal without a feast, even during the seven days of mourning.

2. If one's wife died he should not marry again until three Festivals have elapsed. Rosh-Hashanah, Yom-Kippur, and Shemini 'Azereth are not reckoned as Festivals in that respect. If, however, he had not yet fulfilled the precept " be fruitful and multiply " (Gen.i. 28) or if he had young children, or if he had no one to look after him, he need not wait until the three Festivals have passed. Nevertheless it is proper to wait until after thirty days. A woman whose husband died must wait ninety days before being married again.

Laws Concerning the Time When a Mourner May Leave His House.

1. A mourner is forbidden to leave his house during the entire seven days of mourning, unless a death that required his attention had occurred in the meantime, or even if it occurred somewhere else where the people are destitute of the means wherewith to provide what is required for burial, he is then permitted to leave his house even on the first day, also if there be a matter, which, if he should not go out to attend to, will entail a great loss, he is permitted to go out, but he should put earth in his boots.

2. He is forbidden to leave the house even to go to the Synagogue to pray during the first seven days except on the Sabbath, if it be not possible for him to gather ten adults at his house, and he would be compelled to pray privately, while there is a Minyan in his neighbourhood, he may go there to pray rather than be prevented from participation in public worship.

231

3. If the mourner have to circumcise his son he may go to the house where the circumcision takes place, even during the first three days (of mourning). If a mourner be a Godfather or circumciser he is forbidden on that account to leave his house during the first three days (of mourning); and after these three days he should pray at home although he is allowed to go and attend the circumcision wherever it takes place. If, however, there be no other operator in the city, he is allowed to leave his house to attend the circumcision even on the first day of mourning.

LAW FORBIDDING EXCESSIVE GRIEF.

1. One should not grieve over much. Three days suffice for weeping, seven for lamenting and thirty for abstaining from wearing fully washed garments, and cutting the hair. The foregoing, however, apply only to an ordinary deceased person, but in the case of a scholar, his death should be deplored in proportion to his wisdom. Nevertheless he should not be mourned for more than thirty days.

2. If one of a family had died the entire family should evince sorrow, likewise when a member of a society dies the members of the society should evince grief.

3. He who does not mourn in accordance with the regulations laid down by our Sages is cruel, for it is his duty to bestir himself, and examine his deeds with fear and anxiety and to repent, perchance he may escape the sword of the Angel of Death.

LAW CONCERNING "PART" OF THE SEVENTH DAY AND "PART" OF THE THIRTIETH DAY, ALSO THE LAW CONCERNING THE TWELVE MONTHS.

1. On the seventh day, after the time when the comforters were wont to come, that is after the departure of the worshippers from the Synagogue, the mourner is permitted to do all those things, that were forbidden during the seven days, for, the Rabbis say : "part of a day is reckoned as the entire day." This applies to all things except to cohabitation which is forbidden the entire day (even in a dark room). If the seventh day of mourning occurred on the Sabbath, it is permissible for the mourner to study the Torah, immediately after he leaves the Synagogue.

2. With reference to the thirtieth day, the Sages also say, "part of the day is reckoned as an entire day," and immediately at daybreak, the mourner is relieved from the observance of the laws pertaining to the thirty days of mourning. If the thirtieth day fall on the Sabbath, he is permitted to bathe in warm water on Friday in honour of the

Sabbath, and to wear Sabbath garments, also to resume his original seat in the Synagogue, he is, however, forbidden to cut his hair.

3. With reference to the twelve months of mourning for one's father or mother, the rule stating, " part of a day is reckoned as an entire day " does not hold good, on the contrary, it is customary to add the Jahrzeit day (even if it occur on the Sabbath) to observe thereon all the laws relating to the twelve months. During a leap-year, however, it is not customary to be in mourning for one's parent longer than twelve months, and inasmuch as the twelve months had expired prior to the Jahrzeit day, he is not required to resume mourning on the day of Jahrzeit.

LAW CONCERNING ONE WHO DID NOT OBSERVE MOURNING.

1. A mourner who did not keep mourning during the first seven days, whether inadvertently or intentionally, may make amends for this neglect during the entire thirty days, except with reference to rending the garment, which only applies during the first seven days, but for one's parents one should rend the garments at any time.

2. A child whose relative had died while he was yet a minor need not observe any of the laws of mourning, even if he became an adult, i.e., thirteen years and one day, during the seven days of mourning, inasmuch as he was exempt therefrom when death had occurred. But with reference to the twelve months of mourning for his father or mother, he should observe all the laws of mourning since it is in their honour.

3. An invalid whose relative had died for whom he is required to mourn, if he became aware of it and recovered during the first seven days, he should keep mourning during the remainder of those days, likewise during the thirty days he should keep mourning during the remainder of the thirty days, but he need not make up for the days that had passed while he was ill. This law is also applicable to a woman who had given birth to a child, who is also not required to make up for the days that had passed while she was in child-birth, but she merely keeps mourning during the remaining days.

LAWS CONCERNING TESTIMONY THAT MAKES

MOURNING OBLIGATORY.

1. One is obliged to mourn on being informed of a death by one witness, or by the disinterested statement of a non-Jew. One who received a letter notifying him of the death of a relative, but it failed to mention whether it be within thirty days or after thirty days of mourning, (should be guided by the kind of man the writer is) if the latter be not versed in the Torah, he may take it for granted that his relative was alive shortly before the letter was written, and he is

obliged to mourn. If, however, the writer were a man learned in the Torah, it may be assumed that it is after the thirty days, for if there were a possibility of the letter reaching (its destination) during thirty days, the former would not have written to him regarding a relative, except in the case of a parent, of whose death it is the custom to inform the son immediately, and for whom he is bound to mourn.

LAW CONCERNING MOURNING ON A SABBATH OR FESTIVAL.

1. The Sabbath that occurs in the first seven days of mourning is subject to all the rules regulating the private life a mourner, thus, he is forbidden to cohabit and bathe, he is, however, exempt from the observance of mourning in public, therefore before the recital of מזמור שיר ליום השבת he is permitted to put on his boots, to sit on a chair, and to put on another garment in place of the one he had rent, but the study of the Torah is accounted as a private matter and is not allowed. but he is permitted to read the weekly portion of the Torah twice, and the Targum (Aramaic translation) once, for inasmuch as it is the duty of every one to complete the Torah uniformly with the congregation, he may regard it as the obligation of reading the Shema', or like the reading of another portion of the services of the day.

2. If the mourner were called to the reading of the Torah he must go, as his refusal would indicate public observance of mourning. Likewise one who was accustomed to be called up to the reading of the Torah every Sabbath, should also be called up on the Sabbath during mourning, for inasmuch as he was accustomed to go to the reading of the Torah every Sabbath, his failure to do so on the Sabbath during mourning will arouse the attention of those present, and they will know that he is in mourning, thereby will he infringe the law forbidding the public observance of mourning on the Sabbath. A priest who is in mourning, if there be no other priest in the Synagogue, should be called up to the reading of the Torah, but it would be better for him to leave the Synagogue before the Scroll is taken out of the Ark. Likewise if a mourner have a son who is to be circumcised and it is customary for the former to be called up to the reading of the Torah, as that is his duty, then he should be called up, as the failure to do so will make people aware that he is in mourning, and it will thus be a sign of mourning in public. It were best, however, for him to absent himself from the Synagogue during the reading of the Torah.

3. If the official reader of the Torah on Sabbaths became a mourner, he should not go to that Synagogue on the Sabbath during the first seven days of mourning, as his presence would raise a question of law as to whether he should read or not.

4. The Sabbath day is included in the total of the first seven days, thus, even if he received timely tidings of the death of a relative on Sabbath when he did not begin mourning, it is yet counted as one of the seven days, and he should rend his garment at the termination of the Sabbath.

5. One who buried his dead relative or received " timely " tidings of the death on a Festival itself, or during the Intermediate days of the Festival is not subject to the laws of mourning until after the Festival. The foregoing refers only to the observance of mourning in public, it is customary, however, to observe it in private matters, but one need not change his garments on the Festival, as that would constitute a public observance of mourning, and if he be accustomed to wear Tephillin during the Intermediate days of a Festival, he should wear them on the first day after the funeral.

6. After the Festival is concluded, the mourner should begin to count seven days of mourning, the last day of the Festival (in all countries but Palestine) counting as one of the seven days, after which he should count six days, even the second day of Rosh Hashanah is included in the total of seven days, and if the death occurred on the first day of Rosh Hashanah and the burial took place on the second day, the ecclesiastical authorities should be consulted.

7. Although the period of mourning does not begin on a Festival or during the Intermediate days thereof, nor do the laws pertaining to the thirty days of mourning apply to them, and it is allowed to wear washed garments, they are, nevertheless, included in the total of thirty days mourning, inasmuch as cutting the hair is then forbidden because of the Festival. One should count the thirty days from the day of burial. With reference to Shemini 'Azereth, although it is a Festival by itself, inasmuch as he did not yet begin to mourn thereon, it does not annul the period of mourning and counts but as one day in the total of thirty days.

8. If a bridegroom married before a Festival and celebrated his seven days of rejoicing during the Festival, during which time one of his relatives died, he cannot include these seven days of rejoicing in the total of the thirty days of mourning.

9. Although mourning is not observed during a Festival, still it is right to give to the one who has suffered the loss the attention usual in comforting a mourner, and after the Festival, at the expiration of seven days from the burial, although the seven days of mourning did not yet expire, he may employ others to do his work in their homes, and his workpeople may do his work privately in his home, and after the Festival it is not necessary to comfort him for as many days as he was comforted during the Festival.

LAW CONCERNING THE SEVEN AND THE THIRTY DAYS OF MOURNING THAT ARE ANNULLED BY A FESTIVAL.

1. One who buried his dead relative before a Festival and mourned for him, should cease mourning immediately the Festival begins, and even if the burial took place on the eve of the Festival toward the close of the day, in a manner that makes mourning obligatory upon him, even if he had taken off his boots only for a short

time before the Festival, he should cease mourning, and it is considered as if he had kept the entire seven days of mourning, and the first day of the Festival is counted as the eighth day of mourning, and thus it is reckoned in the sum of the thirty days. Even if the eve of the Festival occurred on a Sabbath, and he received "timely" tidings towards the evening, although only mourning in private matters is customary on that day, being Sabbath, inasmuch as he had observed even that, the Festival annuls the seven days of mourning.

2. One who inadvertently or intentionally did not observe mourning before the Festival, or who could not observe mourning owing to the fact that the burial took place at the approach of night, is not exempt from observing the first seven days of mourning, as the Festival does not annul them, and he is subject to the same law as applies to one who buries his dead on a Festival.

3. If one of the days of mourning (except the seventh day) occurred on the eve of a Festival, he is permitted to wash his garments after noon, but he should not wear them before night, and he is permitted to bathe after the afternoon service towards night-fall (but to cut the hair is forbidden).

4. If the seventh day of mourning fell on the eve of a Festival, inasmuch as we hold that a portion of a day counts as an entire day, the seven days of mourning expire as soon as he had left the Synagogue, and the rest of the day is counted as belonging to the thirty days of mourning, which are annulled owing to the intervention of the Festival, and he is permitted to wash his garments, bathe himself and cut his hair on the eve of the Festival towards night-fall, inasmuch as he does so in honour of the Festival. On the eve of Passover, the mourner is permitted to bathe immediately after noon, as it is partially regarded as a Festival, but he should cut his hair in the forenoon, as another person is forbidden to cut his hair for him in the afternoon.

5. If the seventh day of mourning occurred on the eve of a Sabbath, and this Sabbath was the eve of a Festival, the mourner is permitted to wash, to bathe, and to cut his hair on the eve of the Sabbath.

6. One who had neglected to cut his hair on the eve of the Sabbath or on the eve of a Festival, is forbidden to cut it during the Intermediate days of the Festival, inasmuch as he was able to cut it prior thereto, but he is permitted to cut it after the Festival. If, however, his seventh day of mourning occurred on a Sabbath that was the eve of a Festival, inasmuch as he could have cut his hair as far as the rules of mourning are concerned, but he was only prevented by the intervention of the Sabbath, and was thus compelled to abstain therefrom, he is therefore permitted to cut his hair during the Intermediate days of the Festival.

7. All the foregoing laws referring to the annulment of the thirty days of mourning by reason of the intervention of a Festival

are applicable only in the case of the death of any relative except a parent, as one who mourns for the latter is forbidden to cut his hair until his friends reproach him for abstaining therefrom, such mourning (in this case) is not annulled by a Festival.

8. If one had observed one hour of mourning (not necessarily a complete hour, as less also suffices) before the Passover, that hour (or part of the hour) is reckoned as though he had mourned for seven days, which together with the eight days of Passover are reckoned as fifteen days and he need only mourn for fifteen days thereafter to complete the thirty days of mourning. If one had observed mourning for one hour before Pentecost, that hour is reckoned as seven days, and the first day of Pentecost is also reckoned as seven days, whilst the second day of Pentecost constitutes the fifteenth day of mourning, and the observance of fifteen days more completes the thirty days. If he had observed one hour's mourning before the Feast of Tabernacles, it is counted as seven days, which together with the seven days of Tabernacles are reckoned as fourteen days, the Festival of Shemini 'Azereth counts also as seven days making a total of twenty-one days, the Simchath Torah day completing twenty-two days, and by the observance of eight days more he completes the thirty days.

9. The New Year and the Day of Atonement are reckoned as Festivals with regard to the annulment of the seven days and the thirty days of mourning, thus if one had observed one hour's mourning before the New Year it annuls the seven days of mourning, whilst the Day of Atonement annuls the thirty days of mourning. If he had observed one hour's mourning before the Day of Atonement, the latter annuls the seven days of mourning, whilst the Feast of Tabernacles annuls the thirty days of mourning.

10. Although the Festival annuls the period of seven days mourning, nevertheless the custom of lighting a lamp (or candle) and keeping it in the place where the relative died in honour of his or her soul, should be observed also on the Festival, although the most appropriate course is to do this in the Synagogue.

"*He will destroy death for ever; and the Lord God will wipe away tears from off all faces*" (*Is. xxv. 8*). *May we be found worthy to go up to Zion with rejoicing.*

N.B. The last sentence in vol. i. p. 17 §7 should read: "In some places they appoint a committee to confirm the appointment," etc.

LAWS & CUSTOMS OF ISRAEL.
Vol. 3.

THE
LAWS & CUSTOMS
OF ISRAEL.

VOL· 3.

THE IMPORTANCE OF THE HOLINESS OF THE SABBATH AND ITS
DESECRATION ALSO THE LAWS OF PREPARATIONS FOR SABBATH.

1, The holy Sabbath is the great sign and covenant that the
Most Holy, blessed be His name, has given us to know "that in six
days God made the heavens and the earth and all that is in them and
rested on the seventh day," and that is the foundation of the Faith,
for Sabbath is equal to all other commandments. Observing all the
laws of Sabbath is like fulfilling the whole of the Torah, whilst dese-
crating the Sabbath is like the denial of the Torah in its entirety.

2. Violation of the Sabbath publicly is regarded as the serving
of strange gods. Publicity is constituted through the mere knowledge
by ten Jews of the desecration without their actually seeing same.

3. Hence the praise of the prophet: "Blessed is the man that
doeth this and the son of man that holdeth fast by it: that keepeth
the Sabbath from profaning it," etc. One observing the Sabbath according to its laws, honouring it to his utmost ability, is rewarded in this
world besides the great reward in store for him in the world to come,
as this too is set forth by the prophet: "If thou restrain thy foot for
the sake of Sabbath, not doing thy business on My holy day : and if
thou call the Sabbath a delight, the holy day of the Lord, honourable :
and honour it by not doing thy usual pursuits, by not following thy
own business, and speaking (vain) words. Then shalt though find
delight in the Lord; and I will cause thee to tread upon the high
places of the earth, and I will cause thee to enjoy the inheritance of
Jacob thy father; for the mouth of the Lord hath spoken it."

4. It is written : " Remember the Sabbath·day to keep it holy,"
which means remembering daily the Sabbath day to keep it holy, thus
on coming across a delicious viand of a rare kind, and which is not liable

to be spoilt through keeping, it should be purchased in honour of the Sabbath. It is however preferable to make the purchases in honour of the Sabbath on the eve of Sabbath rather than on Thursday. But articles requiring preparation should be [procured on Thursday. Expression should be given while purchasing that it is in honour of the Sabbath. In accordance to the by-laws of Ezra, the clothes should be washed on Thursday in honour of the Sabbath but not on the Sabbath eve as on that day due attention is needed to the requirements of the Sabbath.

5. It is mandatory upon all, even upon one having numerous domestics, to do something in honour of the Sabbath thereby doing homage unto it, as it was the habit of the Rabbis. Rabbi Chisdo, for instance, used to cut the vegetables very thin. Ruboh and Rabbie Josie used to chop wood. Rabbi Ziro was in the habit of lighting the fire. Rabbi Nachmon put the house in order, bringing all the utensils needed for disposing of [the things used during the week. Others should emulate their example and not regard it undignified, for it is indeed an honour to honour the Sabbath.

6. It is a general custom throughout Israel to bake in their houses loaves in honour of the Sabbath, in order that the woman may be enabled to perform the precept requiring her to separate the dough-cake. Three loaves should be baked, a large loaf, a medium sized one, and a small one; the medium sized one for the evening feast, the large one for the feast in the day-time to show that the Sabbath is entitled to greater honour, the small loaf is left for the third meal.

7. One should prepare choice meat, fish, dessert and good wines, in accordance with his means, for it is desirable to eat fish at every Sabbath meal provided it agrees with him and they are eatable, but not otherwise, for the Sabbath is given us for pleasure and not for sorrow; the [cutlery also in the house should be sharpened and polished in honour of the Sabbath and fresh coverings put on the beds; one should also prepare handsome utensils, and have the household furniture nicely arranged, and the table should be covered with a cloth, which should remain upon the table the entire Sabbath day. He should rejoice with the coming in of the Sabbath, and reflect how the expectation of receiving a distinguished guest would make him active in setting his house in order, how much more so then in honour of Queen Sabbath.

8. Even the poorest of Israel should endeavour with all his might and main to take delight in the Sabbath, he should economise the entire week in order to have sufficient funds wherewith to honour the Sabbath, and if one has no money he should borrow it even upon

a pledge in order to provide for the Sabbath ; of such a one did our Rabbis, of blessed memory, say, " My children borrow for my sake and I will repay " (sayeth the Lord) All that a man disburses for his subsistence is determined and decreed upon the New Year, with the exception of his outlays for Sabbaths and Holidays, for which days, if he increases his outlays, there is a corresponding increase in his income, if, however, one is in needy circumstances, he should be guided by the maxim of our Rabbis, of blessed memory, " Make thy Sabbath as a week-day (not to spend any more for that day) and do not require the aid of the community," nevertheless, if at all possible, he should do some little thing, distinctive for the Sabbath, procure small fishes and such like. One to whom an edible was sent with the express object of having him partake thereof on Sabbath, should eat it on Sabbath and not leave it for a week-day.

9. No work of a fixed character should be pursued on the eve of Sabbath from about 2½ hours before nightfall, but work of a desultory nature is permissible. It is equally permissible when it is required for the Sabbath. When the person is poor and desires to gain sufficient for the requirements of the Sabbath, for him work is permissible all the day as on the Intermediate days of Festivals. Hair-cutting for Israelites is also permissible all day, even in the manner of an artisan, and even for pay, inasmuch as it is obvious that the hair-cutting done then, is for the sake of the Sabbath. It is customary to close shops an hour before Sabbath is due.

10. As soon as a quarter of the day preceding night-fall has arrived, it becomes mandatory to abstain from making a regular feast, even according to one's custom on a week-day, or even a feast of the precepts, if it be possible to make it some other day, it is forbidden to make it the entire day preceding Sabbath, even in the morning. The feast of a precept, however, which has a set time for its performance, e.g., a circumcision or a redemption of the first-born, is permissible. Nevertheless it is proper to hasten its performance in the morning, and not to spend too much time thereon, and one should particularly avoid eating to excess, in order to eat the Sabbath-meal with relish.

11. It is obligatory to conclude each week the weekly portion, viz.: Scripture twice and Targum once. This precept is best performed by reading it on the Sabbath eve in the afternoon, one should read each " Parsha " (sub-division) whether it ends a chapter or not, twice, then its Targum, at the conclusion thereof he should read, after the Targum, one verse in the Torah, in order that he may conclude with a sentence of the Torah. It is well for one not to interrupt the reading with conversation, and it is also customary to read the " Haphtorah." After that is done, some make it a practice to say the " Song of Songs." One who is on the road and has only a Pentateuch, without Targum, should read the Scripture twice, and on arrival at a place where he can obtain the Targum, he should read the Targum. The

more rigorous ought to study Rashi's commentary upon the Law-section, but if he is incapable thereof, he should learn the meaning of the section through a translation in the vernacular.

12. On Sabbath eve it is mandatory to wash face, hands and feet with warm water. And if possible the entire body should be bathed in warm water to be followed by immersion in a ritual bath.

13. It is likewise mandatory to comb the hair, pare the nails, and cut the hair if too long ; but finger and toe nails should not be cut on the same day, nor should the nails and hair be cut on Rosh Chodesh falling on a Sabbath eve. Some object to the paring of nails on Thursday, as the growth would commence on Sabbath, being the third day.

14. All deeds should be reviewed on Sabbath eve and repentance aroused resolving to amend all misdeeds committed during the six days, for Sabbath eve embodies all the week days as does the eve of Rosh Chodesh the entire month.

15. An endeavour should be made to have fine clothes as well as a nice Tallith in honour of Sabbath, for it is written : "And thou shalt honour it" which is expounded by our Rabbis to mean that the garments for the Sabbath should not be the same as those for week-days ; and even while on a journey the attire of Sabbath clothes is desirable for the array is not in honour of the onlookers but in deference to the Sabbath.

16. Victuals must be removed from burning coals before Sabbath begins. In the event of forgetting to do so, it is prohibited for an Israelite to remove it because the burning coals might be touched (and cause to flare up). It is, however, permitted to have it done through a non-Jew.

17. Victuals placed in the oven for consumption on Sabbath, as is customary, is permitted, even though the door of the oven is not closed with mortar. But the door of the oven is not to be opened during the night (Friday) for fear that the food there had not yet properly been cooked and by the subsequent closing of the oven cooking will be accelerated.

18. The permission to place victuals in an oven enclosed by **mortar** refers only to meat, vegetables and other comestibles of a **doughy** nature, but it must be placed there a considerable time before Sabbath begins, so that the food should be cooked a little before Sabbath. If, however, it is placed in the oven close to nightfall then the door must be closed with mortar. This must be strictly observed otherwise it is prohibited to partake of the food till the expiration of Sabbath.

19. It is desirable that the door of the oven which is closed with mortar should be opened by a non-Jew, or, if a non-Jew is not present a child might do it, but in the absence of either it may be done by anyone in a somewhat changed way than would be done on ordinary days.

20. Before darkness approaches the household should be gently asked whether the dough-cake had been separated, and that the candles should be lit.

21. It is obligatory to examine the clothes on Sabbath eve and remove a needle (or pin) that may be sticking there as well as other articles from the pockets; this must be done even in places where there is a "Sabbath Boundary," because the articles might belong to the class that must be "set aside" during Sabbath.

UNDER WHAT CONDITIONS WORK MAY BE DONE ON SABBATH THROUGH A NON-JEW.

1. It is forbidden to allow a non-Jew to do work for a **Jew** on the Sabbath, it being based upon the precept that "no work should be done" which implies even through a non-Jew. But if the work is delivered to the non-Jew on Sabbath eve, even if the latter does it on the Sabbath, it is permissible, but only on the following conditions: That the non-Jew should take the work from the Israelite's house before Sabbath, but not on the Sabbath day.

2. That a stipulated amount should be given the non-Jew in payment for the work, as then the latter does the work for his own sake, in order to get paid, therefore one who employs a non-Jewish

domestic for a stated period, is forbidden to allow the latter to do any work on Sabbath, as the work is solely for the benefit of the Israelite.

3. The non-Jew should be paid a stipulated amount for the entire work and not hired by the day.

4. It is forbidden to engage a non-Jew to do work especially on the Sabbath, even if he does not expressly tell him that he should do it on the Sabbath, but orders its completion immediately after Sabbath, and it is obvious that it cannot be finished by that time unless it is done on the Sabbath, that is forbidden. Likewise if one sends a message through a non-Jew and tells him, "see that you deliver it there on such a day," and it is obvious that it is impossible for him to reach there unless he travels on the Sabbath, this is also forbidden. If a fair (or market) is to be held on the Sabbath-day, it is forbidden to give a non-Jew money on the Sabbath-eve, to buy for him a certain thing, which he surmises he cannot obtain on any other day except on the Sabbath-day, under such circumstances it is also forbidden to give him anything to sell, nevertheless if one does not give the non-Jew explicit instructions to do the work on the Sabbath, it is not forbidden, unless he delivers the work to him on a Sabbath-eve, but previous to that day he is permitted to give him the work to do, or the money to make the purchase.

5. The work should not be of a nature that is connected with the soil, such as in building, or farm-work : indeed, it is forbidden to have a non-Jew work on a building on the Sabbath, even if the Israelite had agreed to pay him a certain amount for the entire work on the building, but in case of urgent necessity one should consult an eminent Rabbi. Even to 'quarry stones, and to prepare beams for building purposes, if it is obvious that they belong to an Israelite, and the non-Jew works thereon publicly in the street, it is forbidden to have it done on the Sabbath. The above is applicable also to farming, i.e., ploughing, or reaping, and the like, even if the non-Jew be hired at a stipulated price for the whole work so that the latter is not a day labourer, it is still forbidden ; if, however, the non-Jew has a share in the crops, and it is also customary in that locality for the worker on the farm to receive a share of the crops, it is permissible, and if the farm is an out-of-the-way place, where there is no Jew in the vicinity within 2,000 paces (a תחום שבת) thereof, it is permissible even if the non-Jew performs the work for a stipulated sum, so long as he is not hired by the day.

6. The owner of a farm or mill may rent them to a non-Jew although the latter works therein on the Sabbath, but one is forbidden to rent a bathing establishment to a non-Jew, but if the Israelite does

not own the bathing establishment, but has only rented it from a non-Jew, he should consult the ecclesiastical authorities how to act as also on other matters arising in this connection.

7. It is forbidden, under any circumstances, to allow a non-Jew to do work at the Israelite's house (on the Sabbath), even a non-Jewish domestic who desires to do some work himself, should be forbidden to do it.

8. If a non-Jewish tailor made a garment to order for an Israelite and brought it to him on the Sabbath, the latter is permitted to put it on, if, however, it be known that the tailor completed it on the Sabbath, it should not be worn, unless in great necessity, but it is forbidden to take utensils or garments from the house of a workman, even a Jewish workman, on a Sabbath or Festival. From a non-Jew who is not a manufacturer, but has a shop where he sells boots, etc., an Israelite who is acquainted with him is permitted to take a pair of shoes and put them on ; there should, however, be no mention of their price, nor should they be of merchandise brought in from without the "Sabbath Boundary" (תחום שבת).

9. It is forbidden to hire to a non-Jew on the Sabbath-eve workman's tools, such as a plough, etc., for although it is not mandatory upon us to cause utensils "to rest" on the Sabbath, nevertheless, inasmuch as he gets paid for it, and has hired it on the Sabbath-eve, it appears as if the non-Jew is his agent, but on a Thursday it is permissible for a Jew to hire it to the non-Jew; lending it, is however permitted even on a Sabbath eve, even utensils with which work is done, the non-Jew however, should take them from the Israelite's house previous to the time of Sabbath, it is permissible even if the former makes the non-Jew agree to reciprocate by the loan of utensils at some future date, and it is not considered as equivalent to hiring it. It is also permitted to hire, even on a Sabbath-eve, utensils with which no work is done, providing the non Jew removes them before Sabbath.

10. Hiring utensils to a non-Jew on the conditions aforementioned, is permissible only, if one does not take the hire for the Sabbath day separately, but is included amongst the rest of the days, e.g., he hires it by the month or by the week and tells him, " you will pay me so much per week, or per month," or even " for every two or three days," but it is forbidden to take hire for Sabbath by itself even if he hired it by the year, but he reckons the hire for each day separately, and says, "I hire you this by the year or by the month, and you will pay me so much per day," even if the non Jew, thereafter, pays him for the entire time in one lump sum, he is forbidden to take hire for the Sabbaths, inasmuch as each day is reckoned by

itself. It is also forbidden to take hire for the Sabbaths which are not included amongst other days, even utensils with which work is not done, even for the rental of a room, the prohibition to take Sabbath-hire is applicable, alike from a non-Jew and from an Israelite.

LAWS CONCERNING EMBARKING ON A VESSEL.

1. A vessel crossing the ocean should not be boarded less than three days before the Sabbath, thus it is forbidden from Wednesday on, but if bound on a sacred mission, it is permitted to embark even on a Sabbath-eve.

2. It is permitted to board a vessel crossing a stream under any circumstances, even on a Sabbath-eve, as long as the Israelite is not required to do any work there on the Sabbath. Even if the barges are pulled by cattle, it is permissible.

3. To board a ship on a Sabbath-eve can only be permitted, if one goes on board on the Sabbath-eve and remains there until nightfall, in this wise, even if one returned home remaining there overnight, it is still permitted to embark thereafter, on the Sabbath, so long as the vessel does not make the trip for Israelites only, but inasmuch as by having remained home on the Sabbath, the "Sabbath rest" had been acquired there, if, therefore the ship had made a longer journey than 2,000 paces and had reached land on the Sabbath, it is permitted to walk no more than 4 paces there, and further than that it is forbidden to go.

4. Boarding a vessel on the Sabbath for the sake of praying in an assembly of ten, or for the sake of performing another precept may be permitted, if the vessel makes the trip also for others, it is nevertheless obligatory upon the Israelite to go on board on the Sabbath-eve while it was yet day, and to remain there until after night-fall, after which he may return home, and come back again on the Sabbath; but to have the vessel make the trip only for the Israelite, should not be permitted. (vide Nessiv Chayim 248).

LAWS CONCERNING THE LIGHTING OF THE SABBATH CANDLES.

1. It is obligatory upon every one to put work aside and to light the Sabbath candles at least half an hour before the appearance of the stars; if מזמור שיר ליום השבת was said in the Synagogue, even if it be

yet two hours before night, the observance of Sabbath is nevertheless obligatory upon the minority from that time, and any manner of work is forbidden. Even an arrival from another city is also obliged to observe the Sabbath immediately מזמור שיר ליום השבת has been said by the congregation. In a city, however, where there are two synagogues, one is not led by the other.

2. It is mandatory to honour the Sabbath by the lighting of many candles. Some are accustomed to light ten, others seven, at any rate, one should not light less than two candles, for it is written, "Remember and observe"; one candle is only allowable in case of necessity; they should be long so that they should burn at least till after the meal, and one should be particular to buy nice candles. It is well that women should give some charity before lighting the candles.

3. It is mandatory to light with olive oil and almond oil which is generally used is also כשר (ritually clean), but there are certain oils that are not כשר. The wick too should be of good quality, such as wool, flax or canvas, for there are kinds that are not suitable for the purpose. It is correct to make candles from tallow as is the general custom in most countries, but it is prohibited to place a quantity of tallow in a vessel, put a wick into it and light it.

4. It is a well-known fact that the blessing relating to a precept is said before the precept is performed, but in the lighting of the Sabbath-candles, inasmuch as by lighting them, the woman assumes the holiness of the Sabbath, and as the blessing is initiative to the lighting, if she would first say the blessing, she would no longer be able to light them, she should therefore first light them, and in order that the blessing be said previous to the performance of the precept she should spread her hands before her face in order to shut out the sight of the candles and pronounce the blessing, she should then put her hands down and gaze upon the candles, it is thus considered as if she said the blessing before lighting them (and in order not to make an exception, this custom also obtains on Holydays). The lighting of the candles that are on the table at which the meal is partaken, is essential to inaugurating the Sabbath, she should therefore light those the last. If she be compelled to go away on account of an urgent matter she may make a mental condition on lighting the candles, that she does not thereby inaugurate the Sabbath, and thus pronounce the blessing before lighting them.

5. The obligation to have candles lit on the Sabbath devolves upon both men and women, but the latter are more beholden therein, inasmuch as they are at home and attend to household matters, another reason assigned is because she caused Adam to sin and thereby darkened his soul, consequently she should take precedence in the performance of that precept, nevertheless it also behoves the man to assist in its performance by preparing the candles and making them easy to light. When a woman is in confinement the husband should light the candles the first Sabbath, but after that, also during mensuration, she should light the candles pronouncing the blessing.

6. It is customary for the women, previous to lighting the candles, to wash themselves and array themselves in Sabbath apparel, " Happy are they ! " it is requisite that they previously say the afternoon prayer, as by lighting the candles they assume the Sabbath, and would therefore be unable to say the week-day afternoon prayers thereafter. If a woman was delayed by her occupation, and reached home about half-an-hour before the Sabbath, and if she should wash herself and change her apparel she would risk profaning the Sabbath, it is more meritorious for her to light them, just as she is, rather than to come to a probable profanation of the Sabbath. If the husband sees that she is tardy in coming, it is most meritorious for him to light them.

7. If the man lights the candles and is afterwards obliged to do some work, it is well for him also to mentally resolve that he does not thereby assume the Sabbath, if he inadvertently omitted to make that condition he is still permitted to do work thereafter, as it is not customary for them by lighting to inaugurate the Sabbath.

8. The candles should be lit where they eat in order that it be apparent that they are lit in honour of the Sabbath, and they should not be lit in one place and then taken to another except in a case of necessity, as for instance when the woman is sick and unable to go to the table, she may light them while in bed, and afterwards they may be placed upon the table in that house, as the entire house is considered their place. Women who light the candles in the Succah and afterwards bring them up to the house are not acting properly. A candle

that burns from the Sabbath-eve should be extinguished and re-lit in honour of the Sabbath, in order that it be apparent that it is lit in honour of the Sabbath.

9. It is necessary to light the candles in every room that is being used. One who is at home with his wife, inasmuch as she pronounces a blessing upon the candles in one room, is not required to pronounce a blessing when lighting the candles in the other rooms ; if, however, he stays elsewhere, and has a separate room there, he is required to light the candles, saying a blessing ; and if several stay in one room, they should all contribute towards the purchase of candles, and one should light them, saying the blessing, and intend to exempt them all by his blessing, but if he has not a separate room, but is in one room with the host who is an Israelite, he is not required to light since his wife lights for him at home. Bachelors who are lodging away from home, are required to light, pronouncing the blessing if they have a separate room, and they should also contribute towards the purchase of candles and one should pronounce the blessing exempting the rest. It is requisite that the candles burn until they arrive there, but if they have not a separate room, inasmuch as they have not wives to light for them, they are required to contribute to the host, and thus acquire a share in the candles. One who eats at the host's table is included with his household and need not contribute towards the candles.

10. It is customary for even many women to light candles in one house, each one pronouncing a blessing upon her own candles, for the increase of light is an increase of joy.

11. No water should be put in the hole where the candle is placed with the object of its extinction on reaching it, but in case of need it might be waived on condition that the water be put in when it is still day : it is, however, strictly prohibited even on Sabbath-eve, to place a vessel fitted with water near the candles so that falling sparks might be extinguished. Bnt it is permitted to put a vessel without water so that the sparks might fall there, sparks not being tangible. But it is forbidden after nightfall to place a vessel near the candles wherein the oil or tallow should drip. But it is allowed to put a vessel for that purpose on Sabbath-eve. If some of the oil or tallow dripped

into the vessel, the latter must not be handled, otherwise it may be removed notwithstanding that it was intended for the purpose.

12. It is well to place the bread upon the table previous to lighting the candles.

13. If a woman is blind and she has a husband, the latter should light the candles, pronouncing a blessing, but if she has not a husband and she lives by herself she should light the candles pronouncing a blessing; if, however, she resides with others in one house, and the others light, the blind woman should light without pronouncing a blessing, but if she be mistress of the house, she should light first, pronouncing the blessing, after which the others should light, pronouncing the benediction.

14. A woman who once forgot to light the candles, should light an extra candle each week, likewise if she forgot several times, she should always light one extra candle, this is in order to remind her to be careful in the future, therefore if she was prevented from lighting by an accident, she need not add to the candles.

LAWS OF THE PRAYERS FOR SABBATH AND HOLYDAYS.

1. It is customary to hold the evening service on Sabbath earlier than on a week-day, this is a proper custom in order to inaugurate the Sabbath as early as possible, but it should be from half of the time for the afternoon service and later. Even those who are accustomed to say the evening prayers during the week-days at the proper time, which is on the appearance of the stars, may pray earlier on the Sabbath, and although, on a week-day, the afternoon prayer is said in the time that the evening prayer is now said, it is of no concern in the evening prayer of Sabbath, inasmuch as it is a meritorious action to take from the week-day and add to the holy day.

2. One should not conclude the blessing השביבנו on a Sabbath or Holyday as he would in a week-day with שומר עמו ישראל לעד, because this blessing refers to the protection of Israel, but Sabbath being itself a protector, the blessing is therefore unnecessary but he should say ברוך . . . הפורס סכת שלום עלינו ועל כל עמו ישראל ועל and close with ירושלים. If, however, he erred and ended it as on a week-day and he was reminded thereof immediately after saying לעד, he should instantly say הפורס סכת שלום, but if he was not reminded thereof until after the time it would take him to say the blessing, he is no longer required to say it.

3. In the תפלה of the Evening Service וינוחו בה is said; of Morning and Additional Services וינוחו בו, and of the Afternoon Service וינוחו בם.

4. After the silent prayer in the Evening Service for Sabbath, the entire congregation say ויכולו; it should be said standing, thus signifying that we are witnesses—for witnesses stand—in the Almighty's creations.

5. After which the Reader says ברוך . . . אלהינו ואלהי אבותינו וכו' then מגן אבות, וכו' and closes with מקדש השבת . . . ברוך the congregation should stand and listen attentively whilst the Reader is saying this blessing, and it is customary for them to say with him מגן אבות until זכר למעשי בראשית but no further.

6. The above blessing is said every Sabbath in the entire year, even when a Festival occurs thereon, also on a Sabbath which occurs at the close of a Festival, but when the first days of Passover occur on a Sabbath, it is not said.

7. It should be said only at a regular place of worship amongst ten, but in a place where prayers amongst ten are only said casually, e.g., at the house of a bride groom, or at the house of a mourner, it should not be said. If ten had appointed a regular place for praying for several weeks, it should be said.

8. It is customary in these countries that the Reader says Kiddush at the Synagogue on Sabbath and Festival evenings, and inasmuch as he is thereby not exempt from saying Kiddush at home, and as he is forbidden to partake of anything previous to saying Kiddush, therefore, in order that his blessing should not be in vain, the wine should be given to a child who had reached the age for being trained in the observances, who having heard the blessing and having been exempted thereby, partakes thereof, and thus the Reader's blessing is not in vain, and if there be not a child in the Synagogue, the one who says Kiddush or another should be intent upon being exempted by the Kiddush, and drink as much as a רביעית in order to say the ברכה אחרונה nevertheless, he may say Kiddish again at his home in order to exempt his wife and family, if they are themselves unable to say it. How he is exempted by the Kiddush in the Synagogue in spite of the fact that Kiddush can only exempt one who says it and then partakes of a meal, is explained by our reliance in an emergency, upon those expounders of the law contending that it suffices if one drank a רביעית

250

of the cup, it is well that he should drink a רביעית besides the mouthful that he swallowed, so that the mouthful be drunk on account of Kiddush and the additional רביעית in place of the meal.

9.   It is customary to say the chapter of במה מדליקין, but it should not be said on Sabbath day, nor on a Sabbath-eve whereon a holiday occurs, nor on a Sabbath of the Intermediate days of a Festival.

10.   It is customary not to come to the Synagogue on the Sabbath as early as on a week day, for sleep is one of the delights of the Sabbaths; this being based on the biblical injunction that the permanent sacrifice should be offered early in the morning but this expression is omitted when referring to Sabbath, thus indicating delay; nevertheless one should take care not to delay the prayers of Shema' and תפלה until their proper time is past.

11.   The time for saying the Additional Service is immediately after the Morning Service, and it should not be delayed later than the end of the seventh hour of the day, and one who says it after that time is called transgressor, nevertheless, he has fulfilled his obligation, as its time is the entire day.

12.   If one had to pray two Shemoneh 'Esrehs, one of the Afternoon Service and one of the Additional Service, e.g., he had delayed saying the Additional Service until six and a half hours, he should first say the Afternoon prayers and then the Additional prayers, because the former is permanent and the permanent is always precedentory, this only applies to one who prays privately, but in a congregation he should not do that.

13.   In the קדושה of the Additional Service when 'שמע ישראל ה אחד 'אלהינו ה is said it is a mistake for the Congregation to follow immediately 'אחד הוא אלוהינו וכו for it is not allowed to utter twice the word אחד consecutively, but it should be said, 'ה. אחד, הוא אלהינו, וכו. Only the Reader who pauses while waiting for the congregation may begin with the word אחד.

14.   In the Afternoon Service previous to the reading of the Law ואני תפילתי should be said. It is not said on a Holyday which occurs on a week-day when the Law is not read, but it is said on a Sabbath

even where there is not a Scroll of the Law to read, it is then said previous to the half-Kaddish in order that there be no interruption between the Kaddish and the שמונה עשרה.

15. After the repetition of the שמונה עשרה by the Reader צדקתך צדק should be said, in memory of Joseph, Moses and David who died on Sabbath afternoon. If, however, the Sabbath is on a date whereon תחנון (Supplications) would not have been said on a week day it should not be said, but when praying in assembly at the house of a Mourner it should be said, for its omission would indicate ths observance of mourning in public, whereas mourning should not be observed publicly on the Sabbath.

16. If one erred on a Sabbath and began saying an intermediate blessing of the week-day service, but was reminded thereof in the middle of the blessing, he is required to conclude the blessing, and then to say the intermediate blessing of the Sabbath or Holyday service; for in fact the blessings of the week-day service should have been said also on Sabbath and on Festivals, only in honour of Sabbath and Festivals the sages reduced the number, and consequently one having commenced a week-day blessing should complete it, since it is in accordance with Law it should be said.

17. If in the Prayers of the Additional Service it is erroneously substituted by a week-day blessing then it should be stopped in the middle of the blessing as soon as reminded thereof and begin the Intermediate Service blessing of the prayer of the Additional Service, because according to the law all the intermediate blessings of the week day are not all essential in this Additional Prayer.

18. Even if one word of the erroneous blessing was said and the mistake at once recognised, it is required to conclude it, the blessing אתה חונן excepted ; for if only the word אתה was said, inasmuch as that word also begins blessings in the evening and afternoon prayers of the Sabbath Service, therefore if during that prayer it was forgotten that it was Sabbath and אתה begun with the intention of saying אתה חונן but immediately recognised the error, it is not necessary to say אתה חונן but קדשת וכו' should be continued, if, however, this occurred during the Morning Prayer, if it was caused by the erroneous impression that it was week-day, it is necessary to conclude the blessing אתה חונן ; but if cognizant of the Sabbath and knowing that ישמח משה should be said, but only through a slip of the tongue due to habit that אתה was said, it

is not necessary to conclude the blessing אתה חונן but ישמח משה should be said, for inasmuch as in the Sabbath Service there are also prayers beginning with אתה it is reckoned as if he had been saying one Sabbath prayer for another, seeing that the word אתה was said though knowing it was Sabbath.

19. If one did not become aware of the error until the concluding blessings (i.e. from רצה, etc.) he should stop in the middle of a blessing wherever he reminds himself, and say the Sabbath or holiday blessing in rotation from beginning to end, but if he only reminded himself after he already began saying יהיו לרצון he should repeat the entire prayer.

20. If one had erroneously substituted one intermediate blessing of the Sabbath prayers for another and became aware thereof before pronouncing the Ineffable Name of the concluding blessing, he should repeat the appropriate blessing, but if he only became aware thereof after he had pronounced the Divine Name, he should conclude by saying מקדש השבת, and is exempted from saying the appropriate blessing, inasmuch as the principle of the intermediate blessings is רצה נא במנוחתנו which is uniform in all the prayers. The above is applicable only to the evening, morning and afternoon services; if, however, he substituted another prayer for the prayer of the Additional Service, he has not fulfilled his obligation, inasmuch as he did not mention קרבן מוסף. Likewise if he substituted the prayer of the Additional Service for the Evening, Morning, or afternoon prayers, he did not fulfil his obligation inasmuch as he mentioned קרבן מוסף and spoke falsely before the Omnipresent, blessed be He.

21. If one erred in the Holyday prayers and instead of concluding מקדש ישראל והזמנים concluded מקדש השבת if he instantly added מקדש ישראל והזמנים he has fulfilled his obligation, but if he did not, he is required to repeat the prayer from אתה בחרתנו, וכו'.

LAWS CONCERNING THE HOLINESS OF SABBATH AND THE FEASTS AT NIGHT AND DAY.

1. It is mandatory to sanctify the Sabbath in words, for it is written: "Remember the Sabbath day to keep it holy," implying an obligation to remember it at its coming in by Kiddush and at its going out by Habdallah, hence our Sages have instituted the ceremony of

sanctification over a cup of wine, both at the coming in and going out of the Sabbath.

2. Kiddush may be said and the meal partaken of although it is not yet night : those, however, who during the week-day scrupulously say the Evening Prayers at the proper time, although saying it earlier on the Sabbath, are forbidden to eat half-an-hour before the appearance of the stars, if, therefore, it is only half-an-hour before nightfall, one should wait till nightfall, when the Shema' and its bene-dictions should be read to be followed by the Kiddush. It is forbidden to partake of anything, even water, before saying the Kiddush.

3. It is mandatory to say Kiddush upon old wine; it is also mandatory to select good wine ; indeed, special effort to obtain choice wine of a good colour should be made. Where grape wine cannot be obtained, Kiddush may be said upon raisin wine. While saying ויכולו one should stand and gaze at the candles, on conclusion thereof he should sit down and gaze at the goblet saying the blessing בורא פרי הגפן and אשר קדשנו, וכו'. If one has no wine, he should say Kiddush upon bread, but not on any other beverage.

4. Kiddush is also obligatory upon women, they should, there-fore, listen attentively when the Kiddush is said and respond אמן but they should not respond ברוך הוא וברוך שמו. A child, even if he had arrived at the age of thirteen, but his religious majority had not been clearly established according to law, cannot (by saying Kiddush) exempt the woman, she should therefore say Kiddush herself, but if she does not know how to say it she should repeat it after the child word by word ; even if she hears the Kiddush said by her husband, or by some other man, it is proper for her to say each word with the one who says Kiddush. If there are several men in one house it is well that one should read Kiddush after the other.

5. One should not say Kiddush upon wine which has turned sour, nor upon wine having a disagreeable odour. Foamy wine should be strained, but if it is impossible to strain it, one must say Kiddush thereon just as it is, but if it is covered by a whitish film, one should not say Kiddush thereon for it has presumably become stale. One may say Kiddush upon wine that has been boiled, or made with honey, but, one should, if possible, seek for different wine.

6. The goblet for Kiddush should be perfect and clean, and it is governed by all the laws pertaining to the cup of blessing for Grace after meals both in the evening and the day-time, as well as the cup of Habdallah. It were well to say Kiddush in the evening upon a large glass (of wine) from which some should be left for Kiddush in the day time and for Habdallah.

7. The bread should be covered whilst the Kiddush is said, even though one says Kiddush on the bread it should still be covered whilst Kiddush is said symbolizing the manna which was covered with dew from above as well as from beneath.

8. The one who says the Kiddush should drink at least a mouthful from the cup without interruption. It is mandatory for all to partake of the cup of blessing. One who does not drink wine on account of having pledged himself to abstain or because it does him harm and the like reasons, should not say the Kiddush upon wine, relying upon others to drink it. Wine of Kiddush, inasmuch as it is one of the essentials of the meal, does not require a concluding blessing to be said thereafter, as that is exempted by the Grace after the meal.

9. On the wine partaken of during the feast one need not pronounce a blessing, as it was exempted by the blessing פרי הגפן of the Kiddush.

10. If one had said Kiddush upon a glass, thinking it contained wine, and then discovered that it contained water or some other beverage, he should repeat the Kiddush upon wine, but if there was wine before him of which he intended to drink during the meal, he is not required to repeat the Kiddush, as it is reckoned to him as if he had said the Kiddush upon that wine, but if there was no wine before him on the table, but there was some in the house of which he intended to partake during the meal, he is not required to say פרי הגפן only אשר קדשנו, וכו' and if the glass contained beer or mead where these are the native drinks, it is not required to repeat the Kiddush under any circumstances, but he should pronounce the blessing שהכל נהיה בדברו and drink, nor is it necessary to repeat it if the saying of Kiddush follows the washing of hands before meals as is the custom in some places.

11. In the day-time at the morning meal, one should say the Kiddush upon a glass (of wine), this Kiddush consists in simply pronouncing the blessing פרי הגפן. This Kiddush is obligatory also upon women. Before this Kiddush is said it is also forbidden to partake of anything, even water, and it is fulfilling the precept in the best manner to say that Kiddush also upon wine, if one, however, is fond of brandy and he says Kiddush thereon, he has fulfilled his obligation, he should be careful to observe that the glass contains a רביעית (the capacity of one and a half egg-shells) and he should drink a mouthful without interruption.

12. Both in the evening and day-time Kiddush should only be said where the meal is partaken of, if one, therefore says Kiddush in one

house and eats in another, although that was his intention when saying the Kiddush he has not fulfilled his obligation concerning Kiddush. One is also required to eat immediately after Kiddush, and if he did not eat immediately thereafter, he has not fulfilled his obligation concerning Kiddush in the day-time. Even if he does not care to eat a regular meal immediately thereafter, still he may say the Kiddush and partake of some pastry, but then he is required to drink a רביעית of the glass in order to say the blessing thereafter על המחיה and על פרי הגפן. A "Mohel" who has to pronounce a blessing upon the "circumcision-cup" but has not as yet said the Kiddush, should drink a mouthful from the glass, then an additional רביעית.

13. After saying the morning prayers, one who feels faint may partake of some slight refreshment previous to saying the prayers of the Additional Service, viz. : of bread no more than the size of an olive (כזית) (or half-egg) but of fruit he may eat plenteously, in order to comfort his heart, he must, however, first say the Kiddush, and drink a mouthful (of wine), than partake of an additional רביעית of wine, or he may drink a רביעית of wine and partake of a כזית food made of the five species of grain.

14. Every Israelite, man or woman, is in duty bound to partake of three meals on the Sabbath, one in the evening and two in the day-time, and at each meal it is obligatory to eat bread (at least) the size of an egg, even during the third meal one should be careful to eat bread, therefore in order to be able to fulfil the precept concerning three meals one should take care not to eat to excess at the morning meal, if, however, one finds it impossible to partake of bread (at the third meal) he should, at least, partake of food made from any of the five species of grain upon which the blessing בורא מיני מזונות is pronounced, but if this also is impossible for him, he should at least partake of that which is eaten with bread, such as meat, fish and such food. and if this also is impossible for him, he should, at any rate, partake of fruit. The time for partaking of the third meal begins from half-an-hour past noon.

15. One is obliged to "break bread" at every meal upon two entire loaves, even if one partakes of many meals, he is required to have "two-fold bread" at every meal, also when saying Kiddush in the morning before meal time, when he partakes of pastry, he should take two entire cakes. Before saying the blessing המוציא, he should divide one of the loaves ; it is customary, before saying the blessing, to make a mark with the knife upon that part of the loaf he desires to cut, and he should lay the loaves in such a way that the one he desires to cut should be before him, so that he need not (by passing a loaf) "leave a precept unfulfilled."

16. If only one of those who are at table has "twofold bread" he should apportion it and exempt them all, they are also exempted from saying the blessing המוציא as it was said by the one who divided the bread. Before saying the blessing המוציא the latter should say ברשות מורי ורבותי and after he had partaken of his portion of the bread on which he had said the blessing המוציא, he should give each one a portion which they should eat.

17. It is forbidden to fast on the Sabbath for the express purpose of fasting, even for a very short time, and to fast until noontime is forbidden at any rate, even if not done for the express purpose of fasting. If one did not read the Law section—Scripture twice and Targum once—on the Sabbath eve, it is mandatory upon him to read it before eating. if he, however, felt faint, or it approached the noonhour, he should read it before the Afternoon Service, and if inadvertently delayed, it may be read until Tuesday evening.

18. One should generously partake of fruit and delicacies also inhale sweet perfumes in order to complete the total of one hundred blessings. Indeed, it is mandatory to take delight on the Sabbath in everything that gives pleasure, and one is forbidden to be distressed about anything, but should pray for mercy to the good God.

19. Sleep is one of the pleasures of the Sabbath, therefore, one who is accustomed to sleep after the meal should not discontinue it ; after which a time should be set aside for the study of the Torah, and assemblies should be formed where the Torah should be taught to the multitude, for thus did our Rabbis, of blessed memory, say : "Sabbaths and Festivals were given to Israel only to devote themselves to the study of the Torah," as there are many who are preoccupied in their work during the week, and have no time to study the Torah regularly, but on Sabbaths and Festivals, being relieved from their work, they can study the Torah properly, hence all those who do not study the Torah the entire week, are all the more obliged to study the Torah on the holy Sabbath, each according to his conception and capacity. One is forbidden to say : "I will sleep and rest myself on the Sabbath so that I may work on the close of the Sabbath."

LAWS CONCERNING THE WORK WHICH IS FORBIDDEN ON THE SABBATH.

1. It is written "These are the things which the Lord hath commanded, that ye should do them. Six days shall work be done, but on the seventh day there shall be to you a holy day, a Sabbath of rest to the Lord : whosoever doeth work thereon shall be put to death." (Ex. xxxv. 1, 2). Our Rabbis. of blessed memory, have expounded the above "work forbidden us to be done on the Sabbath" as having refer-

LAWS AND CUSTOMS OF ISRAEL

-ence to the various works that were necessary for the construction of the tabernacle, which are as follows : (1) Ploughing, (2) Sowing, (3) Reaping, (4) Binding sheaves together, (5) Threshing, (6) Winnowing, (7) Bolting, (8) Grinding, (9) Sifting, (10) Kneading, (11) Baking or Cooking, (12) Shearing fleece, (13) Bleaching it, (14) Beating it, (15) Dyeing, (16) Spinning, (17) Braiding, (18) Knitting two loops cross-wise, (19) Weaving two strands, (20) Separating two strands, (21) Knotting, (22) Un-knotting, (23) Sewing two stitches, (24) Rending for the purpose of sewing two stitches, (25) Snaring a deer, (26) Slaughtering it, (27) Flaying it, (28) Salting its skin, (29) Marking it, (30) Erasing the mark, (31) Cutting it, (32) Writing two letters, (33) Erasing for the purpose of writing two letters, (34) Building, (35) Breaking down, (36) Extinguishing, (37) Kindling, (38) Beating with a hammer, (39) Carrying from one place to another.

PLOUGHING.—Ploughing is forbidden in any form and includes the following : Digging in the field, making a ridge, levelling a small mound, filling up a hollow in the ground, filling up holes wherever the ground is arable. Likewise all that is done to improve the soil, such as manuring it, or casting out the stones in order to enrich the ground, or breaking up its clods, or pasturing his flock upon a field in order that they shall manure it, weeding round the roots of trees, cut-ting off dead leaves from growing plants, severing the fresh branches from the growing stock.

SOWING.—The object of sowing is growth, consequently when growth is the intention, it is considered as sowing and is forbidden in any form. This prohibition applies to one who sows, plants, propa-gates, grafts or cuts the branches of a tree in order to increase them. It also includes one who waters plants, or soaks plants in water or does anything to assist the growth of fruit. Seeds placed in a hollow ves-sel which is standing in such a manner as not to touch the soil, it is forbidden to place it on the soil, because it would thereby be assis-ted in its growth. Likewise if it stood on the ground, it is forbidden to raise it and place it anywhere above the ground, it is even forbidden to handle that vessel.

REAPING.—Reaping, such as detaching anything from whence it grows, whether done by hand or with an instrument, even with one's teeth, is forbidden ; even if the plants are not attached to the soil, but grow on uprooted trees, such as mushrooms or creeping vines, or moss, all that is included in the work of reaping, which is forbidden.

BINDING SHEAVES.—The work of binding sheaves together applies only to that what grows on the earth, and consists in gathering severed ears of corn, or fruit, or saplings where they were raised and heaping them up, as is done with grain. In this prohibition is included gathering fruit together, even where they were not raised, and piling them up in one heap, or tying them with a cord in one mass. It is also forbidden to gather anything together where it was raised even if it is not a vegetation of the earth, such as salt at the place where it is mined.

THRESHING.—Threshing applies only to growths on the soil and consists of crushing ears of corn or removing peas from dry pods, this however is forbidden only when a quantity is treated at one time, but to open one pod at a time and immediately to partake thereof is permitted, as this is a manner of eating. It is permissible to crack nuts, filberts and almonds, and to break open their hard shells, but it is forbidden to peel the soft green husk of the shell.

It is forbidden to press olives, grapes or raisins, likewise other fruit, in order to extract their juice, thus even the squeezing of lemons is forbidden. It is also forbidden to press bread that has been soaked in wine or any other liquid, for by so doing the liquid is extracted.

It is forbidden to milk an animal on the Sabbath, but it is permitted to tell a non-Jew to milk the animal in order to relieve it of its distress. A woman to whom the abundance of milk in her breasts causes pain, is permitted to let the milk out upon the ground.

It is forbidden to scrape snow and hail crushing them into small portions in order to extract the water, but it is permitted to place it in a cup of water, letting it melt of itself. It is even permitted to scrape them with the hands into a cup of water. It is permitted to pour warm water upon sugar, it is also permitted to break ice in order to obtain water for drinking, or for washing the hands.

LAWS AND CUSTOMS OF ISRAEL

It is forbidden to wring out a garment which had absorbed any liquid. If water was spilled it is forbidden to wipe it up with a cloth about which one is particular, as we are apprehensive lest he will wring it out, nor should it be wiped up with a sponge unless there is a handle to it which may possibly guard it against being wrung out, if, however, it has no handle it is impossible to keep from wringing it. It is forbidden to wring out hair on the Sabbath. It is especially forbidden to wash one's head on the Sabbath, as by so doing one transgresses many prohibitions.

WINNOWING.—The work of winnowing which is forbidden consists in scattering chaff to the wind by means of a fan. It is therefore forbidden to expectorate where there is a current of air, as the wind scatters it and it has a semblance to winnowing.

SEPARATING.—The work of separating which is forbidden consists of the following five forms : (1) Separating the worthless matter from the food, even if done with one hand and for the purpose of eating immediately is forbidden, (2) Separating the food from the worthless matter by a fine or coarse sieve or even by any other utensil, even for the purpose of eating immediately is forbidden, it is, however, permitted to separate with the hand that which one desires to partake of immediately in the meal which is to follow ; this is permissible only if the food is more than the worthless matter, as otherwise it is forbidden even to handle the entire mixture, (3) Separating one food from another, if they are two different kinds, such as two sorts of fish cooked together, although they are large pieces and easily distinguishable, nevertheless, the kind one desires to eat immediately is considered as the food whilst the other is regarded as the worthless matter, and it is governed by the laws treated of above in Nos. 1 and 2, (4) Separating one food from another, either large pieces from small or the opposite, whether of the same kind or of two kinds, and selecting of both kinds, either the large pieces from the small or the opposite, that is permitted, (5) The laws concerning separation apply also to that which is not food, such as utensils, wood, garments, and sticks which one separates from what has a resemblance to each other.

It is forbidden to put food which is mixed with worthless matter into water in order that the worthless matter sink to the bottom or float on the top, as that is "separating."

Straining wine or other beverages (except clear water) by means of a cloth is permissible, but the cloth should not be so manipulated as to form a receptacle for the wine, that change being made because of the Sabbath. It is essential, however, that they be entirely clear and without lees, or if it is mostly drunk that way, and it is only strained on account of slivers that fell therein, for inasmuch as it is fit to drink as it is, it does not constitute "separating." If, however, the beverage is thick and one filters it in order to remove the dregs, as that actually constitutes "separating" it is forbidden, it is, however, permitted to drink through a cloth as the laws concerning separating apply only if done previous to eating thereof, but not while eating or drinking thereof.

When drinking coffee care should be taken not to pour out all the clear coffee leaving only the coffee-grounds, as that is equivalent to "separating," this is especially forbidden if the coffee is not drunk immediately, but strained for use during the day and more especially if done by means of a strainer, as that is forbidden even if desired to drink thereof immediately. One should also be careful, when pouring beer and leaving the dregs, or coffee and leaving the coffee-grounds, to leave also some beer with the dregs, or coffee with the grounds. It is also forbidden to skim the fat from soup, unless some of the soup is also skimmed off with it.

It is forbidden to let milk stand in a warm place in order to turn it into cheese as that constitutes "separating." To place coagulated milk in a bag, so that the scrum runs out as in the process of cheese making, is forbidden, as it constitutes "separation." It is also forbidden to put vinegar and the like in milk to curdle it, as that constitutes "separating."

If a fly fell in an edible or beverage, one should not remove the fly itself, but should throw some of the edible or beverage along with it.

It is forbidden to peel garlic and onions and all other fruit, such as nuts, almonds and so forth, in a greater quantity than is necessary for the immediate meal, but to provide for another meal is forbidden.

GRINDING.—The work of grinding which is forbidden consists in pounding spices or drugs in a mortar, one, therefore, who needs to beat pepper or coarse salt should beat them with the handle of a knife, and upon the table or in a plate.

It is forbidden to cut up leek, or horse-radish and the like in very fine slices. as that constitutes "grinding," it is therefore forbidden to cut up onions for the purpose of putting in food excepting immediately before a meal, as that which one grinds to eat at once, does not constitute the grinding of the kind forbidden.

It is forbidden to rub cheese on a grater, but it is permitted during the meal to cut it with a knife, it is also permitted to crumble

261

food even into very small particles in order to eat it at once, because it does not constitute grinding.

It is forbidden to rub off mud from a garment, or to scrape it off with the finger-nail, if, however, it has no consistency, but merely the appearance, it is permitted to reduce it by scraping.

SIFTING.—The work of sifting which is forbidden consists in doing that for the sake of removing the worthless matter, to sift ground מצה and the like in order to immediately partake of the fine flour is forbidden, as that constitutes sifting, inasmuch as the large pieces are regarded as the worthless matter.

It is permitted to put food for an animal in a sieve and place it thus in the crib, although the chaff falls through the holes of the sieve, inasmuch as that is not the intention.

KNEADING.—The work of kneading which is forbidden consists in mixing together flour, bran, clay, earth or ground mustard; included in this prohibition is the mixing up of that which is not even fitted for being kneaded, as ashes, or coarse sand. It is even forbidden to pour water upon any of these as that constitutes kneading.

One desiring to mix horse-radish, or mustard with vinegar on the Sabbath should previously pour in the vinegar and make only a very thin mixture, and should not mix it with a spoon. The same law applies to preparing bran for poultry.

BAKING.—The work of baking which is forbidden consists of baking, cooking, or roasting over a fire, or by heat derived from fire, or even by the heat of the sun, either food, chemicals, or water; even what is partaken of raw, such as fruit and milk, also in melting wax, fat and pitch and the like, or in melting a metal as it is melted in a crucible until it is poured out as a liquid and utensils are made thereof, also in putting clay vessels in a furnace and thus manufacturing earthenware, also in putting a piece of wood in an oven in order to dry, as it is obvious that moisture would evaporate therefrom. The rule is that the softening of a hard substance, or the hardening of a soft substance constitutes the work of cooking which is forbidden.

A vessel which had been used over a fire, so long as it is hot enough to burn the hand by contact has the power of cooking, it is therefore forbidden to put anything therein on the Sabbath, furthermore, it is even forbidden to pour from such a vessel (which is called כלי ראשון "the vessel in which the cooking was originally done") upon anything that may be subjected to cooking, inasmuch as the upper crust is cooked by what is poured therein, thus if one poured (from a כלי ראשון) upon roast meat, or upon bread, he should scrape off the upper crust, as it is forbidden to eat that crust on the Sabbath, it is, however, only forbidden to pour it upon a dry article, but it is permissible to pour hot water into cold water, or vice-versa, on condition, however, that the cold water should be so much more than the hot water that it would be impossible to cook therefrom, but serve merely to temper its coolness. The pouring of cold water into hot water is only permissible if done by pouring a large quantity of water all at once, but it is forbidden to pour little by little as it is immediately cooked, therefore it is of no avail if it cools thereafter.

A vessel wherein one had poured the contents of a vessel in which the cooking was done, if it is so hot as to burn the hand by contact, nothing that may be subjected to cooking should be put therein, hence one should be careful on the Sabbath not to put salt or onions in a plate containing food which is so hot as to burn the hand by contact, but it should be put in a spoon.

It is prohibited on the Sabbath to put an article to which the prohibition of cooking is applicable, against a fire or upon a stove, or even upon another vessel which stands near the fire, or to put it close to the sides of a stove after a fire was made therein (although as yet the stove is cold), or to any place where it will become so heated by standing, as to burn the hand by contact, as that actually constitutes cooking. Even if the object is not to warm it but merely to temper its coolness, it is nevertheless forbidden to place it where by long standing it may become hot enough to burn the hand by contact, as it is apprehended that he may forget and let it cook there.

On the Sabbath it is the general practice to replace the victuals in the oven while still warm, this, however, is forbidden if they become entirely cold, but on a place where, no matter how long it stands, it cannot become so heated as to burn the hand by contact, it is permitted to put an empty pot and place the victuals upon it.

Whatsoever an Israelite is forbidden to do, he is forbidden to have same through a non Jew, it is nevertheless the general practice to have a non Jew place the victuals although they are entirely cold, upon the stove before a fire was made therein, but after a fire was made in the stove, it is forbidden to be done even through a non-Jew, the above, however, has bearing only upon victuals that had already been cooked; but an article that was not cooked is forbidden to be placed, even through a non-Jew, upon a stove even before a fire was made therein, inasmuch as it is cooked on the Sabbath for the sake of an Israelite.

When dishes are washed with hot water, one should not pour the hot water upon the dishes, on account of the prohibition against cooking, but should pour the hot water in another vessel in which the dishes can be put.

It is forbidden to beat eggs in a plate, as it seems that it is done for the purpose of cooking them in a pot. It is likewise forbidden to beat anything. It is also forbidden to beat meal broth and meat together, adding hot water thereto and stirring it thoroughly with a spoon into one mass; it is, however, only forbidden if beaten thoroughly, but if it is mixed with a little water, it is permitted. If one mixes the yolk of an egg with warm water, he should take care that the water is only lukewarm in order that the yolk should not be cooked.

SHEARING.—The work of shearing which is forbidden consists in shearing fleece, or fur, from the skin of a domestic animal or wild beast, whether they be alive or dead, even after the skin was stripped off. Even to pull out a hair from a domestic animal or wild beast is forbidden, moreover, it is forbidden to pluck a feather from a fowl whether living or dead.

It is forbidden to pare the nails, or remove a hair, or an ulcer, either with the hand or with an instrument, either of one's self or of others. It is likewise forbidden to comb the hair with a comb on the Sabbath, and even with a hair (brush) as it is impossible that hair should not be torn out.

It is forbidden to pull out even one (grey) hair from one's head from amongst the black hair so as not to appear old. This is forbidden even on a week-day.

BLEACHING.—The work of bleaching which is forbidden consists in washing a garment of any texture whatsoever, this constitutes bleaching: it does not necessitate rubbing the garment together, as in washing for the mere act of pouring water on a garment is termed washing, and it matters not if the garment be soiled or not. If water was spilled upon a table or chair, one is forbidden to wipe it up with anything about which he is particular, lest he wring the cloth from the water, which act constitutes washing it. Likewise if one's hands were wet he should not dry them with anything about which he is particular, lest he be led to washing the cloth, but if beer, wine or any other beverage was spilled, he is permitted to wipe it up with a cloth, inasmuch as (washing) with any other beverage (than water) does not constitute bleaching, the garment not becoming white thereby.

It is forbidden to shake out a garment which was soaked in water, or upon which rain had fallen, it is even forbidden to handle for fear of wringing it out; but swaddling-clothes which are soiled, as well as a garment which was not altogether soaked in water, if none other is at disposal he is permitted to spread them out and hang them up, as it is obvious that they are not washed. They should not be spread out against a stove where it is hot enough to burn the hand by contact.

It is forbidden to shake from a black garment rain, snow, dust or feathers that had fallen upon it. It is obviously certain that it is forbidden to cleanse a garment with a brush. If there be a stain upon an article made of leather it is permissible to pour water upon it, but it is forbidden to wash it.

Immersion is permissible on the Sabbath, but care should be taken not to wring out the hair.

BEATING.—The work of beating which is forbidden consists in combing wool or flax with a comb, or as wool is beaten out to make yarn, or as is the practice of the scribes in hammering upon the ten dons until they are fit for spinning.

DYEING.—The work of dyeing which is forbidden consists of colouring anything, whether it remains permanent or not. Coloured hands should not be wiped with a garment (thus dyeing it), dyeing, however, is only forbidden with that which it is usual to dye with, but the colouring produced by food-stuffs does not appertain to dyeing.

SPINNING.—The work of spinning which is forbidden consists in any mode of spinning whatsoever; it matters not whether spun by machine, or even if he takes the threads and twists them, or if he makes yarn, all of the above constitutes spinning which is forbidden.

WEAVING.—Any improvement made in a woof constitutes the work of braiding which is forbidden, or of weaving two loops cross-wise.

The work of weaving which is forbidden appertains to a garment, rushes, hair, or any texture. This prohibition also applies to the plaiting of two threads, or two hairs, they are all included in the prohibition against weaving.

SEPARATING.—The work of dividing two threads consists of separating the warp from the woof or vice-versa.

KNOTTING AND UN-KNOTTING.—The work of knotting and unknotting is forbidden if done in the following manner: if he ties two articles together with one knot it is not termed knotting as it does not remain fast unless he ties two knots; one side, however, can be tied with one knot and remain fast. These knots which it is usual to tie and untie each day it is permissible to tie and untie on the Sabbath also, but a knot which one does not at times think of un-knotting every day, although it was originally the intention to un-knot it on that day, it is forbidden to either knot or un-knot it. If something that is usually tied with a slip knot became knotted fast unawares, it is permissible to un-knot it. It is permissible to unfasten any manner of edibles that were tied together, as the law considers them subject to being unknotted daily.

SEWING.—The work of sewing which is forbidden consists in sewing two stitches, that is, in passing a needle and thread through the cloth with a back puncture, so that two stitchings and the knot of the thread are visible on one side, or sewing three stitches. even without a knot constitutes the work of sewing which is forbidden. Likewise the drawing of the thread forming a stitch, that is, if the stitching was slightly separated drawing the thread in order to unite it and make it fast is forbidden.

RENDING.—The work of rending which is forbidden consists in tearing anything. even if not for the purpose of making a vessel thereby. It is likewise forbidden to tear apart two sheets that were purposely pasted together to remain so permanently ; if, however, the pages of a book were accidently stuck together by wax or otherwise, it is permissible to separate them since it was not of a permanent nature.

If the mouth of a vessel was tied round with cord or cloth, it is permissible to cut the cord and tear off the cloth if it is necessary to do so, because it is needed for Sabbath purposes.

SNARING.—The work of snaring which is forbidden consists in snaring anything, whether it belongs to the species which one snares or to a species which one does not snare, as snaring in general is forbidden. hence, it is forbidden to snare a domestic animal, a wild beast, or a fowl. Even those which were raised in one's house and long since domesticated, and even if they freely leave and return to the house, nevertheless, if they left the house it is forbidden to snare them and take them by force, but it is permissible to stand in front of them until they enter a house or go in a secure place, inasmuch as they were long since habituated freely to enter his house, if, however, they were not habituated freely to enter his house, that too is forbidden. If a bird entered a room by the way of a window, it is forbidden to shut the window unless it is cold and there is no intention of snaring it thereby, then it is permissible. If a bird left its cage, although it freely re-entered the cage, it is forbidden to shut the door thereof. On Sabbath it is forbidden to set a trap for catching mice.

SLAUGHTERING.—The work of slaughtering which is forbidden consists in slaughtering or killing anything possessing life. This prohibition also includes the drawing of blood or making a bruise in an animal so that the blood coagulates. If a live fish was in a vessel of water since the eve of Sabbath, even if the vessel was small and snaring is not applicable thereto, it is yet forbidden to take it therefrom, as immediately it becomes dry between its fins, a life is taken on the Sabbath, for even if it is replaced in the water, it cannot live any longer.

FLAYING, SALTING AND TANNING.—The work of flaying which is forbidden consists in stripping the skin off the flesh.

The work of salting and tanning which is forbidden consists in tanning skin by the usual process. It is likewise forbidden to tread leather under-foot in order to harden it, or to soften it by hand after the manner of bootmakers. It is also forbidden to make the skin tender by means of oil or anything else. It is likewise forbidden to smear anything on one's shoes, even if it is only his intention to make a polish thereon.

One should not make much brine for pickling purposes, or for preserving butter, but just sufficient for the requirements of the meal. Meat, fish, cooked eggs and the like which are not improved by salting, it is permitted to salt for the requirements of the meal, but not for the requirements of another meal, however radishes, onions, beans or lentils, which are improved by salting, it is forbidden to scatter salt upon them, but each piece separately can be salted and eaten.

It is forbidden to preserve any manner of vegetables or fruits even in water alone without salt. It is likewise forbidden to salt meat or fish in such a manner as to impregnate them with the salt. It is also forbidden to purge meat which had not been salted and one is apprehensive lest it remain unsalted for three days. (In any event it is permissible to be done through a non Jew.)

INCISING.—The work of incising (scoring) which is forbidden consists in incising leather, paper or any substance at the place one desires to cut, in order to cut it properly. It is likewise forbidden to incise a sheet, parchment, or any substance in order to write letters thereon. In the incising that is prohibited there is no difference between incising with a dye, one's nails, or with anything that makes an impression.

SCRAPING.—The work of scraping which is forbidden consists in removing hair or wool from the skin making the skin smooth, likewise in peeling the skin, hence, one should not scrape his boots with a knife, nor even with his nails, it matters not whether they be new or old, as he thus peels the leather, it is, however, permissible to clean the boots upon the iron scraper in front of the door, providing it is not sharp, but has a blunt edge.

On the Sabbath it is forbidden to rub the shoes in order to polish them, either with the hand or by means of a cloth, and it is obvious that the use of boot-polish is forbidden, inasmuch as it constitutes the actual work of plastering. Plastering, however, as a forbidden work cannot be applied to food.

CUTTING.—The work of cutting which is forbidden, includes all things concerning which one is particular to cut to size, even whittling a chip wherewith to pick one's teeth, constitutes cutting, but in whatever relates to edibles, even in food for beasts, there is no cutting which is forbidden.

WRITING AND ERASING.—The work of writing which is forbidden consists in writing with ink or with any substance upon parchment, paper, or upon any substance, even if one write no |more than two letters of any language, moreover, if one wrote but two marks it constitutes the work of writing which is prohibited. It is likewise forbidden to trace any letter, or picture, even in the beverage upon a table, or in the moisture upon a pane of glass, or in sand. It is even forbidden to make marks upon a sheet of paper with one's nails. Whatever it is forbidden to write it is also forbidden to erase, hence it is forbidden to break sugar-tarts or rolls on which there are coloured pictures, but if the pictures were only impressed with a rubber stamp without paint it is permissible to break them. If wax dripped upon letters it is forbidden to remove it.

It is forbidden to break a seal on which there are letters, it is even forbidden to tell a non-Jew to open for him a sealed letter. If a sealed letter was delivered to him, he should not tell a non-Jew to open it for him, but he might hint to him that he cannot read it, so that the latter should understand. Even this should only be done in an emergency, as aside from this prohibition it is forbidden to read a letter concerning business on the Sabbath. It is forbidden even to look at the writing without reading it, unless ignorant of its contents, in which case it is only permitted to glance at it.

It is forbidden to engage in any business transaction, either to buy or to sell, to hire or to rent on the Sabbath.

BUILDING AND BREAKING DOWN.—The work of building up and breaking down which is forbidden consists in building up or breaking down any structure, whether it is permanent or temporary. It is even forbidden to hang up a sheet or a curtain in a manner that can be termed "partition" according to the code, that is, to tie it on top and at the bottom, in this case it is then forbidden to build it up or to break it down. If, however, it is not fastened at the bottom it is permissible, as it is then not termed "partition," for so long as it cannot stand before a moderate wind it is not a partition. If there be a window or hole in the wall it is permissible to stuff it up with anything that one is not likely to abandon there, such as a garment, but it is forbidden to stuff it with anything that is usually abandoned and left there as that is equivalent to adding to the structure.

Windows or doors of a house even if they hang upon their hinges, are forbidden to be removed from their hinges or to reset them on same. It is forbidden to be done even through a non-Jew.

It is forbidden to dig up or to fill up any hollow place whether in the ground or in loose earth or sand, it is therefore forbidden to sweep the floor on Sabbath, for fear of making the hollow places level, even if the floor is made of boards or stones, it is still forbidden to sweep it, as our Rabbis have made no distinction, unless the sweeping is in a manner different from a week-day, e.g., with goose-feathers, or with a mop, or with a special broom for the use of the Sabbath.

It is forbidden to erect a tent on the Sabbath. It is likewise forbidden to take in one's hand and carry an umbrella, even where carrying to and fro is permissible, inasmuch as the umbrella forms a tent.

Any article which is made up of different sections, and designed to be continually to be taken apart and put together by means of a screw, inasmuch as it was made for that purpose, it is permitted to take it apart and put it together. If, however, it was not designed to be taken apart continually, although it was made with a screw, it is forbidden to take it apart, or to put it together again.

It is forbidden to replace the leg of a chair. It is likewise forbidden to put laces in boots if the holes are too small and there is some difficulty in putting them in, as that constitutes "improving a vessel."

If a vessel become indented it is forbidden to straighten it out. Likewise if a knife became dull it is forbidden to sharpen it, as that constitutes "improving a vessel."

Building is applicable even to articles of food, as for instance, the making of cheese, or putting fruit together with the object of making them long or square, is called "building" and is forbidden. It is forbidden to cause the sounds of a musical instrument to be heard for fear of being prompted to improve it.

EXTINGUISHING AND KINDLING.—The work of extinguishing and kindling which is forbidden consists in extinguishing or kindling any fire, no matter how slight; if, however, there is a conflagration, and danger to human life is apprehended therefrom, even in the slightest degree, then it is permissible to extinguish it. But should it be clear that there is no danger to human life it is forbidden to extinguish it, but it is permitted to call non-Jews and tell them none will lose for extinguishing. One is even permitted to allow those non-Jews who are in his employ to extinguish it, but a child who is aware that it would please his father, should not be permitted to extinguish it.

If a burning candle or sparks fall on a table, it is permitted to shake the table, but not with the intention of extinguishing, and if it can possibly be done through a non-Jew, an Israelite should not do it, but if an oil or kerosine lamp fell, it is forbidden to shake it, as it is extinguished thereby.

It is forbidden to open a door or window if a wood fire or candle burns near them lest on account of the wind, the fire will kindle or the candle will become extinguished, but it is permitted to shut the door or window, as he neither extinguishes nor kindles thereby.

BEATING WITH THE HAMMER.—The work of beating with a hammer which is forbidden comprises all work to which one applies the finishing touch, whether done to vessels or to anything else, it is called "beating with the hammer," hence one who removes the loose threads from a garment or the small pieces of wood which were inadvertently woven therein, if it is his object to beautify the garment thereby and to put the finishing touch, it constitutes the work of "beating with a hammer." It is likewise forbidden to remove the bastings with which the tailor had temporarily pieced the garment together.

Anything that it is impossible to use without making a certain improvement, that improvement is forbidden to be made, inasmuch as he thus repairs articles, even if it is food, as for instance, he had forgotten to separate the dough-cake on the Sabbath-eve, inasmuch as it is forbidden to eat it thus, by now separating the dough-cake, he improves it. If he had forgotten to separate the dough cake on the Sabbath-eve, from the bread baked in lands other than Palestine, he may eat thereof on the Sabbath, but he should leave a slice from each loaf for separating the dough-cake on the close of the Sabbath.

It is forbidden to immerse new vessels unless they are fit for holding water, such as a pot or glass, in which case he should fill them with water from a well and the immersion will be valid, or he should present it to a non-Jew, and borrow it from him again. Nevertheless if all the above are not possible, it is permissible to immerse them.

It is forbidden to go on board a vessel if it is not moored to the shore. but if it is very necessary the ecclesiastical authorities should be consulted.

It is forbidden to wash dishes after the third meal was partaken of, but at night and in the morning it is permitted as he needs to use them on the Sabbath, but drinking vessels it is permissible to wash the entire day, as there is no fixed time for drinking, nevertheless cleaning them with sand or any other cleaning material is forbidden.

Laws Concerning Carrying from One Domain to Another On the Sabbath.

1. There are 4 domains as regards the Sabbath : The private-domain, the public-domain, the semi-private-domain, and the semi-public-domain.

2. By private domain we denominate any place which measures, at least, four hand-breadths square (as that space is sufficiently large to make use of) and is surrounded by partitions at least ten hand-breadths high (even if they are not altogether whole), or an excavation ten hand-breadths deep by four hand-breadths square, likewise a well of a like size, also a mound ten hand-breadths high by four square, and even a vessel, e.g., a chest, if it is ten hand-breadths high, or a barrel, if it measures four square hand-breadths in circumference, all of the above, even if they are in a public or semi-public domain, form a separate division by themselves and constitute a private domain, the open space of a private domain also constitutes a private domain even if it extends to the sky, the tops of the partitions surrounding a private domain are also amenable to the law governing a private domain. Should there be cavities in the partitions toward the side of the public domain, even if they are hollow from side [to side, inasmuch as one can make use of them in the private domain, they are subordinate thereto and are considered as private domains.

3. By public domain we denominate streets and market-places which measure sixteen paces square, and roads leading from one city to another, and which are sixteen paces wide are also public domains, also anything that is in the public domain, if it is not three hand-breadths high above the ground, even if there are not many that walk on them, they are nevertheless subordinate to the ground and are considered as public domains, also an excavation in the public domain, if it is not three hands-breadths deep, it is considered as a public domain. Likewise the cavities in the walls toward the public domain the hollowness of which does not extend toward the private domain, if they are below three hand-breaths from the ground they are subordinate to

the public domain, and are considered as public domains, if, however, they are above three hand-breadths from the ground, their proportions must be taken into consideration, if they measure four square hand-breadths, but are lower than ten hand-breadths they are semi-public domains, if they are higher than ten hand-breadths they are private domains, and if they do not measure four square hand-breadths they are semi-public domains, and it matters not whether they are above or below ten hand-breadths from the ground.

4. Passages leading to a public domain are variously regarded at times as public domains, and at times as semi-private domains, and the laws regarding them are multitudinous and divergent.

5. By semi-private domain, we denominate any place which is not a public thoroughfare, and at the same time is not properly surrounded by partitions, such as fields, a stream which is at least ten hand-breadths deep and four hand-breadths wide and alleys which are partioned off. Booths (erected in front of shops in which merchants sit and a stand (stall) (upon which merchandise is placed) which is in front of the door-posts in the public domain, and is four hand-breadths wide by from three or more (up to ten) hand-breadths high, also a place which measures four square hand-breadths and is surrounded by partitions which are not ten hand-breadths high, and a mound which measures four square hand-breadths and is from three to ten hand-breadths high, a well which measures four square hand-breadths, and is from three to ten hand-breadths deep. There are, besides, many other semi-private domains or כרמלית (which word is compounded of רך and מל, i.e., neither tender nor dry but medium), the same applying here, as it is neither a private domain, inasmuch as it has no proper partition, nor a public domain, inasmuch as many do not go there.

6. By semi-public domain we denominate any place in a public domain which does not measure four square handbreadths and is three or more hand breadths high, or a well which does not measure four square hand-breadths and three or more hand-breadths deep. Likewise a place which does not measure four square hand-breadths and is surrounded by partitions of three or more hand-breadths in height. All of the foregoing are semi-public domains only if they are in a public domain ; if, however, they are in a semi-private domain, they are also considered as semi-private domains.

7. In a public domain and in a semi private domain it is forbidden to carry anything four paces, it is forbidden either to carry, to throw, or to hand it, and to fetch it several times, even at less than four paces, is also forbidden.

8. It is forbidden to carry, throw, or hand anything from a private to a public domain or to a semi-private domain also from a

public domain or a semi-private domain to a private domain. Likewise from a public to a semi-public domain, or from a semi-private to a public domain, but it is permissible to carry out and bring in from a semi-public domain to a private, to a public and to a semi private domain, and from the latter to the former, providing one does not carry the article four paces in the public or semi-private domain. Now inasmuch as there are different laws bearing upon what constitutes a public domain, and what a semi-private domain and what a private domain is, therefore in a city which is not provided with an עירוב (an emblem of inter-community), one who is not well versed in the law should be very careful, as no article should be carried from the place where it lays to a different place, unless it is clear to him that it is permissible to bring it there.

9. The taking of an article from the place where it lies is called "dislodging," and putting down that article is called "depositing." Dislodging without depositing, or depositing without dislodging are also forbidden, hence an Israelite is forbidden to hand to a non Jew any article in order that the latter should take it from a private domain and bring it to a public domain or a semi-private domain, as thereby the Israelite does the dislodging, but the non-Jew himself should take the article. Likewise when a non-Jew brings an article, the Israelite should not take it from his hand, as thereby he does the depositing, but the non Jew himself should put down the article.

10. A court in which there is a breach, if what is left of one side of the partition is four hand-breadths wide by ten hand-breadths high above the ground, or if two sides of the partition are left each measuring a hand-breadth wide by ten hand breadths high, then if the breach does not measure more than ten cubits, no improvement is necessary, as that breach is considered as the door. If, however, the breach measures more than ten cubits, also, if there was not left of one side of the partition the width of four hand-breadths, or of two sides the width of a hand-breadth of each, moreover if it was a complete breach, i.e., no partition having been left on one side, then even if the breach only measures three hand breadths, carrying is forbidden in that court until it be repaired (and the best way to repair it is to give it the form of a door).

11. We have declared that if the breach in the court did not extend to more than ten cubits we could regard it as a door, and it is not necessary to repair it, this applies where there is only one breach, if, however, there are two or more breaches, it is essential that there be, at least, as much left standing as what has been broken down, if however, the breach is more than what remains standing, wherever the breach measures more than three hand breadths it requires repairing.

12. To make the form of a door one should erect two posts on each side (of the breach) not less than ten hand-breadths high and lay a stick or cord upon them. It is essential that the stick or cord lay upon their tops, and not at their sides, and if one drive nails in the heads of the posts and tied the cord around them, it is done properly. It is necessary that neither of the posts be at a greater distance from the partition than three hand-breadths, nor should they be more than three hand-breadths from the ground. In an emergency, where it is impossible to make the form of a door otherwise than by placing the posts at a greater distance than three hand-breadths from the walls, this law may be relaxed.

13. The entrance of a house which opens towards the street and whose door opens inwards, and whose door posts, lintel and threshold are toward the street, is at times a private domain, and at times a semi-private domain, and inasmuch as all are not versed in these laws, therefore because of the uncertainty, the laws applying to a private domain as well as those which apply to a semi-private domain must be rigorously observed in regard thereto. It is forbidden to carry from thence to the street, as that is a public domain, or to a semi-private domain, or from the street to that place, for it may be a private domain. It is likewise forbidden to carry thereto from the house or court, or from thence within, for it may be a semi-private domain ; if, therefore, the door is locked and it is necessary to unlock it, care should be taken to have a non-Jew insert the key in the lock, and after the door is unlocked, the non-Jew should remove the key before the Israelite opens the door, for if the Israelite should open the door while the key is in the lock, he will thereby bring the key from the (entrance) semi-private domain to the (house) private domain.

14. In many places there are houses where the roof projects from the wall of the house, over the street, where it is supported upon pillars. It is prohibited to carry from the house to that place (beneath the projection) or from thence in the house. It is also forbidden to carry anything there four cubits, as it is amenable to the law relating to a street, either as a public domain or a semi private domain, and although the roof juts out upon the pillars making the form of a door, which the law regards as a partition, yet as there are no partitions at the sides thereof, it is not regarded as a partition. It is therefore necessary to erect one post on one side near the wall of the house, opposite the pillar which supports the roof, thus making another form of a door, and another, on the other side. If many houses adjoin each other in a similar manner, it is sufficient to make this at each side of the outermost house, they should also perform the ceremony of establishing an inter-community of courts.

15. It is permitted to place food before a non-Jew in a court or house, although it is known that the latter will carry it outside, so long as he does not give it him in his hand, and thus cause dislodging. The above is permitted only if the non-Jew is permitted to eat it there should he desire, but if he is not permitted to eat it there, or if there be a great deal of food, so that it would be impossible for him to eat it there, also other articles which it is apparent the non Jew will carry out, it is forbidden.

16. A woman may lead her little child, even in the public domain, she should, however, not drag it, but the child should lift up one foot and put the other on the ground, so that it support itself thereon while putting down the foot it has lifted up, thus ever supporting itself on one foot, if, however, she drags the child, trailing both its feet along, it is just as if she carries it, and it is forbidden, even in a semi-private domain, and to actually carry the child is forbidden, even if it is big enough to walk itself, and even in a semi-private domain.

17. It is permitted to pour out waste water in a court-yard which measures four cubits square, although it runs out on the public domain.

18. The partitions with which an enclosure is fenced around do not avail to make carrying permissible therein unless it was fenced around for dwelling purposes. By dwelling purposes we term that which was built for a house to dwell in or an abutment to one's house whose door opens therein, which is fenced around by partitions, after the manner of courts which are built for houses, then, no matter how large the inclosure is, it is an absolutely private domain ; all enclosures, however, that were fenced around for other than dwelling purposes, such as gardens and orchards, fences are only for the purpose of guarding their contents, these are affected by their difference in size. If it is not larger than one hundred cubits in length by fifty cubits in width, if it is a quadrature it is equalled by seventy cubits and four palms by seventy cubits and four palms (six palms equal one cubit). If the area is circular or otherwise circumcribed, it is likewise essential to reckon thus, it should measure thus five thousand cubits square, then it is permissible to carry therein, if, however, the enclosure is larger than that space, or even if it is not larger than that space, but its length more than doubles its breadth, even if only by one cubit, then it is forbidden to carry therein.

19. An enclosure which was fenced around for other than dwelling purposes and which is not larger than the space described above, making carrying therein permissible, if there is a court adjacent

thereto, it is likewise permissible to carry from there to the court and vice-versa utensils which were in the court on the Sabbath, as that enclosure and the court are considered as one domain, the enclosure, however is not considered as of the same domain as the house, hence it is forbidden to carry from thence to the house, or vice-versa, utensils which were in either of these places.

20. An enclosure which was fenced around for other than dwelling purposes, thus, it was previously fenced round by partitions and the dwelling was built afterwards, or he afterwards made a door in his house leading thereto, how can it be converted into an enclosure fenced around for dwelling purposes ? By making a breach in the partitions measuring more than ten cubits (as a breach of ten cubits is regarded as a door, but if more than that it is a breach) thus making them invalid to serve as partitions, after which he should fence it round and it will be considered as having been fenced around for dwelling purposes.

21. If one has planted trees in a court which is larger than the space aforementioned, even a large number of them, it did not thereby cease to be a dwelling, and it is still an enclosure fenced around for dwelling purposes, as one is accustomed to seek the shade of trees. If, however, he planted vegetables therein, and it extended to the greater part of the court (even if it is not in one area, but planted sparingly) it then ceases to be a dwelling, but it is all considered as a garden, if, however, it is planted in the lesser part of the court and the planted place is less than the space described above, it is permitted to carry therein ; but if the planted place is larger than the aforementioned space, it is forbidden to carry in the entire court.

22. A court which only contained the space aforementioned or less, and part of it was planted, should be judged by the greater part thereof. If the greater part thereof be planted, although carrying be permissible therein, inasmuch as it is no larger than the aforementioned place, it is nevertheless forbidden to carry thereto utensils which were in the house on the Sabbath ; it is therefore necessary to make a partition in front of the garden, in order that it be permitted to carry from the house to the court.

LAWS CONCERNING CARRYING BY MEANS OF A GARMENT

OR ADORNMENT.

1. Any article that is neither a garment nor an adornment is forbidden to be carried out in a public or semi-private domain, hence, one is forbidden to go out with a needle or a pin stuck in his garment, even for the requirements of dressing a man should scrupulously abstain from carrying it. But a woman (inasmuch as it is the custom

of women to fasten their bands with pins) is permitted to go out with them for the requirements of dressing, only, however, with a pin, but not with a needle.

2.   A man should be careful not to go out with a ring on which a seal is not engraved ; one should especially abstain from carrying a watch, even if it is attached to a gold chain, because, the watch that lays in the fob is a burden, the carrying of which cannot be permitted.

3.   One who is lame, or convalescent, likewise one who is very old, and unable to walk without a stick, is permitted to go with a stick in his hand ; if, however, it is possible for him to go without a stick, and he does walk without a stick in his house, but takes it in the street to support himself thereon, is forbidden to do so. One for whom it is impossible to go without spectacles, and who also wears them constantly at his house, is permitted to carry them over his eyes, even in the public domain.

4.   It is permissible to go out with two garments on the Sabbath, wearing one above the other, even if one does not need to wear the other garment, and only takes it out for a neighbour who needs it, and the like.   It is permissible only if one be accustomed to wear the two garments on a week-day as well, thus it is his usual costume, if, however, he was never accustomed to wear two such garments, he is forbidden to go out with them on the Sabbath, as the second garment is then considered as a burden.

5.   To carry a handkerchief about the person it is customary to wrap it around under the upper garment above the trousers, but one should be careful not to make two knots therein, one above the other. Some are accustomed to wrap the handkerchief around their necks, this is not permissible unless he wears no other neck-kerchief, and is accustomed to wear a neckerchief at times, if, however he merely throws it around his neck and lets its corners hang loosely in front of him it is positively forbidden.   It is also forbidden to wrap it around one's foot or hand, and thus go out with it.

6.   A garment which has two straps or laces to tie it with, or hooks to fasten it with, if one of them tore off, although the remaining one is of no value, nevertheless if he intends to repair it later, by procuring its mate, the remaining one is not subordinate to the garment and is like a burden, and it is forbidden to go out with such a garment, if, however, he does not intend to repair it later, the remaining one is of no value, and is subordinate to the garment, and permitted to go

out therewith. If it is an article of value, such as a loop or silver hook, even if he does not intend to repair it, it is not subordinate to the garment and is forbidden to go out therewith.

Various Laws Concerning Forbidden Things on the Sabbath.

1. On the Sabbath it is forbidden to place victuals under the cover of anything, even if it does not serve to increase its warmth, hence one who removes a pot in which there are victuals which were cooked or warmed therein, is forbidden to wrap it around or cover it up with anything in order to preserve its warmth.

2. On the Sabbath it is forbidden to soak, even in cold water, any article of food which is impossible to partake of unless it is soaked; it is, however, permitted to soak a herring in cold water, as it was fit for food even previous to having been soaked.

3. If fruit be found lying under a tree it is forbidden even to handle it on the Sabbath, for perchance it fell that very day. Likewise the fruit of a non-Jew, which, it may be surmised, was plucked that very day, is forbidden even to handle it.

4. It is forbidden to take honey which clings to the hive. It is likewise forbidden to crush honey-combs, even if they were removed from the hive a day before, thus if they were not crushed before the Sabbath, it is forbidden to use the honey that flows therefrom on the Sabbath, but it is permissible to take the honey that floats in the hive.

5. It is forbidden to make any use of a tree, no matter whether it be flourishing or decayed, even if he does not shake the tree thereby (as the shaking of a tree is prohibited in itself being one of the things forbidden to be handled on the Sabbath), one should not go up thereon, nor suspend himself therefrom. It is also forbidden to place an article thereon, or take it therefrom, or to tie an animal thereto and the like. It is forbidden to make use of even the sides of a tree.

6. Vessels in which plants or flowers are cultivated, whether for their beauty or fragrance, are forbidden to be plucked on the Sabbath in the same manner that it is forbidden to pluck a tree.

7. One is permitted to say to his neighbour, "fill me up this vessel," even if the vessel is made to measure with, and even if it belongs to the seller, so long as the buyer takes it and brings it home.

it is, however, forbidden to measure in a vessel used for measuring by the seller, and empty same in the buyer's vessel. It is permitted to say to one's neighbour, "give me fifty nuts" and the like, on condition that he shall not mention the name of any measure, nor money, nor shall he reckon up with him, saying "I owe you for fifty nuts, give me fifty more, and I will owe you for a hundred." It is especially forbidden to speak of purchasing, even if a price is not made, and even for the requirements of the Sabbath. On the Sabbath it is forbidden to purchase through a non-Jew; the same law applies to hiring.

8. One is permitted to say to his neihgbour "fill me up this vessel, or give me therein until it reaches this mark, and to-morrow we will measure or weigh it."

9. It is forbidden to produce the sound of any instrument especially designed therefore, e.g., to ring a door-bell, or to press the spring of a watch which is made to sound the hours by the pressure of a spring. This is forbidden on a Sabbath or Holyday.

LAWS CONCERNING THE RESTING OF ONE'S CATTLE ON SABBATH.

1. It is written : "That thy ox and thy ass may repose." Thus has the Torah admonished us that the cattle of an Israelite should also repose, and not alone the cattle, but all animals as well, hence it is forbidden to suffer one's beasts to carry out a burden, thus, even if it voluntarily went out on a public domain, carrying a burden, its owner has thereby transgressed a precept of the Torah, even if it is caparisoned thus, it is nevertheless a burden, if, however, it is for the purpose of curing it, or for guarding it, then it is permissible to let it go out therewith, and only that which is surperfluous as far as guarding it is concerned is forbidden. Likewise anything that is not proper for the guarding of one animal, although another animal is guarded thereby, is considered to the former as a burden and it is forbidden.

2. A horse may go out with a halter or bridle, but not with both. It is permissible to tie the rope of the halter around its neck and it may go out therewith, but it should be tied loosely in order that one may be able to easily slip one's hand in between the rope and its neck to draw it, should it attempt to run off; and it is permissible to handle the halter and to put it on the animal, but not to lean upon it, as it is forbidden to support oneself upon an animal on the Sabbath,

the ass, however, should not go out with an iron bit, as that is a superfluous safeguard for an ass. But an ox and a cow which require no guarding, it is forbidden to let them go out with a rope round their necks, unless they are in the habit of running away. If he tied a rope on the horse's mouth, it is considered a burden, inasmuch as it is not guarded thereby, as it slips from its mouth, and it cannot be compared to the halter which is tied around its head.

3. Neither a horse, nor any animal should be suffered to go out with a saddle. It is also forbidden to let them go out with a bell, even if it does not ring, and even in a city in which an intercommunity was established by an עירוב, it is forbidden to let them go out therewith; but it is permissible to let them go in a court. If, however, the bell is not muffled, and it rings, it is forbidden to let them go therewith even in a court.

4. It is permitted to lead a horse by the rope attached to the bridle, but he should grasp the end of the rope and not let it out of his hand the length of a palm, nor should the rope between his hand and the beast reach as close as a hand-breadth to the ground, if the rope, therefore, is very long, he should coil it around the horse's neck.

5. One who has a non-Jewish domestic who rides upon the beast when taking it to the water, need not be prevented, even if he puts a saddle or garment upon it to ride thereon, as they are subordinate to the rider, but he should not put anything else upon the beast. It is permitted to bid a non-Jew to milk the animals on the Sabbath, in order to relieve the animal's distress, as the milk causes them pain, it is, however, forbidden, even to handle that milk on that day, therefore the non-Jew should put it away where it can retain its freshness. It is also permitted to tell a non-Jew to fatten the geese once on that day to relieve them of their distress.

6. One who lends or hires his beast to a non-Jew should make a condition with him that he should return it to him before Sabbath, and if it happened that he did not return it, the Israelite should make a free gift thereof before the Sabbath, even by himself, in order to save himself from violating a prohibition, it is, however, forbidden to lend or hire originally with such a contingency in view.

7. One should not measure oats in order to give it to his beast, but one should use judgment in averaging it.

8. A bundle of fodder which is not knotted permanently (i.e. doubly knotted) may be unknotted and given to the cattle. It is also permitttd to cut hard cucumbers for the cattle, providing it was torn

up the day previous, but if the cucumbers are tender and they are able to eat them as it is, it is forbidden to cut them.

9. It is permitted to let one's beast stand upon herbage which is connected to the soil, so that it feed thereon, but an herbage which a non Jew had torn up on the Sabbath and is thus מוקצה (forbidden to be handled) it is forbidden to let cattle stand thereon and feed themselves, unless there is nothing else to eat, then it is permitted in order to relieve the animal of its distress. Likewise if it has nothing to drink one is permitted to tell a non-Jew to bring it water from a well in a semi-private domain.

10. One should not hang a bag or vessel around a beast, in order to eat therefrom, inasmuch as it is merely for the pleasure of the beast, so that it need not bend its neck, and it is forbidden to work on the Sabbath for the enjoyment of the beast; bullocks, however, and asses which have short necks and it would cause them distress to eat from the ground it is permitted to hang around them a vessel with food in the court, but they should not be allowed to go out therewith, as it is counted then as a burden.

11. One should not cast corn for poultry on moist ground, as some may possibly remain there and afterwards sprout forth.

12. One who gives bran to cattle or poultry is forbidden to put water therein, and if he had put water therein on the Sabbath eve, he is forbidden to stir it on the Sabbath, but he is permitted to pour it from one vessel into another in order to mix it together.

13. Cattle, beasts and poultry which are raised on one's premises, it is one's duty to provide them with food, and one is permitted to give them food on the Sabbath, but for those who are not raised in one's house and one is not obliged to feed them, it is forbidden to labour in order to provide them with food, it is even forbidden to throw it before them, hence, it is forbidden to put food before doves, as they go and eat in the field. One should place food before a dog, even if it have no owner, it is in some degree fulfilling a commandment to give it some food, for verily, the Holy One, blessed be he, took compassion upon it, for its lack of much food, and caused its food to remain in its stomach (thus nourishing it) for three days.

14. It is permitted to invite a non-Jew to dine at one's house on the Sabbath. Moreover, it is permitted even to serve him alone, as it is regarded as a duty to provide him with food.

15. One whose beast is in pain from over-feeding on cresses and the like, may make it run in the court, in order that the exercise may cure it. If it suffers from a rush of blood, he may let it stand in water to cool off, and if there is a doubt as to whether it will not die unless it is bled, it is permitted to tell a non-Jew to bleed it. Other remedies as well should be applied to it through a non-Jew.

LAWS CONCERNING THAT WHICH IS FORBIDDEN TO HANDLE ON THE SABBATH (מוקצה "SET APART").

1. That which one had intentionally set apart, such as food which one had purposely set apart not to partake thereof on the Sabbath, it being unfit to eat except in an emergency, or that which is fit to eat, even when not in an emergency, but which one had set apart as merchandise even if he stores it away. Likewise, something that is on that day fit food for a dog, although, on the Sabbath-eve it was not intended to serve as such, e.g., cattle or poultry which were rendered as unclean as a carcase, on the Sabbath, likewise a thing that on that day assumed a different appearance from that of the previous day but which is nevertheless still fit for some use, such as utensils which were broken on that day, but are yet, in some manner, fit for the use to which they were put originally as a receptacle for food or drink, also bones from which the meat was picked on that day, and are fit food for dogs, all these it is permitted to handle on the Sabbath, except that which one temporarily rejects, such as figs and raisins (in the process of drying).

2. That which in its original state is absolutely unfit for the food of a human being, even in an emergency, but requires cooking, although it is fit food for cattle or dogs, inasmuch as it will afterwards supply food for man, it does not serve for the use of cattle or dogs, likewise that which is unfit for any use on the Sabbath, such as wood, the feathers of fowls, the skins of animals, and wool and flax, also all animals, even those which are in one's house, and the shells of nuts and of eggs, and hard bones which are not even fit for dogs, and doors and windows (as it is forbidden to hang them up on the Sabbath). Likewise, the fragments of broken utensils which are not fit for any further use, all these and other things it is forbidden to handle, nevertheless it is permitted to remove fragments of broken glass where they may cause injury.

3. Food, the eating whereof is forbidden but of which one is permitted to enjoy, and it is proper food for a non-Jew in its present state, such as cooked meat and the like, and he is able to give it to the non-Jew, as it is his, one is permitted to handle it. If, however, in its present state it is not fit for a non-Jew, such as raw meat, or if he is unable to give it to a non-Jew, because it belongs to someone else, he is forbidden to handle it.

4. A thing "newly born," i.e., that which was evolved on that day, such as ashes from a fire kindled on that day through a non-Jew, likewise an egg which was laid on that day, and water dripping from the trees in April, and even that which did not originate on that day, but was the result of labour which is forbidden on the Sabbath, such as fruit which fell from a tree or which a non-Jew had plucked on the Sabbath, or milk from the milking done on a Sabbath, and the like, is also forbidden to be handled, but bread baked on the Sabbath by a non-Jew in a city where they are mostly non-Jews (and it may be assumed that it was baked for non-Jews), it is permitted in an emergency, or for the requirements of fulfilling a commandment, for an Israelite to partake thereof on the Sabbath.

5. Utensils which are adapted for work that is forbidden to be done on the Sabbath, such as a mortar, a grinder, a hammer, an ax, a trumpet, a candle-stick, a needle, whole candles, either of tallow or of wax, cotton wicks, a garment of linen and woollen thread (Shatnes), which it is forbidden to wear, and all things akin to the above, one is permitted to handle, if the object is needed, e.g., a hammer to crack nuts, an ax to cleave provisions, a whole needle to remove a splinter, (if, however, its eye or point was missing it is forbidden to handle it). It is likewise permitted to handle them if one needs the place they occupy, and as long as one handles them either because he is permitted to do so or through inadvertance he is permitted to continue handling them and to put them down where he pleases, but if one does not need the object itself, nor the place that it occupies, the handling of the object for its own sake, that it be not stolen or damaged, is forbidden. It is likewise forbidden to handle Tephillin on the Sabbath; if, however, they lay in a degrading place, it is permitted to remove them to a place of safety.

6. Articles which one purposely sets apart, not to make use of them because he is anxious that they should not be spoiled, such as workman's tools, of which one is careful that they should not be damaged, a pen-knife, a slaughter-knife, a circumcision knife, writing paper, notes, accounts and letters, all of which one is anxious to keep intact, and precious utensils which he does not use at all, likewise any

article of which he is so careful as to put it away in a special place and not to make use of it, also the vessels that are in one's shop for the purpose of being sold, even if they are culinary vessels, but he is not in the habit of lending them, all of the foregoing and what resembles them, also a purse, are "set apart" and it is forbidden to handle them even for the requirements of the object itself, or of the space it occupies.

7. That which is not designated as a vessel, such as wood, stones, a piece of iron and the like, is forbidden to be handled in any manner whatsoever, even for the requirements of the object itself or of the space it occupies unless it was designed for permanent use on the Sabbath-eve.

8. A vessel that is employed for usage that is permissible, or even for usage that is at times forbidden and at times permissible, such as pots, and even an unclean vessel (it is permitted to handle on the Sabbath what is "set apart" on account of uncleanliness) it is permitted to handle it, even for the sake of the vessel, that it be not stolen or broken, but one is forbidden to handle it if there is no occasion for it, one, however, is permitted to handle holy writ, and victuals, even if there is no necessity therefor.

9. Just as it is forbidden to handle that which is "set apart" or that which was evolved on that day, so is it forbidden to place a vessel underneath them in order that they fall therein, but it is permitted to tie a basket before the young of the birds in order that they walk up and down thereon, as it will be permitted to handle it when the birds will not be upon it. If the birds were on the basket at twilight (on the Sabbath-eve) it is forbidden to handle it the entire day.

10. It is permitted to handle the earth and sand which one heaped up in the corner of the court or house, inasmuch as its laying in a heap is indicative that one had prepared it for his use, if, however, it is scattered about, it became subordinate to the ground and it is forbidden to handle it. If one had cut off the branch of a tree before the Sabbath for the purpose of using it to drive flies away, he is permitted to use it on the Sabbath inasmuch as he had designed it for that purpose and thus made a " vessel " thereof.

11. Boards belonging to a householder which are not for sale it is permitted to handle, but if they belong to an artisan it is forbidden, unless it was his intention when yet day (on Friday) to make use of them on the Sabbath.

12. That which is set apart is forbidden only to be handled, but one may touch them if he does not thereby move them, hence it is permitted to touch a stationery chandelier even if the candles burn therein. It is likewise permitted to take a thing permissible which lies upon a thing that is "set apart," but it is forbidden to touch a

hanging chandelier, or any round thing, as by merely touching it he shakes it. It is permitted to cover an article that is "set apart" with an article that is not "set apart."

13. It is permitted to handle in an indirect manner that which is set apart, hence if he had forgotten a thing "set apart" upon a certain vessel, or if it fell upon it on the Sabbath, if he needs the vessel which is permitted to be handled, or the space it occupies he is permitted to shake it off, or to carry the vessel to another place and shake off the thing "set apart," thus he may also do when he needs to take his garment in which he had forgotten a purse with money, but it is forbidden to be done solely for the sake of the thing "set apart."

14. One is forbidden to carry a child in his arms, even where carrying is permissible if the child has a stone or anything else that is "set apart" in his hand, if, however, the child is very much attached to him and his refusal to take it would sicken it and at the same time it is impossible to throw the stone and the like from the child's hand as it would cry very much, in such case it is permitted to take the child in his arms; it is forbidden to grasp the child's hand if it holds a coin, although it walks by itself, notwithstanding its attachment to him, as we may apprehend that in the event of the coin falling from the child's hand, the former may forget that it is Sabbath and pick it up, thus actually handling a thing "set apart."

15. It is forbidden to handle a dead body on the Sabbath, but it is permitted to remove the pillow from beneath the corpse in order that it shall not become malodorous, providing he does not move any organ, if the mouth of the corpse were open and distending, it is permissible to fasten the jaws that it open no further, but not in a manner as to close what is already open as one would thus move an organ.

16. If a fire broke out, and it is feared that the dead body will be burned, it is permitted to carry it out by means of a thing permissible which should be laid upon the corpse or at its side, such as an article of food, and carry them out together, and if an article of food is not available, a vessel or garment which it is permitted to handle should be laid upon the corpse, but if this is also lacking, it may be carried out by itself, it is however only to be carried where carrying is permissible, but where carrying is not permissible, it should be carried out only by a non-Jew.

17. One is permitted on the Sabbath to place a vessel beneath a liquid that drips down, and when it becomes full it may be poured out and put back in that place, that is, providing that the water is fit to wash with, if, however, the water be filthy it is forbidden to put a vessel there, howbeit if one transgressed and did place it there, and it is a place disagreeable to him, he is permitted to remove it.

LAW CONCERNING THINGS "SET APART" BEING A BASE FOR THINGS FORBIDDEN TO BE HANDLED.

1. If on the Sabbath-eve one had intentionally put a thing "set apart" upon one of his vessels for the purpose of having it lay there on the coming in of the Sabbath, the said vessel becomes a base for a thing forbidden and even if he had removed the thing "set apart" therefrom on the Sabbath, nevertheless, inasmuch as it laid thereon on the twilight (on Friday) at which time it became the base for a thing forbidden, it is forbidden to handle it thereafter the entire Sabbath day, even if one needs that object itself or the place it occupies.

2. If on the coming in of the Sabbath, there also lay on that vessel an article which it is permissible to handle, and the vessel thus became a base for a thing forbidden and a thing permitted, if the thing permitted is of more value to him he is permitted to handle it, but if the thing forbidden is of greater value to him he is forbidden to handle it.

3. If one had money in his garment he is permitted to handle the garment, but he should not wear it even in his house, as we are apprehensive lest he go out with it in the public domain. If there is money in a table drawer it is forbidden to move the table.

4. A vessel is not constituted a base unless the thing "set apart" lay thereon in the twilight on Friday, but if it did not lay thereon in the twilight, but was put thereon thereafter it does not thereby become a base and it is permissible to handle the vessel even when the thing "set apart" lays thereon, hence it is permitted to shake a table or table-cloth from the crumbs, etc., that lay thereon. Nor does it become a base except when he puts it thereon with the intention of letting it remain there in the twilight, if, however he inadvertently left it there or if it fell there of itself it does not thereby become a base, nor does it become a base unless it is his own vessel, but if he put a thing set apart upon another vessel it does not thereby become a base.

Law Concerning Week-Day Matters Forbidden
on the Sabbath.

1. It is written "If thou restrain thy foot for the sake of the
Sabbath, not doing thy business on my holy day"; and it is also said,
"and honour it by not doing thy usual pursuits, by not following thy
own business, and speaking (vain) words"; Our Rabbis have taught
us what is meant by the precept "and honour it by not doing thy
usual pursuits, that is, walk not in the same gait on the Sabbath as
thou art wont to do on a work-day," hence it is forbidden to run on
the Sabbath, for the sake, however, of performing a precept it is permissible to run, and what is meant by the words "by not following
thy own business" our Rabbis have expounded as meaning "thy business is forbidden thee even if thou doest no work," thus one is forbidden even to look after his property to see what it requires on the
morrow; it is also forbidden to promenade through the town in order
to find a horse, a ship or a wagon so as to hire them after the Sabbath, if it is apparent that he went for that purpose, but one is permitted to guard his or his neighbour's property.

2. One is forbidden to go on the Sabbath until the end of the
Sabbath boundary or a lesser distance in order to wait there until dark
so that he will be able to hasten his journey from thence on the close
of the Sabbath, it will be apparent that he went there principally for
that purpose, this, however, is only forbidden if he stays there until
dark in order to go and do something which it is impossible to do on
the Sabbath in any manner whatever, e.g., to hire workmen, or to pick
fruit, or to bring in fruit which is "set apart" as there is no exemption making the doing of these things permissible on the Sabbath. One
is, however, permitted to wait at the Sabbath boundary until dark in
order to bring in his cattle, inasmuch as that would have been permissible even on the Sabbath, in case there were other houses there
no further than seventy cubits from each other, it is likewise permitted to bring fruit that was plucked and not "set apart" inasmuch
as this would also have been permissible even on the Sabbath in case
the entire route be closed in by partitions, and everything of that
character is permitted. It is also permitted to go on the Sabbath
within the limits of the Sabbath boundary to the orchard in order to
pluck the fruit on the close of the Sabbath as it is not recognisable
that he went there for that purpose, but the onlookers may think that
he went there for pleasure or to look for his beast that went astray,
and after being there he bethought himself of remaining until dark in
order to pluck his fruits.

3. From that which is written "and speaking (vain) words," our
Rabbis have inferred that one's words on the Sabbath should not be
the same as on a week-day, hence one is forbidden to say "I will do
this thing to-morrow," or "I will buy that article to-morrow," this,
however, applies only to what cannot be done to-day in any manner,

but if it can be done to-day in a certain way, although that way does not present itself now, it is permissible ; one, therefore, is permitted to say "I will go to yonder place to-morrow," but he should not say it in such a way as to imply that he will ride there nor should he speak much about it. It is likewise forbidden to converse much on trivial matters and it is forbidden to relate on the Sabbath anything to cause distress.

4. One is forbidden to make mental calculations on the Sabbath either of future or past transactions. One is permitted to make calculations from which he derives no benefit, providing he does not make many of them as it is forbidden to speak much on trivial matters on the Sabbath.

5. Inasmuch as it is written "thy own business," our Rabbis, of blessed memory, have inferred that only the business of man is forbidden but heavenly subjects are permitted, hence one waits at the Sabbath boundary until dark for the purpose of performing a precept, it is also permitted to attend to matters of public interest on the Sabbath. It is permitted to speak to a teacher in regard to one's child, if he is willing to take him to teach Scripture or even a trade, as this is also the fulfilment of a precept as the lack of a trade wherewith to earn a livelihood may lead him to steal, but it is forbidden to hire the teacher on Sabbath as the hiring constitutes the violation of a Rabbinical ordinance and it is not permitted even for the purpose of fulfilling a precept as it is only that which is forbidden that is implied in the words "by not following thy own business and speaking (vain) words" which is permissible to be done for the sake of fulfilling a precept. It is permitted to make a public announcement of a loss, inasmuch as returning it to its owner is the fulfilment of a precept.

6. As it is written "and speak (vain) words," our Rabbis have taught us therefrom that only *speaking* is forbidden, but *thinking* is permitted, hence one is permitted to think of his affairs. Nevertheless, in order to delight in the Sabbath it is mandatory not to give them any thought but it should seem to him as if all his work is done. One should especially avoid thinking of that which causes him worry or care.

7. One is permitted to say to a workman, "Do you think you will be able to see me this evening ?" although the latter understands that he needs him in the evening in order to hire him to do some work, as only a direct proposal is forbidden. He should, however, not say, "Be ready for me this evening," as that is equivalent to expressing in plain terms that he desires to hire him.

8. If one has hired a workman to guard anything for him, the workman is forbidden to take pay for Sabbath by itself, if, however, he was hired for a week or a month, he may take pay for the Sabbath inclusive with the pay for the entire time.

9. One is forbidden to give anything to his neighbour as a present or pledge, unless it is necessary for the fulfilment of a precept or requisite for the Sabbath, and he should not say to him "here is the pledge," but simply give it to him.

10. One is forbidden to glance over his bills, accounts or personal letters even without uttering the words, and although he only thinks of the contents it is nevertheless forbidden as thinking is only permissible when it is not obvious he is thinking of forbidden matters, but in the foregoing it is apparent to all that he is thinking of forbidden matters, therefore it is forbidden. One who gets a letter and does not know its contents, is permitted to look at it, for perchance it is necessary for the welfare of his person, but he should not utter the words. If, however, he knows that it relates only to business matters he is forbidden to glance at it, it is also forbidden to handle it, as it is a thing "set apart."

11. One is forbidden to measure whatever he may need on the Sabbath unless it is essential to the performance of a precept.

12. Where one may otherwise sustain a loss it is permissible for him to refer to what is essential either to a Jew or a non-Jew.

13. Whatever the Israelite is forbidden to do he is forbidden to tell the non-Jew to do. One is forbidden even to hint to him that he should do it, even to tell him before Sabbath that he should do it on the Sabbath, is forbidden. It is likewise forbidden to tell a non-Jew on the Sabbath that he should do it after the Sabbath, this, however, is only forbidden when it relates to one's business, but if necessary for the fulfilment of a precept it is permissible.

14. If the non-Jew was going of his own accord to perform some work for the Israelite, the latter is required to prevent him. If one sees that he is liable to sustain a loss, e.g., his cask of wine had sprung a leak and so forth, he is permitted to call in a non-Jew even if he knows that the non-Jew will surely repair it and even in a workmanlike manner, providing he carefully avoids telling him anything that may be construed as a command to repair it, but he is permitted to say in his presence, "Whoever will save me from this loss will not lose thereby," this, however, should not be done unless it may be a great loss.

15. Some have made it a practice to send a non-Jew for refreshments or the like or anything else on Sabbath, even where there is no עירוב this should not be permitted, except in case of necessity where one has nothing to drink but for the mere gratification of one's pleasure it is not permitted. It is not alone forbidden to tell a non-Jew to bring anything from without the Sabbath boundary it is even forbidden to utilise on the Sabbath with whatever was brought. For the prevention of a great loss, e.g., to remove merchandise so that the rain should not damage it is permitted through a non-Jew.

16. When it is cold it is permitted to tell a non-Jew to kindle a fire in the stove as the cold makes people suffer, but if it is not so very necessary this should not be done. It is also forbidden to allow a non-Jew to kindle a fire in the stove on the Sabbath after noon-time that it may be warm at night.

17. If a non-Jew brings grain to an Israelite in payment of his debts and the Israelite gives him the key to his storehouse and the non-Jew measures and counts what he puts in there it is permitted, inasmuch as he works for himself, as the grain does not belong to the Israelite until after it is measured; furthermore the Israelite is permitted to stay there and see that he does not cheat him, providing he does not speak to him at all concerning that business, if, however, they brought him his own grain he is forbidden to tell them to unload it from the wagon and place it in his store-house, even if they are about to unload it of their own accord he is required to prevent them.

18. When a non-Jew is engaged in making cheese from his own milk and an Israelite watches the process of milking and cheese-making with a view of making it permissible for him to buy it after the Sabbath, although the non-Jew makes it purposely for the sake of the Israelite in order to sell it to him it is permissible, inasmuch as the cheese belongs to the non-Jew who makes it for his own benefit; it is even permitted for the Israelite to tell him to make it although it is Sabbath, as an Israelite is permitted to tell a non-Jew, "Do your work" although the Israelite also derives a benefit therefrom.

LAW CONCERNING ONE IN PAIN, OR BEING ILL BUT NOT DANGEROUSLY.

1. One who is in pain but is able to walk around as if in good health is forbidden to take any treatment even if there is no work performed therein. He should neither treat himself nor let another, even a non-Jew, treat him.

2. It is permitted to eat and drink edibles and beverages which are the food of healthy people as remedies although in some respects it is hard to partake of them and it is obvious that he partakes of them medicinally it is permitted to partake of same. What is not food and drink for healthy people it is forbidden to partake of medicinally.

3. One who suffers slightly from tooth-ache but is not in great pain should not absorb vinegar or other beverages in his teeth as a remedy and then expel the liquid out of his mouth, but he should drink and swallow it, or dip bread in it and eat it in the usual manner, likewise one who has a pain in his throat should not gargle it with any liquor, but he should swallow it and he may be cured thereby. If one is in pain and he needs to rub himself with oil, he is forbidden to do so on the Sabbath.

4. One who has abdominal pains is permitted to apply thereto a vessel from which hot water has been poured out although it still retains the heat. It is also permitted to warm cloths and put it thereon.

5. If one has hurt his hand or foot he may bathe it in wine in order to staunch the bleeding, but not in vinegar as that is strong and is akin to medical treatment, and if he is sensitive the wine is also considered as vinegar and it is forbidden, but if the wound is on the back of his hand or foot, or it was caused by an iron, he is permitted to apply any remedy thereto, as it is dangerous.

6. On a wound in which there is no danger one should not place a plaster, even if it was made the previous day, nor anything else medicinally, but he may put something thereon to guard it against breaking open. If there was a plaster thereon from the previous day he may slightly raise it from each side and cleanse the wound, but he should not wipe the plaster itself as he thus plasters. If the plaster fell from the wound on the ground he should not restore it, but if it fell upon a vessel he should restore it. If, however, it cause him great pain he is permitted to tell a non-Jew to restore it, but he is forbidden to tell a non-Jew to make a plaster on the Sabbath, as plastering is a work forbidden through the Torah and it is even forbidden to be done through a non-Jew unless his entire body suffers.

7. It is forbidden to place a cloth upon a wound from which the blood flows as the blood colours it, and more especially a red cloth which he improves thereby. It is also forbidden to compress a wound

in order to extract blood, but one may bathe it in water or wine to staunch the flow of blood, then bandage it and if the blood does not stop flowing through the bathing, he should have it treated by a non-Jew.

8. It is customary for doctors to open up the wound in order to extract the matter, this is forbidden on the Sabbath, but if he opens it only in order to remove the matter which causes him distress and he does not care if it immediately closes up again it is permissible because of the distress he is in, but only with a needle and the like is he allowed to pierce but not with his nails as he would thereby tear some of the skin of the wound. If possible, the piercing should be done by a non-Jew.

9. On a wound which had healed one may put a plaster that was made the previous day as it is only for the purpose of preserving it. It is permissible to remove the skin that peels off the wound. If a splinter ran into one's flesh, he is permitted to remove it with a needle, but he should take care not to draw blood, as he would thus make a bruise.

10. One who was compelled to take to bed owing to his sickness, although he is not in danger, or if his pain is so great that he suffers in his entire body, then although walking about, a non-Jew may be told to apply a remedy, also to cook for him, but on the close of the Sabbath, he is forbidden to partake of the victuals if he can obtain others.

11. It is also permitted to take medicine either solid or liquid, whether applied as a remedy for oneself, or have others apply it, providing, however, that no work that is forbidden even by Rabbinical prohibition be performed therein, but whatever necessitates a violation of even a Rabbinical injunction it is forbidden to do except through a non-Jew; in the absence of a non-Jew, it may be permitted an Israelite to do it, but only if it is a Rabbinical prohibition, and done in a different manner from a week-day.

Law Concerning One Dangerously Ill, also Regarding One Forced to Transgress a Precept.

1. The compliance with every precept of the Torah (with the exception of those prohibiting idolatry, immorality and bloodshed) must be superseded by the exigency arising from danger to human life, hence it is mandatory to disregard the Sabbath for the sake of

one who is dangerously ill, providing the person is of good character, even if he is occasionally led by desire to transgress a precept, also even for the sake of an infant a day old it is mandatory to desecrate the Sabbath and if the sick person will not allow it, he should be compelled to submit, as it is very iniquitous not to be cured because it would necessitate the violation of a prohibition, indeed, one who exceeds in disregarding the Sabbath for the sake of one dangerously ill is praiseworthy, and even if a non-Jew be present the work should be done preferably by an Israelite, and he who disregards the Sabbath for the sake of one who is dangerously ill even if his exertions prove unnecessary has earned a reward, e.g., if a certain thing was ordered by the physician, and nine men ran and procured it, they have all earned a reward, even if the invalid became well from the first that was brought; this applies to every case of danger to human life, even where it is doubtful whether human life is endangered it is mandatory to disregard the Sabbath and perform all work involving a violation of a prohibition of the Torah, as there is nothing that supersedes the saving of a human life.

2. Any one regarding the condition of a sick person as dangerous and there be no competent physician present to gainsay him, he is credible, and the Sabbath be disregarded, even if he does not make a positive assertion, but says "I believe that he is in danger," he should be heeded and the Sabbath should be disregarded, as the law should be relaxed when there is probability of danger to human life. If one physician thinks there is danger and requires a certain remedy and another physician says he does not require it, they should pay heed to the physician who says he does require it. If the sick person says that he requires a certain remedy, and the physician says he does not require it, they should heed the sick person, if, however, the physician declares that that remedy will do him harm, they should heed the physician.

3. If a physician or another who understands, says that although the sick person is in no immediate danger the sickness may nevertheless assume a dangerous form unless a certain remedy is applied therefor, even if the invalid says that he does not require it, the physician should be heeded and the Sabbath should be disregarded. Likewise if the physician says that if a certain remedy will not be applied he will surely die, but if applied there is a chance that he might live, the Sabbath should be disregarded.

4. For a wound in the interior of the body, that is, from the lips inwards, the teeth included, and for the injury caused by a wound or for the swelling caused thereby and the like, the Sabbath should be disregarded, nor does it require the giving of an opinion, thus, even if experts are not there, and the sick person does not object, everything

should be done for him, the same as is done on a week-day, if they, however, know that according to the nature of that illness, it is possible to wait and there is no necessity of disregarding the Sabbath, it should not be disregarded. Pains are not considered as wounds, and one whose tooth aches to such an extent that he suffers therefrom in his entire body, is permitted to tell a non-Jew to extract it.

5. If one has pains in both eyes, or if some substance entered one eye, or if they were watering or bleeding, or other matter oozed therefrom which endangered sight, the Sabbath should be disregarded for their sake.

6. If one who is dangerously ill requires meat, and only forbidden meat is obtainable, an animal should be slaughtered for his sake in order not to feed him with forbidden meat, as it is apprehended lest he will become aware of having been fed on forbidden meat and he will be nauseated thereby, when, however, there is no fear of it causing nausea, as in the case of a child, or of one whose mind is distracted, he should be fed with forbidden meat, and not slaughter an animal for his sake on the Sabbath.

7. One who is well is forbidden to partake of the victuals that were cooked on Sabbath for an invalid, but even one who is well is permitted to partake thereof immediately on the close of Sabbath, providing it was cooked by an Israelite.

8. If one is forced to temporarily transgress a precept, even if it be an extreme offence, the Sabbath should not be disregarded for the sake of saving him from the transgression. If one, however, is forced to apostatize and become alienated from the Jewish community, even if it be a little boy or girl, one is duty bound to exert all his efforts in order to save him, even disregarding the Sabbath if necessary, and perform work thereon forbidden by the Torah, even if it is doubtful whether the efforts will be of avail or not; however, for a transgressor who deliberately becomes an apostate, the Sabbath should not be disregarded so far as to violate a prohibition of the Torah. But when it only involves the violation of a Rabbinical prohibition, e.g., to go beyond the Sabbath boundary, and to ride on horse-back, or in a wagon, also to handle money, or other such prohibitions, it is permissible to disregard them in order to save him.

LAWS CONCERNING CHILDBIRTH.

1. As soon as a woman begins to feel the symptoms of childbirth, even if she is not certain thereof, a mid-wife (or doctor) should be brought immediately, even from a place many miles away.

2. A woman at child-birth is equal to one who is dangerously ill, therefore the Sabbath should be disregarded for her sake in providing all that she requires. If, however, it can possibly be done in a different manner than on a week-day or through a non-Jew it should be done so. As soon as she is in travail, or as soon as there is a downward flow of blood, or as soon as she is unable to walk alone, she is considered as a woman in child birth. One who has had a miscarriage forty days after her immersion (טבילה) is amenable to the same law that governs a woman at child-birth.

3. During the first three days, even if she says she does not require it the Sabbath should be disregarded for her sake, and thereafter if she have no other pains than the after pains of child-birth until seven days if she says that she requires it, the Sabbath should be disregarded for her sake but it should not be diregarded if she says she does not require it. These days should be counted from the day of child-birth and not from the twenty four hours, thus if she gave birth on Wednesday towards the evening the Sabbath will complete the three days, and if she gave birth on the Sabbath toward the evening, the coming Sabbath completes the seven days, if, however, there be any possible danger, the woman being weak on the seventh day, it is not acting wrongly in relaxing the law and beginning to count these days from the first twenty-four hours.

4. After the seven days even if she says she requires it the Sabbath should not be disregarded for her sake, but until thirty days she is like one who is ill but not in danger, and all necessary work should be done for her through a non-Jew, to make a fire in a stove for her sake is permissible even through an Israelite (when a non-Jew is not easily found) and even in Tamuz, inasmuch as a woman in confinement is in danger from cold for thirty days.

5. One may cut the navel-string of a newly-born infant, bathe it, and straighten out its limbs, and do everthing that it requires.

LAWS CONCERNING THE INTER-COMMUNITY OF COURTS.

1. Two or more Israelites who reside in one court each in a room by himself, are forbidden to carry from the house to the court, or vice-versa, or from one house to another, even if they do not need to pass the court, as for instance if there is a door or window between one's house and the others, they are forbidden to carry through them, and it is mandatory upon them to establish an inter-community of courts, in order that they stumble not into transgression.

2. The tenants of two courts if there be a door between them, may establish if they desire a separate inter-community for each, thus making it permissible for them to carry, each in their respective courts; they are, however, forbidden to carry from one court to the other, vessels which were in the house over Sabbath, all the tenants of both courts can if they desire establish one inter-community in order that they should be permitted to carry also from one court to another even such vessels as have remained in the house over Sabbath. If there is only a window at least four hand-breadths wide by four hand-breadths high between the courts, and furthermore is within ten hand-breadths above the ground, and it has no lattice they may also establish an inter-community in common (inasmuch as being a house it is considered as if the gap is filled).

3. The tenants who occupy different apartments in a house containing many apartments to which they have access by means of a vestibule which is the entrance to the various apartments, are forbidden to carry anything even from the house to the vestibule. Even if an apartment is divided for two tenants although the one who occupies the inner rooms has no other exit than the door of the outer room, which door leads into the court, they are nevertheless forbidden to carry even from one room to another until they establish an " Erub " (inter-community).

4. The " Erub " is established as follows :—One of the tenants of the court takes one entire loaf of his bread the size of which should be about the capacity of eight egg-shells, and makes all the tenants of the court share therein, through another, by saying in whatever language he understands, as follows : " Take this loaf and acquire a share therein on behalf of all the Israelites dwelling in this court," or "(these courts," the latter then takes the loaf and raises it up a hand-breadth, then the one who makes the " Erub " takes it from him and says the blessing, adding בּרוך אתה ה' אלהינו מלך העולם אשר קדשנו במצותיו וצונו על מצות עירוב " By virtue of this ' Erub ' it shall be permissible for us to take out and to carry in from the houses to the court and from the court to the houses, and from one house to another, for us and for all Israelites who dwell in the houses of this court."

5. It is essential that he grant them proprietary rights only through another, he should therefore not grant it through his son and daughter who are minors, even if they do not eat at his table, inasmuch as their hands are considered as his own, but he may grant it through another's child. If possible he should not grant it through

nis wife as he supports her, nor through his grown son and daughter if they eat at his table as they are also considered as his own hand, but if there is no other, he may grant it through them, but if the son is married although he eats at his father's table, the latter may grant proprietary rights through him.

6. It is essential not to be niggardly about the food supplied for the "Erub" to care if his neighbour ate it, for if he should be concerned thereat the "Erub" is not valid, he should therefore take care not to make the "Erub" with food that he had prepared for Sabbath use.

7. The inter-community of courts should be established every Sabbath-eve, and the loaf of bread used in that ceremony may be cut up on the Sabbath (as it only needs to be whole on the entering of the Sabbath). If he be apprehensive lest he sometimes forget to perform that ceremony, he may make the "Erub" with one loaf of bread to apply to every Sabbath until Passover by changing the formula as follows : When saying "By virtue of this ' Erub ' etc., he should conclude "for every Sabbath until the Passover which comes to us for good." It is requisite that the loaf be thin and well-baked in order that it should not spoil. For the Sabbath during Passover, the "Erub" should be made with unleavened bread that was prepared according to the law.

8. The ceremony establishing an inter-community of courts should not be prepared on a Festival, hence if a Festival occurred on the Sabbath-eve, it should be performed on the eve of the Festival.

9. If an Israelite resides in one court with a non-Jew, the latter does not restrict him and he is permitted to carry from the house to the court and vice versa, if, however, two or more Israelites who are required to make an "Erub" reside there with a non-Jew, the latter restricts them, and they are not allowed to make an "Erub" until they pay him for a temporary rental of his premises, and if two or more non-Jews live there the Israelites are required to rent the premises of each of them. An Israelite who publicly profanes the Sabbath, is in that regard considered by the law as a non-Jew and the Israelites are required to rent his premises from him.

10. Even if the non-Jew resides in another court but his only egress to the public domain lies in that court where Israelites reside, or if he lives in a garret but the staircase leads to the court, he also restricts them.

11. If the court is owned by an Israelite who hired or rented a dwelling therein to a non-Jew or to an Israelite who profanes the Sabbath, the latter does not restrict him inasmuch as he does not hire

or rent to him with the intention of restricting his co-religionists, even if the owner of the court does not reside there himself.

12. How should the hiring be done ? The Israelite says to him, "Rent me your premises at such a price," and he is not required to explain to him that it is in order to make carrying permissible, if, however, he said to him, "Allow me the use of your premises," although he explains to him "in order that I may be permitted to carry in the court" it is not valid. He may rent the premises even from his wife, and even from his servant.

13. If he rented the premises for an indefinite period it is valid so long as the non Jew or Israelite who profanes the Sabbath does not repent thereof, and he still resides there. If he removes and another lives there it is necessary to renew it from the latter. If he rented them for a certain time, and during that time the occupant rented his premises to another non-Jew or Israelite who profanes the Sabbath, the original rental is sufficient, if, however, the occupant died or sold the premises to another during that lease, he is required to rent it anew from the heir or purchaser. If he rented it from his servant, if he did not stipulate a time it is valid only as long as that servant remains there, if, however, he rented it for a certain time, then, even if the servant is no longer there, the rental is valid until that time expires. Whenever the rental ceases and a new rental must be made, the ceremony of lre-establishing an inter-community of courts is essential.

14. If it be impossible to rent the premises from him (the non-Jew) one of the Israelites should borrow a special place on his premises for the purpose of putting an article there, the Israelite thereby acquires proprietary rights in that place and even if he removed the article from thence before the Sabbath it is nevertheless considered as if he had a share in the premises inasmuch as the Israelite had a right to let the article remain there on the Sabbath as well, thus the Israelite may rent the premises to all the residents in the court.

15. In many communities an inter community is established between all the thoroughfares and streets (by making the form of a door and the like) and they rent the franchise from the head of the municipality in order that they may be enabled to carry throughout the city. It is essential that all the necessary observances be performed through a learned Rabbi well versed in these laws. In these communities the "Erub" should be put away in the synagogue, in those places, however, where the city is not provided with an "Erub," each court yard is required to have an "Erub" of its own ; when an "Erub" is made for the residents of the court wherein there is a

synagogue, the "Erub" should not be put away in the synagogue, but put away in one of the dwellings.

16. If the "Erub" of a city became defective on a Sabbath, the tenants of every court which is properly partitioned and in which there is no breach making it invalid—even if that court contains many houses—are permitted to carry the entire Sabbath. Even if the "Erub" lay in another's premises which is now separated from that court, it is yet permissible, as it is said in connection therewith, "once it was allowed on that Sabbath," it continues to be allowable. But as there is great risk of many stumbling into the transgression of carrying also where it is forbidden, having become habituated to carry everywhere because allowable, therefore, if possible to have the same repaired by a non-Jew, it is permissible. If the cord across the form of a door was torn and it is possible for a non-Jew to repair it by looping it together or by making one knot and a loop above it, it is proper to have it done.

LAWS CONCERNING THE INTER-COMMUNITY OF BOUNDARIES.

1. On a Sabbath or Festival it is forbidden to walk a greater distance than 2,000 cubits "and a man's space," which is four cubits, from the place where one had acquired the Sabbath repose. Thus, if on Friday in the twilight one was in a field where there was a solitary house where he had acquired the Sabbath repose, his boundary should be measured from the outer wall of that house and beyond. If he had reposed in the city the entire city is considered as his space also the purlieu of the city which is a space of 70²/₈ cubits in the vicinity of the city, even if no building be there (it is called the city enclosure) belongs to the city and from its outskirts the measurement to the boundary line should begin.

2. A walled city even if it is very large, may be traversed throughout, also through its purlieu and from thence is measured the Sabbath boundary. Likewise a city which is not surrounded by a wall, if there be no vacant space between one house and another for a greater distance than 70²/₈ cubits, they are all reckoned as of the one city even if it would take many days to traverse it, and from the last house the city enclosure and the Sabbath boundary should be measured.

3. If there were two cities near each other, an inclosure should be added to each, hence if the distance between the two cities was no greater than the dimensions of two inclosures they should both be considered as one city. There are many laws concerning the measuring of a Sabbath boundary, and it should only be done by one proficient in these laws.

4. One who needs to go further than the Sabbath boundary on a Sabbath or Festival is required to put down a "Boundary 'Erub'" on the eve of the Sabbath or Festival : he is required to put it within the boundary lines of the city in a place where he would be permitted to go; the place where he puts the "Erub" is considered as his habitation, thereby acquiring the right to walk from thence 2,000 cubits in each direction. Of course it is understood that what he gains on the side where he puts the "Erub" he loses on the other side.

5. How should the "Erub" be made ? One should take bread as large as the capacity of eight egg-shells, or that which is eaten with bread, enough to eat therewith bread of the capacity of eight egg-shells (excepting salt and water with which an "Erub" is not made) and go into the place where he desires to put it, and pronounce the blessing ברוך אתה ה' אלהינו מלך העולם אשר קדשנו במצותיו וצונו על מצות עירוב then add, "By virtue of this 'Erub' shall it be permissible for me to go from this place two thousand cubits in each direction," and then return to his house. He may let an "Erub" lay for many Sabbaths but he should put it in a safe place so that it should not get lost or spoiled.

6. He may send the "Erub" through a messenger who can put it down on his behalf, the latter should pronounce the blessing and say "By virtue of this 'Erub' shall it be permissible for——(naming the principal) to go," etc. It is essential that the messenger be an intelligent adult. Even if he does not know whether the messenger had fulfilled his mission, he may take for granted the accomplishment of his mission.

7. Many people may obtain dispensation by means of one "Erub," if it consists of sufficient food to make it valid for each. If one puts an "Erub" down for all of them he should make them acquire a right therein through another in the same manner as is done with the "Erub" of courts. The "Erub" for boundaries should not be made for any one without his knowledge. The one who puts down an "Erub" as an agent for many should say, "It shall be allowable for this and that one" if he puts it down for himself as well he should say, "for me and for this and that one."

8. It is essential that the "Erub" shall lay in a place where it is possible to partake thereof on Friday in the twilight without transgressing a prohibition of the Torah, hence if he placed it in a pit and covered it with earth the "Erub" is not valid. If he covers it with a stone the "Erub" is valid. If he placed it upon a tree, if it is a hard tree the "Erub" is valid. If he put it upon a soft tree or stalk the "Erub" is not valid.

9. If he placed the "Erub" in the midst of the city, it is considered as if he is a resident of that city and he may traverse the entire city even if it is large, also without the city the length of its purlieu until the Sabbath boundary.

10. If within the bounded district there be a city which is surrounded by walls, or in which an inter-community was formed by means of an "Erub" that city is not measured and does not count for more than four cubits, providing, however, that the boundary line extends beyond the outskirts of that city, e.g., if there are five hundred cubits from the "Erub" until the city, and the length of the city is one thousand cubits, the city is not figured at more than four cubits and he has yet 1,496 cubits beyond the city (unto the Sabbath boundary). If, however, the boundary line ends in the middle of the city he is forbidden to walk any longer as beyond that is without the boundary line; in that regard the entire city is not reckoned to him as four cubits. The law applies to him also who has put the "Erub" down at a place which is near to 2,000 cubits without the city, if when afterwards returning to his city the 2,000 cubits from the place where he had put the "Erub" end, where the city begins before his house, he is forbidden even to return to his house.

11. An "Erub" for boundaries should be made only for the purpose of performing a precept, e.g., to pray in an assembly of ten, or to meet one's Rabbi or friend who had returned from a journey, or to go to a feast of the precepts, or to attend to matters in the interest of many, or if he had returned from a journey and he desires to go to his house and the like.

12. The "Erub" for boundaries should not be put down on a Sabbath or Festival, if, therefore, a festival occurred on the eve of the Sabbath and he desires to go (beyond the boundary line) on the Sabbath, he is required to put the "Erub" down on the eve of the Festival. Likewise on a Festival after the Sabbath, if he desires to go on the Festival, he is required to put the "Erub" down on the Sabbath-eve.

13. The property and live-stock of a man are governed by the laws which restrict his own feet, thus, it is forbidden to take them where he is not allowed to go, if, however, he had loaned them to another, or hired them out, or delivered them to another's care they are governed by the law applying to the one in whose charge they are, even if he be a non Jew, the cattle and the property have acquired the Sabbath-rest at his place, furthermore, even the property of a non-Jew acquires the Sabbath-rest wherever they are on Friday in the twilight.

14. If a non-Jew brought an article regarding which one need not apprehend that any labour was performed therein on that Sabbath, only that it is forbidden on account of having been brought from beyond the Sabbath boundary, if the non-Jew brought it for himself or for another non-Jew, it is at once permitted to make use of it, even to partake thereof; only that it is forbidden for him to carry it more than four cubits unless it was brought into the house, or if the city is supplied with an "Erub," then it is permissible to carry it in the entire city. If, however it was brought especially for the Israelite, he and his entire family are forbidden to make use thereof the entire Sabbath and on the close of the Sabbath they must wait the length of time it would take to bring it. Nevertheless it is permissible for him to carry it within a space of four cubits, or in the entire city, if it is surrounded by a wall or provided with an "Erub." When it is a matter of conjecture as to whether it was brought from beyond the Sabbath boundary it is also forbidden unless it may be more readily surmised that it was not brought from beyond the boundary.

15. There are no boundaries above ten hand-breadths from the ground, therefore one who boarded a vessel on the Sabbath-eve before the coming in of the Sabbath and the vessel sailed away, even on a long voyage, if it reached port on the Sabbath and he landed, he has the right to go from that place a distance of 2,000 cubits in any direction, as it is presumed that during the entire voyage of the vessel, he is always above ten hand-breadths from the ground, and he does not acquire the Sabbath rest until he reached land, if, however he had left the vessel during the Sabbath and returned thereto after having been on shore during the Sabbath he had then acquired the Sabbath-rest, and if the vessel afterwards sailed beyond the boundary-line, he has only four cubits on board as he is governed by the law applying to one who went beyond the boundary-line. Likewise if a vessel reached a port on the Sabbath where it is not ten hand-breadths above the ground he had there acquired the Sabbath-rest. If he is in doubt whether it was at such a place or not the law may be relaxed.

LAWS CONCERNING THE CONCLUSION OF THE SABBATH.

1. The Evening Service should be said at a later hour (than on a week-day) in order to add from the profane to the sacred. In the prayer of שמונה עשרה one should include אתה חוננתנו, but if one forgets to say it, and he recollected it before he pronounced the Divine Name of the blessing חונן הדעת he should say אתה חוננתנו, וכו' and וחננו. If, however, he did not recollect it until after he had pronounced the Divine Name, he should conclude the blessing חונן הדעת and he need not repeat the שמונה עשרה as he will afterwards pronounce the "Habdalah" upon a goblet, but he should not not do any manner of work nor partake of anything before he will have pronounced the

302

"Habdalah" upon the goblet, and if he did some work or partook of something, he is required to repeat the prayer.

2.   After the שמונה עשרה, portion of the Kaddish is said followed by ויהי נועם should be said.   It must be said standing, and it is customary to repeat the last verse אורך ימים, וכו' afterward ואתה קדוש should be said, also the verses of sanctification.   In the event of a Festival occurring in the week that follows, ויהי נועם and ואתה קדוש should not be said.   After ויהי נועם and ואתה קדוש the entire Kaddish should be said followed by ויתן לך.

3.   It is mandatory to sanctify the Sabbath on its conclusion upon a cup of wine, that is the "Habdalah."   Blessings should also be pronounced upon spices and upon the light.   Women also are in duty bound to hear the blessings of the Habdalah.   When wine cannot be procured the Habdalah should be pronounced upon another beverage which is the "national drink," water excepted.

4.   From sun-set it is forbidden to eat or drink anything except water [previous to pronouncing the "Habdalah," one, however, who prolongs the third Sabbath-feast until the night is permitted to eat and drink inasmuch as he began it when allowable, he is also permitted to drink from the goblet of Grace, as that also forms part of the feast, this however, is permissible only when it is his invariable custom to say Grace upon a goblet of wine, but one who sometimes says Grace without such goblet is forbidden to drink from the goblet of Grace before having pronounced the "Habdallah."

5.   No work should be performed previous to the saying of the "Habdalah."   Women who need to light up before the saying of the "Habdalah" should first say, ברוך... המבדיל בין קדש לחול, בין אור לחשך, בין ישראל לעמים, בין יום השביעי לששת ימי המעשה, ברוך . . המבדיל בין קדש לחול and if a Festival occurs on Sunday, the blessing should be concluded with המבדיל בין קדש לקדש.

6.   One who delays saying the Evening Prayers on the conclusion of the Sabbath or who prolongs his meal into the night is permitted to tell even an Israelite who had already prayed and said אתה חוננתנו in the שמונה עשרה to do some work for him

7.   One should fill up the goblet of Habdalah to its very brim, letting it slightly overflow as a token of blessing then take the goblet

in the right hand and the spice box in his left and hold them thus until after pronouncing the blessing בורא פרי הגפן : then he should transfer the cup to the left hand and the spice-box to the right and pronounce the blessing בורא מיני בשמים, then he should pronounce the blessing upon the light after which he should again take the goblet in his right hand and pronounce the blessing המבדיל and on concluding he should resume his seat and drink the entire contents of the goblet.

8. It is well to put some of the spice called "pizam" among the spices as all are agreed that the blessing בורא מיני בשמים should be pronounced thereon. One should also take an "Hadas" (spice-box for ritual use) inasmuch as a precept was once performed therewith it is fitting that another precept be performed therewith.

9. It is mandatory that the light for the "Habdalah" should be made of wax and consist of several strands twisted together, but if he has none, he should pronounce the blessing on two candles which should be held together so that both flames should merge in one like a flambeau, after saying בורא מאורי האש he should look upon his finger-nails.

10. One who cannot smell should not pronounce a blessing on spices, nor should one who is blind pronounce a blessing upon the light.

11. If after having pronounced a blessing upon the wine while holding the spices in his hand and intending to pronounce a blessing thereon, he had erred in the words and said בורא מאורי האש but instantly became aware of it and concluded בורא מיני בשמים it is a valid blessing upon the spices, and he should afterwards pronounce the blessing upon the light, if, however, it was his intention to pronounce that blessing upon the light, it is a valid blessing upon the light and he should afterwards pronounce the blessing upon the spices.

12. It is mandatory to light up on the conclusion of Sabbath somewhat more brilliantly than usual and to chant the appropriate hymns, and thus accompany the Sabbath upon its departure; the name of Elijah the prophet should also be mentioned and prayers should be said that he may come to bring us the glad tidings of redemption.

13. It is mandatory to partake in the "feast of accompanying the Queen" of bread and warm victuals. One should set a good table in honour of accompanying the Sabbath. One who is unable to partake of bread should at least eat cake or fruits.

14. One who had already said the Habdalah may repeat it for the sake of his sons who has reached the age of religious training, in order that they may thus fulfil their obligations, and all the more so for the

sake of a grown person. One who pronounces the " Habdalah " for the sake of others should inhale the perfume of the spices when saying the blessing בורא מיני בשמים so that the blessing be not pronounced in vain. One who had already said the " Habdallah " should not repeat it for the sake of women alone.

15. If one had forgotten or was prevented by an accident, or had wilfully neglected to say the " Habdalah " on the conclusion of the Sabbath, he should say the " Habdalah " at any time until the end of the third day, but he should not say a blessing on the spices nor on the light and only say the blessing בורא פרי הגפן and המבדיל, after Tuesday the " Habdalah " should not be said.

LAWS CONCERNING THE NEW MOON AND THE CONSECRATION OF THE MOON.

1. On the eve of the New Moon a fast is observed by the pious and special services called " Services for the Minor Atonement-day " are held, for on this day pardon is accorded for the sins of the past month.

2. It is mandatory to regale oneself at the meal of the New Moon. If it occurs on the Sabbath an extra dish should be prepared in its honour. It is forbidden to fast, to deliver a funeral eulogy, and to say צדוק הדין (services for the dead) on the New Moon.

3. Hallel should be said in the Morning Service; it should be said standing and without interruption. One should endeavour to say it together with the congregation, hence if one arrives at the synagogue when the congregation is about to begin saying Hallel, he should join them and pray afterwards; if he is then saying פסוקי דזמרה he should say Hallel with the congregation but he should not say the blessings before and after Hallel, as the blessings ברוך שאמר and ישתבח will answer the same purpose for the Hallel. This, however, may be done only on the New Moon when parts of the Hallel are omitted, likewise during the Intermediate and last days of Passover but when the entire Hallel is said this cannot be done. One who was saying Hallel without the congregation, if two more are there he should say הודו לה' before them in order that they should respond, for the saying of הודו implies an exhortation to another. After the Hallel, the entire Kaddish is said and two Scrolls of the Law are taken out, four persons being called up to its reading.

4. It is obligatory each month to consecrate the moon. It should not be consecrated before it is actually night, when its light is reflected upon the ground and one may enjoy of its light. If it was obscured by a cloud it should not be consecrated unless the cloud is light and filmy. If one began the blessing and a cloud obscures the moon he should

conclude it, if, however, he thinks that he will be unable to conclude the blessing before the moon will be obscured he is forbidden to begin it. It should be consecrated only in the open air, and not under a roof; if, however, he has no clean place or is unable through some cause, he is permitted to consecrate it also in the house through a window. It is permissible for a blind person to consecrate the moon.

5. It is mandatory to consecrate it on the conclusion of the Sabbath, but if it will then be more than ten days from its conjunction, or it is apprehended that he will then be unable to consecrate it, one need not wait until the conclusion of the Sabbath. It is mandatory to consecrate it in the midst of a multitude, he, however, should not postpone it on that account.

6. It should not be consecrated before at least three days had elapsed from its conjunction, nor should it be consecrated after 14 days and nights, 18 hours and 22 minutes had passed since its conjunction.

7. It should not be consecrated on a Friday night, nor on a Festival night, unless in an emergency when the time for its consecration will have passed on the conclusion of the Sabbath.

8. If the moon was visible in the beginning of the night before the Evening Prayers had begun and there yet remain several nights to consecrate it, Evening Prayers should first be said and then consecrate it, but if there remain only two or three nights the time being so short, it may be apprehended lest it will be obscured by clouds, and in a rainy season even if four nights yet remain, it may be apprehended lest it be obscured by clouds and the consecration of the moon should therefore take precedence. If the moon were not visible while reading the שמע and its blessings, and the time for its consecration be so limited that it will have passed after שמונה עשרה is said then prayers may be interrupted even in the midst of the blessings, or in the midst of reading the שמע in order to consecrate it between the sections.

9. If during the month of Adar the moon was not visible until the night of the 14th, which is the time for reading the Book of Esther, the moon should be consecrated first and the Book of Esther read thereafter. If it became visible during the reading of the Book of Esther, if it be at such a time that it will be valid to consecrate it also after the reading is concluded, the reading of the Book of Esther

should not be interrupted, but if the time for the consecration of the moon will have passed before the reading of the Book of Esther is concluded and the entire congregation had not as yet consecrated the moon, they should interrupt the reading of the Book of Esther and consecrate the moon, concluding the reading thereafter, but an individual should not interrupt same.

LAWS CONCERNING THE MONTH OF NISSAN.

1. During the entire month of Nissan תחנון (supplications) should not be said, nor should צדוק הדין (funeral services) be held, nor should צדקתך be said on Sabbath in the Afternoon Service. One should not fast in Nissan even on a Jahrzeit, but one may fast to propitiate an evil dream. The first-born should fast on the eve of the Passover, a bridegroom and bride should also observe their fast even on the New Moon of Nissan. Beginning with the New Moon on each day should be read (privately) the section of Num. vii. treating of the offerings of the prince on that day, and on the thirteenth day, section בהעלותך should be read until כן עשה את המנורה (Num. viii. 1-5). On Sabbath Haggodol it is customary to omit ברבי נפשי and to substitute therefor עבדים היינו, וכו'.

LAWS CONCERNING THE WHEAT AND FLOUR FOR
UNLEAVENED BREAD.

1. It is written "And ye shall observe the unleavened bread," hence it is inferred that it is requisite to observe the wheat intended for the unleavened bread of the precept in order that no water come thereon from the time that it is taken to the mill and thenceforth. It would be well if it were possible for one to use (during the entire Festival) unleavened bread of wheat that was under observation from the time of reaping. If this is impossible, one should at least embellish the two "Seder" nights by using such unleavened bread thereon.

2. If there was found in the wheat some that were split, or had sprouted, it is permitted to use the rest, providing they had separated them or were very particular about there being at least sixty times as much good wheat as split ones, or as those that had sprouted. One should originally be careful to separate wheat from that which was devoured by mice, or see that there are sixty times as much good wheat. Wheat brought by a vessel, or stored in pits if it is dry and hard and its appearance is not changed, it is valid for unleavened bread, but if it was stored in a garret and the rain had dripped down

upon it in several places through the roof, it is forbidden to use them, if, however, a little snow or rain fell on it in one place, then only the doubtful wet wheat should be removed, and the rest is permitted to be used.

3. The utmost care should be taken to cleanse the mill and make it fit to grind the grist for unleavened bread. One should, therefore, thoroughly cleanse the mill in the most scrupulous manner, and provide new receptacles for the flour, and yet as the laws relating thereto are numerous, and great knowledge is required for their application, it has long been the custom in Israel not to consider the mill valid for use unless it was inspected by erudite Rabbis who vouched for its fitness in a proper manner. The flour of the first grinding after the mill was approved should not be partaken of on the Passover. If grist that was soaked was also being ground in that mill, it should be separated from the other by a partition in order that none of its powder mingle therewith.

4. If a bag of flour was moistened by water and a part only affected, it does not matter whether it is still wet or already dry, one may hold that part in his hands while emptying the bag of the rest of the flour, the use of which is permitted, but the use of that which became moist is forbidden. If, however, many places became wet, so that it is impossible to proceed as aforementioned, if it is still moist, one should sift the flour and that alone which remains crumbling upon the sieve is leaven, but the use of the rest is permitted; likewise if mice devoured some of the flour, it should be sifted, but if it had already become dry sifting is of no avail and the use of the entire flour is forbidden.

5. It is forbidden to bake the flour on the same day that it was ground as the flour is then warm and will readily turn sour when water is added to it, therefore one should defer baking for at least 24 hours after the grinding.

6. It is proper to make new bags for holding the flour, or at least to take the seams apart and to wash them thoroughly with warm water, ashes, and by rubbing them.

7. It is forbidden to place a bag of flour upon a beast except with the intervention of thick leather, as otherwise it will get warm and moist from perspiration. One should also be as careful as possible not to place many bags one on top of the other, as the flour will be heated by friction and turn sour in the kneading.

LAWS AND CUSTOMS OF ISRAEL

Laws Concerning the Water with which the Unleavened Bread is Kneaded.

1. Unleavened bread should be kneaded only with water that stood over night, i.e., drawn in the twilight (or a little earlier, but not much earlier) filtered, then placed covered in a cool place and let stand the entire night. Even if the night is longer than twelve hours, still it is forbidden to knead it before daylight, and if the night is short and there are not twelve hours to daylight, it is required to wait until twelve hours will have passed since it was drawn. When bringing it to his house he should be careful that the rays of the sun do not reach it.

2. One may draw at one time enough water to last several days, but it is mandatory to draw water daily for each day's use.

3. As the streams in Nissan are generally cooler than the wells, one should draw water from a stream, at times, however, the streams are swollen from the melted snow and are not so cold, it is then preferable to draw water from the wells.

4. Only an Israelite should draw the water. It should not be placed in a vessel that had contained honey or other fruit-extracts, unless it had been previously scoured it should specially be avoided placing it in a vessel which had contained something having a pungent taste even if it is not leaven, because on account of that which is pungent it will more readily turn sour, and even scouring will not avail, nor should the water be placed in a copper vessel, as it does not keep it so cool as other vessels.

5. If the water that stood over night does not suffice, it is permitted to add water thereto, providing most of the water be that which stood over night, and it should be a primary object to have two thirds of the water of that which stood over night. One should if possible endeavour to obtain the added water from a sheltered place, where the rays of the sun do not reach it.

6. If the baking is done on Sunday, it is necessary to draw the water on Thursday evening, and if not drawn on Thursday, it should be done on the eve of Sabbath (Friday) after the Afternoon Service, or on the Sabbath through a non Jew. The water that stood over night should not be poured out on account of a death if it occurred, or on account of the equinox, for it is written that "no evil will befall upon him that guardeth the precept."

LAWS AND CUSTOMS OF ISRAEL

LAWS CONCERNING THE KNEADING AND BAKING OF THE UNLEAVENED BREAD.

1. If it is desirable to bake unleavened bread in an oven where leaven had been baked it is required to make it legally proper by glowing it so much as to make sparks fly therefrom. Great care should be taken to spread the coals upon its entire surface; after glowing it it is highly proper to remove the ashes and clean it carefully waiting until it will become slightly cooler, he should then make a new fire therein for baking unleavened bread.

2. If the oven is made of earth, it is customary for some to plaster it with fresh earth in order to make it valid for use without requiring to glow it. A thick coating, however, of plaster (the thickness of one's finger, or thicker) should be put upon the entire oven, as a thin coating is of no avail.

3. The unleavened bread should be kneaded and made only in a room that has a roof, and not opposite an open window, even if the sun does not shine through, but if the sun shines through, the glass window-panes are of no avail, but it is necessary to spread a curtain to shut out the sun's rays. Care should also be taken that the room should not be heated or warm.

4. No greater quantity of dough should be kneaded than that requisite for the separation of the dough-cake. When the flour is measured it should not be stuffed into the measure. If the dough kneaded was soft, flour may be added thereto to harden it.

5. One should be careful not to place the flour near water so that the flour-dust should not fall therein. Likewise one who measures the flour should not go near the dough or the water. It is well to take care not to needlessly handle the flour, as it might warm it slightly.

6. There should be neither crack nor crevice in the vessel used for kneading wherein any particle of dough might remain and turn into leaven, nor should the vessel be placed upon cushioned articles while in the act of kneading lest it become warm; the vessel must be thoroughly cleansed every 18 minutes when the hands too must be carefully washed. The boards, rollers and machines should also be free from crack or crevice, and should be thoroughly cleansed at least

every 18 minutes. The peel with which the unleavened bread is thrust into the oven should be critically examined that there be no crack therein where a particle of dough might enter and become sour.

7. If anything calorific fell in the dough, such as salt, spices or quick-lime, even a particle thereof, and was kneaded therein, the use of the entire dough is forbidden, inasmuch as it became heated thereby. If a grain of corn was found in the dough, a mass of dough as thick as one's finger should be removed from all around that grain and thrown away and the use of the rest is permitted.

8. Care should be taken not to let the dough lay for a moment without working upon it and if the unleavened bread cannot change process with sufficient celerity, the kneading of the dough should be kept up as it should not lay idle for a moment.

9. Those who are engaged in the work should perform their tasks speedily and see that there are no particles of dough upon the boards or machines, and that none of it stick to their hands ; should they find any dough sticking to them, they should instantly cleanse them and remove same.

10. Immediately after the unleavened bread was prepared, it should be put in the oven as quickly as possibly, the utmost care should be taken not to delay it for a moment opposite the mouth of the oven, as there it will quickly turn sour, hence it is necessary that the one handing the unleavened bread to the baker should be versed in the law and pay scrupulous attention to it.

11. A God-fearing man should take care before baking his unleavened bread to have the oven heated anew and the coals spread upon its entire surface.

12. The baker should most carefully see to it that none of the unleavened bread be doubled up, nor that one should touch the other. In the event of one having doubled up or become inflated (that is, if the unleavened bread was divided at its thick parts, and the hollow part is as wide as a thumb) it is requisite to break off that portion as it is leaven, and it is permitted to use the rest, if, however, they touched each other while still moist in the oven, their use may be permitted.

13. Care should be taken not to take the unleavened bread out of the oven so long as it is not baked to such a degree that one may break it without drawing strands of dough therefrom as previous to that condition it is only like dough which being taken out of the oven readily turns sour, the peel upon which such unleavened bread was

taken out, is also thenceforth forbidden to use for unleavened bread. If it is impossible to tell whether strands of dough can be withdrawn therefrom or not, because of the doubt, the law should be enforced, but if it became brown the law should be relaxed.

14. It is proper for every God-fearing man to personally supervise the making and baking of his own unleavened bread and admonish the workingmen to use due care and diligence. This was the method of the great men of Israel, of blessed memory, and this is also the method of the pious in our own times.

15. The unleavened bread wherewith to perform the precept of its eating on the two first Passover nights will be fulfilled, is called "the unleavened bread of the precept" and it should be made "for the sake of the precept" by an adult male Israelite of intelligence, aged at least thirteen years and one day. or by a female aged at least twelve years and one day, and at each stage of its process, even when drawing water, the worker should say "for the sake of the unleavened bread of the precept."

LAWS CONCERNING THE SEARCH FOR AND

NULLIFICATION OF LEAVEN.

1. On the night preceding the eve of Passover, immediately after dark, a search for leaven should be made, and it is forbidden to begin eating or doing any manner of work half-an-hour before nightfall.

2. The search should be made only with a single wax-candle, but in an emergency, if one has no wax candle he may search with a candle of tallow.

3. All the rooms wherein it is surmised leaven was brought, should be searched, even the wine-cellars, garrets, stores and wood-shed: all those vessels in which leaven was kept should also be searched. Before the search all these places should be carefully swept and cleansed from leaven in order to facilitate the search thereafter.

4. A stall in which the cattle are fed with corn, likewise a coop in which the fowls are fed with corn do not require searching, if, how-ever, corn was given them therein, they require searching.

5. It is essential to search every nook and cranny in these places with the utmost care. One should also search his pockets also the children's garments as sometimes leaven is placed therein, and in the morning when the leaven is being burnt they should be thoroughly shaken out.

6. The rooms which are sold to the non-Jew with the leaven, inasmuch as the sale will not be made before morning, the obligation to search devolves upon him in the night.

7. Before beginning the search he should say the blessing אשר קדשנו במצותיו וצונו על ביעור חמץ and he should not interrupt same between saying the blessing and beginning the search; it is well not to interrupt until the search is completed, excepting for that which relates to the search. One may search many houses by the one blessing that was pronounced.

8. Previous to making the search, it is customary to lay pieces of bread in places where the searcher may find them, so that the blessing should not be in vain, one, however, who does not make a proper search but simply gathers up these crumbs, does not fulfil the commandment of searching and has pronounced the blessing in vain.

9. Previous to making the search, one should put away in a safe place all the leaven which he leaves for food or to sell. The leaven which he has found in his search should likewise be put away in a safe place, it should first be carefully tied round and then put it in a prominent position where it can be seen in the morning and one should not forget to burn it.

10. Immediately after the search he should nullify it. The essential of nullification is the hearty resolve to consider all the leaven in his domain as non-existent, entirely valueless, and comparable to dust, and as something for which he has absolutely no use, our Sages have furthermore ordained that one should give expression to these thoughts by saying כל חמירא, וכו' and if he does not understand it, he should say it in any language he understands. In the morning after one has burnt it, one should again nullify it, including all the leaven by that nullification and say כל חמירא, וכו' or a translation of same.

11. If one desires to use as a store-house for fruit, wood, or other things a room which requires to be searched for leaven, and the above-mentioned articles will prevent him from searching that room on the night of the 14th of Nissan, he should previously search it in the night-time in the same manner that the search is made on the night of the 14th, even if there be yet ample time before the Passover, and even a year in advance. If, however, by inadvertance one did not search it before he had transformed it in a store house, and it is his intention to remove the things before the time will come for the search of leaven,

he need not trouble himself to remove them just then and search the room, but if he intends to remove them during the Passover, he must remove them and search the room even if it involves great trouble and entails a loss of money.

12. If one fills up a store-room with the intention of not emptying same until after Passover, there is a distinction as to the time. If it is before 30 days preceding Passover he need not previously search the room (except to burn anything that is positively leaven that may be there) and the formula of nullification at the proper time will also avail for that room, if, however, it is within the 30 days preceding Passover, it devolves upon him to search the room, thus, even if he inadvertently did not make the search, he is required to empty the store-room and search it in the night time immediately he was reminded thereof.

13. If one stores wheat that was not sour in a pit, but afterwards the wheat on the bottom and sides of the pit turned sour on account of its dampness, even if he had stored it there within the 30 days, he need not empty the pit on the night of the 14th in order to search same, as the nullification is sufficient, inasmuch as he had stored it away in a manner that was permissible, and if there be some sour wheat amongst them, there are diverse laws in regard thereto and one should consult the ecclesiastical authorities.

14. One should not cast corn-seeds to fowls in a moist place during the 30 days as he may forget to burn them.

15. One who sets out upon a journey should previous to starting, appoint one as his agent to search and nullify his leaven, and he should tell him expressly that he is appointing him his agent to search and nullify. The agent when pronouncing the [formula of nullification should mention the name of the owner; nevertheless the owner himself, wherever he may be, should nullify the leaven on his premises on the morning of the Passover-eve.

16. If one finds leaven in his house during the Intermediate Days of Passover, he should take it and burn it, and if it be the size of an olive he should previously pronounce the blessing על ביעור חמץ. If he found it on the Festival, or on the Sabbath in the Intermediate Days, likewise on the Sabbath which occurs on the Passover-eve, when it is forbidden to handle it, as it is "set aside," he should cover it with a vessel until the conclusion of the Festival or Sabbath and then burn it. If he had found it on the last days, as the Passover will end on the conclusion of the festival days, he need not say a blessing when burning it, although it is the size of an olive.

314

LAWS AND CUSTOMS OF ISRAEL

Laws Concerning Articles Forbidden, and those Permitted to be Found in an Israelite's House on the Passover.

1. Everything which has a mixture of leaven in it, even if the leaven is not actually there, i.e., if it was removed therefrom, but the taste of the leaven remains, it is nevertheless forbidden to keep it on the Passover, but an article in which there was no leaven, only that it was cooked in a vessel used for leaven, even if cooking was previously done therein on that very day, or an article that was pickled in a vessel used for leaven, it is permitted to keep it on Passover providing the cooking or pickling was done before the Passover. If, however, it was cooked or pickled on the Passover in a vessel used for leaven it is obligatory to burn it.

2. Corn in which there were grains that had sprouted, or were split, even if but a few were mingled in a large quantity, likewise corn upon which water had fallen, or had been saturated with water, it is forbidden to keep that as well as everything that was prepared therefrom. One who sells his neighbour corn that became moist is required to inform him thereof in order that he should not keep it on the Passover, but it is forbidden to sell it to a non-Jew when it may be apprehended that the non-Jew will sell it to an Israelite, who will keep it during the Passover.

3. One is permitted to wear on the Passover garments which were washed and prepared with starch, but one should not spread a cover upon the table if there be any of the starch upon it which may be apprehended to crumble therefrom, and it is most decidedly forbidden to put Passover flour therein.

4. It is permissible to use paste made of the five species of flour, even during the 30 days preceding Passover, providing the leaven is not visible, inasmuch as the paste is not absolutely leaven, and it is also covered up, the law is not stringently enforced therein; if, however, it is visible on the surface it is forbidden, but before the 30 days it is permitted in any manner.

5. The leaven which became spoiled and was entirely damaged before the Passover, it is permitted to utilise it also to keep it on the Passover.

LAWS AND CUSTOMS OF ISRAEL

6. All vessels which were not made valid for the use of Passover should be thoroughly scoured and washed on the Passover-eve before 12 o'clock in such a manner that no leaven be recognizable upon them, and secreted in a secluded place. But it is best to lock them up in a separate room and hide the key until after Pascover.

LAWS CONCERNING PASSOVER-EVE.

1. On Passover-eve neither מזמור לתודה nor למנצח should be said.

2. It is forbidden to eat leaven after a third of the day, (i.e. a third of the time from dawn until the stars appear), but one may utilise it for another hour; thus he is permitted to sell it to a non-Jew; after that time, any use thereof is also forbidden. It is requisite to burn the leaven and to nullify it while it is yet permitted to utilise it.

3. After noon-time such work only is permitted as that which is permitted during the Intermediate Days of the Festival. One is permitted to have his hair cut by a non-Jew. Paring the nails should also be done before noon, one, however, who forgot, may also pare his nails after noon, but he is forbidden to have his hair cut except by a non-Jew.

4. It is forbidden to eat unleavened bread the entire day. It is forbidden to give unleavened bread even to children capable of understanding the subject of the exodus from Egypt, but all are permitted to partake of victuals made of the meal of the unleavened bread until the last quarter of the day. From that time it is forbidden to eat, save in a case of necessity, when fruit, meat or fish may be partaken of, but one should be careful not to eat too much in order that he may relish the un leavened bread of which he is about to partake in the night.

5. The first-born, whether on the father's or on the mother's side, should fast on Passover-eve, even if it occurred on a Sabbath-eve. One who was born after an abortion should also fast. While the child is small the father should fast in its stead. At a feast of the precepts they are permitted to eat.

6. A first born who fasts should say עננו in the Afternoon Service. If there are many of the first born and they pray with the congregation, none of them should officiate as Reader as עינו is not said in the loud repetition of the prayer owing to the month Nissan.

Laws Concerning the Baking of the "Unleavened Bread of the Precept."

1.   The very pious bake the "unleavened bread of the precept" on the Passover-eve after noon-time which is the time when the Pascal sacrifice was offered, and inasmuch as leaven is then forbidden, it is proper to nullify the crumbs by saying as follows: "All the crumbs that will fall during the kneading and preparing, as well as the dough which will cling to vessels, I hereby nullify and make free to all."

2.   The water with which the vessels are washed should be poured out where it can flow down, a stone flooring should not be there, so that it might be quickly absorbed in the ground, for, by emptying it where the the water cannot flow down, or even in a steep place but there is a stone flooring it may be apprehended that it will gather in one place and turn sour before it is absorbed in the ground, thus there will be leaven on his domain.

The Selling of the Leaven.

1.   An Israelite possessing "leaven" is perpetually transgressing the law which precludes such possession.   Therefore it is needed that all leaven should be sold to a non-Jew before Passover.   But the selling must be real and not nominal.   If the buyer does not pay for the goods, it is permissible to retake it from him after Passover.

LAWS AND CUSTOMS OF ISRAEL

2. The leaven that is sold to a non-Jew must not remain in the house of the Israelite. But if the buyer connot take it away, then the room in which the leaven is found must be let to him.

3. The Israelite may have a key to the room which he nominally lets to the non-Jew with the contents of leaven but it is prohibited to put a seal on the leaven, for that would imply that he still regards himself the owner of the leaven, which is forbidden.

4. If the Israelite is unable to let the whole room containing the leaven, it being indispensable for his own use then a partition should be made between the place occupied by the leaven and the rest of the room and the specified place may nominally be let to the non-Jew buying the leaven.

5. If the place containing the leaven is not the property of the Israelite selling the leaven, but belongs to another Jew then permission must be obtained from the latter to sub-let it to the non Jew for the Passover week.

6. It is prohibited to make a condition with the non-Jew buying the leaven, that he must re-sell it after Passover. But the Israelite may promise the non-Jew that he will re-buy again the leaven after Passover and give him some profit. It is prohibited to sell leaven before Passover to an apostate or even the second generation of an apostate.

7. One possessing leaven in distant places or laden on waggons or on ships he can likewise transfer it to a non-Jew.

8. As to an Israelite possessing leaven in the house of a non-Jew, or vice versa, then the learned in the law should be consulted and judge according to the circumstances.

9. Care should be taken not to benefit after Passover of such leaven that had not properly been transferred during Passover.

Laws Concerning the Passover-Eve
Which Falls on the Sabbath.

1. On the Passover-eve which falls on the Sabbath, the leaven should be searched for on Thursday night, on concluding the search one should nullify it and say כל חמירא " All leaven " etc., as at another time, and on Friday he should burn it at the same time that he burns it every Passover-eve, he, however, need not say כל חמירא excepting on the Sabbath after the meal when he should nullify it and say כל חמירא " All leaven " etc.

2. The first-born should fast on Thursday, and if it is difficult for him to fast until after the search for leaven is concluded, he may take some slight refreshments previous to the search, or else appoint one as his agent to make the search.

3. An article of food prepared with flour should not be cooked for this Sabbath, inasmuch as it may cling to the plate, and it is forbidden to wash it (being Sabbath) therefore only victuals that are not pasty should be cooked ; after the meal the cloth should be well shaken and hid away with the vessel used for leaven in a room to which one is not accustomed to go during the Passover ; if he have any bread left he should give it to a non-Jew, but he should not give it to him to take it to the public domain. The house should be swept by a non-Jew, or with something permissible.

4. The Morning Service should be held at an early hour in order not to delay in eating while it is yet permissible to eat leaven. It is proper to divide the meal as follows, he should say Grace and pause for a short time, then wash the hands again, and eat a little, then repeat the Grace, thus fulfilling the precept regarding the third meal.

5. On the Sabbath-eve one should be very careful to inquire whether the dough-cake was separated from the loaves that were baked in honour of the Sabbath. If the separation of the dough-cake was forgotten on the Sabbath-eve, the ecclesiastical authorities should be consulted.

LAWS OF PURGING.

1. For all earthen vessels which have been used for leaven, neither purging nor glowing will avail ; for ovens, and ranges for saucepans built of stones and brick glowing may be used.

2. For wooden, metal and stone utensils, purging is available, but if it be an article that will be damaged by hot water, such as a vessel which is glued together, even if only the handle is glued on, purging does not avail.

3. Before the vessel is purged, it should be thoroughly cleansed from rust and the like, and made perfectly clean, but stains do not matter. If the vessel is indented, it should be carefully scraped. If it is made of metal, hot coals should be placed upon the dents to glow them, and the vessel should be purged thereafter, if, however, it be impossible to thoroughly cleanse the dents and cracks, also to glow them, it cannot be made valid for use, hence it is necessary to carefully observe whether purging will avail for knives with handles. It is best, if one can afford it, to buy new knives for Passover.

4. Utensils in which water is not generally put when used over the fire (such as frying pans and the like) require glowing. One should originally glow them to the extent of making them emit sparks. A wooden spoon cannot be made valid for use.

5. A vessel on which there is a patch should be examined to ascertain if there is any apparent leaven under the patch, in which case it is necessary to glow that place until it is positive that any leaven there was consumed, it should then be purged, but if there is no fear of there being any apparent leaven, then, if the patch was put on before it was used for leaven, he may purge it just as it is, as the purging will cause it to reject the leaven it has absorbed. If, however, the vessel was used for leaven before the patch was put on, the purging is not enough, but it is necessary to place hot coals upon the patch to glow that place before purging it; if the patch was soldered with lead or silver and the like, it may be purged just as it is, as the leaven that was absorbed was used in the soldering. A mortar, which it is customary to use for pounding pungent spices together with leaven requires a slight glowing, thus it should be filled up with burning coals until it is hot enough for straws to be burnt on its surface, but where it is customary to pound therein only pepper and the like, purging is sufficient.

6. A vessel which was permanently used to hold brandy does not reject the odour or taste of brandy through purging, and only if it was previously thoroughly boiled in water and ashes until its odour was entirely dissipated, does purging avail it.

7. The purging of a cask should be done in the following manner: One should place therein stones that he had made glowing hot, and pour upon them boiling water from the vessel in which it was boiled, and then roll the cask in order that it be purged everywhere. The casks commonly used that are made of many staves confined by hoops, if they had contained leaven such as brandy, or if flour was kept therein, cannot be made valid by purging.

8. Any article that requires purging cannot be made valid by scraping, but must be purged.

9. A vessel that cannot be thoroughly cleansed, such as a sieve, the receptacle of a mill, a basket used for leaven, and a grater as well as any vessel that has a narrow neck which makes it impossible to cleanse it from within, e.g., tubes, cannot be made valid by purging.

10. A larder in which eatables are kept the entire year and in which leakage from the pots is possible, require a slight purification, such as hot water poured upon them from the very vessel wherein it was boiled. The water should not be thrown suddenly, but poured upon the shelves and made to run all over them. Tables are best purified by having stones made glowing hot placed upon them, boiling water poured over the stones which should then be moved from place to place in such a manner that the boiling water should cover the entire surface. The table should previously be scoured, then purified at the end of twenty-four hours.

11. Handles of vessels also require purification, nevertheless if they do not protrude into the pots the pouring of water thereon is sufficient.

12. Vessels used for drinking and for measuring also require purging, glass vessels cannot be made valid by purging.

13. Purging is done only in water, and nothing should be mixed therewith, not even ashes and the like. If one had purged many vessels in one boiler, so that the water became turbid, no more purging should be done therein.

14. If one purges a vessel by means of a pair of tongs with which he takes hold of it, he should loosen its hold on the vessel, and then again take hold with it. It is better to put the vessels in a net or basket. One should not place many vessels at one time in the vessel wherein he purges them, so that they should not touch each other.

15. One should not purge a vessel unless twenty-four hours had passed since leaven was cooked therein. Likewise the boiler in which the purging is done should not have been used for leaven that same day, he should carefully observe each time that he puts a vessel in the

boiler that the water comes up boiling hot. If it is requisite to purge the boiler, then it must be full when the water is boiling therein and hot stones should be thrown therein in order that the boiling water should overflow its border; purging should only be done until noon.

17. After the purging it is customary to wash the vessels with cold water.

VARIOUS LAWS CONCERNING PASSOVER WHICH IT IS NECESSARY

FOR EVERY ISRAELITE TO KNOW.

1. On Passover-eve until night-fall the prohibition against leaven is amenable to the same law that governs all dietary prohibitions which is nullified if the forbidden food is but a sixtieth part of the proper food, hence if a corn seed was found within a fowl or in victuals, it should be thrown away, and it is permitted to partake of the rest even during Passover. But as during the Passover even a particle of leaven makes food prohibited, even to benefit thereby, thus wherever a corn-seed of the five species of grain is found, or any particle of leaven, it is necessary to consult the ecclesiastical authorities.

2. If corn seeds were found in a well, the water thereof should not be used unless in a case of urgent necessity, e.g., if no other water can be obtained, but if a piece of bread was found therein, its use is forbidden even if there is no other water, and straining does not avail to make it fit for use.

3. Poultry should not be singed with straws bearing ears of corn, as it is apprehended that a leavened grain may be amongst them, hence, singeing is done with paper or herbs, or the ears of corn are detached from the straw, if, however, by inadvertence the singeing was done, it does not invalidate the poultry. One should be careful to remove the crop from poultry previous to singeing it.

4. All kinds of legumes, likewise all kinds of dried fruits are forbidden unless it is known that they were dried in a proper manner by the sun, or in a stove that was made proper for the use of Passover. Even dried figs and raisins are forbidden, whether they are large or small, also the rinds of oranges, nevertheless it is permitted to drink during Passover a beverage prepared from raisins that was made before Passover.

5. Neither cloves nor saffron should be put in victuals, as there is a taint of leaven about them, other spices in which there is no taint of leaven, salt included, should be carefully examined to see if there is not a corn-seed therein.

6. Honey should not be partaken of excepting of that which was not detached from the combs, or of that which was not detached by an Israelite especially for the use of Passover.

7. In a case of necessity, as for instance for the requirements of a sick or an aged person it is permitted to take unleavened bread with extract of eggs or other fruit extracts such as milk, wine and so forth. This is called מצה עשירה (unleavened bread prepared in a rich manner) care, however, should be taken not to mingle any water wfth it, no matter how little, but on the first two nights of Passover only the actual unleavened bread should be partaken of, and one does not fulfil one's obligation with מצה עשירה. Where there is no great necessity it is forbidden to bake מצה עשירה even before Passover for use during Passover.

8. One who places corn or bran before fowls should be careful to put them in a dry place so that they should not become moist, but it is forbidden to give bran to cattle, as it becomes moist from their saliva, and if one does give them corn, he should be careful to give a little at a time so that they leave none that is moist, and if any were left it should be instantly burnt.

9. On Passover-eve from the time when it is forbidden to benefit by leaven as well as during the entire Passover, it is forbidden to benefit even by the leaven of a non-Jew, hence an Israelite is forbidden to transport or to guard the leaven of a non-Jew, and it is assuredly forbidden to purchase leaven for a non-Jew even with the non-Jew's money. It is also forbidden to hire a beast to a non-Jew for the purpose of carrying leaven, or to rent him a room for the purpose of keeping leaven therein, but it is permitted to hire him a beast for the Passover week without any stipulations, it is also permitted to rent him a room to live in during Passover, although he knows that he will bring in leaven.

10. One is forbidden to deliver his beast to a non-Jew, even a long time before the Passover, if he knows that he will feed it with leaven on the Passover.

11. It is permissible for one to say to his non-Jewish domestic on the Passover, "here is money, go buy yourself some food and eat," although he knows that he will buy leaven. In a case of necessity, one is also permitted to say "go and eat by the non-Jew, and I will pay him," or to say to another non-Jew "Give my domestic something o eat and I will pay you," but he is forbidden to pay him the money in advance for whatever he will give to his domestic.

12. If it is necessary for one to feed a child with leaven, the child should be carried to a non-Jew and the non-Jew should give it the leavened food, the Israelite should pay him afterwards. The Israelite should not himself feed the child with the leaven, but if the child is in a dangerous condition, everything is permitted.

Laws Relative to Preparing the "Seder" (סדר).

1. It is mandatory to acquire choice wine of a fine appearance and rich flavour wherewith to perform the precept of drinking four goblets. For the first dipping termed "Carpas" כרפס one should take a species of fruit which grows on the ground. For the bitter herbs one should take salad or horse-raddish, but inasmuch as the latter is very pungent, it may be grated, care, however, should be taken that it become not entirely tasteless, therefore it might be grated on arriving from the synagogue, but on the Sabbath it should be grated before night, and kept covered until the night.

2. All the species valid for the precept can be counted together to make up the size of an olive (כזית) and either the leaves or stems can be used, but not the growing roots which peel off here and there, the large root, however, upon which the leaves grow, although it is hidden in the earth, is classed with the stem. Nevertheless, it is best to take the leaves and the stem which protrude above the ground. The leaves are not valid for the precept unless they are tender, but the stems are valid whether they are tender or dry, but not if cooked or pickled.

3. The "Charoseth" (חרוסת) should be made of figs, nuts, dates, pomegranates, apples, almonds, cinnamon and ginger. It should be mixed thickly, and when necessary to dip the bitter herbs therein, one should pour in wine or vinegar in order that it be soft and fit for dipping therein. On the Sabbath one should not pour the wine or vinegar in the "Charoseth," but one should put the "Charoseth" in the wine or vinegar. The salt water should be prepared on the eve of the Holiday, and if one makes it on the Holiday he should first pour in the water then add the salt.

4. During the recital of the Hagadah it is necessary that there should be on the table the meat from the part called the shoulder which has been broiled over the fire, also a fried or cooked egg, prepared on the Passover eve while it is yet day, if, however, one did not fry or cook them while yet day, it may be done at night on the Festival in which case he should eat them on the first day of the Festival. Likewise on the second night, if he fried or cooked them on

327

the Festival he should eat them on the Festival day, as it is not allowable to cook on one Festival for another, more especially on a Festival for a week-day. Now, inasmuch as roasted meat is not partaken of on the Passover nights, if he roasted it on the Festival, he should eat it on the following day. Even if it was roasted on the eve of the Festival, it should not be thrown out thereafter, but it should be placed in the victuals that are cooked on the second day of the Festival and eaten.

5. He should arrange his seat while it is yet day, using nice spreads to the full extent of his means, and place it in such a manner that he will be able to incline his body and recline on the left side. Even if he is left-handed, he should recline on the left side. The "dish" too should be set while it is yet day in order that immediately on his arrival from the synagogue he may proceed with the "Seder" without any hindrance. It is good to make use of as many beautiful vessels as one can afford, and even the vessels that he does not use for the meal he should arrange nicely on the table to beautify it and to symbolize freedom.

6. The "dish" should be set as follows : Three Matzoth should be placed upon the dish and covered with a nice cloth, near that, towards his right hand the זרוע (shank bone) should be placed, and the egg towards the left hand, the bitter herbs on which a blessing will be pronounced in the centre, the Charoseth below the shank-bone, the "Carpas" below the egg, and the bitter herbs for eating with unleavened bread in the centre.

7. The wine goblets should be whole, without any flaw, and thoroughly washed, and they should hold at least a רביעית (the capacity of one and a half egg-shells).

8. It is customary to don the ritual garment called "Kittel" which should also be prepared while yet day, but one who is in mourning should not don it but is obliged to recline. if, however he did not in any wise observe mourning before the Festival, as for instance, if he had interred his dead on the Festival, then it is not customary to recline, but he should say the Hallel, inasmuch as it is obligatory to say the Hallel.

9. The son at his father's table is obliged to recline, but the disciple at the table of his Rabbi is not required to recline.

LAWS CONCERNING THE NIGHT OF PASSOVER.

1. The precept to eat unleavened bread on the Passover is to be performed especially at night as also the precept to drink four goblets which is also to be carried out especially at night, hence "Kiddush" should not be said until it is positively night. He should don the

"Kittel" and take his seat to arrange the "Seder." It is mandatory to distribute nuts, almonds and the like amongst the children in order that they shall note the change and ask the cause, their curiosity will then lead them to enquire also the cause for having unleavened bread, and bitter herbs, and the reason for reclining. If the children have the capacity to comprehend the sacredness of the Festival, and understand what is related concerning the Exodus from Egypt, goblets of wine should be placed before them as well from which they should drink. It is customary to fill up one goblet more than the number at the table, this is called "the goblet of the Prophet Elijah."

2. The domestic or one of the household should fill up the goblets, and whenever it is necessary they should be filled by another than himself to symbolize freedom. He should urge his household to drink at least the greater part of each cup at one time, and of the fourth cup they should drink a רביעית at one time and they should all bear in mind that they are thus performing the precept to drink four goblets, to relate of the going out from Egypt, to eat unleavened bread and bitter herbs, as women also are in duty bound to perform these precepts, excepting the custom of reclining. He should recite the "Kiddush" as it is written in the Hagadah, and drink while reclining on his left side. If it is possible for one to do so, it were well to drink the entire contents of each of the four goblets.

3. After that he should wash his hands without pronouncing the blessing, dry them, and cut up the "carpas" for himself and the members of his household, less than a כזית should be given to each, it should be dipped in salt water, and the blessing בורא פרי האדמה should be said thereon, they should bear in mind that this blessing will exempt them from saying one on the bitter herbs, he should eat thereof whilst reclining on his left side. After that he should take the unleavened bread that lies in the middle and divide it in two parts, he should take the larger part and put it upon his seat (it is right to wrap it in a cloth) for the Afikomon. The smaller portion he should put back in its place on the dish, the company present should then say הא לחמא עניא די אכלו until לשנה הבאה בני חורין.

2. The cup should be filled a second time and the youngest son should ask his father מה נשתנה "Wherefore is this night different, etc." If the son has no knowledge (how to ask) his father should teach him. If he has no son the wife should ask him, otherwise he should recite the questions himself. Even the learned should ask one of the other מה נשתנה. After that עברים היינו should be said, and it is proper to explain the Hagadah to the household in the language that they understand; if he himself does not understand the Holy language, he should say the Hagadah with the translation in the vernacular, particularly the section ר' גמליאל היה אומר where it is essential to understand the reason for the pascal lamb, the unleavened bread and the bitter herbs. At והיא שעמדה he should cover the unleavened bread

and they should take the goblets in their hands and say כהיא שעמדה
until מידם, after which he should again uncover the unleavened bread.
At זו מצה he should take the half Matzoh from the dish, and showing
it to his household, say זו מצה. Likewise at זה מרור he should raise the
bitter herbs, but when saying פסח שהיו אבותינו אוכלים he should not
raise the shank bone which is commemorative of the pascal lamb. At
לפיכך he should cover the unleavened bread, and they should each take
their cups in their hands and hold them aloft until they conclude
saying גאל ישראל, they should then say the blessing בורא פרי הגפן and
drink whilst reclining on their left sides.

5. After that they should wash their hands and say the blessing
על נטילת ידים he should then take the two whole Matzoth with the
broken one between them and pronounce the blessing המוציא, then lay
down the lower Matzoth and retain only the upper and the broken
Matzoth and pronounce the blessing על אכילת מצה, then break off a
piece the quantity of half an egg both of the upper and the broken
Matzah (and give the same to each member of his household) he should
eat both pieces whilst reclining on his left side. If it is difficult for
him to eat both at one time, he should first eat the pieces on which he
had pronounced the blessing המוציא, then the piece from the broken
Matzah, but he should not delay between them and eat both whilst
rec'ning, neither the Matzah of המוציא nor that of מצה should be
dipped in salt.

6. One who is unable to masticate Matzah is permitted to soak
it in water to soften it, providing it does not become entirely dissolved,
but a sick or old person who cannot eat it if soaked in water may soak
it in wine or other beverage. When soaking the Matzah wherewith
one intends to fulfil his obligations, care should be taken not to let it
soak for twenty-four hours, as then it would be considered as if it was
cooked and the precept could not be performed therewith. Care
should also be taken that it does not lose its right to be classed as
bread through other means.

7. He should then take bitter herbs the quantity of an olive,
(and give as much to each of his household) and dip it in Charoseth,
which he should shake off therefrom and eat it without reclining, after
that he should take from the Matzah on the bottom also a like quantity of a half egg and about the quantity of half-an-egg of bitter herbs,
and he should also dip it in the Charoseth and shake it off therefrom
and put the bitter herbs between the Matzah and say זכר עשה הלל וכו'
and eat about the size of half-an-egg whilst reclining. One who is
indisposed and cannot eat any bitter herbs should at any rate
chew a little of the species with which the obligation can be

fulfilled, or any other bitter herb until he will feel a bitter taste in his mouth just as a commemoration, without saying a blessing thereon.

8. The feast should then be partaken of. It is proper to recline during the entire feast. It is customary to partake of some eggs. When feasting one should bear in mind that he has to partake of the Afikoman, according to the precept, which is, not to be food in excess of his desire. Roast meat should not be partaken of on either night, not even poultry, nor even if it was first boiled and then roasted. On concluding the feast the Afikoman should be eaten. It is proper to eat thereof about the size of an egg. At any rate one should not eat less than the size of half-an-egg. It should be eaten whilst reclining. After the Afikoman it is forbidden to partake of anything. The third cup for the Grace should then be filled up but if it is not clean it requires washing and rinsing. It is mandatory to make an effort to say Grace in a company of three, but they should not go from house to house in order to look for a company to say Grace. It is customary that the Grace be said by the master of the house, after it is said a blessing should be said on the third cup which should be drunk whilst reclining. It is forbidden to drink between that and the fourth cup.

9. After Grace the wine cup is filled up for the fourth time, the door is opened according to the custom, and שׁפוֹך חמתך וכו׳ is said, after that they begin to recite לא לנו and continue Hallel until הודו which, if there are three, should be said by one and responded to by two, as it is said in the congregation (the same may be thus recited even where one's wife and children who had reached the age of training compose the three). A full רביעית should be drunk from the fourth cup and the ברכה אחרונה (final blessing) said thereafter, the Hagadah should then be continued until concluded. After the four goblets it is forbidden to drink any beverage except water. If one is not too somnolent, he should say the Song of Songs after the Hagadah. It is customary on the two first Passover nights to omit the reading of קריאת שמע with the exception of the section שמע and the blessing המפיל before retiring.

10. One who abstains from wine during the year because it is injurious to him should at any rate strain himself to drink the four goblets, and in any event he may dilute it with water or he may drink raisin wine or mead.

11. If the Afikoman was lost and there yet remains Matzah of that which was made for performing the precept, he should eat thereof about the size of half an egg otherwise he should eat that amount of another Matzah.

331

22

12. One who had forgotten to eat the Afikamon and became aware of it previous to saying Grace, although he had already laved his hands on the conclusion of the meal, or said "Let us say Grace" he may eat it without being required to say the blessing המוציא, he should at any rate wash his hands without saying על נטילת ידים. If he did not become aware of it until after Grace, before pronouncing the blessing on the third goblet he should wash his hands without saying על נטילת ידים, but he should say the blessing המוציא and eat about the amount of half-an-egg, he should then say Grace, say a blessing on the third cup and drink thereof, if, however, he only became aware of it after he had already said the blessing בורא פרי הגפן on the third goblet, he should partake thereof, he should then wash his hands and eat the Afikoman and say Grace without a cup of wine.

LAWS CONCERNING THE COUNTING OF THE OMER AND LAWS ABOUT THAT PERIOD.

1. The counting of the Omer begins from the second night of Passover. It is counted whilst standing. This precept is performed in the beginning of the night, yet the entire night is the proper time for its performance. On the nights of Sabbath and Festival, the Omer is counted in the synagogue after the Kiddush has been said. At the conclusion of Sabbath and Festival it is counted before the Habdallah is said. When the last day of the Festival occurs at the conclusion of the Sabbath when Kiddush and Habdallah is said on the one goblet, the counting is also done previously in order to say the Habdallah at the last.

2. If one had forgotten and did not count the entire night, he should count in the daytime without saying a blessing thereon, but the following night he should say a blessing when counting, but if he had forgotten to count that entire day he should count every night thereafter without saying a blessing. If he is in doubt as to whether he had counted the previous night or not, although he did not count on the following day he may nevertheless say a blessing when counting on the remaining nights.

3. If one is asked at twilight or later previous to counting the Omer, how many days are to be counted on that day, he should tell him the number of days that were counted on the previous day, for by mentioning the number of days to be counted on that day he will afterwards be forbidden to pronounce a blessing when counting the Omer.

4. Before he pronounces the blessing he should know the number of days to be counted, if, however, he did not know it, and said the blessing with the intention of counting as he will hear his neighbour count, he has also fulfilled his obligation, likewise if one said the blessing with the intention of counting four days and was afterwards reminded that he must count five days, he need not repeat the bles-

sing. Likewise if one erred in counting and instead of saying "six days" said "five days," if he was immediately reminded thereof, he should count properly and is not required to repeat the blessing, but if he had paused slightly he must repeat the blessing.

5. On every Festival, if the first night occurs on the Sabbath when special Festival compositions ("Maaravith") are not said, the " Maaravith " of the first night are said on the second night, the Passover excepted, when even if the first night occurs on the Sabbath, nevertheless, on the second night the "Maaravith" pertaining to that night is said, inasmuch as it treats of the cutting of the Omer (sheaf) which took place on that night.

6. Neither men nor women should do any work during the days that the Omer is counted, from sundown until after the Omer has been counted.

7. One should not marry on the days that the Omer is counted, nor should one have his hair cut, but the Sandek, the Mohel and the father of the child are permitted to have their hair cut on the day before the circumcision towards evening. It is permitted to make betrothal parties, even to have a feast thereon is permissible on the days of counting the Omer, dancing and music however are forbidden.

8. On Rosh Hodesh, Log Be'Omer (the 33rd day of the Omer) and the three days before Pentecost (שלשת ימי הגבלה) one is permitted to marry.

9. On the first night of "Shevuoth" the Evening Service should be put off until the stars appear.

LAWS CONCERNING THE MANNER OF WORK PERMITTED
AND FORBIDDEN TO BE PERFORMED ON A FESTIVAL.

1. Any work which one is forbidden to do on the Sabbath, one is forbidden to do on a Festival, even through a non-Jew it is prohibited. On a Festival it is also mandatory that one's cattle repose. In the observance of a Festival it is different from the Sabbath only as regards supplying food for human beings, thus kneading, baking, slaughtering and cooking are permissible on a Festival, and carrying from place to place, also kindling a fire are all permissible on a Festival even when not required for supplying food, but for another purpose.

2. The making of cheese or butter or the curding of milk by placing something therein to cause it to coagulate is forbidden on a Festival. It is likewise forbidden to separate the cream from the milk, unless one lets some of it remain with the milk on the surface, and even in this manner it is only allowable for as much as he needs on

that day, but it is forbidden thus to separate it for the following day. If, however, he apprehends that he will sustain a loss he may have a non-Jew separate it in the manner aforementioned.

3. On a Festival it is allowable to pound spices if done in an unusual manner, e.g., to lay the mortar on its side, or to pound them on the table and the like, likewise when rubbing horse-radish on a grater, one should not rub it in a plate in the manner usual on a week-day, but on a cloth. Coffee, too, should not be ground in a mill but crushed in a mortar and done in an unusual manner, it is, however, better to prepare all these on the eve of the Festival. Articles of food whose flavour does not spoil should surely be ground on the eve of the Festival, but if one had forgotten, they also may be prepared in an unusual manner. All of the foregoing is permitted only as much as is required for the day, but not for the morrow. One should even be scrupulous and not prepare any more than is necessary for the immediate use of the meal. In pounding "Matzah" one should also observe the foregoing rules.

4. It is forbidden to split wood or even to break it by hand. It is also forbidden to collect wood that is scattered about.

5. It is permitted to separate peas, all that one needs for that day, but not with a sieve, nor should they be placed in water in order that the worthless matter or the edibles should float on top, but he should separate them by hand and gather up what is most convenient for him. If it is easier for him to gather the worthless matter, he may gather it, and if it is easier for him to gather the edibles, he may gather that.

6. If one desires to bolt for a second time flour that had already been bolted, he should bolt it through a non-Jew or in an unusual manner, e.g., by bolting it through the back of the sieve. The same should be done with ground Matzah. Flour that was not bolted, it is forbidden to bolt excepting through a non-Jew and in an unusual manner.. It is forbidden to separate worthless matter from flour, as for instance, if some foreign substance fell therein. It is even forbidden to separate the large pieces from the broken Matzah.

7. Kneading is permitted on a Festival, nevertheless one should not measure the flour, if, however he does not measure it exactly but diminishes or increases the quantity, it is permissible.

8. The dough that is cut up in order to cook it with soup should be kneaded on the eve of the Festival, as it is improved by standing, but if one did not knead it on the eve of the Festival he may do so on the Festival in an unusual manner, thus if he usually kneaded upon a board, he should knead it on a cloth and the like, likewise victuals that do not become stale, such as dried fruits and the like should be cooked on the eve of the Festival.

9. One who kneads dough on a Festival is permitted to separate the dough-cake therefrom, but is forbidden to burn it, he is also forbidden to bake it, inasmuch as it is not right to use it as food, the handling thereof is also forbidden, but directly following the separation he should lay it down in a safe place until the conclusion of the Festival when he should burn it. It is forbidden to separate the dough-cake on the Festival, but he may bake it and partake thereof, and leave some bread from which to separate the dough-cake on the conclusion of the Festival. He should leave sufficient bread for separating therefrom and still have some left.

10. Poultry which is in one's house or yard which is to be used for food and which have been domesticated for some time, that though they go away from the house they come back in the evening, it is permissible to catch them, even if they are outside of the yard, for the requirements of the Festival in order to kill them, but if not for the requirements of food it is forbidden to catch them. If they are new and unused to the house it is forbidden to snare them even for the requirements of food, and even while they are within the house, but at night as they are sitting it is permitted to take them ; but care should be taken on the eve of the Festival to select those which it is intended to kill on the Festival. Poultry which is not kept for food but for laying purposes are " set apart " (and not to be handled). It is forbidden to snare even those domesticated doves who are accustomed to come to their nests, although he had them in readiness from the eve of the Festival.

11. It is permitted to cut or burn the cord from the feet of poultry after they were killed. It is also permitted to sew stuffed poultry providing the needle is threaded on the eve of the Festival. If it was not threaded on the eve of the Festival it is forbidden to thread it on the Festival. After it was sewn it is permissible to burn the remaining thread.

12. It is forbidden to catch fish from a fish pond if it is impossible to catch them with one's hands, if, however, one is able to catch them with one's hands he is permitted to catch them even with a vessel. If there are many fishes there he should prepare on the

Festival-eve, that which he desires to take on the Festival by making a certain sign thereon, and if he needs all, he should prepare all, that is, he should say on the Festival-eve, "I prepare all these fishes for the Festival."

13. It is forbidden to use that of which there is a doubt as to its being snared or prepared, but if very necessary this law may be relaxed on the second day of the Festival, but not on Rosh-Hashana.

14. It is forbidden to give to drink or feed any living creature that is "set apart" when close to it, it should be done at a slight distance.

15. If one had killed poultry and then found it unfit for use, טרפה, he is forbidden to handle it as it is like any other thing that is "set apart," if, however, he slaughtered an animal and it was found unfit for use, he is permitted to hide it where it will not get spoiled but if he cannot hide it where it will not get spoiled, he is permitted to sell it to a non-Jew, providing he does not mention the price and does not weigh it.

16. An animal should not be slaughtered on a Festival unless it is very necessary. It is forbidden to sell the meat by weight and at a fixed price, but one can give another any quantity on payment after the Festival.

17. It is proper for one who slaughters an animal not to examine the lung until after he strips the skin, and he is permitted to handle the skin of an animal that he had slaughtered that day in order to put it away, but not to spread it out to dry, but it is forbidden to handle other skins. It is also permitted to handle the feathers of a fowl which was killed on that day in order to put them away but it is forbidden to handle other feathers.

18. It is permitted to salt meat to purify it of its blood even if it was possible to salt it on the previous day, providing it is needed on that day, and if he has more meat which he fears might be spoiled, he is permitted to salt it all together, even if it is a large quantity and it is not required for that day as it is all the same labour. Meat, however, that was salted and cleansed of its blood and fish that it were possible to salt on the eve of the Festival it is forbidden to salt on the Festival.

19. When baking pastry on a Festival it is forbidden to make figures thereon through a mould or by hand.

20. It is forbidden to warm a wax or tallow candle in order to make it stick to the candlestick lest he plasters it. If the socket of the candle-stick is filled with tallow he is permitted to clean it.

21. It is forbidden to quench a fire on a Festival, it is even forbidden to cause it to be quenched, consequently it is forbidden to place a lighted candle where the wind may blow it out even if there is no wind blowing at the time ; it is likewise forbidden to open a door or window opposite a lighted candle.

22. It is permitted to cover the fire with a vessel or with ashes that were prepared previously, although it is likely that it may be slightly quenched by being covered, providing it is necessary for that day.

23. Vessels which are forbidden to be used should be neither purged nor glowed on a Festival. The law concerning the washing of dishes on a Festival is the same as on the Sabbath. It is forbidden to wash them on the first day of the Festival for the use of the second day of the Festival.

24. It is permitted to heat water wherewith to wash one's hands, but not for the entire body, but when required for an infant, a larger quantity may be heated for his own use, thus although only a little water is needed for cooking, it is permitted to heat even a large boiler, but all the water should be poured in before placing it upon the fire, and nothing added thereafter. If the child is ailing it is permitted to heat the water for his sake through a non Jew.

25. It is forbidden to draw fire either from a flint, a piece of glass, or a match, it is forbidden even to ignite the match by putting it near a hot iron, but it is permitted to ignite the match upon a live coal.

26. It is forbidden to scatter spices upon the coals either for inhaling the odour or for perfuming the house or vessels.

27. All things which one is forbidden to do on the Sabbath as a remedy for one who is sick but not in danger, are also forbidden to do on the first day of a Festival, also on the two days of Rosh-Hashana, except through a non-Jew, but on the second day of the Festival one is permitted to do it through an Israelite as well, but a complete work one is forbidden to do for a sick person who is not in danger even on the second day of a Festival except through a non-Jew.

Laws Concerning Things "Set Apart" מוקצה on a Festival.

1. Everything that is "set apart" and forbidden to be handled on the Sabbath is forbidden also on a Festival. An egg which was laid on a Festival is forbidden even to be handled, but it is permitted

to cover it with a vessel to keep it from breaking. If it was laid on the first day of the Festival its use is permitted on the second day, but if the second day is on the Sabbath its use is prohibited on that day. Likewise if the first day on which it was laid is Sabbath its use is prohibited also on the following day (the second day of the Festival) also whenever the Sabbath is next to the Festival, whether preceding or following it, if laid on one day its use is prohibited on the other day. On Rosh Hashana, if laid on the first day its use is prohibited also on the second day. If Rosh Hashana occurs on Thursday and Friday, even if it was laid on the first day, its use is prohibited also on the Sabbath. If one had killed poultry and found eggs within, even if they are perfect, their use is permitted even on the same day.

2. The handling of wood is permitted only when required for kindling a fire, but when not required for burning it is forbidden to handle it, therefore one should not support a pot or a door with a wooden wedge.

3. It is permitted to handle on a Festival the ashes of wood that was burned on the eve of the Festival, and if it was from a fire made on the Festival, if the ashes are still hot it is permitted to handle it, but if it became cold it is forbidden to handle it.

LAWS CONCERNING THE BENEDICTION OF THE PRIESTS (כהנים).

1. It is mandatory upon the Priests, according to the Torah, to bless the people, thus if a Priest who can validly perform the functions of Priesthood (כהונה) is called to go up and bless the people and he does not go he transgresses a positive precept. It is customary in all countries except Palestine and Egypt (where the Priests daily raise their hands in benediction) not to raise their hands in benediction excepting on a Festival during the Reader's repetition of the Additional Service, likewise on Rosh-Hashana and the day of Atonement. Regarding a Festival that falls on the Sabbath there are various customs, therefore the ecclesiastical authorities should be consulted.

2. The Priests should not raise their hands in benediction excepting in a congregation of ten, themselves included. Previous to raising his hands in benediction the Priest should not drink wine nor any other intoxicating beverage, and if he feels weak and desires to partake of some cakes previous to saying the Additional Services he should hear another say the Kiddush.

3. Before the Priests pronounce the benediction, they should divest themselves of their boots, then lave their hands until the wrist. A Levite should pour water upon the hands of the Priests, the water being poured at the junction of hand and arm. If no Levite be present a first-born son, the first-born of his mother should pour the water, and

if there be no first born, it is best for the Priest to do the laving himself, and not to have it done by an Israelite. If the hands of the Levite or first-born who is to pour water upon the hands of the Priests are unclean, he should previously wash his hands.

4. When the Reader begins the prayer רצה all the Priests should leave their seats in order to go up to pronounce the benediction, and their hands should then be proper to raise in benediction, they should therefore lave their hands before רצה, if, however, they laved their hands thereafter, it is also valid.

5. After going up to pronounce the benedictions, they stand facing the Holy Ark in the east and say מודים of the Rabbins with the congregation after which they say יהי רצון מלפניך ה' אלהינו שתהא ברכה זו שצויתנו לברך את עמך ישראל ברכה שלימה, ולא יהא בה שום מכשול ועון מעתה ועד עולם they prolong the chanting of this prayer until the Reader concludes with ולך נאה להודות in order that the congregation should respond אמן also to this prayer. The Reader says או"א ברכנו וכו' in an undertone, but the word כהנים he says aloud as that is a call to the Priests to pronounce the benedictions, then he resumes in an undertone עם קדושיך כאמי. After the Reader has called כהנים the Priests begin the benedictions, all say in unison ברוך אתה ה' אלהינו מלך העולם אשר קדשנו בקדושתו של אהרן then, turning their faces toward the people, they conclude וצונו לברך את עמו ישראל באהבה to which the congregation responds אמן, but the Reader should not respond אמן. From the conclusion of the blessing with the word באהבה signifying " with love," it is inferred that if the congregation hate the Priest or vice versa he should not raise his hands in benediction, he should therefore leave the synagogue. If there is only one Priest in the synagogue the Reader should not say כהנים in a loud voice, but the Priest should himself turn his countenance.

6. They raise their hands toward their shoulders and spread them out, and separate their fingers so that there be five open spaces between them, thus, between each two fingers there is one open space, and between two fingers and the thumb there is another open space, the same with the other hand, making four open spaces, between the two thumbs there is also an open space, which makes five open spaces. It is requisite to raise the right hand slightly above the left, the right

thumb being above the left thumb, they should, however, not touch each other and they should spread their hands so that the palms be turned toward the ground and their backs raised heavenwards.

7. When the Priests bless the people they should neither look around nor divert their thoughts, but their eyes should be directed downward as when praying, and the people should pay attention to the benedictions. They should face the Priests but they should not gaze at them, nor should the Priests themselves gaze at their hands, thus they have made it a custom to let the folds of their Talethim drop over their faces and hands and the congregation do likewise in order not to gaze (at the Priests).

8. The people standing behind the priests are not included in the benediction unless they are compelled to stand thus, but the people who stand on the sides and facing them are included in the benediction therefore where the Holy Ark projects from the wall, the people who stand near the eastern wall are at the sides which are behind the Priests and they should leave their places and stand where they can be at least at the sides which face the Priests, but if it is impossible, they are as those who are compelled to stand there and are included in the benediction.

9. The Reader recites the benedictions word for word, and the Priests repeat each word until they conclude the first verse and the congregation respond אמן, thus also after the second and third verses. The Reader should not recite from memory but from a prayer-book. At the following words the Priests turn towards the South and towards the North שלום, לך, אליך, ויחנך, אליך, וישמרך, יברכך, while the Priests prolong the chanting of the words ending the verses, that is וישמרך, ויחנך, שלום, the congregation (not the Reader) say רבש"ע, יהי רצון ובו'. The Priests should chant only in the appropriate air; when the Priests say the words the congregation should not say any verse, but should listen attentively to each word pronounced by the Priests.

10. The Reader then begins שים שלום and the the Priests turn their faces towards the holy Ark and say רבון העולמים and prolong the chanting of this prayer until the Reader concludes המברך את עמו ישראל בשלום in order that the congregation should respond אמן also to their prayer, if they cannot prolong it till then they should also say אדיר

LAWS AND CUSTOMS OF ISRAEL

במרים. On Rosh Hashana and Atonement Day when היום תאמצנו is sung, the Priests should not begin רבון העולמים until that prayer is nearly concluded, in order that they conclude their prayer at the same time as the Reader. Neither the Reader nor the Priests nor the congregation should begin their respective prayers before those preceding had concluded theirs.

11. When the Priests turn their faces either at the beginning or at the end, they should turn only towards the right. When they descend on concluding the benediction, their faces should be towards the Holy Ark, they should therefore walk backwards. If they had touched their boots when putting them on they are required to wash their hands.

12. An effort should be made not to appoint a Priest as Reader but if there is none better than the Priest, the ecclesiastical authorities should be consulted as to how he should manage with raising his hands in benediction.

13. If a Priest who had raised his hands in benediction had later gone to another synagogue, he may, if he desires, go up to pronounce the benediction again, but if he is not so inclined he is not obliged to go up even if he hears the call of כהנים inasmuch as he had already gone up.

14. One who does not know how to say the letters distinctly and pronounces שׁ the same as שׂ should not raise his hands in benediction excepting where the entire congregation read the same way ; a Priest who does not raise his hands in benediction should leave the Synagogue before רצה is said and remain outside until the Priests have concluded the benedictions.

15. One who had wilfully killed a human being, even if he had repented, should not raise his hands in benediction, but if he had slain unwillingly and had repented, he should raise his hands in benediction, likewise a renegade or one who had profaned the Sabbath in public, and had repented, should raise his hands in benediction. One who had married a woman put away from her husband, or a widow termed חלוצה (see Lev. xxv.) or one who became defiled by contact with the dead, for whom he is forbidden to defile himself, should not raise his hand in benediction until he will have repented as directed by a learned man. The transgressions of other precepts do not debar one from raising his hands in benediction. A son of a woman who has done any of the foregoing is also prohibited from raising his hands in benediction.

16. A mourner, before his dead was interred should not raise his hands in benediction, nor should a mourner during the twelve months of mourning for his parents, or during the thirty days for other relatives, raise his hands in benediction, but he should leave the synagogue.

before רצה is said until the benedictions are concluded, if, however there are not two other priests in the synagogue, the mourner is permitted to raise his hands in benediction during the twelve months' mourning for his parents, or during the thirty days for other relatives, but during the seven days, e.g, if he has interred his dead on a Festival, he should not raise his hands in benediction, even if two other Priests are not there.

Laws Concerning the Preparation of Food on a Festival.

1. All work that is permitted to be performed on a Festival is permitted only if required for that day. Preparing on the first day for the second day, even on Rosh-Hashana, especially for a week day is forbidden. If, however, one needs to cook for that day he is permitted to cook in a large pot and leave some for the night or the morrow, this is only permitted with victuals, but it should not be said expressly that the remainder is for the night or the morrow, but cook without making mention thereof, where, however, the preparation of the victuals entails considerable labour, it is forbidden to prepare in excess of what is required for that day.

2. It is forbidden to bring water or even wine, in order to prepare (for the following day). It is likewise forbidden to put the candles in the candle-stick on the first day of the Festival for the requirements of the night-time unless they are needed for use before night, or in a synagogue for the honour thereof.

3. If a non-Jew brought fish or fruit on the first day of a Festival and it is apprehended they were caught or plucked on that day or brought from beyond the Sabbath-boundary, they are forbidden to be handled on that day, but permitted in the evening (if the non-Jew knows him and gives it to him without mentioning a price) excepting on the first day of Rosh-Hashana, when if it was brought on the first day it is forbidden even on the second day. This law applies only if the non-Jew brought it for himself, if, however he brought it for the Israelite, it should be prohibited also on the second day, and it is only when the Festival occurs on Thursday that it is permitted, if very urgent, to handle and cook it on Friday in honour of the Sabbath, but on Rosh Hashana this is also forbidden.

4. Milk which a non-Jew milked on the first day of the Festival (in the presence of an Israelite) is permitted to be used on the second day, but if the milking was done on the Sabbath and the Festival occurs on Sunday, its use is forbidden on Sunday. The milk of the milking done on the first day of Rosh-Hashana is also forbidden to be used for the second day and also on the Sabbath if that is the next day.

Laws Concerning the Mingling of Victuals (עירובי תבשילין).

1. On a Festival (whether it be the first or second day of the Festival) that occurs on Sabbath-eve it is forbidden to bake or to cook in a separate pot for the Sabbath unless the ceremony of עירובי תבשילין was performed on the Festival-eve. It should be performed as follows : One should take the quantity of a כזית of food, cooked or roasted, such as meat, fish or eggs, also bread the quantity of an egg (ביצה) and pro- nounce the blessing אשר קדשנו במצותיו וצונו על מצות עירוב, then he should say בהדין עירובא יהא שרי לנא לאפויי ולבשולי ולאדלוקי שרגא ולמיעבד כל צרכנא מיומא טבא לשבתא " By virtue of this Eirouv be it permitted us to bake, cook, keep the victuals warm, light the candles, and do all the work that is necessary on the Festival for the Sabbath." If one does not understand Hebrew one should say it in any language one under- stands. One should make an effort to let the victual be of the choicest food in honour of the precept, the bread also should be whole, it should be laid on the table on the Sabbath as two-fold bread, and at the third meal it should be divided and the blessing said thereon.

2. Everything that is necessary to be done for the Sabbath should be done on the Festival early in the day. It is therefore the custom when a Festival occurs on a Sabbath-eve to hasten and com- mence the Evening-service of Sabbath when it is still day so that due diligence may be observed, and that everything be promptly done before מזמור שיר ליום השבת is said. The victuals that are kept warm for the Sabbath should be done in broad daylight, that is at least one third before twilight. It is requisite that the Eirouv remain intact while all the necessaries have been prepared for the Sabbath, and if the Eirouv was lost or eaten up, the learned should be consulted.

3. Only on the Sabbath-eve is it permitted to bake or cook by means of " Eirouv-Tavshilin," if however, the Festival occurs on Thursday and Friday it is forbidden to cook and bake on Thursday for the Sabbath.

4. Every master of a house is required to make "Eirouv Tavshillin" for himself. Even a woman who has not a husband is required to do so. One who forgot to make "Eirouv-Tavshilin" should consult a learned man.

LAWS CONCERNING HOW TO HONOUR, DELIGHT IN AND REJOICE ON A FESTIVAL.

1. It is mandatory to honour all the Festivals and to take delight in them as it is mandatory to honour the Sabbath and to delight therein.

2. It is mandatory for one to cut his hair on the eve of the Festival, thus not inaugurating the Festival with an untidy appearance. It is also mandatory for one to wash oneself with warm water and to comb one's hair, also to pare one's nails on the eve of the Festival as on the Sabbath eve. It is mandatory too to knead bread in the house on the eve of the Festival as on the Sabbath-eve. It is likewise forbidden to eat on the eve of a Festival from the time of Afternoon Service and later, the same as on the Sabbath-eve. If the eve of the Festival occurred on the Sabbath, the third meal should be taken before the latest time for the Afternoon Service; this law also applies to the first day of a Festival, as that is the eve of the second day of the Festival.

3. It is obligatory to partake of two meals each day of the Festival, one at night and one in the day. It is likewise obligatory to pronounce the Kiddush upon wine before the meal and to divide the portions of two entire loaves, the same as on the Sabbath. One should be lavish with meat, wine and confectionery as far as means permit.

4. On every Festival when saying Kiddush at night, the blessing שהחינו should be said thereafter, with the exception of the seventh and eighth nights of Passover when the blessing שהחינו is not said.

5. It is obligatory upon one to gladden his wife and his children, also all who are dependent upon him, in the manner appropriate to each. Thus he should give the little children nuts and confectionery, and gladden the women-folk with new apparel and ornaments according to his means, and the men with meat and wine. One should fare more sumptuously on a Festival than on a Sabbath; the Festival garments should also be costlier than those of the Sabbath.

6. On the second day of Passover one should add something to the meal as a remembrance of the feast of Esther that took place upon that day. On the first day of Pentecost it is customary to partake of food prepared with milk, also with honey. Now, inasmuch as milk-food is partaken of and it is also necessary to partake of meat, it being

mandatory on every Festival, great care should be observed in order not to violate a prohibition.

7. Although by eating and drinking on a Festival one fulfils a commandment, yet one should not spend the entire day in eating and drinking, but should divide half to the service of God and half to his own use.

8. When one is eating and drinking, it is a duty to feed also the orphan and the widow as well as others who are in poverty, but he who locks the door of his house in order to eat and drink alone with his wife and children, and does not give food or drink to the poor, and to those whose souls are embittered, behold, this is not rejoicing in performing a precept, but gluttony, and such rejoicing is a disgrace.

9. When one rejoices on a Festival, one should not prolong in wine-drinking, jesting and levity, for drunkeness, jesting and levity is not rejoicing but mere foolishness, which is not according to the command. The rejoicing should be consistent with the worship of the Creator of the universe.

10. Every man should take care of his household lest they seek their pleasures in companionship with the thoughtless, which might lead them to levity; they must be holy, for the day is holy.

11. At the conclusion of the Festival, when it will be followed by a week-day or by the Intermediate days of the Festival, one should say אתה חוננתנו in the silent prayer and say the Habdallah over a cup of wine, but should not say the blessing on the light nor on the spices.

12. On the day following each of the three Festivals, one should fare somewhat better than ordinarily; that day is called אסרו חג, and there should be no fasting on that day, not even by a groom and bride on their wedding-day, nor should one who observes Jahrzeit fast on אסרו חג.

LAWS CONCERNING THE INTERMEDIATE DAYS OF A FESTIVAL.

1. On the Intermediate days of a Festival there is certain work that is forbidden and work that is permitted, thus all work necessary in the preparation of food for those days or for the Festival, as well as any work that can save one from loss, that is, if by not doing it a loss will be sustained, it is permitted to do it, but great care should be taken not to do any work that is forbidden on the Intermediate days of the Festival, for our Rabbis have taught us the severity of the sin of one profaning or despising the semi-Festivals.

It is one's duty to honour the semi-Festival by better food and by costlier attire than ordinarily, according to one's means.

2. Any work the non-performance of which would entail a loss, and it was impossible to have done it before the Festival, is permitted to do it on an Intermediate day of the Festival, it may also be done through another Israelite, even for pay. If, however, no loss be entailed, only that it is needed for the semi-Festival, it should not be done through another Israelite for pay but through a non-Jew, but if he cannot get a non-Jew and is himself unable to do it, he is permitted to have it done even through another Israelite for pay.

3. Work that it is forbidden to do in the Intermediate days of a Festival may be done through an Israelite who has not enough to eat for the Intermediate days and for the Festival, so that he might have what te eat, but it should be done privately. When the work is required for the performance of a precept it is permissible to have it done even through a non-Jew.

4. The work that is permissible should not be done in the Intermediate days of a Festival for any but an Israelite.

5. It is forbidden to manure one's field; even to let sheep therein in order that they furnish manure is forbidden. Sowing is forbidden, if, however, one has seeds which will be entirely spoiled unless one puts them in water, it is permitted to soak them.

6. It is forbidden to pull or cut off anything from whence it grows, if the fruit will not be spoiled or otherwise endangered, until after the Festival, excepting whatever he requires as food for the semi-Festival, and one need not confine himself to the exact amount, but may pull off a liberal quantity, and if there is some left it does not matter. Likewise if one needs wood to make fire on the same festival, he is permitted to chop it off from whence it grows.

7. If one has fruit which will be spoiled unless he does a certain work for it, he is permitted to do all that is necessary, even to press grapes and make wine, and what is similar thereto, providing he did not purposely leave that work for the Intermediate days of the Festival.

8. It is forbidden to have one's hair cut in the Intermediate days of a Festival, even if he had cut his hair on the eve of the

Festival. Paring the nails is also forbidden on the eve of the Festival, but if one had pared them on the Festival eve he is permitted to pare them also in the Intermediate days of the Festival. It is permissible for a woman to have טבילה.

9. It is forbidden to wash anything, even if required for the semi-Festival unless it was impossible for one to wash it before the Festival, it is likewise permitted to wash infant's diapers, but one should be careful to wash them privately.

10. What is required medicinally, either for man or beast is permitted to be done.

11. It is permitted to write accounts and the like, which if not written will be forgotten. It is likewise permitted to write what is requisite for the semi-Festival, but it is forbidden to write anything else. A letter of friendship may be written but in a slightly different manner, the first line, for instance, might be written unevenly. For such writing as permissible, it is also permitted to prepare pen and ink.

12. One who is in need of funds, even though it is not for the requirements of the semi-Festival, but he is apprehensive lest he will not obtain the loan after the Festival and he cannot obtain it without a note, is permitted to write such note.

13. One should not marry during the Intermediate days of a Festival, but he is permitted to be re-united in marriage to the woman he had divorced. It is permitted to make a feast for the celebration of a circumcision, the redemption of the first-born, also for an engagement.

14. One is permitted to hire labourers, even Israelites, to do work for him after the Festival.

15. It is permitted to go outside of the Sabbath-boundary, either on foot, in a vehicle, or on horse-back.

Laws Concerning Things that are Forbidden
on Account of the Hard Work.

1. One is forbidden to remove and carry his chattels and furniture during the Intermediate days of a Festival, from a dwelling in one court to a dwelling in another court, even from a humble to a handsome dwelling, but from one house to another in the same court

347

it is permissible. Likewise if the two courts adjoin each other, and there is a door between them, it is permissible to carry the articles out through that way, where, however, a loss may be otherwise sustained, it is permissible, even from one city to another. One is likewise permitted to remove from a dwelling not his own, to a dwelling on his own property, in order to rejoice on the Festival, as it is one's joy to dwell on one's own property.

2. If it is necessary for one to take in his merchandise for fear of loss, it should if possible be done privately, although it is allowable to take it publicly.

Laws Concerning Buying and Selling

During the Intermediate Festival Days.

1. During the Intermediate days of a Festival it is forbidden either to buy or to sell any merchandise unless there is a chance for one to profit greatly, then it might be done privately, but he should spend in honour of the Festival more than it was his intention to spend.

2. If one has merchandise of which he may be apprehensive that unless it is immediately sold its value will be reduced to less than its cost, he is permitted to sell it, if, however, there is no fear of loss only lack of profit, one is forbidden to sell it.

3. If the market-day occurs during the Intermediate days of the Festival and it is a rare occasion, and also results in the gathering of many purchasers it is permissible to sell it, for inasmuch as it is an unusual occasion the lack of profits is also considered as a loss, and when merchants or ships occasionally arrive, who sell cheaply or buy dearly (which is an unusual occurrence) it is likewise permitted to purchase from them and to sell to them.

4. Whatever is required for the semi-Festival as food and drink it is permitted to sell as usual, even publicly. During the Intermediate days of the Festival one is permitted to collect his debts for fear of loss.

5. It is forbidden to sell merchandise to one who is not a regular customer, but it is permitted to sell to a regular customer, as otherwise a loss may be entailed by the latter becoming accustomed to purchase elsewhere.

Laws Concerning a Public Fast Day.

1. It is mandatory to fast on the days commemorating sorrowful occurences to our ancestors, the purpose of this fast being to stir the hearts and to open the eyes to the ways of repentance, hence it is every man's duty to take this to heart in those days and to search out

the evil of his deeds and repent thereof, for the principal thing is not the fast, but the preparation for repentance.

2. These are the days on which all Israelites fast. The fast of the fourth month, that is the seventeenth of Tammuz; the fast of the fifth month, that is the ninth of Ab; the fast of the seventh month, that is the third of Tishri, which is called the Fast of Gedaliah, and the fast of the tenth month which is the tenth of Tebeth. Even a groom and bride during their seven days of feasting are obliged to fast on these fast days.

3. If these fasts fall on a Sabbath, they are postponed until after the Sabbath. When the tenth of Tebeth occurs on a Sabbath-eve the fast is observed the entire day.

4. On the seventeenth of Tammuz, the Fast of Gedaliah, and the tenth of Tebeth one may partake of food on the previous night until the break of day providing one does not sleep as usual, but one who has one's regular sleep is forbidden to eat or drink thereafter unless one so determines before going to sleep, but one who is accustomed to drink after sleeping need not previously have set the mind upon drinking. On the ninth of Ab, however, it is necessary to abstain from food on the preceding day while it is yet day. They differ also in this: on the three fast-days above-mentioned, washing, anointing, wearing boots, and cohabitation are permissible, but on the ninth of Ab they are all forbidden. The former three fast days are also less stringent as regards their observance by pregnant and nursing women, who, if they would suffer therefrom are exempt from fasting. Likewise a sick person, even if he is not in danger should not fast. Nevertheless, even the one for whom it is permissible to eat should not take pleasure therein but should eat only as much as is essential for the preservation of health. Children, also, although it does not devolve upon them to fast, nevertheless if they are of sufficient intelligence to mourn, it is proper to train them (not to give them other food than bread and water) to mourn with the community.

5. On a public fast-day one is forbidden to rinse his mouth in the morning, it is also forbidden to taste food even if one ejects it. On a fast day which one voluntarily undertakes, one is permitted to rinse one's mouth, also to taste food and eject it.

6. It is mandatory upon every Jewish community whenever they are in distress, Heaven forfend, to fast and to pray for relief

from their distress to the Holy One, blessed be His name, but if it is not an appropriate time for fasting they should resolve to fast a certain number of fasts when they will be saved, and it is reckoned unto them as if they were now fasting.

Laws Concerning the Interval Between the Seventeenth of Tammuz and the Ninth of Ab.

1. From the Seventeenth of Tammuz until after the Ninth of Ab, one should not marry, but a betrothal is permitted, even accompanied by a feast until the new moon of Ab; but from Rosh Chodesh Ab although a betrothal is permitted, it is nevertheless forbidden to make a feast (but they are permitted to partake of preserves and the like). An Israelite whose vocation is that of a musician is permitted to play in the house of a non-Jew to make a living thereby until Rosh Chodesh, but he is forbidden to play from Rosh Chodesh until after the Fast of Ab. It is likewise forbidden to play on the Fast of the seventeenth of Tammuz, also on the tenth of Tebeth.

2. The blessing שהחינו should not be said during these days, therefore one should neither purchase nor put on a new garment, as that would necessitate saying the blessing שההחינו, but on celebrating the redemption of the first-born the blessing שהחינו should be said in order not to "sour" the precept (delay its fulfilment). If a new fruit will not be obtainable after the ninth of Ab, one should say the blessing שהחינו thereon either on a Sabbath or even a week-day.

3. One should not cut his hair during these days, neither the hair of the head, nor of the beard, nor any hair of the body. Adults are also forbidden to cut the hair of children.

4. The paring of nails is forbidden only during the week in which the ninth of Ab occurs, but a woman for the requirements of טבילה is permitted to pare them even then. A Mohel is likewise permitted to fix up his nails for the requirements of פריעה.

5. On the three Sabbaths between the seventeenth of Tammuz and the ninth of Ab the three chapters in the Prophets foretelling the chastisements, viz: דברי ירמיהו, שמעו דבר ד׳, חזון ישעיהו are read for the Haphtorah. If by error one had read on the first Sabbath the Haphtorah of the regular weekly section, on the Sabbath that follows both sections should be read שמעו and דברי ירמיהו, as they are near each other. If Rosh Chodesh Ab fell on the Sabbath, the Haphtorah השמים כסאי should be read.

6. When the month of Ab has come there should be a decrease of mirthfulness. One should not build an edifice for pleasure, or even only for profit. If one had contracted with a non-Jew to decorate one's house, if one can induce the contractor through some slight emolument to wait until after the ninth of Ab, it is proper to do so, but if it is not possible it is permissible.

7. One should not eat meat nor drink wine in the nine days from Rosh Chodesh until after the ninth of Ab, it is forbidden even to partake of victuals wherein meat was cooked, or in which there is fat, even the flesh of poultry is forbidden, but for the requirements of a sick person all that is permissible, nevertheless if it is not hard for the invalid, abstention should be practised from the seventh of Ab. On a feast of a precept such as a circumcision, the repemption of the first-born, and the conclusion of a Talmudical treatise, it is also permissible to partake of meat and wine, and besides one's parents, brothers and children, as well as those who are concerned in the performance of the precept, one may invite six more men for friendship's sake, but only those who would have come to one's feast at another period; all of the foregoing is permissible even on the eve of the ninth of Ab before noon, but not after that time.

8. Concerning the goblet of wine for Habdallah on the conclusion of the Sabbath, if there be a child who is able to drink the greater part of the goblet, it should be given him, otherwise he who says the Habdallah may drink it himself.

9. One should not have any washing done during these nine days, even a garment which one does not wish to wear until after the fast is forbidden to be given to a non-Jew to be washed. A Jewess is permitted to wash garments for a non-Jew, nevertheless in the week that the ninth of Ab occurs she should take care not to do so. During the nine days it is likewise forbidden to put on or to spread even those garments or cloths that were washed previously, but for the honour of the Sabbath one is permitted to put on linen garments, and to cover the table with white cloths, and to change towels in the same manner as on other Sabbaths, but it is forbidden to lay white spreads. A woman who requires to put on white lingerie in order to count seven clean days is permitted to wash them and to put them on. It is also permitted to wash infants' diapers, as they are continually soiled.

10. During the nine days one should not have new garments or new boots made even by a non Jewish workman, but if very necessary, e.g., for a wedding that will take place immediately after the ninth of

Ab, it is permissible to have them made by a non-Jewish workman, but not by an Israelite; before Rosh Chodesh it is in every wise permissible to give them to be made even by a Jewish workman, who is permitted to make them even after that time.

11. During the nine days one should not bathe even in cold water, excepting as a remedy, as for instance a woman who had given birth, or a pregnant woman nearing parturition, for whom bathing is beneficial; likewise one who is feeble and was medically advised to bathe—these are permitted to bathe even in warm water. A woman who was menstrually unclean may bathe and immerse herself as usual. If she will perform the immersion on the night after the ninth of Ab, and it will be impossible for her to bathe then, she is permitted to bathe on the eve of the Ninth of Ab. Likewise when putting on lingérie, she may bathe somewhat, as usual, inasmuch as she does not do so for pleasure.

12. On Rosh Chodesh Ab occurring on a Sabbath-eve, one who is accustomed to bathe every Sabbath-eve is also permitted to bathe then, even in warm water, but on the eve of the Sabbath on which the Haftora חזון is read, bathing in warm water is forbidden even for one who is accustomed thereto, and he is permitted to bathe only his face, hands and feet. Likewise one who is accustomed to brush his hair every Sabbath-eve is also permitted then, but not with soap. One who is accustomed to immerse every Sabbath-eve is then also permitted to do so in cold water, but one who sometimes abstains therefrom is forbidden to do so.

13. A mourner whose thirtieth day occurs on the eighteenth of Tammuz or thereafter until the eve of Rosh Chodesh Ab, is permitted to have his hair cut. but from Rosh Chodesh he is forbidden, even in that circumstance, either to bathe or have his hair cut.

14. At a circumcision that occurs during the nine days, it is customary for the Mohel, the Sandek and the parents of the son to don Sabbath-attire, but the one who brings in the child is forbidden. The woman, however, who assists in that ceremony is accustomed to wear her Sabbath-apparel, as that is the only ceremony in that rite which is mandatory upon her.

LAWS CONCERNING THE EVE OF THE NINTH OF AB.

1. When the covenant of circumcision, or the redemption of the first-born is celebrated on the eve of the ninth of Ab, the feast should take place before noon.

2. One should not go out for pleasure on the eve of the ninth of **Ab**, nor should any enjoyment or festivity mark that day, hence it is customary not to study in the afternoon other subjects than that of mourning and distress.

3. The regular meal is partaken of before the Afternoon Service, after that the afternoon prayers are said, but תחנון is omitted. At the approach of evening one should sit on the ground; it is not necessary to remove the boots. Three should not sit down together, and only bread and a cold hard-boiled egg should be partaken of, a portion of bread should be dipped in ashes and eaten. Care should be taken to finish this meal while it is yet day.

4. One who fasts on Mondays and Thursdays during the entire year, and the eve of the Ninth of Ab occurs on one of those days, should consult a learned man regarding his vow. One who has Jahrzeit on the eve of the Ninth of Ab should make a resolve on the first occasion not to fast any longer than until noon, then he should say the afternoon prayers מנחה גדולה (half-an-hour after noon) and partake of a meal, afterwards, at the approach of evening he should eat the concluding meal.

5. All that is forbidden to be done on the Ninth of Ab is forbidden in the twilight, it is therefore necessary to remove the boots before twilight.

Laws Concerning the Ninth of Ab.

1. In the evening all enter the synagogue and take off their boots. The vail is removed from the Holy Ark and but one light is lit in front of the Reader, the evening prayers are then said in a low tone with a weeping intonation, mourning-like. נחם is not said until the morrow in the afternoon prayer. After the prayer of שמונה עשרה the entire Kaddish and תתקבל is said. All should be seated on the ground. A few lights are lit just sufficient to enable them to say איכה and the קינות which is said also in a low and weeping intonation; when saying איכה a slight pause is made between one verse and the other, and a slightly longer pause between each איכה. At each succeeding איכה the Reader raises his voice slightly and the last verse of each איכה is read in a loud tone. When the verse השיבנו is reached, the congregation say it in a loud tone, then the Reader concludes and the congregation repeat השיבנו in a loud tone and the Reader follows suit. On conclusion of the קינות, אתה קדוש is said, then the entire Kaddish, but not תתקבל. On the morrow in the morning service תתקבל is also omitted and is only said in the afternoon service. One who prays privately having no assembly of ten to pray with also says איכה and קינות.

2. Neither the Talleth nor the Tephillin are put on in the morning but the Arba Kanfoth (טלית קטן) should be worn as usual, no blessing however being said thereon. All arrive at the synagogue a little earlier than usual. There is no " light of prayer " lit (in front of the Reader) and the prayers are said also in a low tone with a weeping intonation. מזמור לתודה is said. The Reader in the repetition of the שמונה עשרה says עננו between גואל and רופא as on every public fast day, but he does not say ברכת כהנים ; after the שמונה עשרה he says half Kaddish. Neither תחנון nor אל ארך אפים is said. A Scroll of the Law is taken out of the Holy Ark and the section כי תוליד בנים (Deut. iv. 24) is read for three persons. On conclusion of the reading of the Torah half-Kaddish is said, and the Haftorah אסוף אסיפם (Jeremiah viii. 13) is read in the tone of איכה ; the Scroll of the Law is then replaced in the Holy Ark the congregation being seated on the ground and קינות are said. The saying of קינות should be prolonged till close to noon. After that אשרי is said but not למנצח, only ובא לציון and the verse ואני ואת וגו' is omitted, אתה קדוש is said, then the entire Kaddish, but תתקבל is omitted, after which עלינו then the orphans' Kaddish is said. Neither the שיר היחוד, the שיר של יום nor פטום הקטרת is said.

3. A mourner during his seven days of mourning goes to the synagogue on the night of the Ninth of Ab, also in the daytime until the קינות are concluded, and it is permissible for him to go up to the Torah and to read the Haphtorah, since all are mourners.

4. On the Ninth of Ab it is forbidden to study excepting such subjects that sadden the heart, such as the prophecies of evil in Jeremiah ; it is likewise permitted to study the Book of Job, Midrashi איכה, in the Talmud the chapter אלו מגלחין which treats of the laws of a mourner, and a מנודה (one who is disgraced by the Rabbis) and in the Hagada הנזקין פ', and in the Talmud of Jerusalem the last part of the Treatise תענית which treats of the destruction of the Temple, and even in these it is forbidden to study therein and solve the problems they

present, or find the inference they suggest, as these things cause satisfaction ; all that one is himself permitted to learn, he is also permitted
to teach to children. One is permitted to read the entire order of the
daily sacrifices, even אינהו מקומן, but the order of מעמדות one should not
say even if one is accustomed to say it daily.

5. A pregnant woman or one nursing who suffers very much are
required to complete the fast, unless, God forbid, danger may be
apprehended, but one who is ill, even not dangerously, should not
complete the fast, but only fast for a few hours, this also applies more
especially to one who is naturally weak. A woman who had given
birth, from seven days thereafter to the thirtieth day, even if she is
not ill is amenable to the law that governs one who is ill but not
dangerously, yet those who are obliged to eat on the Ninth of Ab
should not regale themselves with viands, but eat just enough to preserve their bodily health.

6. Bathing is forbidden, whether in hot or cold water, even to
put one's finger in water is forbidden, only to bathe for pleasure is forbidden, but if not for pleasure it is allowable, hence one washes his
hands in the morning, but should be careful not to wash more than
the fingers, and after having dried them slightly while they are still
moist one may pass them over the eyes, but if one's eyes are filmy
after sleep and one is accustomed to bathe them every morning, one
may then also bathe them as usual. One whose hands are stained is
likewise permitted to wash them at the stained spot. One should
also lave the fingers for the Afternoon Service.

7. One who cooks and is obliged to rinse the edibles is permitted
to do so inasmuch as the purpose is not to wash the hands.

8. Although only bathing for pleasure is forbidden, nevertheless,
a woman whose time for מבילה occurred on the night of the Ninth of
Ab should not perform the "immersion," inasmuch as cohabitation is
forbidden.

9. Anointing also is only forbidden if done for pleasure, but if
necessary as a remedy, anointing is permitted.

10. Wearing boots is forbidden only if they are made of leather,
but if they are made of cloth or the like and they are not trimmed
with leather it is permissible to wear them. One who goes amongst

non-Jews is permitted to wear boots, but those who stay in shops are forbidden to do so. One who walks for a considerable distance is permitted to wear boots, but on nearing a city they should be removed; one who rides in a vehicle is forbidden to wear boots.

11. Cohabitation is forbidden and it is proper to be scrupulous as not even to embrace one's wife.

12. One is forbidden to greet his neighbour on the Ninth of Ab, even to say Good Morning and the like is forbidden, and if greeted by an ignoramus or a non-Jew he should respond in a low tone in order to avoid offence. It is likewise forbidden to send a present to one's neighbour on the Ninth of Ab. Smoking in the privacy of one's house is permitted in the afternoon.

13. All work which takes some time to do, even if it is not the work of a skilled artisan, but the work of an ordinary person, is forbidden to be done in the night-time and in the daytime until noon, but a thing that it does not take long to do, such as lighting candles and the like is permitted to be done. In the afternoon all work is permissible. The transaction of business is also forbidden until noon, after that time it is permitted. All manner of work is permitted to be done through a non-Jew, and if it is of a nature which if not done at once might occasion a loss, one is permitted to do it himself. The milking of cows ought to be done by a non-Jew, but when that is impossible, one may milk them himself.

14. One should not sit on a chair, neither at night nor in the daytime until noon, but only on the floor; after noon it is permissible. Of the other things that are forbidden to be done one is forbidden to do them until the appearance of the stars.

15. One should not prepare the requirements for a meal until the afternoon, but for the requirements of a precept it is permissible.

16. A circumcision may be celebrated on the Ninth of Ab after the קינות are concluded, and the parents of the son, also the Sandek and the Mohel are permitted to don their Sabbath attire in honour of the circumcision; after the circumcision they divest themselves of those garments. Candles are lit in honour of the circumcision, and the goblet of wine is given to a child to drink.

17. In the Afternoon Service the Talleth and Tephilin are put on and the blessings said thereon, the שיר של יום and other portions that were omitted in the Morning Service are said. אשרי is said and the Half Kaddish thereafter, then the Torah is read and the same Haphtorah is read as on any other public fast-day, the Torah is then replaced in the Holy Ark, the Reader says the Half Kaddish, the prayer of שמונה עשרה is said, and in the blessing ולירושלים—נחם is said, if it was then omitted, it should be said after עינינו but it should not be concluded with ברוך מנחם but with כי אתה שומע, but if he did not become aware of the omission even then until after he had said ברוך אתה ה' he should conclude the blessing שומע תפלה and he need not repeat the שמונה עשרה. The Reader when repeating the שמונה עשרה says the ברכת כהנים and after the שמונה עשרה the entire Kaddish also תתקבל, the Tephillin are then removed and the evening prayers are said.

18. One should scrupulously abstain from eating meat or drinking wine on the night of the tenth of Ab, also on the tenth until noon, excepting at a feast of a precept, also the blessing שהחינו should not be said. Neither should one bathe, cut his hair, or wash anything until noon of the tenth. If the tenth occurs on the Sabbath eve one is permitted to bathe, cut the hair, and wash immediately in the morning in honour of the Sabbath.

LAWS CONCERNING THE NINTH OF AB THAT OCCURS
ON THE SABBATH OR ON SUNDAY.

1. If the Ninth of Ab occurs on Sunday or on the Sabbath and it was postponed to Sunday, meat and wine is partaken of even at the third meal; after the Afternoon Service eveything is permitted, but one should not at that time feast with a company (if a circumcision was celebrated the feast should take place before the Afternoon Service) but one is permitted to partake of a meal with one's household, and he may say Grace by appointment with three; the meal should be finished while it is yet day, as eating, drinking and bathing are forbidden in the twilight, the boots, however, should not be taken off until after ברכו is said, but the Reader takes them off before he begins והוא רחום, first saying the blessing המבדיל בין קדש לחול without pronouncing the Divine name and Royal attribute.

2. Cohabitation is forbidden on the Sabbath-night on which the Ninth of Ab occurs unless it is her time to go טבילה.

357

3. אב הרחמים is said and the Memorial Service is held in the morning, but in the Afternoon Service neither צדקתך צדק nor פרקי אבות is said.

4. למנצח בנגינות is not said before the evening prayers, nor is ויהי נועם said before ואתה קדוש nor is ויתן לך said. At dark when one sees the candle lit, he should say the blessing בורא מאורי האש, and in the שמונה עשרה he should say אתה חוננתנו, but the Habdallah on a goblet of wine should not be said until the conclusion of the Ninth of Ab, at which time he should say the blessing of Habdallah on a goblet of wine, but he should not say the blessing on spices nor on a candle, even if he did not say it on the conclusion of Sabbath, he should warn his house not to do any work before they say המבדיל קדש לחול omitting the Divine name and Royal attribute.

5. When the Ninth of Ab occurs on the Sabbath and is postponed to Sunday, it is forbidden to partake of meat and wine on the night after the fast, but on the morrow everything is permitted very early.

6. When a postponed circumcision is celebrated on the Ninth of Ab, the parents of the son, the Mohel and the Sandek are permitted to say the afternoon prayers about half-past-twelve, and then they are allowed to say the Habdallah over a goblet of wine and eat as well as to bathe, but a feast should not be held until the night. Likewise at the celebration of the redemption of the first-born, the father and the Priest need not complete the fast.

THE COMMANDMENT TO COMMEMORATE THE DESTRUCTION OF THE HOLY TEMPLE.

1. After the destruction of the Holy Temple our sages of blessed memory established that on every occasion of rejoicing, this desruction of the Holy Temple should be commemorated, as it is said, "If I forforgot thee, O Jerusalem, etc. If I prefer not Jerusalem above my chief joy." Thus, when one's house is decorated or painted, a square cubit near the entrance should be left unfinished commemorative of the destruction of the Holy Temple, also before a bridegroom stands under the nuptial canopy, ashes are placed upon his head at the place the Tephillin are worn, nor should any silver or gold thread be

interwoven in the veil with which the bride is covered. It is also customary at the writing of a marriage-contract (after it has been read) to shatter a broken earthen vessel, commemorative of the destruction of the Holy Temple, a glass vessel is also broken under the nuptial canopy by the bridegroom.

Laws Concerning a Private Fast-Day.

1. If one is in distress, as for instance, if one of his family is ill, or if he goes astray in his travels, or if he is confined in prison on a false charge, it is mandatory upon him to fast and to pray to God and to beg for mercy from Him, blessed be His name, that He should help him.

2. If an individual desires to fast, he should make that resolve on the previous day in the שמונה עשרה of the afternoon prayers, thus in the blessing שמע קולנו he should think in his heart that he takes it upon himself to fast, and before saying יהיו לרצון he should say רבון העולמים הרי אני לפניך בתענית וכו׳, if he eats and drinks thereafter until break of day it does not matter. Likewise if one desires to fast several days consecutively, although he will eat and drink in the intervening nights, still the one resolve is sufficient, but if one takes it upon himself to fast certain days which are not consecutive such as Monday, Thursday and Monday, he should make that resolve for each day respectively in the Afternoon Service of the preceding day.

3. One who is accustomed to fast during the ten days of penitence, or on the first day of סליחות and on the eve of Rosh-Hashana, need not make a resolution to do so. Likewise a fast on account of an evil dream does not require to be preceded by a resolution, nor do the fasts of the Monday, Thursday and Monday which follow Passover and Tabernacles require any other resolution than the responding of אמן and the mental resolve after the מי שברך announcing these fasts. Nevertheless if he regrets that thought, and does not desire to fast, he is released inasmuch as he did not verbally undertake to fast.

4. Although one did not verbally undertake to fast, but merely thought of fasting on the morrow, and that even if not in the after-

moon-prayer, but previous thereto or afterwards, while it was yet day it is a resolution, and he is obliged to fast.

5. If one had undertaken to fast without specifying until when, he is required to complete it until the stars appear, even if it is Sabbath-eve.

6. One who fasts should not make known that he is fasting. If, however, he is urged to eat, he is permitted to reveal that he is fasting.

7. One who fasts even a private fast, whether it is a voluntary fast, or a fast on account of a dream, should say עננו in the שמונה עשרה of the afternoon prayer, in the blessing שמע קולנו, the same as on a public fast day and before יהיו לרצון he should say רבון העולמים.

8. One who had vowed to fast one day or several days, and did not specify on which day or days, even if he had resolved in the afternoon prayers to fast on the morrow and it became urgently necessary for him to eat, he may substitute the fast day, that is, he may eat on that day even if he had already begun to fast, and in lieu thereof fast on another day, this is permissible only providing that he had undertaken to fast on that day only in order to fulfil his vow, if, however, he did not originally make a vow, but merely took it upon himself in the Afternoon Service to fast on the morrow, then, even if it causes him great distress thereafter, he is not allowed to substitute his "fast day" and repay it by another day. Likewise, if, while making the vow, he had specified certain days, and also took them upon himself in the Afternoon Service, he can no longer substitute the fast-day.

9. One who resolved to fast but the fasting caused him great distress, may redeem it with money according to his means, but the money should be distributed to the poor; if the fast is undertaken because of a vow he had made, redemption is of no avail, nor does redemption avail on a fast day decreed by the congregation unless the congregation made that a condition thereof.

10. One who had vowed to fast Monday, Thursday and Monday may change it and fast Thursday, Monday and Thursday, but not on other days.

11. The fasts of the Monday, Thursday and Monday after the Passover and after the Tabernacles, likewise of the ten days of peni-

tence, which one did not resolve upon in the afternoon prayers, if a circumcision or the redemption of the first-born, or another feast of the precepts occurred then, it is mandatory for him to eat (and he does not require absolution) and the fast ceases entirely, and he is permitted to eat thereafter at his own house also, but before the feast he is forbidden to eat. The father of the son on the day of the circumcision, also the Sandek may eat also before the feast, inasmuch as to them it is similar to a Festival.

12. If one ate on a fast day without having been absolved, whether unwillingly or presumptuously, he is also obliged to complete the fast after the eating, and he must fast thereafter on Monday, Thursday and Monday as an atonement for having eaten on the fast day; especially if the fast was undertaken because of a vow is it requisite to complete it thereafter.

13. If an individual fasted because of his distress and it passed by, or if he fasted for one who was ill, and he became well or died, he is required to complete the entire fast that he had taken upon himself, but if he became aware that the reason for fasting had passed by before he undertook to fast he is not required to complete it.

14. Fasting and repentance are efficacious in nullifying the prognostication of an evil dream, and particularly on that very day, nevertheless one is not obliged to fast, it devolves, however, upon him to repent and to spend that entire day in the study of the Torah and in prayer.

LAWS CONCERNING THE MONTH OF ELLUL.

1. The forty days from the New Moon of Ellul until after Atonement Day are days of acceptance, for although in the entire year does the Holy One, blessed be He, accept the repentance of those who turn unto him with a perfect heart, nevertheless these days are more choice and appropriate for repentance, inasmuch as they are days of mercy. It is proper to fast on the Eve of the New Moon of Ellul and to say the prayers of יום כפור קטן and if the New Moon occurs on the Sabbath, the fast is held on the preceding Thursday.

2. On the second day of Rosh Chodesh Ellul the blowing of the Shofar is begun and is continued daily after the morning service שחרית excepting on the eve of Rosh Hashana, when it is interrupted in order to make a distinction between the voluntary blowing and the blowing that is mandatory. The reason for blowing the Shofar in

this month is to stir up the people to repent. From the second day of Rosh Chodesh Ellul until שמיני עצרת Ps. xxvii. (לדוד ה' אורי וישעי) is said every morning and evening after the respective prayers.

3. From the Sunday preceding New Year and onwards daily all rise early and attend to Propitiatory Prayers (סליחות); if, however, the New Year occurs on Monday or Tuesday, they are begun from the Sunday of the preceding week. When rising early the hands should be washed and the blessings על נטילת ידים and ברכת התורה should be said. After the סליחות the hands should be washed again without a blessing being pronounced.

4. The Reader intoning the סליחות should borrow a Tallith from another and wrap himself therein before saying אשרי. He should not pronounce the blessing upon the Tallith. If a Tallith cannot be obtained, the סליחות and the שלש עשרה מדות may be said without wearing a Tallith. It is proper that the one who intones the סליחות should also read the morning and afternoon prayers as well as the evening prayers of the preceding night, wherein he takes precedence over a mourner, a mohel and a Yahrzeit.

5. It is well to stand whilst saying the סליחות, and one who finds it difficult should stand at least whilst saying אל מלך יושב וגו' and שלש עשרה מדות.

6. It is proper that the Reader who recites the סליחות, and who conducts the services on the awe-inspiring days (Rosh Hashana and the Day of Atonement) should be a man of eminent respectability, greatly learned in the Torah and excelling in goodness, as good a man as can be found, he should be at least thirty years old, married and having children, likewise he who blows the Shofar on Rosh Hashana, and he who prompts him should be men of learning in the Torah and in the fear of God. Howbeit, every Israelite is eligible for every sacred office, if he but suits the congregation. If, however, one sees that his election will cause dissension, he should withdraw his candidature, even if an improper person will be chosen.

7. One who is in the twelve months of mourning for his parents should not officiate as Reader on Rosh Hashona and Atonement Day, nor should he blow the Shofar on Rosh Hashana unless there be none else so suitable for the office as he, during the entire period in which סליחות are said, even on Rosh Hashana eve, a mourner is permitted to act as Reader, but not during his seven days of mourning.

8. One who says the סליחות is not allowed to say שלש עשרה מדות as a prayer, and supplication, but as one who reads it in the Torah

in the same air and with the same intonations, he should also omit the passage wherein the שלש עשרה מדות are mentioned, such as וכור לנו היום ברית שלש עשרה and the like, as well as the entreaties in the Aramean language such as מחי ומסי should be said only amongst an assembly of ten.

9. A mourner, during the seven days of mourning, is forbidden to go from his house to the synagogue to say סליחות excepting on the eve of New Year, when many סליחות are said.

10. Many are accustomed to fast on the ten penitential days ; but inasmuch as they lack four days on which there is no fasting, that is the two days of New Year, Sabbath and the eve of Atonement Day, there are therefore four other fast-days in the days of סליחות before New Year to take their place, viz., the first day of סליחות, the eve of New Year and yet two intervening days, preferably Monday and Thursday. If a feast of the precepts occurred therein, one may partake thereof, and he can fast on another day in its stead.

11. On the eve of New Year it is a general custom to fast until after Afternoon Service, at which time some food is partaken of in order not to inaugurate the Festival whilst fasting.

12. One should wash himself and cut his hair on the eve of New Year in honour of the Festival, care, however, should be taken to cut the hair before noon, the ceremony of immersion is also performed and Sabbath garments are put on, on New Year.

13. On the Eve of New Year התרת נדרים " the abolution of vows " is said. One who does not understand it in the Holy Language should say it in the vernacular.

LAWS CONCERNING NEW YEAR.

1. In each Kaddish that is said from New Year unto the Day of Atonement, the word לעילא is repeated, thus, לעילא לעילא.

363

2. In the entire year in the שמונה עשרה—האל הקדוש and מלך אוהב צדקה ומשפט is said, with the exception of that interval from New Year until after the day of Atonement when it is requisite to say המלך הקדוש —המלך המשפט. If one erred and said האל הקדוש, or if one is in doubt whether he said האל הקדוש or המלך הקדוש, if in the time that it would take to say it he became aware of his error, he should say המלך הקדוש and is not required to repeat from the beginning; this law applies also to המלך המשפט. If, however, he was not reminded thereof until after the time that it would take to say it, then at המלך הקדוש he is required to turn to the beginning of the שמונה עשרה. Even a Reader during the repitition of the שמונה עשרה is required to turn to the beginning and it is necessary to say the קדושה again; at המלך המשפט, however, even an individual need not turn back to repeat even that blessing. If during the year one had erred and said המלך הקדוש—המלך המשפט it is not necessary to repeat the שמונה עשרה.

3. In the Evening Service of Sabbath, in the blessing מגן אבות— המלך הקדוש is said also in place of האל הקדוש, and if the Reader erred and said האל הקדוש, if he became aware of it immediately, in the time that it would take to say it, he should turn to say המלך הקדוש, but, he need not turn back thereafter.

4. If one forgot to say זכרנו or מי כמוך and וכתוב and בספר חיים, and was not reminded thereof until he had mentioned the Divine name, he concludes the blessing and continues the prayers. Likewise if he forgot to say ובכן תן פחדך and concluded המלך הקדוש, even if he had only said ברוך אתה ה' he concludes המלך הקדוש and says אתה בחרתנו and so on.

5. At the conclusion of the שמונה עשרה some conclude עושה שלום and some do not change, but say המברך את עמו ישראל בשלום and only in Kaddish do they say עושה שלום במרומיו וכו'.

6. After the Evening Service on the first night of New Year, it is customary for one to say to a friend לשנה טובה תכתב ותחתם and to a female תכתבי ותחתמי, but this is not said in the day.

7. In the feast made at night, it is customary to make the auguries of a good year, thus, a portion of the bread on which the

blessing המוציא has been said is dipped in honey, and after a כזית thereof is eaten, יהי רצון שתחדש עלינו שנה טובה is said : after this, a piece of sweet apple is dipped in honey, the blessing בורא פרי העץ is said thereon, after eating, the יהי רצון is also said. It is also customary to partake of the head of a sheep in commemoration of the ram of Isaac. One should also endeavour to partake of fish, but it should not be cooked in vinegar, as sour or bitter food is not partaken of on New Year. Rich meats and all kinds of confectionary are partaken of. It is also customary not to partake of nuts and almonds. It is proper to study the Torah whilst at the table, some make it a practice to study the Mishna, the treatise relating to the New Year.

8. On the New Year, when saying אבינו מלכנו חטאנו לפניך one should not beat one's breast as on a week-day or as on the Day of Atonement, as one does not confess the sins on New Year it being a Festival.

9. When the Scrolls of the Law are taken out of the Holy Ark, the שלש עשרה מדות and רבונו של עולם is said, but on a Festival which occurred on the Sabbath neither of the foregoing are said.

10. The sounds of the Shofar should be, primarily as follows : the תרועה is the blowing of nine short sounds, the שברים should be blown thrice in succession, the sound of each שבר should be as long as three short sounds of תרועה, thus the שברים also is equal to nine sounds ; one should be careful not to prolong the blowing of the שברים until each שבר equals nine sounds, for otherwise the obligation is not fulfilled even when already accomplished. The תקיעות are simple sounds and in the order of תשר"ת the sound of each תקיעות should be as long as the שברים and a תרועה, that is, as eighteen sounds, the same in the order of תר"ת. In the תקיעות preceding the Additional Service, the שברים and the תרועה should be sounded in one breath, but in the תקיעות during the repetition of the תפלה they should be sounded as in two breaths, nevertheless, one should not pause between them, but they should sound in immediate succession.

11.   When the one who blows Shofar pronounces the blessings, the congregation should not respond ברוך הוא וברוך שמו, but they should listen attentively and after each blessing devoutly respond אמן, and from thence it is forbidden to permit any interruption until after all the תקיעות during the repetition of the תפלה.

12.   At the repetition of the תפלה when the Reader says ואנחנו כורעים the congregation say it also with him, as well as to bow and to postrate themselves; the Reader also bows and postrates himself, but he is forbidden to leave his place during the תפלה, it is therefore customary for the Reader to stand at a slight distance from the desk in order that he may be able to bow and postrate himself without leaving his place, and those who stand near him should assist him to rise, that he be not compelled to move his feet.   The תקיעות during the repetition of תפלה should not be sounded by the Reader, unless he is confident that he will not become confused (in his prayers) thereby.

14.   At the repetition of the תפלה the Shofar is blown after the blessings of מלכיות in the following order, תשר"ת—תש"ת—תר"ת, the same order being observed after the blessings זכרונות, likewise after the blessings שופרות, and after the תפלה, the above order תשר"ת—תש"ת—תר"ת is thrice repeated repectively, and on conclusion thereof תשר"ת—תש"ת—תר"ת— is sounded, making thirty sounds before the Additional Service, and thirty sounds at the Reader's repetition of the תפלה and forty sounds after the תפלה making one hundred sounds in all.   On conclusion of all the תקיעות the Shofar should be hidden, and even one who desires to act as תוקע on the second day should not blow on the first day to practice.

15.   If a circumcision is to take place at the synagogue, it should be performed after the Haphtora, before the blowing of the Shofar, and if it be a Sabbath, the circumcision should take place after אשרי : if necessary that the circumcision should be performed at the house of the mother, it should take place after leaving the synagogue.

16.   One who had fulfilled his obligation as regards the blowing of Shofar, and desires to blow for the sake of others, may also say the blessing, nevertheless it is more proper that one requiring to fulfil this obligation should pronounce the blessings.   One who blows the Shofar for the sake of women, should blow it before hearing the תקיעות in the synagogue, and he should pronounce the blessings thereon with

the intention of fulfilling his obligation thereby, this, however, should not be done in the first three hours of the day, as one should not, then, blow the Shofar privately, or else he should either blow the Shofar for them at the time it is blown in the synagogue, or after the תקיעות in the synagogue, but he should bear in mind not to be exempted by these תקיעות, but only by those תקיעות which he will blow for the women, and he should say a blessing thereon, and although he afterwards goes to the synagogue to say the prayers of the Additional Service, and to hear the תקיעות in the תפלה, the interruption does not oblige him to repeat the blessing, as all the תקיעות constitute one precept. A weak woman who cannot abstain from food until after the תקיעות may eat before.

17. When leaving the synagogue it is proper to go with quiet decorum and with a heart full of happy confidence that the Lord had mercifully heard the voice of their prayers and the sounds of the Shofar, and they should eat and drink according to the bounty of the Lord which he had bestowed upon them, yet it is proper for one to guard oneself against eating to excess, and the fear of the Lord should be upon his countenance. It is also proper to study the Torah at the table. After Grace has been said, one should not go to sleep but should go to the synagogue and say תהלים with the congregation until the Afternoon Service, and only one who has headache may sleep a little before going to the synagogue.

18. After the Afternoon Service it is customary to go to a stream, preferably to one which is outside the city, and in which fish abound, if, however, a stream containing fish is not there, one goes to one without or to a well, and says מי אל כמוך וכו' in the סדר תשליך as it is set out in prayer books. If the first day of New Year falls on the Sabbath, one goes to the water on the second day.

19. Authorities differ as to whether שהחינו should be said at the Kiddush of the second night, therefore a new fruit is laid on the table in order that the blessing שהחינו said in the Kiddush should also apply to the fruit, or one should put on a new garment, yet if he have done none of these, it does not bar the fulfilment of his obligation, and the blessing שהחינו is said in Kiddush. A woman likewise when lighting the candles on the second night, should, if possible, put on a new garment, or lay a new fruit on the table in order that the blessing שהחינו should apply also to these, yet if she have none of these, it does not bar the fulfilment of her obligation. Likewise the one who blows the Shofar on the second day, should, if possible, put on a new garment; if, however, the first day falls on Sabbath, this is not necessary, inasmuch as he did not, as yet, say the blessing שהחינו on the Shofar.

LAWS AND CUSTOMS OF ISRAEL

LAWS CONCERNING THE TEN DAYS OF PENITENCE.

1. The purpose of the Ten Days of Penitence is demonstrated by its name which indicates that they are devoted to repentance, hence it devolves upon a man during these days to search into his deeds, and to turn from all evil actions. For the transgressions of which one is in doubt, more penitence is necessary than for that deed which one knows positively that it is a transgression, as one feels more regret if he knows that he had committed a transgression, than if he does not know it. One should exceed in the study of the Torah, in the performance of the precepts, and in the distribution of charity, but more than all, a man should make amends for all the wrongs that he had committed against his neighbour, for which there is no atonement unless he makes restitution of the thing stolen, or obtained by oppression, and he conciliates him until he forgives him.

2. It is proper for a man during these days to be more scrupulous than the entire year, by rigidly adhering to the precepts, for we also pray to God, blessed be his name, that He deal with us with lovingkindness.

3. It is customary not to marry in these days.

4. On the Sabbath whereon the section שובה is read for the Haftora, an eminent man should be called up as Maftir.

LAWS CONCERNING THE EVE OF ATONEMENT DAY.

1. On the Eve of Atonement-day, a cock is taken by a male, and a hen by a female, and for a pregnant woman both a cock and a hen, and the verses בני אדם וכו' is said, and the fowl is turned around his (or her) head while saying זה חליפתי וכו' and if saying for another זה חליפתך should be said. One should perform the ritual for oneself before doing it for another. One should not imagine that the fowl atones for oneself, but should think that everything that is done to that fowl should properly be done to oneself because of one's iniquities, and one should lament because of his sins, and the Holy One, blessed be He, in His mercy, will accept his repentance. If chickens cannot be obtained a goose may be taken, or another live thing, but neither turtle doves nor pigeons. Some are accustomed to give the redemption fowls to the poor, but it is more proper to redeem them with money and to give the money to the poor.

2. Neither מזמור לתודה, nor תחנון, nor למנצח is said, nor is אבינו מלכנו said, excepting when Atonement Day falls on the Sabbath, then

368

אבינו מלכנו is said in the Morning Service on the day previous to Atonement Day.

3. It is mandatory to feast sumptuously and to fare generously as it is accounted a virtue to him who eats and drinks on the Eve of Atonement Day, just as if he had fasted on that day. It is mandatory to partake of fish in the first meal.

4. The Day of Atonement does not atone for transgressions one commits against one's neighbour unless he conciliates his neighbour, one should therefore be very particular to return to others that which he may unlawfully have belonging to them and conciliate them. If one has money, his right to which is in doubt, he should notify his neighbour that immediately after Atonement Day he desires to appear with him before a Jewish tribunal, and he should in all sincerity be resolved to be guided by the verdict in accordance with the edicts of the holy Torah. Likewise if one sinned against his neighbour only with words, he is obliged to conciliate him, and it is his duty to go personally and conciliate him, if, however, that is a difficult thing for him to do or if he understands that he will more easily be reconciled through another, he should conciliate through another, and the one whose forgiveness is sought should forgive with a perfect heart and not be cruel, and even if he has been grieviously wronged, he should not seek vengeance, nor bear a grudge against the other. On the contrary, if the offender does not arouse himself to come unto him to sue for forgiveness, the offended one should present himself to the offender in order that the latter may beg his pardon. If one does not let his enmity pass away, his prayers are not heard on Atonement Day, Heaven forfend, and one who is magnanimous and forgives, has all his own sins forgiven.

5. If the one whom he had offended had died, he should bring ten men and assemble round his grave, and say, " I have sinned unto the God of Israel and to this man (name) have I sinned," to which they should respond, " Thou art forgiven," three times ; he should walk barefoot and also detail the offence if it is not a shame for the dead. If the grave is beyond three leagues from the place where the offender resides, he does not need to go there himself, but he may send another who should take ten men with him to assemble round the grave and say, " I am the agent of this one (name), who publicly confesses, and who sent me to beg for forgiveness for his sin, etc." If one had vilified another after his death he is not required to go

369

on his grave, but he should beg his forgiveness in the place where he vilified him, if, however, he libelled him, he is required to take upon himself to do penance for having transgressed the ordinance of the Ancients—not to utter a libel against the dead.

6. It is mandatory for one to immerse himself on the Eve of Atonement Day, he should then be particular to see that nothing intervenes between any part of his body and the water. The afternoon is the time essential for the performance of the immersion. A mourner, even during the seven days, may bathe and immerse himself about an hour or two before night, even before the Afternoon Service, but the other laws of mourning, such as sitting on the ground and not wearing boots, he should observe until the night.

7. It is customary for the master of the house to have one candle made for his house and another for the synagogue, for the sake of the souls of his deceased parents, to atone for them. It is customary to light one in the house and to let it burn until the time to say the Habdallah has arrived, when it should be used as the Habdallah light, and the other candle is lit in the Synagogue.

8. In the Afternoon Service of the Eve of Atonement Day after the week-day שמונה עשרה has been said, the וידוי (confession) is read, that is before אלהי נצור וגו', the verse יהיו לרצון וגו' is said, and the words אלהינו ואלהי אבותינו תבוא לפניך are begun, as in the prayers of Atonement Day; if, whilst saying the וידוי the Reader repeats the תפלה, inasmuch as he has already said יהיו לרצון, he may respond אמן and say קדושה and מודים.

9. The וידוי should be said standing and in a bowed attitude as when saying מודים. When he mentions the sin he should beat his breast. The confession should be said by all alike according to the version printed in the prayer books; one, however, who is conscious of a sin he had committed which is not mentioned in the וידוי, inasmuch as he says the וידוי inaudibly, should properly mention that sin, and acknowledge his guilt thereof with bitterness of heart, and with abundant tears. Likewise if that sin is one that is mentioned in the וידוי, he should, when coming to it, groan deeply over it. The sins that one had acknowledged in the foregoing Atonement Day, although he is conscious that since then he was not guilty of them, nevertheless, he should repeat his acknowledgment thereof.

10. On conclusion of the Afternoon Service אבינו מלכנו is not said, and it matters not whether the Atonement Day occurs on a week-day or whether it falls on a Sabbath.

11. Towards evening the final meal is partaken of, and it is customary to dip the piece of bread on which the blessing המוציא had been pronounced in honey as on New Year. One should eat no food but that which it is easy to digest, such as the flesh of fowls. Fish should not be partaken of at this meal. One should neither eat nor drink any food or drink that warms, such as victuals in which spices and saffron are mingled. It is requisite for one to be exceedingly careful to add from the profane to the sacred, that is, he should conclude the meal while it is yet day, a short time before twilight, the zealous hasten to end their meal at about an hour before nightfall. One who had finished his repast while the day is yet long and he intends to eat and drink thereafter is required to make that provision before Grace after the meal, and he should say explicitly, or at least bear it in mind that he does not as yet inaugurate the fast.

12. It is mandatory to honour the Holy Day with clean apparel and with lights; hence, in the synagogue also beautiful covers are spread and many lamps are lit. Before twilight the table-cloths are spread upon the tables and the lamps are lit as on a Sabbath-eve. It is proper also to light candles in the bed-room, and the blessing להדליק נר של יום הכפורים is said upon these lights. If it occurred on Sabbath one says the blessing להדליק נר של שבת ושל יום הכפורים.

13. It is customary to wear a Kittel, which is the garment of the dead, as through that the heart of man is humbled and broken. A mourner may also wear it. Inasmuch as it is a garment made for the special purpose of praying therein, one should remove it before entering a lavatory. Women also wear white clean dresses in honour of the day, but they should not adorn themselves with ornaments, because of awe for the judgment.

14. It is customary for parents to bless their children before entering the synagogue and to pray in that blessing that they may be sealed for a happy life, and that their hearts may be steadfast in the fear of God.

15. It is customary to put on the Tallith, one should be careful to put it on while it is yet day, and say a blessing thereon, if, however, he delayed in putting it on until twilight he should not say a blessing thereon.

LAWS AND CUSTOMS OF ISRAEL

Laws Concerning Atonement Eve (כל נדרי).

1. Previous to כל נדרי the most venerable of the congregation
take the Scrolls of the Law from the Holy Ark and walk therewith
round the Reader's platform (בימה), whilst the people bow and press
their lips reverently to the Sacred Scroll and plead for pardon and
forgiveness for having been lax in honouring the Torah, and they
should resolve that henceforth they will be guided by it, and the verse
אור זרוע וגו' is repeated many times; then two respected men of the
congregation stand near the Reader, at his right and at his left, and
the three say בישיבה של מעלה וכו', then the Reader says כל נדרי thrice,
and all should say it in an undertone together with the Reader. It
is proper to begin saying כל נדרי while it is yet day, and continue it
until night.

2. When the Reader says the blessing שהחיינו it should be his
object to exempt the congregation from saying it, nevertheless, it is
proper for the listener to bear in mind that he is not exempted by the
Reader's blessing, but he should himself say the blessing in an undertone, and should hasten to conclude it before the Reader, so that he
may respond אמן, but the women who have already said the blessing
שהחיינו when lighting the candles or likewise if a man lit the candles
and said שהחיינו then, they should not repeat same.

3. On the Atonement Eve and day ברוך שם כבוד מלכותו לעולם ועד
should be said in a loud voice.

Laws Concerning the Day of Atonement.

1. On the Day of Atonement, eating, drinking, bathing, anointing, wearing boots and cohabitation is forbidden. It is likewise forbidden to do any work, or to carry from place to place, as on a Sabbath. Inasmuch as it is necessary to add from the profane to the
sacred, all of the foregoing are forbidden while it is yet day, a short
time before twilight, likewise on the conclusion of the Day of Atonement until a short time after the appearance of the stars.

2. The Priests who go up to say the benediction are permitted, nay, required to wash their hands up to the arm. One who is ill, even not dangerously, may wash in the usual manner.

3. Anointing is forbidden, even on part of the body, but one who is ill, even not dangerously may anoint in the usual manner.

4. The wearing of boots made of leather is forbidden, but it is permissible to wear them if they are made of cloth; if, however, it is very distressing for one to go in a muddy, clayey or wet place and it is impossible for one to go there unshod, boots or slippers may be worn, but they must be removed at the door of the synagogue, care being taken that the hands do not touch them either when putting them on or taking them off, so that one be not required to wash the hands.

5. It is permitted to stand on coverings or spreads, even if they are made of leather. One who is in any wise indisposed, although not in danger, or one who has a bruise upon the foot, or a woman within thirty days after her confinement may wear boots.

6. One is forbidden to caress his wife, even in the daytime, but he should consider her as though menstrually unclean the entire Atonement-Day.

7. Pregnant and suckling women fast until the conclusion like other people. A suckling woman whose infant is dangerously ill, and will not suckle from anyone but her, and if she should fast, it will jeopardize the child's life, she should not fast.

8. If a pregnant woman was affected by the odour of a certain edible and desired it, and it is certain that unless she partakes thereof she and the child may be in danger, therefore, if she said, "I must eat," even though her face did not undergo a change, or if it is noticeable that her face had undergone a change, although she did not say anything, she is quietly told that it is Atonement Day, which has often the effect of allaying her desire, if, however, her mind is not soothed thereby, she is fed in the following manner. At first she is given just a taste, thus—the finger is dipped in the soup or the like, and applied to her mouth, for one drop will often tend to allay her desire, if, however this is ineffectual, she is given less than the required quantity, but if her mind is not yet calmed thereby, she is given as much as she requires. This applies as well to any man who

was affected by the smell of food and his face had undergone a change, he is in danger and is treated as described above, but as long as his face had not undergone a change he is not fed, although he says, "I must eat."

9. A woman in confinement, likewise one who is dangerously ill, are governed, concerning the profanation of Atonement Day by eating and drinking, by the same laws that govern Sabbath-profanation, but in the matter of eating and drinking, even if many doctors say he or she does not require it, nay more, even if they say that the eating or drinking will prove injurious to him, whilst the sick person say she does require it, and even if he says that he is not in danger as yet, but if he will not eat he will become worse and be in danger, he should be heeded and food should be given him, for in the matter of eating and drinking his judgment concerning himself is more reliable, as the sufferer is the best judge of his position.

10. When food is given to a woman in pregnancy or in confinement, or to a sick person, it is placed before them, and they are told as follows: "If you are sure that you may possibly be in danger unless you eat as much as you require, you may eat ordinarily until you feel satisfied, if, however, it is possible for you to eat less than the required quantity at one time, then act as follows: Eat at one time no more than the quantity of two-thirds of an egg, and rest somewhat, then eat the same quantity again, rest at least nine minutes between each time of eating." When drinking one should take less than a mouthful at one time and rest for about seven minutes before drinking again.

11. One who was overcome by hunger in such a manner that his eyes grew dim so that he could not see, is fed until his eyes regain their lustre.

12. One who is fed on account of being in danger may in the lack of permitted food, be given forbidden food, but in that case, he should be given less than a כזית at any time.

13. If his mind is composed, he should say a blessing both before and after eating but he should not say the Kiddush. In the Grace after the meal he should say יעלה ויבוא, and if it occurs on the Sabbath he should also say רצה, if he omitted it, he is not required to repeat the Grace.

14. A child less than nine years old should not be permitted to fast, in order that they should not risk their health, but as soon as

374

they are !fully nine years old and in good health, they are trained to fast a little, thus, they should not eat until several hours later than they are accustomed to eat. In abstaining from wearing boots, bathing and anointing they should be trained even before the age of nine years.

15.   On Atonement-Day memorial prayers for the dead are read, and offerings of charity are made for the sake of the souls of the departed. These prayers are also said on the last day of Passover, on the second day of Pentecost, and on the eighth Day of Tabernacles. It is customary for those whose parents are living to leave the synagogue whilst the memorial prayers for the dead are being said, it is also customary for one whose father or mother had died within that year to likewise leave the synagogue.

16.   If there is an infant to be circumcised, it should be performed before אשרי is said, a blessing is said upon the cup of wine and some of it given to the circumcised infant, besides what is given him when בדמיך חיי is said, but none of it should be given to another child. One who was used to sprinkle wine when extracting the blood should not sprinkle it with his mouth but with his hand, he then extracts the blood with his mouth as usual.

17.   One is forbidden to prostrate himself on ground that is tesselated with stones, and should therefore spread something thereon to intervene between himself and the ground.

18.   The time for the נעילה (Conclusion Service) is when the sun is seen above the tree-tops, in order that it may be concluded at the appearance of stars; at times it is prolonged even into the night, even then חתמנו should be said. If the stars appeared the Reader should not say היום יפנה, but he should say היום פנה, השמש בא ופנה, the Reader says the ברכת כהנים and שים שלום even if it is night.

19.   After the נעילה prayer is over, אבינו מלכנו is said, even if is a Sabbath Day and still day when נעילה is concluded, then שמע ישראל is said once, ה' הוא האלהים three times, ברוך שם כבוד מלכותו לעולם ועד seven times, the Reader then says the entire Kaddish in a joyful tone, after which the Shofar is sounded once. It may be sounded even though the stars have not yet made their appearance and it is but

twilight, even if it is a Sabbath Day, but it should not be sounded in the daytime. After it is sounded, all say, thrice לשנה הבאה בירושלים.

20. After the appearance of the stars, the Evening Service is held, and אתה חוננתנו is said in the שמונה עשרה. If it had occurred on a Sabbath ויתן לך is said, but ויהי נועם and ואתה קדוש are not said. Friendly greetings are then exchanged with rejoicing and a merry heart as on a Festival.

21. When saying the Habdallah on the conclusion of Atonement Day it is requisite to say the blessing only on a light that was kindled before Atonement Day, and not upon a light that is now produced by means of a match, and the like, nor with what was lit by them; the best way is to light a candle by the light of a candle that had been lit in the house the day before, and say a blessing upon both, and if there is no light in the house one should bring a burning candle lit by the candle of a non-Jew, or by the light of a match and the like. The Habdallah is not begun with the words הנה אל ישועתי, but the blessings are said upon the goblet (of wine), and upon the candle, and המבדיל is said, no blessing is pronounced upon the spices, if, however, it was Sabbath, then a blessing on the spices should be said, and Habdallah is also begun with הנה אל ישועתי, as on the conclusion of an ordinary Sabbath.

22. On the conclusion of Atonement Day, there is eating, drinking and rejoicing. On the conclusion of Atonement Day, the erection of a Succah is immediately begun. On the day after Atonement Day it is customary to rise early and to go to the synagogue, and on the days between the Day of Atonement and Tabernacles none should fast, not even the fast of a Jahrzeit, nor is תחנון said therein.

LAWS CONCERNING THE SUCCAH.

1. It is mandatory to erect the Succah immediately upon the close of Atonement Day, even if it is a Sabbath-eve. A clean place should be chosen for its site. Each one is commanded to personally attend to the making of the Succah and the laying of the covering, even if one is an eminent man it is an honour to him to personally attend to the fulfilment of a precept. One should do his best to embellish the Succah and to adorn it by placing therein fine furniture and beautiful coverings according to his means.

2. It is essential that the walls of the Succah be entire and strong in order that they be not shaken by the wind, also that the wind should not extinguish the candles. One who has not enough boards for walls, had best make three complete walls, rather than four incomplete walls.

3. Anent the covering of the Succah, care should be taken not to cover it with anything but the branches of trees, or with reeds, in which are fulfilled the following four conditions : it should be a production of the soil, and severed therefrom, and not subject to defilement, and not tied together. It is primarily proper that one should be scrupulous not to lay upon the Succah anything that is subject to defilement as a support for the covering ; e.g., ladders of which the rungs are subject to defilement, and especially other utensils, such as a hatchet and shovel. One should scrupulously abstain from even putting them upon the covering to secure it, if, however, it was put there, or if he have nothing else, it is permitted to keep the covering firm with something that is subject to defilement.

4. It is requisite to put enough of a covering to make the Succah more shady than sunny, for if it is more sunny than shady, it is not valid, it is therefore necessary to put on so much of the covering, that even if it will dry up, there will still be more shadow. It is also essential to be careful not to leave an open space of three cubits in one place, but it is primarily necessary to leave open spaces between the covering in order that the stars may be visible, nevertheless if it was so thickly covered that the stars were not visible, it is valid, If, however, it was so thickly covered that even if there would be a heavy rainfall it would not enter therein, it is thus like a house and not valid.

5. Sometimes the boards project above the walls, and upon them are laid the poles on which the covering is placed. If the board is not four cubits wide it does not invalidate the Succah, and it is considered as if the partition sloped upwards, but one neither sits nor sleeps under the board, as the law does not recognise it as a Succah, even if it is only four cubits wide, but the rest of the Succah is valid ; if, however, boards that are four or more cubits wide lay near the partition, they invalidate the entire Succah, but if this is the case only on one side, and there yet remain three valid partitions upon which there is a valid covering, it is valid providing there is the requisite space for a Succah, which is at least seven hand-breadths square, but they should not sit under the boards.

6. A Succah that is made under the branches of a tree is not valid, and even if the branches cause it to have more shadow than sunshine, thus making the Succah complete by means of the covering that he put on it, it is nevertheless invalid, and even if the branches of the tree are afterwards cut off, the Succah nevertheless continues to be invalid, and it is necessary to raise each branch of the covering and to lay it down again expressly for the sake of the Succah which is then valid. It is likewise forbidden to lay the covering before the walls are made, as it is essential that the laying of the covering make the Succah valid. When a Succah is made by raising the roof, it should be raised before the covering is laid. In such a Succah it is also necessary to take care that the roof should be wide open and stand in line with the wall of the Succah, for if it is not perpendicular, but inclines slightly on the covering, even in such a degree as not to invalidate the Succah, it is nevertheless necessary to be careful not to sit in that place where the roof slopes, as one thus sits under the roof.

7. The Succah made for the Festival is exempt from a Mezuzah during that period, but a Succah that is built and made use of during the entire year and must consequently have a Mezuzah, is not exempted therefrom during the Festival, and it is not necessary after the Festival to fasten the Mezuzah anew.

8. One may fulfil his obligation with a borrowed Succah, but not with a stolen one, hence, it is forbidden to make a Succah on the public domain; in an emergency, however, when one has no other Succah, he may sit therein and say a blessing thereon.

9. Care should be taken that the Israelite should not cut the covering for his Succah himself, but should purchase it from another, if unable to do so he may procure it himself.

10. It is permissible to make a Succah during the Intermediate days of the Festival.

11. It is forbidden to benefit by the wood of the Succah, either of the walls or of the covering until after שמחת תורה, inasmuch as they were set apart for the performance of a precept, it is forbidden to take even a splinter therefrom for any use whatever; even if they fell down they are unconditionally forbidden, and if שמחת תורה occurred on Sabbath Eve, it is forbidden also on the Sabbath. It is also forbidden to benefit by the ornaments of a Succah, even if they fell down, and inasmuch as it is forbidden to benefit by them, it is likewise forbidden to handle them on a Sabbath and Festival because they are set apart; it is nevertheless permitted to inhale the fragrance of a Citron that is hung up in a Succah as an ornament as it is not set

378

apart as far as smelling is concerned. Even if a provision was made to benefit by the ornaments suspended from the covering it is the practice not to use them. Painted tapestries that are hung up in the Succah for ornament it is customary to remove them when it is feared they may be spoiled by rain, even if one did not make an express provision therefor, as it is presumed that it was hung up on that condition.

12. Those ornaments of a Succah which it is one's purpose to remove during the Festival, one should be careful not to tie with a knot, but merely with a slip-knot.

13. When taking the Succah apart after the Festival one should not tread upon the boards nor make a degrading use of them.

14. It is forbidden to engrave or write any verse of the Torah upon an ornament of the Succah because it might subsequently be degraded.

15. On the Succoth-eve in the afternoon one should not partake of bread so that he should eat with relish in the Succah. It is proper to dispense much charity on the Succoth-Eve.

Laws Concerning Dwelling in a Succah.

1. It is written בסכות תשבו and correctly translated, "In booths *shall ye dwell seven days,"* meaning thereby that one should dwell in the Succah seven days even as he dwells in his house the entire year, thus his principal abode should now be in the Succah, therein he should take his fine furniture and household linens, he should eat, drink, study, amuse himself and sleep in the Succah, even intercourse with a friend should be had in the Succah. Likewise when praying privately one should pray in the Succah, and the mind should be centred on the fact that he is abiding in the Succah because the Holy One, blessed be He, had commanded us to dwell in the Tabernacle as a memorial of the departure from Egypt.

2. One should maintain the Succah in honour, hence he should not bring therein vessels that are not for usage of honour. After the meals the plates should be removed from the Succah (but drinking vessels should remain in the Succah). One should not perform any menial service therein, if, however, one brought degrading vessels

379

therein, it is not thereby invalidated, only that, while they are therein, one should not say the blessing לישב בסוכה until they are removed.

3.   On the first night it is obligatory to eat in the Succah at least a כזית of bread, and even if one is distressed he is obliged to eat in the Succah, if, however, it rains, and it appears that it will stop in a short time, he should wait, and then say the Kiddush and eat in the Succah in a proper manner, but if it seems that it will not stop so soon, or if he had waited and it did not stop, he should say the Kiddush in the Succah, also say the blessing שהחיינו and bear in mind that שהחיינו also applies to the Succah, but the blessing לישב בסוכה should not be said ; hands should be washed and the blessing המוציא said, then a כזית of bread is eaten without interruption and one may then proceed to the house to complete the meal ; when washing the hands and saying the blessing המוציא one should bear in mind that one intends to eat in the house ; if the rain stops before Grace after the meal is said one should return to the Succah and say the blessing לישב בסוכה and eat slightly more than a כביצה of bread, and then say the Grace after the meal.   If it stopped raining after he said Grace, he should also go to the Succah and wash his hands again and eat a little more than a כביצה of bread, saying the blessing לישב בסוכה thereon, after which he should say Grace.

4.   On the second night it is also obligatory to eat in the Succah, even if it causes him distress, and it is governed by the same law that applies to the first night, as above described, with the difference that if it appears that the rain will not stop so soon, Kiddush should be said in the house, and the meal eaten there, but before saying Grace he should go to the Succah and eat there at least a כזית of bread without saying the blessing לישב בסוכה, one then returns to the house and says the Grace after the meal.

5.   In the evening, on his return from the synagogue he should enter the Succah and immediately say the Kiddush, but he should not say the Kiddush unless it is positively night.   When saying the blessing לישב בסוכה in the Kiddush, he should bear in mind that in that blessing is included the meal he is about to partake of, as well as his sleeping and other requirements that he will attend to in the Succah until he will again say Kiddush on the following morning.   When saying the blessing שהחיינו he should bear in mind that it applies to the Festival and also to the Succah, therefore on the first night, he should first say the blessing לישב בסוכה and שהחיינו thereafter, so that the blessing שהחיינו should also apply to the Succah, but on the second night he should first say the blessing שהחיינו and then the blessing לישב בסוכה.

6. On the remaining nights and days, it is not obligatory to eat in the Succah, unless one desires to eat a regular meal, or to sleep in the Succah, then he may do so. By a regular meal is meant bread more than כביצה, even if he had made no appointed time for eating it, and even if it was baked in a pan, likewise made of the five species of grain, if more than a כביצה and if he pre-arranged a time for eating it, these it is obligatory upon one to eat in the Succah, and to say the blessing לישב בסוכה, but one is allowed to eat fruit outside the Succah, even if he eats much of it. It is likewise permitted to drink wine or other beverages, and to eat meat or cheese outside of the Succah, providing it was not pre-arranged. If, however, he desire to pre-arrange for drinking wine or other beverages, or for eating meat or cheese, he requires a Succah, but he should not say the blessing לישב בסוכה thereon. It is best that he previously partake of bread in order to say a blessing. All this is according to the law, but with the more praiseworthy, one is so scrupulous that he does not even drink water outside the Succah.

7. For sleeping, even for taking a nap, the Succah is the place required, and those who are scrupulous in the observance of the precepts make a practice thereof. Now, however, there are many who are lax in the observance of the law as regards sleeping, but every God-fearing man ought to be scrupulous and make a Succah fit for the habitation of himself and wife, just as he lives the entire year.

8. If it rains one is exempt from entering the Succah. To make one exempt from the Succah, it must rain so hard as to lead one to judge that if it rained thus into a victual it would spoil it, or if he judges that if it would thus rain into his room, he would leave it and go into another room, then one should also go from the Succah to the house. If after one began to eat in the Succah the rain descended and one went into the house and began to eat there, or if one had begun to eat in the house on account of the rain, which ceases thereafter, the meal is finished in the house and one is not obliged to leave the house in the midst of the repast in order to enter the Succah. When the weather is cold and the victuals freeze in the Succah, one is exempt from entering the Succah, but eats in the house.

9. Regarding sleeping in a Succah, even a little rain causes distress when one sleeps, and one may leave it on that account, and if

one left and went to sleep in the house on account of the rain, and afterwards it ceased, one is not put to the trouble of going to the Succah the entire night, but he should sleep in the house till morning.

10. When one is exempt from the Succah and he does not leave it, he is called a common person, and obtains no reward therefore, and he is not permitted to say a blessing, as it is a blessing said in vain. When one leaves the Succah on account of the rain, he should not do so with disgust, but should go out meekly.

11. When entering the Succah to partake of a regular meal, one should first say the blessing המוציא then לישב בסוכה before he tastes anything, then everything that he will eat in the Succah the entire day, and whatever he will do while staying therein, even if he will sleep there, all that will be exempted by this blessing until he will eat another regular meal. If he does not leave the Succah between the meals, inasmuch as he had once said that blessing (לישב בסוכה) he need not repeat it in the meal that follows, nor even the entire seven days, for as he did not leave the Succah he does not need to say the blessing more than once, his attention not having been diverted from the Succah, and even if he went out temporarily with the intention of returning immediately, it is not considered as diverted attention, and is not required to say the blessing at the second meal.

12. One who goes to a friend's Succah in the midst of the meal and partakes there of an amount sufficient to make a Succah obligatory, is required to say there also the blessing לישב בסוכה.

13. If one had forgotten to say the blessing לישב בסוכה and was reminded thereof in the midst of the repast, or even after he had finished his meal he is required to say the blessing.

14. Women are exempt from dwelling in a Succah, yet they are permitted to say a blessing. Children are also exempt, nevertheless it is obligatory upon the father of a boy of five years of age and over, to train him to eat in the Succah.

15. A sick person and his attendants are exempt from dwelling in a Succah. If he is not dangerously ill, the attendants are not exempt excepting when he needs them, but if the invalid is dangerously ill, they are exempt even when he does not need them so urgently.

16. One whom it causes distress is exempted from dwelling in the Succah (with the exception of the first two nights of the Festival); likewise if the lights in the Succah were extinguished on a Sabbath and

LAWS AND CUSTOMS OF ISRAEL

it is very difficult for him to go to a friend's Succah, he may return to his house, where the candles are lit, providing he had originally made the Succah in a proper manner, and it is only an accident that caused him distress when sitting or sleeping therein, but if he had originally erected it in a place where there is an obnoxious effluvia and the like, or in a place where he fears to sleep therein, he does not fulfil his obligation therewith even when eating there in the daytime. If the wind penetrates the walls and is about to blow out the candles, it is permitted to spread there a sheet or a garment.

17. Those who go into the country during the Intermediate days of the Festival, if they are unable to get a Succah there, they should scrupulously return to their houses every night in order to perform the precept of Succah.

18. Those who stay in a shop, even if they reside out of town and the shop is in town, and they are mostly accustomed to eat there in the daytime during the entire year, nevertheless on Tabernacles they are obliged to eat in a Succah.

Laws Concerning the Lulav and Appurtenances.

1. One who bought an Esrog and Lulav and knows not the laws concerning them, it is customary to show them to a Rabbi, to learn whether they are valid or not. An effort should be made to purchase a fresh Lulav, as a dry Lulav (whose greenness has gone) is not valid excepting in an extremity.

2. The required length of a Lulav is that its stock besides its upper leaves, should measure four hand-breadths. In an emergency, the length of thirteen-and-one-third thumbs is sufficient.

3. The "Hadas" should be three-leaved, that is, there should be three leaves in one even row on each stem, thus, one should be neither higher nor lower than the other. It is also requisite that the leaves cover the wood, that is, the top of each leaf should lap over the stem of the leaf that is above it, and he who fears the word of the Lord should endeavour to purchase fresh and green "Hadasim" which are three-leaved and beautiful, and he should investigate whether they had not been grafted, and if they did not grow in a pot having no orifice. If one cannot obtain three-leafed "Hadasim" those that are not three-leafed should be taken, but a blessing should not be said thereon.

383

4.   The requisite length of an "Hadas" is three hand-breadths. In an emergency the length of ten thumbs is sufficient. The entire "Hadas," from the bottom to the top, should be three-leafed; in an emergency, however, if part thereof at the bottom is not three-leafed, and the greater part thereof at the top is three-leaved, it is also valid. If part of the leaves had fallen out, a learned man should be consulted One should also be particular that the "Hadasim" are not broken off, and if the tops are broken off, a learned man should be consulted.

5.   The Arava is known through its leaf being drawn out, its edge is smooth, and its stem is red, and even while it is green it is also valid, inasmuch as it turns red when on the tree. The greater part of this species grows near streams. The required length of the Arava is the same as that of the Hadas.

6.   An Arava which is dried up or of which most of the leaves had fallen, or the top of the stem is broken off is not valid. An Israelite should be careful not to detach one of the four species from the tree himself in order to connect them, even if the owner of the ground had given him permission, but a non-Jew or another Israelite should detach them and he should purchase it from them.

7.   Three Hadas and two Arava branches are taken in the way they grow, with the cut edges downwards, and bound together with the Lulav so that they all form a single band. The Hadas should be bound on the right side of the back of the Lulav, and the Arava on the left, that is, when taking the Lulav with its back towards his face, the Hadass should be towards his right hand, and the Arava towards his left, and at the bottom thereof they should all be even so that by taking the Lulav he should grasp all, nevertheless, one should see that the Hadass is a little higher than the Arava, and one should be careful to see that the stock of the Lulav is at least a hand-breadth higher than the Hadas. They should be bound all together with a perfect band, with say, two bands, one above the other. Besides binding these species together. three more bands should be placed on the Lulav, but the upper hand breadth of the Lulav should be without a band, so that it might rustle when waived. If a cord is twined round the Hadass it should be removed before binding it (with the Lulav) in order that nothing intervene. If the band becomes loose on the Festival it is forbidden to bind it again by making a knot, but only by making a loop, or as the practice is, to wrap them round and to insert the edge of the binder into its folds.

8. An Arava that was plucked on a Festival, whether on the first or second day, is forbidden to be handled on that day, as it is absolutely "set apart," but if it is plucked on the first day of the Festival, it is valid for use on the second day thereof, but if the first day occurred on the Sabbath and it was plucked then, it is forbidden also on the second day. If an Esrog or any of the other species were brought from beyond the Sabbath boundary, it is permitted to handle them and to take them out, but if the city is not provided with an Eirouv, it is forbidden to handle them outside of the house where they are, and all must go there in order to fulfil one's obligation with them

9. One who has not a choice set of the four species should rather fulfil the precept with his friend's, nevertheless it is mandatory for one to have also four species of his own, as good as he can afford to buy, with which to perform the ceremony of waving in the Hallel and Hakafoth.

LAWS CONCERNING THE TAKING OF THE LULAV AND THE

ORDER OF HAKAFOTH (PROCESSION IN THE SYNANGOGUE).

1. The Lulav, Hadasim and Aravath, bound together, should be taken in the right hand, and the Esrog in the left hand, the three species being taken in the position in which they grow, the place where they have been cut being downward, but the Esrog, on the contrary, should be taken with the stamen upward, and the apex downward and the blessing ברוך אתה ה' אלהינו מלך העולם אשר קדשנו במצותיו וצונו על נטילת לולב should be said, then the Esrog, too, should be turned towards the position in which it grew with the apex upward and they should be waved.

2. On the first day the blessing שהחינו should also be said, but if the first day occurs on a Sabbath, when the Lulav is not taken, the blessing שהחינו should be said on the second day. One should be careful to hold the Esrog close to the Lulav, there being no separation between them; they should be waved towards the four points (of the compass) also upwards and downwards. Likewise when waving them during Hallel and in the Hakafoth he should be careful to bring the Esrog close to the Lulav. If he had done the opposite, and took the Esrog in his right hand and the Lulav in his left, he should again take them, but without saying a blessing.

3. One who is left-handed should take the Lulav in *his* right hand, (i.e., that of the normal) and the Esrog in *his* left hand. If he did the opposite, he should take them again without saying a blessing. The general law applies to one who is ambidexterous.

4. It is proper to remove the phylacteries before taking the Lulav, one should at least remove the strap from his hands that there should be nothing to intervene. It is also proper to remove the rings from the fingers.

5. The order of " waving " in Hallel is as follows : There are six words in הודו besides the Name, waving should be done at every word in a different direction, but at the mention of the Divine Name, there should be no waving. The Reader waves only in הודו and in יאמר נא ישראל, but the congregation waves each time they say הודו. When saying אנא the Reader waves as well as the congregation, but in אנא ה' הושיעה נא as it has but three words besides the Name, the waving should be done in two directions at each word. In the הודו at the end of Hallel, the Reader and the congregation also wave. When waving downwards, only the hands should be lowered, but the Lulav and the other species should remain in the position in which they grow, nor is he required to turn his face in the direction in which he waves, but the top of the Lulav only need be waved, nor is he required to wave it with force, only to shake it gently in order to make the leaves rustle.

6. It is forbidden to partake of food before taking the Lulav. One who is travelling and hopes to arrive at a place where there is an Esrog and a Lulav, likewise those who dwell in country places where an Esrog and Lulav are sent to them, are required to wait until noon, but no longer, as it is forbidden to fast on a Festival and during the Intermediate days of a Festival ; one, however, who feels faint and cannot wait until noon, may partake of some refreshment previous thereto.

7. It is permissible to put the Lulav back in the water on the Festival, and to add water thereto, but not to change the water. During the Intermediate days of a Festival, it is, however. mandatory to change the water in order that the Lulav remain fresh and bright. It is also mandatory during the Intermediate days of a Festival to take a new Arava for the Lulav each day.

8. It is forbidden to inhale the fragrance of the Hadas with which the precept is performed during the entire seven days of the Festival, even on the Sabbath, but an Esrog the fragrance is permitted to be inhaled on the Sabbath and the blessing הנותן ריח טוב בפירות is said, and during the other days its fragrance should not be inhaled, even during the time that it is taken to fulfil the precept therewith. It is forbidden to handle the Lulav on the Sabbath even for the requirements of itself or of its place, inasmuch as it is "set apart," but the Esrog, since it is permissible to inhale its fragrance is not "set apart." and it is permissible to handle it ; it is also permitted to put it in the cotton wherein it was before the Festival, which

had already become impregnated with its fragrance, but it should not be placed in new cotton or in cloth, as an odour will be created.

9. On the first two days of the Festival, one's obligation is not fulfilled with a Lulav and the species that were borrowed but they must actually belong to him, but if one presents them to him on condition that he return it, it is a gift, and he fulfils his obligation therewith, even if they are merely given to him in order to fulfil his obligation, it is considered as if he had told him plainly that he gives it to him on condition that he return it. If the husband is not at home and the wife desires to give them to another to fulfil his obligation therewith, its validity depends on the disposition of the husband, whether he be likely to be displeased thereat or not.

10. If two bought an Esrog and the rest of the species in partnership, it is presumed that they bought them with the intention of mutually transferring their share in it to each other when each will perform the precept therewith, hence it is customary for the congregation to buy an Esrog wherewith the entire congregation may fulfil their obligation and whoever can afford it is obliged to pay the price of the Esrog. In spite of that it is best for one to fulfil his obligation with the Esrog of an individual which has a superior assortment of appurtenances, for what an individual transfers to his neighbour is more select.

11. On the first day children should not be allowed to take the Lulav and Esrog until after the adults have taken it.

12. Every day during the Festival when the Hoshanoth are said, a Scroll of the Law is brought up on the Reader's desk, and all those possessing a Lulav and an Esrog walk in procession encircling the Reading desk whereon is the Scroll of the Law, whilst the Holy Ark is left open until after the saying Hoshanoth when the Scroll of the Law is returned thereto. Every day the Reader's desk is encircled once, but on the seventh day which is Hoshana Rabba, every Scroll of the Law is taken out and brought up on the Reader's desk, and it is encircled seven times. The Hakafoth should be made towards the right, therefore they encircle it in a northerly direction. One who has an Esrog and Lulav and does not encircle the Reading Desk acts wrongly, but a mourner does not encircle the Reading desk.

13. On the Sabbath the Reading desk is not encircled, for that reason a Scroll of the Law is not brought upon the Reading desk, but the Holy Ark is kept open until after the Hoshanoth have been said.

LAWS CONCERNING HOSHANA RABBA, EIGHTH DAY OF SOLEMN

ASSEMBLY AND REJOICING OF THE LAW.

2. The fifth day of the Intermediate days of the Festival is Hoshana Rabba. It is customary to be awake the whole of the preceding night and to study the Torah. In the Morning Service there is a

slight increase in the number of candles burning, as on the Day of Atonement, and the Reader wears a white robe (קיטל). למנצח is said as on a Festival; מזמור לתודה is also said; נשמת is not said; אין כמוך is said, also שמע ישראל, as on a Festival. In the קדושה of the Additional Service נעריצך is said.

2. It is a custom instituted by the Prophets for each to take on that day a special Arava, besides the Arava which is in the Lulav. All that invalidates the Arava in the Lulav applies also to that Arava. (an Israelite should not cut it for his own use) only that if most of the leaves fell out, and even if there be but one leaf on a stem it is valid, nevertheless it is a glorification of the precept if it possesses many leaves and long stems. It is a fine custom to take five stems and tie them together with the leaves of a Lulav.

3. It is not taken together with the Lulav, but when תענה אמונים is said, the Lulav and the Esrog are put down and that is taken up. On conclusion of the הושענות it is waved and then beaten against the ground five times, which is sufficient, even if its leaves are not lessened thereby. After the beating, it should not be cast upon the ground, in order not to treat a precept with contempt.

4. On the night of שמיני עצרת one should wait until night before saying the Kiddush. The blessing שהחינו is said in the Kiddush, inasmuch as it is a Festival in itself; the blessing לישב בסוכה is not said.

5. On the night of שמיני עצרת and during the entire day, the eating is done in the Succah, only that the blessing לישב בסוכה is not said. Before leaving the Succah the יהי רצון as printed in the prayer books is read.

6. On the Eighth day, at the approach of darkness, the furniture may be removed from the Succah to the house, but it should not be put in order while it is yet day, as it is like preparing on one Festival for another.

7. The last day of the Festival which is also שמיני עצרת is called שמחת תורה, because the Torah is concluded on that day, and we rejoice therewith. In the evening after the service, the Reader's desk is encircled, after which the Scrolls of the Law are replaced in the Holy Ark, and one is left out, wherein the law is read. After the reading of the Law the Scroll is replaced and עלינו is said.

8. In the daytime after the Hakafoth are over, three Scrolls of the Law are left out, and many are called up for whom the section from וזאת הברכה until מעונה is read many times. At the conclusion thereof all the boys are called up. It is proper for the eldest among them to say the blessing and for the rest to hearken thereto, then the section המלאך הגואל is read for them. After that the חתן תורה is called up, and the portion from מעונה until the conclusion is read. The חתן בראשית is then called up, and after the portion of בראשית is read for him in the second Scroll, half-Kaddish is said, then the Maftir is called up, and a portion is read for him in the third Scroll. It is proper to call up an eminent person as חתן תורה, even one who had already gone up to the law when וזאת הברכה was read, may nevertheless be called as חתן תורה or to חתן בראשית. Where there are only two Scrolls of the Law, וזאת הברכה is read in one, and בראשית in the other, then the first is again taken and the portion for the Haftorah is read therein.

9. It is customary for the חתן תורה and the חתן בראשית to make donations, also to invite all their friends to a banquet of rejoicing on the occasion of ending the Torah and its commencement.

LAWS OF CHANUCAH (חנוכה).

1. On the twenty-fifth of Kislev, the eight days of חנוכה begin; these are days of rejoicing and praise, and on every night of these eight nights lights are lit near the doors of the houses in order to display and reveal the miracle that was performed for Israel in those days. It is mandatory to slightly increase the meals on חנוכה. It is customary to eat milk food on חנוכה and it is proper to relate to one's household the story of the miracles that were performed for our ancestors in those days. On חנוכה charity should be generously dispensed, especially to those who are poor and study the Torah in order to maintain them.

2. Nobody should fast on חנוכה, but it is permissible to pronounce a funeral oration, also to fast on the day before and on the day after חנוכה. It is permitted to do work during חנוכה, but women observe the custom not to work whilst the Chanucah lights are burning in the synagogue.

3. All kinds of oil are valid for the Chanucah lights, nevertheless, the most proper way of performing the precept is to take olive oil. If it cannot be obtained, other oil which gives a clear and bright flame should be selected, or else wax candles, as their light is also clear, but there should not be two candles stuck together, but each candle by itself. (It should not be made of wax that was used in the place of worship of another people).

4. All wicks are valid for the use of Chanucah lights, but the most preferable way of performing the precept is to take cotton. It is not necessary to take new wicks every night, but one may light the original wicks until they are consumed.

5. One should procure a beautiful metal candle-stick, and one who can afford it should buy a silver candle-stick in order to perform the precept in a glorious manner.

6. Each one of the household should light one candle on the first night, and two candles on the second night, and add thus until the eighth night when eight candles are lit. Care should be taken that each one should place his candles in a separate place in order that it be recognisable how many candles are lit; they should not be lit in a place where candles are lit the entire year in order that it be discernible that they are Chanucah lights.

7. It is mandatory to light the Chanucah lights within the door that is near the public domain in order to make the miracle known. As at the present period we dwell amongst other nations, each one lights in the house wherein he dwells, and if there be a window towards the public domain they should be lit there, if not they should be lit near the door, and it is mandatory that they be placed within the handbreadth that is near the left side of the door, so that the Mezuzah be on the right and the Chanucah light on the left, thus one finds himself surrounded by precepts. It is preferable to place them within the hollow of the door.

8. It is mandatory to place them higher than three hand-breadths above the ground and lower than ten hand-breadths, if, however, he places them higher than ten hand-breadths he has fulfilled his obligation, but if one places them above twenty cubits from the ground the obligation is not fulfilled. One who dwells in a garret may place them in the window even if it is higher than ten hand breadths above the ground, if, however, the window is more than twenty cubits above the ground of the public domain, then it is better to place them near the door.

9. The lights should be in an even row, one should not be higher and the other lower, and there should be an open space between one light and the other in order that one flame should not merge into another; between wax candles there should also be an open space in order that one should not become heated by the other, so that the wax should not drip down and the candles be spoiled.

10. A candle-stick that has two or more branches should not be lit by two even in the first night as it would not be recognisable how many candles are lit.

11. The time of lighting them is immediately at the **appearance** of the stars, and it should not be delayed. It is forbidden to do anything before the lighting, even to study the Torah, but the evening prayers should be said before lighting them. The entire household should be assembled in order to give the matter publicity. It is requisite to pour in oil sufficient to burn at least half-an-hour, but if by inadvertance one did not light them immediately, he may light them saying a blessing, as long as the household is awake, but after the household is asleep the miracle is no longer given publicity, and he should light without saying a blessing. If he will have no time to light at night, he may hasten himself and light them at $\frac{5}{8}$ of the day or about one hour and a quarter (where the day is twelve hours) before the stars appear, providing he pours in sufficient oil to make them burn until half-an-hour after the appearance of the stars, and if they do not burn until then he has not properly performed the precept.

12. The following is the order of lighting them : On the first night the light toward the right should be lit, and on the second night he should add one light toward his left, the one that is added should be lit first and then turn and light toward the right.

13. On the first night the one who lights them says three blessings previous to lighting them : להדליק שעשה נסים, and שהחינו, and on the other nights he does not say the blessing שהחינו : after the blessings have been said, one light is lit and while lighting the others הנרות הללו וכו׳ is said. A convert to judaism says שעשה נסים לישראל, if, however, he said לאבותינו his obligation is fulfilled. A mourner before his dead was interred should not light if there be another to do so, but if there be no other, he should light without saying the blessings.

14. In regard to Chanucah lights, the act of lighting them constitutes the performance of the precept, it is therefore essential that during the lighting the lights be in their place and in accordance with their proper quantity, hence, we infer that if he had lit them when they were lower than three hand breadths above the ground, or higher than twenty cubits, and after being lit they were properly placed, they are invalid, likewise, if when lighting them there was not the proper quantity of oil. and it was added thereafter, it is of no avail. Likewise, if one placed them where the wind is blowing and they are in danger of being extinguished. the precept is not properly performed, and it is incumbent to light them again, but no blessing should be said, if, however, they are placed properly and they were accidently extin-

guished, it is customary to re-light them. It is also customary scrupulously to abstain from lighting one candle by the other, but they should be lit by the candle provided for that purpose.

15. During the time prescribed for the performance of the precept, which is half-an-hour, it is forbidden to make any use of their light, hence it is customary to place near them the candle with which the lighting is done, so that if he does anything near them, it is done by the light of that candle. It should be placed slightly higher than the lights in order that it is apparent that it is not of the number of candles.

16. The Chanucah lights are lit in the synagogue to give publicity to the miracle, and a blessing is said upon them. They are placed near the southern wall, and are lit between the Afternoon and Evening Services, no one is however exempted by the lights in the synagogue, but is required to light them again in his house. A mourner should not light them in the synagogue the first night, as he is required to say the blessing שהחיינו in public, but in his house he says the blessing שהחיינו.

17. The observance of Chanucah lights is obligatory upon women, and a woman may light them on behalf of her entire household, it is obligatory also upon a lad who had reached the age proper for being trained in the precepts. For a blind person it is best if he can contribute something towards the purchase of the candles with another. If he has a wife, she lights them for him, but if he has no wife, and has a separate dwelling where he has none with whom to join in purchasing them, he should light through the aid of another.

18. On the Sabbath-eve, the Chanucah-light is lit first, then the Sabbath-light, but it should be $\frac{5}{8}$ of the day (about an hour and a quarter) before night, and the afternoon prayers should be said previous thereto. It is necessary to pour in oil sufficient to keep them burning until half-an-hour after the appearance of the stars, as otherwise his blessing will have been said in vain. If he lit them near the door, he should place something between them and the door, to prevent their being extinguished by the opening and closing of the door.

19. On the conclusion of Sabbath the Chanucah light is lit, and the Habdallah is said thereafter. In the synagogue it is lit before ויתן לך.

20. One who is out of town, if he knows that his wife lights them at his house, he should light them wherever he is without saying a blessing. If possible, it were well for him previously to hear the

blessings said by another who is lighting them there and he should bear in mind that he is fulfilling his obligation by the other's blessing, and should respond אמן, after which he should light them without saying the blessings. But if his wife does not light them at his home, likewise the guests in hotels and the like, they are required to light them, saying the blessings, or else they should become " partners " with the head of the hotel and the like by giving him a coin in order that they shall also have a share in the oil and wick, and the head of the hotel and the like should add a little more oil than the required quantity for the share of the partners, they, however, should glorify the precept by each one lighting for himself. One who is in his city but in a different house should return to his house at the time of lighting them.

21. The oil that is left in the lamps after Chanucah, also the wicks, should be gathered together and burnt, inasmuch as they were set apart for the performance of the precept ; it is forbidden to make use of them unless he had originally made it a condition that he does not set apart that which will be left.

22. During the eight days of Chanucah, על הנסים should be said in the שמונה עשרה, but if one had inadvertently omitted it, and was reminded thereof before saying the Name in the blessing הטוב שמך it should be repeated, beginning with על הנסים, but if he was not reminded thereof until he had uttered the Name, he should conclude the blessing and it need not be repeated.

23. During the eight days of Chanucah, the entire Hallel is said. Neither תחנון, nor אל ארך אפים, nor למנצח, nor צדקתך צדק, nor צדקתך is said. Each day a section of the portion נשא (Nu. iv. 21) is read for three persons, as follows : On the first day the reading is begun for the Priest from ויהי ויהי המקריב ביום until ביום כלות משה, for the Levite from ויהי המקריב ביום until מלאה קטרת, until הראשון, for the Israelite from פר אחד until בן עמינדב. On the second day for the Priest and the Levite—ביום השני, for the Israelite—ביום השלישי ; thus, on each day, for the Priest and the Levite the יום at which they left off and for the Israelite the יום that follows. On the eighth day for Priest and Levite—ביום השמיני and for the Israelite the reading is begun from ביום התשיעי and the entire Portion is concluded, the reading is then continued in בהעלותך until בן עשה את המנורה.
24. On Sabbath Chanucah two Scrolls of the Law are taken out, in one the weekly portion is read, and in the other the portion for the Haphtora which is the יום of that day, and for the Haphtorah רני ושמחי is read. If there be yet another Sabbath, for the Haphtora, part of the chapter (Kings i. 7.) treating of the candlesticks of King Solomon is read thereon. On ראש חדש שבת which occurs on a week-day two Scrolls

of the Law are taken out ; in one the usual section for Rosh Chodesh
is read for three persons who are called up, after which a fourth is
called up and the יום relating to that Chanucah Day is read for him in
the other Scroll of the Law. If by error the section of Chanucah was
read first—even if the reading had not yet begun, but the one who
went up had already said the blessing, it need not be interrupted, but
the reading of his portion may be concluded, and for the rest who are
called up, the section of Rosh Chodesh is read. If it was read in the
section of Rosh Chodesh in a proper manner, but by error it was read
also for the fourth person in the section of Rosh Chodesh, even if they
immediately became aware of their error after the one who was called
up had said the blessing, if only one Scroll had been taken out, they
need not read further therein, if, however, two Scrolls of the Law were
taken out, for fear lest the honour of the Scroll will be slighted, a fifth
person should be called up and the portion for Chanucah should be read
therein. After the fifth person has been called, the half-Kaddish
should be said.

25. If Rosh Chosdesh שבת occurred on the Sabbath, three Scrolls
of the Law are taken out, in the first the weekly section is read for six
persons ; in the second the portion of Rosh Chodesh is read for the
seventh person. It is begun from וביום השבת, then half-Kaddish is said
In the third Scroll of the Law, the יום belonging to that Chanucah
Day is read for the Hophtorah, and רני ושמחי is read for the Haphtorah.

26. On the fifteenth of Shebat תחנון is not said, and it is customary to eat thereon different kinds of the fruits of trees.

LAWS CONCERNING THE "FOUR PORTIONS" (ארבע פרשיות).

1. The Sabbath prior to Rosh Chodesh Adar (the month before
Nissan in a leap year) is called שבת פרשת שקלים. If Rosh Chodesh
occurs on the Sabbath, פרשת שקלים is on that day. Three Scrolls of
the Law are taken out. In the first the weekly section is read for six
persons, in the second the portion of Rosh Chodesh is read for the
seventh person, the reading is begun from וביום השבת, then the half
Kaddish is said. In the third פרשת שקלים is read for Maftir, and the
Haphtorah of שקלים is read. If by error the reading was first begun
in פרשת שקלים, it is concluded, and the portion of Rosh Chodesh is read
for the Maftir, and the Haphtorah of Sabbath Rosh Chodesh is read.

2. The Sabbath before Purim is פרשת זכור. The Sabbath before Rosh Chodesh Nisan is פרשת החדש. If Rosh Chodesh occurs on the Sabbath, פרשת החדש is on that day, and it is governed by the same law that applies to Rosh Chodesh Adar that occurs on the Sabbath. The Sabbath before פרשת החדש is פרשת פרה.

3. It is obligatory to hear the reading of פרשת זכור and פרשת פרה from the one who reads in the Torah, and a minor is not called to the Maftir. Country people who have no Minyan are required to go to a place where there is a Minyan, and if that be impossible for them, they should at least read the Parshioth with the proper intonations.

Laws Concerning the Megillah (מגילה).

1. As soon as Adar arrives all should exceed in being joyful.

2. All Israel have taken upon themselves the thirteenth day of the month of Adar as a public fast-day. This is called the Fast of Esther. Nevertheless this fast-day is not as obligatory as the four fast days which are ordained in the Scriptures, hence, it may be relaxed in an emergency; thus pregnant and nursing women, or even one suffering slightly with his eyes, if the fast would cause them distress, should not fast. Likewise a woman within thirty days of giving birth, also a bridegroom in his seven days of rejoicing, need not fast, and they should afterwards make up for that fast, but other persons who are well, should not separate themselves from the congregation, and even one who goes on a journey and it is hard for him to fast, is nevertheless required to fast.

3. Purim is on the fourteenth of Adar. If Purim occurs on Sunday the fast is held on Thursday, if a circumcision is celebrated on that day, the feast should be held at night, but the Sandek and the father of the son are permitted to eat in the daytime, and they are not required to fast on Friday, but if another forgot and ate on Thursday, he should fast on Friday.

4. In honour of the Megillah one should attire himself in Sabbath garments in the evening, and on his return from the synagogue he should find the lights burning in his house and the table set. In

the evening after שמונה עשרה the entire Kaddish is said, also תתקבל, then the Megillah is read, after which ואתה קדוש is said, then the entire Kaddish is said, but תתקבל is omitted. If it is the conclusion of a Sabbath, ויהי נועם and ואתה קדוש is said, then the entire Kaddish without תתקבל is said, then ויתן לך, the Habdallah is then said upon a goblet of wine, and עלינו is said.

5. Before Purim has set in, it is customary to give half of a standard coin current in that place and at that time. This is called מחצית השקל (half a shekel), it is customary to give three half shekels, it is given in the evening before the Megillah is read, and that money is distributed among the poor. A minor is exempted from contributing a half-shekel, but if his father once gave on his behalf, it is ever obligatory upon him.

6. On Purim in the שמונה עשרה of the evening, morning and afternoon services על הנסים is said, and if it was omitted, it is governed by the same law that applies to Chanucah.

7. It is obligatory upon all, both male and female, to hear the Megillah read at night and in the daytime, hence, maidens too should go to the synagogue, and for those who do not go it is necessary to read in the house. Children also should be trained to hear the Megillah read, but very young children should not be taken to the synagogue as they divert the attention of the listeners.

8. At night it is forbidden to read the Megillah before the stars have appeared, even if one is much distressed on account of the fast, but some slight refreshment might be partaken of before the Megillah is read, in order to somewhat overcome the weakening effect of the fast.

9. The best way of observing the precept is to hear the Megillah read in the synagogue where there is a "multitude of people." One should at least endeavour to hear it in a Minyan (of ten), but if it is impossible to read it in a Minyan, each individual should read it out of a valid Megillah with the blessings that precede it. If one knows how to read it, and the others do not, the one who knows should read it, and they should hear and thus fulfil their obligations, even if they are not ten, but the blessing at the conclusion should not be said, excepting amongst ten, but if the Name is omitted an individual may also say it.

10. He who reads the Megillah for the congregation spreads it out and folds it folio upon folio like a letter, but the listeners are not required to spread it out.

11. He who reads the Megillah, whether in the daytime **or at** night, pronounces three blessings previous thereto, ‎שעשה‎ ‎על מקרא מגילה‎, ‎נסים‎ and ‎שהחינו‎, and after he had read it, he rolls it completely together, and places it before him, and says the blessing ‎הרב את ריבנו‎.

12. If a mourner reads the Megillah, another should say the blessings because of the blessing ‎שהחינו‎.

13. When saying the blessing ‎שהחינו‎ in the daytime, it should be borne in mind that it has reference also to the sending of portions, the making of gifts to the needy, and the Purim feast, the Reader should likewise bear in mind that he is causing the congregation to assume the obligations concerning these precepts as well.

14. He who reads the Megillah is required to have his mind centred upon causing all the listeners to fulfil their obligation, the listener also should bear in mind that he is thus fulfilling his obligation, hence he should hear every word, for if he did not hear even one word, his obligation is not fulfilled, the reader, therefore, is required to be very careful to cease reading altogether while there is a tumult at the mention of Haman, and wait until the commotion is entirely over. Nevertheless it is perfectly proper for each to have a valid Megillah in order that he himself should say word for word in an undertone, as perchance he may not hear a word from the Reader.

15. The Reader should say ‎עשרת בני המן‎ including the word ‎עשרת‎ all in one breath. It is the custom to begin with ‎חמש מאות איש‎ and say all in one breath, if, however, one inadvertently paused between ‎עשרת‎ ‎בני המן‎, his obligation is fulfilled. At night, when the Reader says ‎בלילה ההוא נדדה‎ he should raise his voice, and when saying ‎האגרת הואת‎ he should wave the Megillah.

16. One who has a Megillah that is not valid, or a Bible, should not read with the Reader, nor should anyone verbally assist the Reader, therefore the four ‎פסוקי גאולה‎ which the congregation say in a loud voice, the Reader is required to repeat from the valid Megillah.

17. One who had already fulfilled his obligation concerning the reading of the Megillah, and reads for the sake of another, if the one who is required to fulfil his obligation knows himself how to say the

blessings, he should say it himself, but if it is read before a woman, it is best that the Reader should say the blessings and say אשר קדשנו במצותיו וצונו לשמוע מגילה.

18. It is permitted to handle a Megillah on the Sabbath, nevertheless, if Purim falls on Sunday the Megillah should not be brought to the synagogue on the Sabbath, even in a city that is provided with an "Eirouv," inasmuch as it is preparing from a Sabbath to a weekday.

19. If a congregation has not a Reader who is able to read with the intonations, he may read it without any intonations, providing he reads the words properly, so that the subject matter is not changed, for if he read instead of ומרדכי יֵצֵב—יוֹיֵב or instead of נָפַל—והמן נוֹפֵל and the like, even if it has already been said, his obligation is not fulfilled.

20. If a congregation has not a Megillah that is legally valid, nevertheless if it is written upon parchment according to the law, only that some words in the middle are missing, but an entire subject is not missing, it may be read from and the blessings said thereon, and when coming to the error the Reader should repeat from memory, or one should say it for him from a Bible; but if they have no Megillah at all, or an entire subject is missing, each one should read for himself from a Bible, but the blessings are not said. An individual who has only a Megillah that is not valid should read therein without saying the blessings.

21. A mourner in the seven days should observe all the laws of mourning, and is forbidden to witness any manner of festivity, but is permitted to put on his boots and to sit on a chair. At night if he can gather a Minyan at his house to read the Megillah, it is well; if not he should pray at his house and go the synagogue to hear the Megillah. (If it occurs on the conclusion of the Sabbath, he should go to the synagogue after the third meal while it is yet day) and on the morrow he should go to the synagogue to pray and to hear the Megillah.

22. One who has lost a member of his family on תענית אסתר and is an אונן, at night, before the interment, he should hear the Megillah read by another, and if he heard the Megillah read before the interment, his obligation is fulfilled, nevertheless it is proper for him to

read it again without saying the blessings, he should not put on the phylacteries even after the interment. An אונן is permitted to eat meat and to drink wine on the Purim-day.

23. In the morning it is customary to arrive early at the synagogue. After the שמונה עשרה half-Kaddish is said, and the law is read in section ויבא עמלק and three persons are called up, after which half-Kaddish is said. After the Scrolls of the Law is replaced in the Holy Ark the Megillah is read. On conclusion of שושנת יעקב—האל המושיע is said, then אשרי ובא לציון, then the entire Kaddish with תתקבל. The phylacteries should not be taken off until after the Megillah is read If there is a circumcision it takes place before the Megillah is read.

24. In a city that is surrounded by a wall since the days of Joshua the son of Nun, it is read on the fifteenth.

LAWS CONCERNING THE SENDING OF PORTIONS,

GIFTS TO THE NEEDY AND THE PURIM FEAST.

1. It is incumbent upon each to send at least two presents to one person, and he who exceeds in sending portions to his friends is praiseworthy. Nevertheless it is better to exceed in taking gifts to the needy than to make a great feast for himself and to send portions to friends, for there is no greater and more glorious joy before the Holy One, blessed be He, than to gladden the hearts of the poor, the orphans and the widows.

2. By portions is meant that which may be eaten as it is without preparations, such as cooked meat and fish, confectionery, fruit or liquid and the like. Even the poorest Israelite who accepts charity is obliged to give at least two gifts to two persons, that is, one gift to each. One should not be particular when distributing the Purim monies, but to everyone who puts forth his hand to take charity, money is given. If one is in a place where there are no poor, he should keep that money until he will come across some poor people, or he should send it to them.

3. Women are also obliged to send portions and make gifts to the needy. The sending of portions should be done by one woman to

another, and by one man to another, but no distinction are made in the gifts to the needy.

4. It is obligatory to eat, drink and be merry on Purim. On the night of the fourteenth one should also rejoice and make somewhat of a feast, nevertheless one does not fulfil his obligation by the feast that he makes at night, as it is mandatory to make the feast principally in the daytime. On the night of the fifteenth one should rejoice somewhat. Portions to one's friends and gifts to the needy, should be sent in the daytime.

5. The Afternoon Prayers are said while it is yet broad day, and lights are lit as on a joyful and festive occasion, and the feast is held after the Afternoon Service, at least the greater part of it should be held while it is yet day. When it occurs on a Sabbath-eve it is held in the morning in honour of the Sabbath. It is well to engage in the study of the Torah for a short time before beginning the feast.

6. "One is obliged to regale himself on Purim," that is, he should drink more than he is accustomed to of wine or of another intoxicating beverage; one, however, who is of a weak disposition, likewise one who knows that it will cause him to despise some precept, a blessing or a prayer, or that it will lead him to levity, it is best not to become intoxicated.

7. A mourner, even in the seven days, is obliged to send gifts to the needy and portions to his friends, he, however, should not send anything of a joyful nature, but to a mourner, portions are not sent the entire twelve months, even a thing that is not of a joyful nature. If he is a poor man it is permissible to send him money or another article that is not of a joyful nature, and if only the mourner and another are at that place, it is obligatory to send to him, in order to perform the precept of sending portions.

8. No work should be done on Purim, but it is permissible to be done through a non-Jew. It is also permissible to attend to business, and it is likewise permitted to write even a letter of friendship, also one's account and everything that does not require any close attention, and especially to write something for the sake of a precept, or to perform a precept, likewise for the requirements of Purim it is permitted to perform even entire labours.

9. The fifteenth of Adar is termed שושן פורים. Neither תחנון, nor אל ארך אפים, nor למנצח is said thereon. It is also forbidden to hold a.

funeral address and to fast thereon, and it is customary to make somewhat of a feast and to rejoice thereon, but עֵל הַנִסִים is not said, and it is permitted to marry on that day, but on the fourteenth of Adar no marriage should take place.

10. On the fourteenth and fifteenth of Adar Rishon, neither תחנון, nor אֵל אֶרֶךְ אַפַּיִם, nor לַמְנַצֵּחַ is said, and it is forbidden to hold a funeral address or to fast thereon. On the fourteenth somewhat of a feast is made.